Community Rights, Conservation and Contested Land

In memory of Alan Rodgers (1944–2009):
ecologist, activist and mentor to several
generations of conservationists in
East Africa and beyond

Community Rights, Conservation and Contested Land

The Politics of Natural Resource Governance in Africa

Edited by
Fred Nelson

publishing for a sustainable future

London · New York

First published in 2010 by Earthscan

Copyright © IUCN 2010

All rights reserved.

ISBN: 978-1-84407-916-2 hardback
ISBN: 978-1-415-52036-2 paperback

Typeset by
Bookcraft Ltd, 18 Kendrick Street, Stroud, GL5 1AA

Cover design by Andrew Corbett

For a full list of publications please contact:

Earthscan

2 Park Square, Milton Park, Abingdon, Oxon OX14 4RN
Simultaneously published in the USA and Canada by Earthscan
711 Third Avenue, New York, NY 10017
Earthscan is an imprint of the Taylor & Francis Group, an informa business

First issued in paperback 2011

Earthscan publishes in association with the International Institute for Environment and Development

A catalogue record for this book is available from the British Library

Library of Congress Cataloging-in-Publication Data

Community rights, conservation and contested land: the politics of natural resource governance in Africa / edited by Fred Nelson.
    p. cm.
Includes bibliographical references and index.
    ISBN 978-1-84407-916-2 (hardback)
    1. Nature conservation–Government policy–Africa. 2. Conservation and natural resources–Government policy–Africa. 3. Biodiversity–Government policy–Africa. 4. Land tenure–Africa. 5. Community development–Africa. 6. Political participation–Africa. 7. Africa–Environmental conditions. 8. Africa Politics and government. I. Nelson, Fred, 1976-
    QH77.A4C56 2010
    333.72096–dc22

                                                                    2010000821

At Earthscan we strive to minimize our environmental impacts and carbon footprint through reducing waste, recycling and offsetting our CO_2 emissions, including those created through publication of this book.

Contents

Part I   Introduction

Part 2   Political Economies of Natural Resource Governance

Part 3   Local Struggles and Negotiations across Multiple Scales

Part 4   Looking Forward

List of Figures, Tables and Boxes

Figures

Tables

Boxes

List of Contributors

Simon Anstey was born in Tanzania and has spent most of his working life in western and southern Africa, with three years in central Asia and the Middle East. In 1992, he initiated IUCN's Mozambique programme, supporting post-conflict protected area rehabilitation and pilot community natural resource management initiatives until 2002. He has a doctorate on the politics of natural resource governance and Yao history in northern Mozambique from the University of Zimbabwe and is currently the Director of ResourceAfrica UK.

Tom Blomley is a community-based natural resource management specialist, with a strong background in east Africa. From 2003 to 2008 he advised the Tanzanian government on the development of a national multi-donor programme in support of participatory forest management. He currently lives in the UK and works as a freelance natural resource management consultant.

Brian Child is Associate Professor in the Geography Department at the University of Florida, and editor of *Parks in Transition* (2004). He worked for wildlife departments in Zimbabwe for 12 years, subsequently supported park and community-based initiatives in Zambia's Luangwa Valley, and has worked within the wildlife sector in Uganda, Kenya, Namibia and South Africa.

Chaka Chirozva is currently studying for a PhD with the Communication and Innovation Studies Group of Wageningen University, The Netherlands. He is a Lecturer at the Centre for Applied Social Sciences at the University of Zimbabwe and is also Facilitator with the IDRC-funded Scenario Planning, Iterative Assessment and Adaptive Management Project, a regional research and development initiative which uses participatory scenario planning methodologies with communities in the Great Limpopo Transfrontier Conservation Area.

Maxwell Gomera is a resource economist with experience in community development issues, biodiversity conservation, commercialization of natural products and community-based natural resource management. He managed the IUCN Regional Office for Southern Africa's engagement with the mining and extractive industries and was co-chair of the International Working Group on Mining and Metals that produced the mining and metals supplement to the Global Reporting Initiative. Currently, Maxwell is working with the United Nations Environment Programme based in Nairobi, Kenya.

Brian Jones is an environment and development consultant and researcher, working mainly on CBNRM policy and governance issues in Namibia and the Southern African Development Community (SADC) region. He worked as a government official in the Namibian Ministry of Environment and Tourism for ten years where he coordinated the ministry's CBNRM programme, and has recently worked as a CBNRM policy advisor and protected area co-management policy advisor to the Ministry.

Ngeta Kabiri is a political scientist specializing in African politics and conservation policy. He has been a lecturer at Kenyatta University, completed his PhD dissertation at the University of North Carolina-Chapel Hill on community conservation in cross-border areas of Kenya and Tanzania, and most recently was a post-doctoral fellow at Yale University.

Rodgers Lubilo is a natural resources management facilitator with 13 years of experience in community mobilization and facilitation. He has worked for the Luangwa Integrated Resource Development Project in Zambia's Luangwa Valley, supporting 45 Village Action Groups and 6 Community Resources Boards. He runs Luangwa Management Services, a consultancy in CBNRM development.

Masego Madzwamuse is trained in environmental sciences and sociology and has over ten years' experience in conservation and development in southern Africa. She worked for IUCN as the Botswana Country Programme Coordinator (2001–2006) then later as Regional Programme Development Officer with IUCN ROSA and UNDP on the TerrAfrica Programme. She has over the years undertaken research and written publications on the land rights and development challenges of ethnic minorities in various parts of Botswana; livelihood security in dryland ecosystems; community-based natural resource management and adaptive livelihoods. She is currently an independent consultant and researcher based in South Africa.

Brian Maguranyanga is sociologist and independent consultant in organization and environment in southern Africa. He has consulted for IUCN, WWF and TRAFFIC in the area of policy and community-based natural resource management. He is part-time dissertation supervisor at the Graduate School of Management, University of Zimbabwe. Brian holds a doctorate from the University of Michigan, Ann Arbor (USA) and his dissertation explored transformation and black empowerment in the South African national park system.

Partalala Meitaya is a resident of Ololosokwan village, Loliondo, northern Tanzania. He has worked as Programme Officer for the Ujamaa Community Resource Trust, based in Arusha and Loliondo, for more than ten years.

Marta Monjane has over 15 years' experience in conservation and development in southern Africa. She has worked for IUCN for the past seven years, first as a programme officer (2002–2007), then subsequently as the Head of IUCN Mozambique Country office (2008). Presently she coordinates the IUCN Forest Regional Programme for East and Southern Africa, based in Nairobi, Kenya.

James Murombedzi is a property rights and resource governance consultant. His main research interests include agrarian political economy, land tenure, natural resources management and climate change in Africa.

Fred Nelson has worked on community-based natural resource management, ecotourism, and conservation policy in eastern Africa since 1998. He presently directs Maliasili Initiatives, a consulting firm working to address biodiversity conservation and natural resource management challenges using innovative, collaborative and market-based strategies.

Maanda Ngoitiko is a Maasai activist, development expert and community leader originally from Soit Sambu village, Loliondo, in northern Tanzania. She is the founder and Coordinator of the Pastoral Women's Council, based in Loliondo, was one of the first Maasai NGO activists working with the NGO, KIPOC, in Loliondo in the early 1990s, and is also a founding Programme Officer with the Ujamaa Community Resource Trust.

Liz Rihoy currently resides in Kenya and is the Programme Director of the Zeitz Foundation. She has worked with non-governmental organizations in a number of African countries on community development and natural resource management issues. Her particular interests lie in governance in relation to CBNRM and she is completing a PhD thesis on related policy processes in Zimbabwe and Botswana for the University of the Western Cape.

Makko Sinandei is from Arash village, Loliondo, in northern Tanzania and works as Programme Officer with the Ujamaa Community Resource Trust, based in Loliondo and Arusha. He has worked as a community development facilitator, organizer, and activist for nearly 20 years in northern Tanzania.

Webster Whande, an environmental geographer, is the Programme Coordinator for the 'Human Mobility, Networks and Institutions for the Management of Natural Resources in Africa' programme, operating from the Institute for Ethnology at the University of Köln and also Research Associate and Consultant with RUZIVO Trust, a land, natural resource and agrarian reform research institute in Zimbabwe.

Preface

This book has come together during the past three years, starting with its initial genesis at a meeting of the International Union for Conservation of Nature (IUCN) Southern Africa Sustainable Use Specialist Group (SASUSG) in May 2007. During this time, the volume's core subject – local and national institutional struggles over natural resource use, tenure and control – has increasingly been a subject of debate and public attention, both within African countries and more widely around the world.

During the past year, a string of studies and media reports in newspapers from Tanzania to India to Britain have highlighted the rapidly growing global demand for African lands and resources. Attention is increasingly focused on this emerging 21st century 'land grab', driven by global market interest in African landscapes desired for agriculture, biofuels, wildlife tourism and other natural resource-based investments. While many African economies have recorded strong levels of macro-economic growth during the past decade, in stark contrast to the economic malaise of the 1980s and 1990s, it remains an open question as to what degree this growth has improved the livelihoods of the majority of people living in rural areas. Is Africa entering a new era of investment, growth and prosperity, or an unprecedented period of resource alienation, rural marginalization and consolidation of undemocratic political relationships between states and citizens?

Similar dynamics are evident across the wider developing world. For example, as the book was nearing completion in mid-2009, Peru was engulfed by violent protests pitting central government policies allocating oil and timber concessions against the land and resource rights of indigenous communities in the Amazon basin.

This book arose from widespread concerns amongst scholars and field practitioners across east and southern Africa that the efforts undertaken during the past 20 years to empower local communities with greater rights over lands and resources have not had the envisioned impacts, and that these efforts have generally been undermined by forces which are at root political and institutional in nature. Natural resource governance reform efforts that seek to strengthen local rights and tenure cut across conservation, developmental and political aims and interests throughout the region. The core aim of this volume is to strengthen the political understanding of those governance processes as a way of understanding natural resource management outcomes, including existing barriers to change or, where applicable, the reasons underlying successful institutional transformations.

The book represents a call to take political institutions and dynamics seriously as a core element of understanding natural resource management outcomes in their multi-faceted social, economic and ecological dimensions. In other words, politics is central to efforts to promote sustainable development and the sustainable use of natural resources.

The book has been carried out as a project of SASUSG, with most of the contributors being long-term members of the network and, in many cases, collaborators through a range of community-based natural resource management initiatives across the region. Support for the project has been provided by SASUSG through funding from the Norwegian Ministry of Foreign Affairs. Additional financial support for the volume has been provided by the Sand County Foundation Bradley Fund for the Environment. Both sources of financial support are gratefully acknowledged.

The development of the volume has been a collaborative effort throughout, starting with the initial concept. In particular, two of the contributing authors, Simon Anstey and Liz Rihoy, also played a central role in contributing ideas to the initial conceptual framework and objectives for the volume and in identifying and recruiting a number of the other authors to the project. Marshall Murphree played a key role in providing early encouragement to the initiative as well as invaluable feedback on initial concept notes and a number of the draft chapters. Beyond the SASUSG network, Jesse Ribot and Ashwini Chhatre also provided helpful suggestions and feedback as the volume's structure and objectives took shape.

Other individuals who provided critical feedback and helpful comments on earlier drafts of various chapters include the following: Liz Alden Wily, Tor Benjaminsen, Ivan Bond, Bram Büscher, Mike Jones, Patience Mutopo, David Peterson, Chris Sandbrook, Michael Schoon and Geir Sundet.

Support to the project has also been provided by the IUCN South Africa office, and in particular Ditse Mduli enabled the smooth logistical preparation and execution of the authors meeting held in Johannesburg in August 2008. Additional support from within IUCN and SASUSG during the course of this initiative has come from Brian Child, Kule Chitepo and Masego Madzwamuse. At Sand County Foundation, Mike Jones and Kevin McAleese provided helpful feedback and facilitation in developing the proposal to the Bradley Fund for the Environment.

Fred Nelson
October 2009
Arusha

Acronyms and Abbreviations

AA	Appropriate Authority
ACORD	Agency for Cooperation and Research in Development
ADC	Area Development Committee
ADMADE	Administrative Management and Design for Game Management Areas
AGM	Annual General Meeting
AWF	African Wildlife Foundation
BDP	Botswana Democratic Party
BOCOBONET	Botswana Community-Based Organizations Network
CA	CAMPFIRE Association
CA	Cooperative Agreement
CAMPFIRE	Communal Areas Management Programme for Indigenous Resources, Zimbabwe
CBFM	Community-based forest management
CBNRM	Community-based natural resource management
CBO	Community-based organization
CCA	Conservation Corporation Africa
CCG	CAMPFIRE Collaborative Group
CDM	Clean Development Mechanism
CEO	Chief Executive Officer
CI	Conservation International
CKGR	Central Kalahari Game Reserve
CNP	Contractual National Park
CPA	Communal Property Association
CRB	Community Resource Board
CTT	Cgaecgae Tlhabololo Trust
DfID	Department for International Development
DNPWM	Department of National Parks and Wildlife Management
DWNP	Department of Wildlife and National Parks
EAWLS	East African Wildlife Society
FAO	Food and Agriculture Organisation of the United Nations
FBD	Forestry and Beekeeping Division
FDI	Foreign direct investment
FPK	First People of the Kalahari
FZS	Frankfurt Zoological Society

GDP	Gross domestic product
GHG	Greenhouse gas
GLTFCA	Great Limpopo Transfrontier Conservation Area
GLTP	Great Limpopo Transfrontier Park
GMA	Game Management Area
GNU	Government of National Unity
GPA	Global Political Agreement
GRZ	Government of the Republic of Zambia
GTZ	German Development Agency
IBEAC	Imperial British East Africa Company
IFAW	International Fund for Animal Welfare
IPCC	Intergovernmental Panel on Climate Change
IRDNC	Integrated Rural Development and Nature Conservation
IUCN	International Union for Conservation of Nature
JMB	Joint Management Board
JVP	Joint venture partnerships
KANU	Kenya African National Union
KCWCM	Kenya Coalition for Wildlife Conservation and Management
KDT	Khwai Development Trust
KIPOC	Koronkoro Indigenous Peoples Oriented to Conservation
KWS	Kenya Wildlife Service
KWWG	Kenya Wildlife Working Group
LIFE	Living in a Finite Environment
LIRDA	Lupande Integrated Rural Development Authority
LIRDP	Luangwa Integrated Resource Development Programme
LLS	Livelihoods and Landscape Programme
MCC	Mahenye CAMPFIRE Committee
MDC	Movement for Democratic Change
MEA	Millennium Ecosystem Assessment
MET	Ministry of Environment and Tourism
MMD	Movement for Multiparty Democracy
MNRT	Ministry of Natural Resources and Tourism
MoU	Memorandum of Understanding
MP	Member of Parliament
MWCT	Ministry of Wildlife, Conservation and Tourism
NACSO	Namibian Association of CBNRM Support Organisations
NCA	Ngorongoro Conservation Area
NCAA	Ngorongoro Conservation Area Authority
NGO	Non-government organization
NPWS	National Parks and Wildlife Service, Zambia
NRMP	Natural Resource Management Program
OBC	Ortello Business Corporation
OCT	Okavango Community Trust
ODA	Overseas development aid
OKMT	Okavango Kopano Mokoro Tru
OWS	Okavango Wilderness Safaris
PES	Payments for ecosystem services

PPF	Peace Parks Foundation
RDC	Rural District Council
REDD	Reduced Emissions from Deforestation and Forest Degradation
SADC	Southern African Development Community
SADF	South African Defence Forces
SANDF	South African National Defence Forces
SANParks	South Africa National Parks
SAP	Structural Adjustment Programme
SASUSG	Southern Africa Sustainable Use Specialist Group
SIDA	Swedish International Development Cooperation Agency
SNP	Serengeti National Park
SNV	Netherlands Development Organization
SWAPO	South West Africa People's Organization
TANAPA	Tanzania National Parks
TBL	Tanzania Breweries Limited
TFCA	Transfrontier Conservation Area
TFCG	Tanzania Forest Conservation Group
TGLP	Tribal Grazing Land Policy
TLA	Traditional Leaders Act
TOCADI	Trust for Okavango Cultural and Development Initiatives
UNDP	United Nations Development Programme
UNFCCC	United Nations Framework Convention on Climate Change
USAID	United States Agency for International Development
VAG	Village Action Group
VLFR	Village Land Forest Reserve
VTC	Village Technical Committee
VTC	Village Trust Committee
WADCO	Ward Development Committee
WIMSA	Working Group for Indigenous Peoples of Southern Africa
WMA	Wildlife Management Area
WWF	World Wide Fund for Nature/World Wildlife Fund
Z$	Zimbabwe Dollar
ZANU-PF	Zimbabwe African National Union-Patriotic Front
ZAWA	Zambia Wildlife Authority

Part 1

Introduction

Introduction: The Politics of Natural Resource Governance in Africa

Fred Nelson

The land is the economy, the economy is the land.
>Zimbabwe African National Union-Patriotic Front (ZANU-PF)
>election slogan

Wildlife is our oil.
>Tanzania National Parks official (quoted in Sachedina, 2008)

Power concedes nothing without a demand. It never did and it never will.
>Frederick Douglass, 1857

Few matters are more central to the daily lives of African societies than the use and governance of natural resources. The majority of Africa's human population relies on the resources that grow or live on the land, and the ecological services which underpin agricultural and pastoralist livelihoods. Patterns of resource use are fundamental to rural and national economies, as well as to local and global concerns about environmental conservation. In the political sphere, the desire of Europeans to capture and exploit African resources played a key role in the transformative process of colonialism. Natural resource governance issues such as land tenure continue to underpin evolving relations between citizens and states in the post-colonial era.

Institutional histories and political interests fundamentally shape rights over natural resources, which in turn are central to the way those resources are used. The core characteristic of Africa's colonial era was the imposition of new forms of centralized political authority over access to land and resources that had previously been controlled by more localized institutions. After independence arrived in most of sub-Saharan Africa in the 1960s, this centralized authority over natural resources was generally reinforced as states sought to consolidate the political authority needed to drive modernization processes and to control patronage resources.

During the past several decades, a diverse array of factors have challenged these prevailing historical patterns of natural resource policy and management practice across sub-Saharan Africa, and indeed much of the world. Central state agencies have often mismanaged natural resources, due to both insufficient capacity and misaligned incentives which lead to appropriation of public assets for private gain and patronage. In many African countries, centralized state ownership of resources such as wildlife, forests and fisheries has led to conditions of open access exploitation, as central capacity to enforce restrictions on use has not matched the state's claims of ownership. Local communities whose livelihoods depend directly on natural assets continue to lack the formal authority to conserve and manage those resources. As knowledge has grown over the past 20 years about the durability and sustainability of many local collective resource governance institutions (e.g. Ostrom, 1990), numerous initiatives have emerged in developing countries to reform centralized resource management systems by vesting more secure rights and responsibilities at the local level (Ribot, 2004; Batterbury and Fernando, 2006). In Africa, these reforms have been driven not only by concerns about developing more sustainable and participatory resource governance systems, but also by broader political economic changes. These include the declining capacity of bureaucratic agencies in many states following the economic crises of the 1970s and 1980s, which led to externally driven policy reform processes (e.g. 'structural adjustment'), as well as the spread of democracy and multi-party politics throughout Africa in the 1990s following the end of the Cold War (Bratton and van de Walle, 1997).

In some east and southern African countries, innovative reforms granting local communities greater rights to use and manage resources have led to tangible development and conservation gains on the ground and catalysed broader enthusiasm for reforms (Suich et al, 2008). Zimbabwe's CAMPFIRE programme has been particularly influential, resulting in over US$20 million in revenues from wildlife being captured at district and community levels during 1989–2001 (Frost and Bond, 2008). Namibia's communal conservancies adapted some of the key lessons, including both successes and limitations, from CAMPFIRE, and this has resulted in widespread wildlife recoveries and rapidly increasing local revenues from wildlife and tourism on communal lands (NACSO, 2008). In Tanzania, policy and legal reforms carried out in the 1990s which enable local communities to formalize collective rights over forests have resulted in both widespread ecological recoveries and new local benefits (Blomley et al, 2008; Lund and Treue, 2008). Globally, evidence is increasing that local communities are often able to manage and conserve resources more sustainably than state protected areas, and often at a fraction of the costs (e.g. Hayes, 2006). Local experiments such as CAMPFIRE have provided the empirical basis for the widespread support that has emerged since the 1980s for more decentralized and participatory forms of natural resource management such as 'community conservation' and 'community-based natural resource management' (CBNRM) (Adams and Hulme, 2001; Suich et al, 2008).

Such efforts to reform natural resource governance policies and institutions highlight not only the potential and importance of local management regimes on ecological and socio-economic grounds, but also the practical barriers facing such changes. In an influential global review, Ribot (2004) finds that most of the natural resource decentralization reforms being promoted are effectively 'charades' due to the lack of real reform and implementation on the ground. Around the world, governments have adopted the rhetoric of decentralization, devolution and local empowerment, but rarely has this change in language been matched by the substantive depth of institutional reforms. By contrast, numerous measures ensure that centralized government agencies across Africa, Asia and Latin America maintain discretionary control over valuable natural resources, and local tenure remains insecure (Ribot et al, 2006).

In eastern and southern Africa, numerous studies, project reviews and practitioner reflections are evidence of the illusory nature of many natural resource reforms and the difficulty of achieving real change (IIED, 1994; Barrow et al, 2000; Shackleton et al, 2002; Jones, 2004; Jones and Murphree, 2004). The lack of progress on the ground has in some instances caused erstwhile supporters of community-based approaches to natural resource management to shift to other narratives and strategies, or to argue that community-based natural resource management initiatives have broadly failed to live up to their promise (Hutton et al, 2005; Blaikie, 2006).

If there has been a broad failure of these community-based approaches, it has been not in the performance of their operational principles, which have rarely been put into practice (Murphree, 2004), but in the recognition of the nature and depth of resistance to reform that exists across the region. This resistance is political in nature, and relates to the interests and incentives that central agencies and individuals possess for maintaining or expanding control over natural resources (Gibson, 1999; Nelson and Agrawal, 2008). Land and natural resource reforms are often not carried out because, as Alden Wily (2008a, p6) puts it, in relation to competing state and private commercial interests, 'these resources are too valuable to allow ordinary people to own'. With rapidly growing financial interests in African natural resources, driven largely by global patterns of commerce and capital interacting with national and local governance institutions, the political-economic stakes in African landscapes and ecosystems are rapidly rising.

These political-economic realities and trends create an axiomatic conundrum facing natural resource governance reform efforts in sub-Saharan Africa: crafting more sustainable resource management arrangements requires reforms that secure greater land and resource rights at the local level, but the policy-makers that control such reform processes generally have substantial disincentives to implementing such measures (Murphree, 2000). If local groups of people are to become better able to use, manage and conserve the resources that their livelihoods depend on, this paradox must be better understood and ultimately negotiated. This is no small challenge for the diverse array of parties with a stake in rural Africa's environmental and economic future.

This volume examines these political dimensions of natural resource governance, in the hope of generating an improved understanding of how and why reform efforts play out the way that they do, and ultimately contributing to the development of more effective strategies for influencing institutional changes that empower local groups of people to secure their livelihoods, territories and environments. While this book's scope is limited to east and southern Africa, these case studies and regional syntheses will likely be relevant to efforts elsewhere to craft more sustainable natural resource governance arrangements in a world of increasing human demands and depleted ecological capacity.

African economies and natural resource use

Patterns of use and control over natural resources have been a core thread tying together the course of human history, and in few places is this more the case than in sub-Saharan Africa. The importance of natural resources in African states' political histories is a function of the central economic role that such resources play in agrarian societies. Although African countries are rapidly urbanizing, the economic foundation of most nations across the region remains their natural resource base. In rural areas, people rely on agriculture, livestock and a range of natural products for food and income. Because much of sub-Saharan Africa is semi-arid with erratic patterns of rainfall and with ancient and infertile soils, less than 10 per cent of the subcontinent is classified as arable land (FAOSTAT, 2009). Many groups of people continue to rely on extensive pastoralist livestock production systems, from the Sahel to the Rift Valley to the Namib.

Forests, rangelands, lakes and coastal ecosystems provide a wide range of valuable natural products which generate economic activity and underpin people's livelihoods. The World Health Organization estimates that up to 80 per cent of Africa's human population uses traditional medicines from natural products as a key form of primary health care (Roe, 2008). In central Africa, wild meat accounts for between 30 per cent and 80 per cent of rural households' overall protein intake (Nasi et al, 2008). In Kenya, pastoralist livestock production, in the form of milk, meat and hides, is estimated to be worth about US$800 million to the national economy (Hesse and MacGregor, 2006). A recent World Bank (2008) study from Tanzania suggests that informal natural resource uses at the local and national level could be worth up to US$100 per capita, or about 30 per cent of existing mean national incomes. Even in relatively industrial South Africa, communal resources, such as non-timber products from forests and woodlands, provide an annual subsistence value estimated at a mean of nearly US$450 per household, or a total national value of US$800 million per year (Shackleton and Shackleton, 2004).

Renewable resources provide the basis for Africa's growing forestry, tourism and fishing industries. Commercial timber production in Cameroon was worth over US$345 million by 2002, while Uganda's lake fisheries generate an estimated US$200 million per year and provide employment for over 800,000 fishermen and small-scale processors (Oyono et al, 2007; Roe, 2008). Forests also provide key ecological services in the form of water supplied from highland catchment areas, which serve not only the domestic water needs of urban centres such as Johannesburg and Dar es Salaam, but also the hydroelectric generation that is a key component of many African countries' energy supplies.

International tourism receipts to sub-Saharan Africa amounted to US$14 billion in 2004, with annual rates of growth consistently above 8 per cent from 2000 to 2005 (World Bank, 2006). Tourism industry growth in Africa reflects the growing global demand for nature-based ecotourism, and the competitive advantage that Africa possesses for delivering such tourism products as a result of its wildlife and other unique natural assets. As Sachedina (2008) highlights in a recent study of community-based conservation in northern Tanzania, as captured by the quote placed at the outset of this chapter, wildlife's role in the tourism industries of countries such as Kenya and Tanzania gives wildlife resources a political economic salience analogous to that of oil in other nations.

Alden Wily (2008b) estimates that up to 25 per cent of the total African land mass consists of communally managed lands, such as forests and rangelands, with a conservatively estimated real estate value of at least US$70 billion. Moreover, she also estimates that 'over 90 percent of the rural population access land through indigenous customary mechanisms, and around 370 million of them are definably poor' (Alden Wily, 2006, p2).

The centrality of natural resources and ecosystem services to African economies at scales from rural households to entire nations is a important factor in the convergence of environmental and developmental concerns during the past 20 years. The economic value of these natural resources also places debates over land rights and resource use on centre stage politically. Before proceeding to outline these political economic factors and the way they shape natural resource policies and management practices, it is important to briefly review the key role that institutions play in natural resource governance and management outcomes.

Institutional dimensions of natural resource use

Institutions are the rules, both formal and informal, that govern society and which underpin human economic activities and social interactions (North, 1990). As such, institutions provide the substantive basis of 'governance', both analytically and operationally. Formal institutions include laws, policies, and constitutions, which all serve to define, distribute and delimit the powers of states and citizens. Informal institutions include norms, customs and ethical beliefs, which are all collective means of governing human behaviour through 'rules' of social interaction. Institutions such as property rights determine who may use a resource and access or capture that resource's value. Formal property rights enable the formation of large-scale markets for trade in the resource itself as well as the rights to a given resource's value in the future.

The institutional arrangements, including both formal legal rules and informal social norms, that define the distribution of rights over natural resources shape patterns of resource use and conservation in fundamental ways. Where rights over resources are either completely undefined or unenforced, conditions of 'open access' tend to encourage the depletion of the resource because nobody possesses incentives for conserving a resource which is available for appropriation by any prospective user. This may be the case where resources are physically situated at the global scale, such as pelagic fisheries or the atmosphere, but where institutions have not been formulated and adopted to govern the use of these shared global resources. Alternatively, open access scenarios may exist where the state (or any other actor such as an absentee landowner) claims ownership of a resource but does not in fact enforce that right; this is the case with wildlife across most of sub-Saharan Africa and elsewhere in the tropics. As a result, wildlife tends to be exploited in an unsustainable manner because local users do not have rights over the resource and thus lack incentives for investing in conservation measures that would restrain exploitation and promote sustainable use (Nasi et al, 2008).

Resources which are subject to open access are effectively ungoverned; that is to say, there are no functional rules which govern who may use a resource and no institutions that allocate rights over resources amongst different groups or individuals. Such open access scenarios have often been conflated – most influentially by Hardin (1968) in his seminal article on 'The tragedy of the commons'– with communal or common property regimes. In such communal regimes, rights to use resources are shared by a group of people, with membership of that group somehow defined and rules mutually adopted which govern resource use (Ostrom, 1990). Rates of resource use which exceed rates of resource renewal – the definition of 'unsustainable' – may be prevented by collective enforcement of such rules.

The ability of groups of people to devise and maintain collective resource governance institutions thus has a critical influence on the sustainability of resource use patterns. As the understanding of common property regimes and collective resource governance systems has blossomed around the world since the 1980s, the importance of local institutions in sustaining natural resources has become increasingly recognized (Dietz et al, 2003). For example, a wealth of evidence from long-term studies of forests in different parts of the world suggests that local management institutions may perform as well or better than state protected areas (Hayes, 2006; Ostrom and Nagendra, 2006). Agrawal (2007, p123) summarizes the evolving understanding of the relationship between sustainable forest management and local institutions as follows:

> *Rules that are easy to understand and enforce, locally devised, take into account differences in types of violations, help deal with conflicts, and help hold users and officials accountable are most likely to lead to effective governance.*

Similarly, the rules that govern the exploitation of fisheries have a critical influence on patterns of use. A recent global study of fisheries management outcomes demonstrates that fisheries which are managed based on clear and enforceable property rights over a defined catch volume have largely avoided the kinds of collapses in stock that characterize many modern fisheries (Costello et al, 2008).

Institutions shape the way people use resources in fundamental ways by distributing rights, authority and responsibilities amongst different layers of society. Importantly, though, institutions are inherently the outcome of the political negotiations whereby people devise governance systems from local to national to global scales (North, 1990). In order to understand natural resource management outcomes, we must understand the political processes that determine the shape of resource governance institutions and how those institutions change over time.

Negotiating reform: The promise and limitations of community-based natural resource management

Most of African history since the onset of the colonial era in the late 19th century has been characterized by the transfer of formal authority over lands and natural resources from local communities to national political jurisdictions (Adams, 2004; Alden Wily, 2008b). Colonialism resulted in sweeping institutional changes in the way resources were governed, with authority shifting over time away from local resource users towards a remote and unaccountable colonial state with objectives that were very different from those of local communities. This undermined local resource governance systems, and served to shift many resources from a status as common property to that of de facto open access. The result has been extensive conflicts over rights and tenure amongst different local, national, and global resource users, as well as widespread degradation of renewable natural resources such as forests and wildlife.

Even while colonial and post-colonial measures were extending centralized authority over lands and resources throughout most of sub-Saharan Africa, the seeds of alternative decentralized approaches were being planted in some countries. Starting in the late 1960s, southern African countries such as South Africa, Zimbabwe and Namibia progressively adopted wildlife management policies which brought about devolved proprietorship of wildlife and generated local economic incentives for conservation. This initially occurred between 1965 and 1975 in those three countries, all of which were ruled by white minority governments at the time, and this first wave of reforms was concerned solely with alienated freehold lands. White landowners were given conditional rights to manage and utilize the wildlife on their properties, which resulted in new incentives for stewardship and increases in both the number of animals and the economic productivity of wildlife as a form of land use in all three countries. In Zimbabwe, about 27,000km^2 of commercial farmland gradually shifted, through voluntary landholder choice, towards wildlife as the main form of land use, with some areas undergoing a broad shift from cattle ranching to wildlife production (Bond et al, 2004). In Namibia, wildlife on private lands increased by an estimated 80 per cent between 1972 and 1992 (Barnes and de Jager, 1995).

These experiences with institutional reforms devolving proprietorship over wildlife from the state to private landholders provided the conceptual, and ultimately political, basis for attempting to extend similar reforms to the communal lands in Zimbabwe and Namibia after those countries' transitions to majority rule in 1980 and 1990, respectively. In Zimbabwe, this resulted in the development of the Communal Areas Programme for Indigenous Resources (CAMPFIRE), which sought to devolve rights over wildlife in communal lands to the local level (Martin, 1986). CAMPFIRE was, at the time, a highly innovative experiment in community-based natural resource management. Although the architects of CAMPFIRE within Zimbabwe's wildlife bureaucracy were able to gain support for reforms which in principle aimed to devolve authority over wildlife to the local level, they were constrained by the institutional context of the country's communal lands, where no community-level governance institutions existed with rights over a defined area of land (Murphree, 2005). This led to a strategic compromise whereby authority would be transferred to the level of Rural District Councils rather than the community or village level as had been envisioned (Ibid.).

This compromise played a central role in CAMPFIRE's performance and impacts on the ground, as well as in the broader evolution of ideas about natural resource governance in southern Africa since the 1980s. From 1989 to 2001, the CAMPFIRE programme expanded from two districts to 37 districts, with a total of 43,000km^2 of communal lands being allocated for wildlife management (Frost and Bond, 2008). During this same period CAMPFIRE generated over US$20 million in direct income from wildlife, with about 50 per cent of this revenue going to the communities themselves, and the other half being captured by the Rural District Councils (Ibid.).

The capture of such a large proportion of wildlife revenues at the district level under CAMPFIRE meant that the essential principle of matching local proprietorship over wildlife with control over benefits had occurred imperfectly at best. The direct control over wildlife revenues by the district governments weakened local incentives for investing in wildlife production and conservation, and this emerged as the chief critique of CAMPFIRE. Reflecting on the program's first decade, Murombedzi (2001, pp247, 255) concludes that:

> *CAMPFIRE has not sufficiently devolved rights in wildlife to local communities to the extent where these communities can use these rights to gain an increased stake in the wildlife utilization enterprise at its multiple levels of value...the top-down preferences of central government on communities have merely been replaced by the top-down preferences of local governments on communities.*

In neighbouring Namibia, the lessons of CAMPFIRE were absorbed and influenced the design of Namibia's own wildlife management reforms following independence from apartheid South Africa in 1990. Namibia also sought to extend authority over wildlife to communal lands, but unlike Zimbabwe it did so with legislative reforms passed in 1996 that enabled communities to form their own self-defined 'conservancies' which would be granted direct proprietorship over wildlife. Since those reforms were adopted, community conservancies have spread rapidly, and by 2007 over 50 conservancies containing 118,000km^2 – over 14 per cent of Namibia's total land area – had been established (NACSO, 2008). The rights granted over wildlife in conservancies enable local communities to develop joint ventures with private tourism and hunting companies and to keep 100 per cent of revenues generated through such commercial enterprises (Jones, this volume). In sharp contrast to most countries in Africa and the world, the local incentives created through this devolved governance framework have helped enable Namibia to sustain broadly increasing wildlife populations, including rare species such as black rhinos, across private, state and communal lands (Nelson, 2008).

Experiences such as those of CAMPFIRE in Zimbabwe and the communal conservancies in Namibia have played an important role in catalysing further experimentation throughout east and southern Africa, and outside the region as well (Hulme and Murphree, 2001). Natural resource managers and rural development and conservation practitioners elsewhere in the region also developed similar models independently. In Kenya, efforts to develop models of community-based conservation which integrated wildlife management with local livelihoods are traceable to initiatives in the 1960s around Amboseli National Park (Western, 1994). Experiments with decentralized forest management arose in countries such as Uganda and Tanzania in the early 1990s, drawing as much on experiences with joint forest management in southern Asia as on initiatives elsewhere in Africa.

As a result, during the 1990s, community-based natural resource management (CBNRM) or 'community conservation' strategies became a widely promoted narrative for achieving interconnected conservation, rural development and local governance aims (Adams and Hulme, 2001). But by the end of the decade the tone had begun to change in many quarters, with growing doubt both within the region and amongst external donors and supporters as to the efficacy of these community-based approaches. The core problem has been that for effective local management regimes to emerge, institutional reforms need to shift authority over natural resources from state bureaucracies to local communities (Alden Wily and Mbaya, 2001; Shackleton et al, 2002; Nelson and Agrawal, 2008). With some notable exceptions, this has rarely occurred. Surveying southern Africa, Murphree (2002, pp1–2) concludes that:

> ...*most initiatives lacked the critical ingredient for success: the devolution of authority and responsibility through societally sanctioned entitlements. Government and agency implementation retained ultimate power to shape objectives and control benefits; 'involvement' became compliance and 'participation' became co-option.*

These constraints are common to natural resource reform efforts outside of southern or sub-Saharan Africa. A vast academic literature and chronicle of field experiences from around the world testifies to the challenges of shifting rights over resources from central bureaucratic agencies to local resource users (Ribot, 2004; Ribot et al, 2006; Sunderlin et al, 2008). These diverse experiences also testify to a main common cause of the failure of reforms: unwillingness at the political centre to divest authority over resources.

Natural resources and the African state: The politics of reform

Most experiences with natural resource decentralization reforms to date, in east and southern Africa and elsewhere as well, serve to highlight the inherently problem-atic nature of bringing about institutional changes that increase local authority and tenure over resources (Batterbury and Fernando, 2006). The underlying barriers to change lie in the institutional structures and political interests that govern socie-ties, and the incentives that those interests create in the context of policy formu-lation. Modern African states possess a number of general characteristics which fundamentally influence institutional reform processes and their outcomes.

Africa's colonial states were established in order to control labour, capital and resources for external, European purposes. This set of political objectives resulted in the concentration of central bureaucratic and executive power, with the states' powers of coercion used to limit independent forms of social organization. Governance was not, self-evidently, democratic, representative or accountable. Opportunities for people to self-organize in civic institutions such as unions, cooperatives or political parties were heavily curtailed. States claimed wide powers over natural resources, particularly land, which was generally placed under discretionary bureaucratic control with customary rights subordinated to claims explicitly recognized by the colonial administration (Toulmin and Quan, 2000). Even where colonial authorities claimed to operate in a decentralized manner, as in British 'indirect rule', this functionally meant concentrating fused executive, legislative and judicial powers in externally-recognized local authorities who were bolstered by what Mamdani (1996) calls 'the fist of colonial power' (see also Murombedzi, this volume).

African independence leaders inherited these political structures from their European predecessors. Domestic administrative capacity tended to be extremely low at the time of independence in most countries, while developmental aspirations and expectations were high. In many states regional or ethnic cleavages had been exacerbated by colonial indirect rule arrangements. Post-independence leaders faced the challenge of consolidating state authority over scattered populations and pursuing ambitious modernization agendas (Boone, 2003). In pursuing this agenda of consolidation and expansion of central authority, the colonial state was de-racialized but rarely democratized (Mamdani, 1996). Ihonvbere (2006, p10) states that African nationalist struggles 'culminated in the consolidation, rationalization, and reproduction of unequal and exploitative neo-colonial relations.' With discretionary power heavily concentrated in the hands of the executive, and limited means of democratically contesting that authority, control of the presidency in post-colonial African states became a path to power, wealth, and, through networks of patronage, social and ethnic security (Ake, 1996). The tremendously high stakes attached to control of the executive branch have led to many of Africa's civil wars and conflicts during the past 50 years, and remain clearly visible in events such as Kenya's disputed 2007 general election, and the violence that followed it (Wrong, 2009).

With tremendous private economic opportunities linked to groups' or individuals' control of the executive branch, and, at least until recently, limited opportunities for private accumulation elsewhere, politics becomes 'a means of entry into business' through a 'winner-take-all game in which power allows private appropriation of state resources' (Szeftel, 1998, p237). The result is that 'the state remains a battleground where individuals fight for whatever power or resources they can capture,' as Ake (1996, pp67–70) has put it.

An essential characteristic of this intense political struggle in sub-Saharan Africa is the degree to which it takes place outside the bounds of formal institutions. Political processes often revolve around kinship ties and relationships based on personal and communal patronage, rather than formal public discourses and institutions (Hyden, 2008). Chabal and Daloz (1999, p158) highlight the 'extent to which vertical and/or personalized relations actually drive the very logic of the political system...the overall aim of politics is to affect the nature of such personal relations.'

The importance of informal patronage in structuring political power in African countries is central to the region's governance dynamics. The high degree of informality of African polities underlies the region's high levels of corruption, which verge on what some term the 'criminalization of the African state' (Bayart et al, 1998). What is important to grasp in relation to the institutionalization of corruption in African societies is that, in contrast to much of the global discourse on 'good governance', corruption is not an aberrant malignancy of these systems, but is rather central to the operation and stability of political relations. Corruption simply reflects the dominance of private interests within the public political realm in most African countries, be it in the formulation of public policy or the use and allocation of public resources. In states dominated by informal patron–client relations, 'corruption' is simply a normative term contrasting the prevalence of informal processes with the more marginal role of formal legal institutions (Chabal and Daloz, 1999). As Kelsall (2008, p642) notes, 'this is the essence of neo-patrimonial governance; the rules are merely a screen, or else they are cynically used to create opportunities for rent-seeking.'

This emphasis on informality can, however, lead to ascribing all public policy and political dynamics in African states to informal goals and motivations. Part of the challenge of studies of African public policy and governance is to untangle the complexity of interacting formal and informal institutions and processes. Van de Walle (2001, pp51–52) highlights this 'hybrid' nature of the neo-patrimonial African state:

> ...*most African states are hybrid regimes, in which patrimonial practices coexist with modern bureaucracy. Outwardly the state has all the trappings of a Weberian rational-legal system, with a clear distinction between the public and the private realm, with written laws and a constitutional order. However, this official order is constantly subverted by a patrimonial logic, in which officeholders almost systematically appropriate public resources for their own uses and political authority is largely based on clientelist practices, including patronage, various forms of rent-seeking, and prebendalism.*

The key point is that both informal patronage relations and formal state institutions such as laws and policies are relevant to governance, and that ignoring either the formalistic, bureaucratic, 'visible' realm, or the informal, personalized, 'hidden' realm is likely to lead to misunderstandings and misinterpretations of governance processes and outcomes.

The pervasiveness of informal patron–client relations set within a context of centralized but often highly contested state authority fundamentally influences the way public resources are used and governed in African states. Bates (1981, p96), in his study of the political economy of agricultural policy-making in African countries, concludes that 'public institutions no longer embody a collective vision, but instead reinforce a pattern of private advantage.' Governance decisions and institutions are thus often oriented towards the production of private gains and rents, rather than towards producing public goods. Ake (1996, p42) locates these political economic dynamics at the centre of contemporary development outcomes in Africa:

> *Instead of being a public force, the state in Africa tends to be privatized, that is, appropriated to the service of private interests by the dominant faction of the elite… Given a choice between social transformation, especially development, and political domination, most African leaders choose the latter.*

Natural resources, with their historic mooring in the public domain and their high economic values, are central to the patronage interests that allow governing élites to maintain powers and privileges. VonDoepp and Villalón (2005, p18) note that 'control over resources translates into political advantage as incumbent elites obtain the ability to dispense patronage, run viable party organizations, and mount effective campaigns.'

This political logic of state control over lands and resources shapes natural resource governance patterns across Africa. Agricultural policy in Africa's largely agrarian nations has evolved according to political interests bent towards controlling producers' access to markets and inputs in order to extract rents (Bates, 1981; see Cooksey, 2003, for a more recent example). Forest policy and management institutions from Senegal to Cameroon to Tanzania are crafted according to central patronage interests in controlling and extracting rents from both formal and informal patterns of trade and utilization in products such as timber and charcoal (Oyono, 2004; Milledge et al, 2007; Ribot, 2008). Keely and Scoones (2003, p91) quote an Ethiopian government policy advisor framing the fundamental political importance of land tenure institutions with disarming simplicity: "'if you control the land you control the people.'"

Gibson (1999, p3), in a relatively unique comparative study of the political economy of wildlife policy in Zambia, Kenya and Zimbabwe, frames wildlife governance as a struggle amongst different social actors to control wildlife's economic value:

> *…because wildlife is an important economic and political resource…individuals and groups have sought to structure policy to secure its benefits for themselves. These actors operate in an arena composed of numerous institutions that affect their strategies and choices. The outcome of their efforts is wildlife policies that do not necessarily protect animals…Rather, wildlife policies and their outcomes reflect attempts by individuals and groups to gain private advantage.*

Gibson's somewhat understated conclusion is that 'although rural residents respond to incentives, bureaucrats do not appear interested in creating policies that undercut their own authority' (Gibson, 1999, p160).

The political economic barriers to natural resource reforms are merely one component, albeit in the rural African context an important one, of broader struggles over rights and accountability in African nations. Many natural resource management reforms emerged during the 1990s, during the same decade when democratic reforms were sweeping across sub-Saharan Africa in the 'second liberation' following the end of the Cold War (Bratton and van de Walle, 1997). As with natural resource reforms, the extent of these broader changes in governance has often been limited and invariably contested (Ibid., VonDoepp and Villalón, 2005). While new forms of political pluralism widely emerged during the early and mid-1990s, it has often been followed by efforts on the part of incumbent élites to reconsolidate political authority. Despite the spread of regular multi-party elections across African states in the 1990s, Ihonvbere and Mbaku (2006, p2) note that 'in no instance have elections been able to drastically alter the status quo and deepen the political process.' National elections in Kenya and Zimbabwe in late 2007 and early 2008, respectively, further demonstrate the substantial barriers that remain in the basic exercise of citizens' democratic rights even in the context of multi-party electoral contests, and the explosive social ramifications that continuing struggles over those rights can bring to bear at national and local scales. While such events provide dramatic illustrations of the ongoing nature of struggles for democracy in African societies, contests over land tenure and resource rights provide a less sensational but perhaps more substantive daily window into these same processes. As Ribot (2004) suggests, natural resource governance in developing nations constitutes the basic substance of democracy in agrarian and natural resource-dependent societies. Shivji (1998, p48), reflecting on the centrality of struggles over land tenure to Tanzanian democracy and political freedom, notes:

> *There is a deep structural link between the use and control of resources and the organisation and exercise of power. Control over resources is the ultimate source of power.*

Once one has set natural resource governance and policy formulation within sub-Saharan Africa's broader political context, it becomes apparent that efforts to decentralize or devolve authority over lands and resources are, to borrow from Kelsall (2008), 'going against the grain' of prevalent governance patterns and power relations. The widely noted failure of many natural resource reform efforts that have sought to strengthen local rights over resources in African countries is a function of the incongruity between such reforms and the political interests governing these states, combined with a democratic deficit with regard to rural communities' ability to demand rights and privileges. Arguments supporting decentralization based on technical criteria which emphasize production of public goods – such as increasing wildlife populations, more sustainable resource use patterns, or greater tax revenues – tend to overlook the informal private interests that underpin many or most policy decisions. In other words, the function of natural resource management in Africa is not necessarily to sustainably manage public resources in a way that contributes to public interests, just as Ake (1996, p70), speaking more broadly of African economies, observes that 'a national development project in most African countries is not a rational undertaking.' Hence natural resource governance outcomes may be politically rational in the private realm while environmentally degradative and economically destructive in the public realm. This misalignment between the personal interests and political logic which underlie policy formulation and implementation, and public environmental and economic interests, is central to the full spectrum of conservation and development issues in contemporary Africa.

Global influences: Aid and investment

The African political arena wherein natural resource management decisions are made and governance institutions shaped is not, however, inhabited solely by contending state and local actors. Now more than ever, African governance processes are fundamentally influenced by forces and actors operating at the global scale (Ferguson, 2006). The two most prominent elements of these global political-economic forces in relation to natural resource governance are development aid and private investment.

Aid agencies and transnational NGOs

The spread of natural resource decentralization and community-based approaches to conservation within sub-Saharan Africa has been heavily influenced by foreign development aid agencies (Adams and Hulme, 2001). This includes both multilateral organizations such as the World Bank and the many bilateral donor agencies such as the United States Agency for International Development (USAID), the German Development Agency (GTZ) and the British Department for International Development (DfID). In east and southern Africa, USAID and the four Scandinavian national development agencies have been particularly active in supporting and promoting community-based natural resource management, participatory forest management and related approaches. The emphases among different national agencies inevitably vary, with for example USAID tending to have greater interest in biodiversity conservation, while European donors generally prioritize poverty reduction and the social dimensions of local participation in resource governance.

During the past three decades, western development efforts have embraced and propagated a 'neo-liberal' set of ideas, narratives and policies for guiding global economic development (Ferguson, 2006). These emphasize private investment, reduced governmental regulation, transnational patterns of trade, and access to global capital flows as keys to economic growth and development in African countries, and have been steadily promoted, particularly by the multilateral development agencies such as the World Bank and the International Monetary Fund through its Structural Adjustment Programmes. Decentralization of government services, secure property rights and promotion of efficient and democratic governance are all additional elements of this neo-liberal set of policy prescriptions. These broader development policy narratives have strongly influenced natural resource management and conservation policy and account for much of the enthusiasm on the part of foreign donors for natural resource decentralization and community-based approaches (Brockington et al, 2008).

Linked to the governmental aid agencies and prevalent neo-liberal policy narratives through organizational, financial and political relationships are international or transnational non-governmental organizations (NGOs). Transnational private NGOs and foundations are particularly important players in the development and conservation arena in sub-Saharan Africa. Prominent development NGOs such as Oxfam and CARE International are deeply involved in issues of land tenure and natural resource management, at both local and policy levels. Conservation

NGOs such as the World Wildlife Fund, Conservation International, Frankfurt Zoological Society and African Wildlife Foundation pursue conservation agendas by attempting to work with state bureaucracies, private investors and local communities. Scholfield and Brockington (2008) estimate that conservation NGO funding in sub-Saharan Africa amounts to a total of at least $200 million annually. These private NGOs often function as implementing agents of governmental aid agencies, since a significant amount of their funding comes from aid, but they also influence broader development and conservation public policy debates within developed countries.

Multilateral and bilateral aid agencies and transnational development and conservation NGOs comprise a diverse set of actors and influences, with a wide range of complementary and conflicting interests. These organizations have played a key role in promoting natural resource governance reforms in Africa, but also in determining the shape that reform efforts take. Aid agencies and transnational NGOs have particular general structural characteristics and organizational interests which influence the way they conceive and pursue their activities in African countries.

A critical factor shaping actions by both aid agencies and transnational NGOs is the political reality of operating in foreign countries. Aid agencies themselves are effectively diplomatic entities, and are part and parcel of the efforts of national governments to pursue their interests outside their sovereign boundaries. In this context, development narratives promoted by aid agencies tend to minimize or obscure the political dimensions of policy choices; indeed, for most of its history the World Bank contended it did not involve itself in 'political' matters but was solely a technocratic organization, despite the inherent implausibility of any structural economic policy choices being apolitical in their scope or impacts. This apolitical culture and outlook continues to pervade the world of development aid, as memorably characterized by Ferguson (1994) as 'the anti-politics machine'. Even since the 1990s' incorporation of 'good governance' as a central element of effective economic development policy, considerable efforts are made to treat 'governance' as a set of technical prescriptions, rather than a fundamentally political process.

Aid agencies' apolitical treatment of governance processes shapes natural resource reform efforts. First, reform processes are framed as technocratic efforts designed to enhance production of public goods. For example, a USAID report on community-based natural resource management describes the process as a relatively technocratic set of sequential governance measures, with reform being driven by action at the political centre:

> *CBNRM is fundamentally based on the devolution of responsibilities, rights and authority from central government to local communities…Several milestones must be crossed to create the full enabling environment for better natural resources management. The first milestone is crossed when there is sufficient national political will to move toward CBNRM by enacting enabling policies, legislation, and regulations to support the devolution of power, and the policy, legal and institutional framework for supporting CBNRM. A second milestone requires establishing clear, simple and transparent procedures for mutual accountability between local, district/ provincial and national levels.*

(Alcorn et al, 2002, p*iv*)

While it is clear from the above narrative that CBNRM is a governance reform process, what is not interrogated is what might lead to the emergence of 'political will', which has been self-evidently elusive in so many African and global CBNRM initiatives. Other aid agency analyses are less grounded in the empirical realities of African governance:

> *...is devolution good for the government? The answer to this question appears to be positive. Most CBNRM schemes involve some revenue-sharing mechanism with the government. Many authors contend, therefore, that CBNRM facilitates a rural wildlife tax. The state, as the 'owner' of natural resources, is simply obtaining resource rents on its assets. To the extent that involving the community increases these rents, it is a win-win situation for the state.*
>
> (Shyamsundar et al, 2005, p42)

The above World Bank report quotation is conventional in its underlying assumption that natural resource policies are constructed according to states' interests in generating public goods such as tax revenues, rather than according to political élites' private interests. Those informal political interests, despite their centrality to policy-making in African states, rarely feature in donors' analyses of CBNRM and their strategic approaches to natural resource governance reform.

Because natural resource policy choices and governance patterns are shaped by conflicting interests which are negotiated in formal and informal political arenas, it is highly problematic when resource governance issues are framed in an apolitical manner, or based on dubious assumptions about policy-makers' motivations. This has been an important contributor to the unsuccessful outcomes of many natural resource reform efforts supported by donor agencies and transnational NGOs in Africa (Nelson, 2009).

This problem is compounded by the reality that African governments effectively mediate the interactions between foreign aid, and the local communities that are nominally the target 'beneficiaries' of CBNRM and related resource governance reform efforts. Aid itself is managed according to bilateral country agreements and thus African governments exert strong influence over the shape of foreign development efforts (van de Walle, 2001). This influence is amplified by donors' own organizational incentives, which are related to the inherently limited domestic accountability that western nations' citizens can exert on aid agencies operating overseas, making them very difficult to monitor effectively (Martens et al, 2002). Because of this weakness of citizens' ability to provide oversight of their government aid programmes' impacts, development agencies tend to measure and report their performance according to criteria such as the volume of expenditures, which do not correlate well with actual impacts achieved (Gibson et al, 2005). This creates an entrenched agency problem in the operation of government aid agencies, and is a central factor in the observed incentives that aid agencies have to spend large volumes of money over relatively short periods of time (Ibid.).

A related factor is the disincentives that aid agencies possess for applying punitive sanctions to recipient countries, such as withholding funds or terminating grants or lending programmes, which would have the undesirable internal effect of reducing aid expenditures. These disincentives have tended to render ineffective donors' efforts to use 'conditionality' in aid programmes as a way to influence policy reforms in recipient states (Collier, 1997; van de Walle, 2001).

Thus one may generalize that donors' efforts to finance natural resource governance reforms in African states often have not been based on a sound conceptualization of the political dimensions of governance processes, and in fact many aid agencies have organizational incentives to resist deeper interrogation of these political elements. Development agencies also are institutionally tied to African governments and have limited means of forcing reforms where there is insufficient domestic constituent demand (see also Devarajan et al, 2001). In addition, when reform efforts do not yield the intended results, aid agencies face limited sanction from their own constituent governments and citizens due to difficulties with monitoring, and have incentives to continue to maximize their expenditures (Gibson et al, 2005).

This structure of incentives also applies to many transnational NGOs, which as noted often function as implementing agents of donor agencies, and partners of host governments, rather than as autonomous agents of 'civil society' (Edwards and Hulme, 1996). Sachedina (2008) provides a thorough account of how these interests have played out in relation to the efforts of the African Wildlife Foundation (AWF) to support community-based conservation in Tanzania:

AWF wanted donor money and to be independent from the State. But in order to achieve growth, AWF needed to position itself as a close government partner in order to gain legitimacy, influence and funding.

(p330)

AWF undertook a strategic decision: it adopted an approach of working through government to enhance its legitimacy, networks of power, and donor relations. This approach compromised its ability to function as an independent civil society organization [and resulted in a] withdrawal from politically-laden conflicts over land tenure, money, and resource rights between pastoralists and the state.

(p355)

Thus the relationships between donors, the state and NGOs can exert a profound influence on the shape of natural resource institutions and power relations amongst different actors, and specifically on the outcomes of efforts to empower local communities with greater rights and privileges.

Global commerce and African resources

Up until recently, the defining feature of Africa's position within the global economy was its almost complete irrelevance (Ferguson, 2006). This is now changing, with rapidly increasing levels of foreign direct investment (FDI) as well as changing patterns of trade and commerce. In 2007, FDI in Africa as a whole reached an all-time high of US$53 billion, an increase of over 80 per cent from inflows of $29 billion received in 2005, and with US$30 billion of the 2007 total amount going to sub-Saharan countries (UNCTAD, 2008).

Increasing investment in African countries is driven by technological changes as well as increasing global demand for commodities. Resource shortages and growing affluence both play a role. Chinese demand for unprocessed logs has led to a dramatic shift in patterns of timber trade from Africa–Europe to Africa–Asia, with Indian Ocean countries such as Tanzania and Mozambique particularly affected (Nelson and Blomley, this volume). Concerns about domestic agricultural production and food security are driving a range of Asian and Middle Eastern countries to attempt to acquire large areas of land in African countries for exporting food (Cotula et al, 2009). European countries seeking to develop alternative fuel sources for their domestic markets have been the leaders in the sudden surge of biofuel investments in Africa during the past three years, which have acquired or proposed to acquire large areas of land (Cotula et al, 2008).

Africa's rapidly growing tourism industries are also a resource-based land use attracting capital to new areas or expanding within established markets and landscapes. While most tourists continue to come from North America and Europe, increasingly tourism properties throughout Africa are as likely to be owned and managed by Arabian, Indian or South African companies and investors.

The result of these trends is rapidly increasing demand for African resources, including not only transportable commodities such as timber but also land itself. The rapid growth in the market value of land and resources often is accompanied by escalating conflict over control of increasingly valuable resources. As some scholars have pointed out, resource-based conflicts are not necessarily driven by resource scarcity as such, but can equally arise from the high market value of resource-rich landscapes (Peluso and Watts, 2001; Duffy, 2006). As resource values rise in rural parts of Africa, so do the number of claimants competing to use and control those lands and resources.

Recent accounts portray an African landscape which is rapidly being allocated to transnational corporations, potentially at the expense of the long-term interests of both national economies and local communities (Vallely, 2009). For rural communities, there are important potential opportunities to benefit as custodians of lands and resources, for example through joint venture partnerships for tourism developments between local communities and external investors. In countries such as Kenya and Namibia, such models for wildlife-based ecotourism have generated considerable revenue for local communities, and may enhance local willingness and capacity to advocate for their resource rights and claims.

In many cases, though, the penetration of commercial trade into rural landscapes simply acts as a mechanism for foreign companies and national political élites to dispossess local groups. Patterns of commercial resource trade and economic value can be a key factor in the interests that policy-makers and governing élites have for maintaining control over those resources or in allowing local groups to strengthen their own tenure claims (Nelson and Agrawal, 2008). As Ribot (2004) points out, the general pattern across the developing world has been for governments to decentralize control over resources with low commercial values, and to retain or recentralize control over valuable resources. Ultimately the changing patterns of commercial investment and trade based on African lands and resources are likely to have substantial implications for ongoing struggles over resource rights and tenure.

In search of change, reform and sustainability

The political-economic context for natural resource governance in African nations encompasses a wide range of actors operating across multiple scales from local to global. Existing patterns of natural resource governance generally remain centralized, and are influenced by the legacy of colonial history, in élites' political interests in maintaining privileged control over valuable resources and discretionary authority, and extant patterns of commercial trade and investment. Reforms that would devolve or decentralize rights over resources to the local level, and which could provide the institutional basis for local common property management regimes, are frequently incompatible with other more powerful actors' interests. The efforts of external aid agencies and transnational NGOs may reinforce existing power relations because of those organizations' own interests and ties to the central government of the states in which they operate. Expanding capital penetration into rural Africa, through evolving global markets and trade patterns, can create stronger incentives to alienate local lands and resources. In the face of these established and potentially growing barriers to local resource rights and tenure, many parties, ranging from local communities to conservationists to development agencies, are left searching for effective measures that can achieve reforms which deliver more equitable and sustainable resource governance arrangements.

This dilemma is both a practical and conceptual one. Pragmatically, it is clear that numerous natural resource reform efforts across sub-Saharan Africa have not produced the intended results, and that the ability of practitioners to catalyse such changes often remains limited or ineffective. The practical question that arises is therefore: how can greater local authority over natural resources be effectively supported and promoted?

Conceptually, there are important flaws with the way that a wide array of local and international practitioners tend to frame processes of institutional reform. A central conceptual problem with the narratives used to describe these reform processes is that they generally presume that change will be driven from the centre, in the interests of the local. The discourse on natural resource decentralization is overwhelmingly predicated on central agency and initiative, with decentralization defined by way of central governments' actions to formally cede powers to lower levels within a political and administrative hierarchy (see Manor, 1999; Ribot, 2004). Anstey (2005, p144), writing about Mozambique, observes that the reforms which seek to enable local natural resource governance regimes tend to be founded on 'the premise of ordered dispersal of governance downwards (power, accountability, authority) from an enabling effective centre.' A related prevalent assumption made in most reform efforts is that natural resource governance in the region is oriented towards sustaining resources in the public interest based on technical considerations of efficiency, sustainability and productivity.

These kinds of assumptions (that natural resource reforms which decentralize or devolve rights to local communities will occur because they will result in more efficient, sustainable, and resilient resource governance regimes) are at best incomplete and at worst highly misleading. Narratives which presume that central bureaucrats will enact reforms designed to enable greater local authority over lands and resources often fail to capture the critical political interests of those authorities. As a result, institutional reform processes are framed within incorrect assumptions that misconstrue fundamental aspects of African governance. This problem is not restricted to natural resource reforms but more broadly characterizes contemporary efforts to promote 'good governance' in African states (Hyden, 2008; Kelsall, 2008). More effective efforts to promote decentralization, devolution and democratization require a better understanding of governance processes if reform efforts are to have greater impact. Practitioners, external supporters in both public and private organizations, and local activists need to develop conceptual frameworks for institutional change which more accurately and realistically describe how such changes may, or do, occur. To continue framing reform as a technocratic and apolitical process of delegating rights from the political centre to the local level, often in direct contradiction to the political interests that actually structure the choices and decisions of key state and non-state actors, is merely to invite further disappointment. This volume is an effort to develop a more informed and systematic framework for understanding natural resource governance in African countries, and the factors that underlie changes in resource management institutions.

Searching for the roots of reform: Democracy and decentralization

The motivating question that lies at the centre of this volume is: where does institutional change in natural resource governance come from? Using case material from India but a theoretical perspective which is of universal utility, Chhatre (2008, p12) provides a useful starting point for approaching this critical question: 'Political commitment from above is considered crucial for the success of decentralisation reforms, but where does this commitment come from?'

This poses the self-evident but often unacknowledged point that actions by the political centre which transfer power to other levels of society are unlikely to occur in the absence of political forces which create incentives for central actors to take such actions. In the case of decentralization, the source of such incentives is logically the local groups of people who are the beneficiaries of such changes and consequently demand reforms. Such local demand, often accompanied by the use or threat of violence, has been the underlying driver of many democratic reforms during the past several centuries, as Frederick Douglass, the 19th-century African-American antislavery activist, famously noted in the quote reproduced at the beginning of this chapter (see also Moore, 1966; Acemoglu and Robinson, 2006).

Chhatre (2008, p12) states the answer to his own question regarding the roots of decentralization accordingly: 'Decentralisation in natural resource management is about community agency,' meaning the ability of communities to 'mobilize to oppose the imposition of institutional forms that they deem inappropriate' and to advocate for their own resource use interests. Change at the centre is thus inextricably linked to action and agency at the local level. Natural resource decentralization depends on the broader political context and in particular the ability of local groups of people to influence central decision-makers through democratic mechanisms for representation and accountability.

The importance of this democratic context is a recurrent theme in the cases presented in this volume. In Namibia, reforms devolving rights over wildlife on communal lands were crafted by a relatively small technocratic élite within the bureaucracy, but this was only made possible by the sea change of independence from South Africa achieved in 1990. In South Africa, post-apartheid land tenure reforms enabling communities to claim alienated lands have re-shaped negotiations over resource rights, protected area governance and accountability at the local level. In Kenya, civil society has been able to play a much more influential role in crafting legislative reforms and public policy following the watershed 2002 general election which ended the long KANU (Kenya African National Union party) monopoly on executive power. Those changes in the macro-political context have had major consequences for the ability of local communities and non-state actors to influence natural resource governance. In all those instances, the broader democratic changes were not initiated solely or principally by the political centre. In contrast, macro-political change was an outcome of generational struggles over democratic rights, which in many cases were pursued through violent resistance movements that demanded change.

Analytic framework and content of this volume

This volume's analytic approach revolves around a set of national and local case studies, and uses those to attempt to explain the factors that account for natural resource governance outcomes and negotiations over resource rights and tenure in a range of settings in east and southern Africa. Such rights are inevitably contested and negotiated amongst different actors with diverse interests and differential powers and forms of political capital. The case studies, taken together, aim to contribute towards developing a deeper and more systematic understanding of the political variables that drive the outcomes of these institutional negotiations.

All the case studies are guided by two basic questions:

- What factors account for the outcomes of negotiations or distributive contests over natural resource rights and authority?
- How are these contests or negotiations over natural resource governance contributing to changes in the wider local governance arena?

Thus the cases examine both the variables that explain the general patterns of institutional change, and the impacts that those changes are having on local governance institutions and the capacity for collective resource governance.

In examining these processes, we adapt the analytic framework of Keeley and Scoones (2003) on African environmental policy formulation. Their framework takes a usefully broad view of policy processes, recognizing the importance of the instrumental interests of policy-makers and other key actors in shaping policy, as well as the importance of ideas framed through narratives and discourses, in determining certain policy outcomes. Both of these conceptual lenses are valuable, and as the chapters demonstrate, their relative importance varies across different cases. Incorporating both helps the cases avoid a more narrow disciplinary focus and to account for the diversity that one encounters in trying to distil the key drivers of complex institutional processes.

Natural resource governance processes are shaped, in large part, by the interests and relative powers of different actors. Political scientists frame decision-making processes according to this 'rational actor' assumption, which holds that people pursue their own economic interests. An important element of this theoretical framework is the assumption that people are able to, with a reasonable degree of efficiency, calculate their own interests in the face of numerous possible courses of action. The work of North (1990) on institutional change and economic performance employs this framework to illustrate how the social rules and norms that govern markets are constructed according to the interests and relative bargaining power of different societal actors. Ostrom (1990) also employs the 'rational actor' framework, and earlier work on human cooperative behaviour developed through game theory modelling, in her work on collective natural resource governance institutions. Gibson (1999) applies this political economic framework to the formulation of African wildlife policy, demonstrating how wildlife governance outcomes are a function of the relative interests and powers of key actors including members of parliament, government bureaucrats, local communities and foreign donors. The cases in this volume build on this work in political economy by identifying the key actors that influence the outcomes of local and national-level contests over resource rights and governance, and describing the interests which lead those actors to pursue various courses of action.

Although people tend to pursue their own interests within a certain economic and social context, people's own ideas, perceptions and actions can be strongly influenced by narratives and discourses which frame issues in particular ways. Roe (1991) provides the seminal definition of policy 'narratives' as stories that provide a compelling description of cause and effect in terms of a particular social or environmental outcome. In Africa, such narratives play a powerful role in shaping people's ideas, often independently of scientific evidence on the ground (Anderson and Grove, 1987; Keeley and Scoones, 2003). Examples of environmental narratives that have had a powerful influence on policy in Africa during the past 30 years include the tragedy of the commons; desertification; deforestation and erosion; and overgrazing and rangeland degradation (Leach and Mearns, 1996). During the past 20 years, community-based natural resource management has also become a narrative used to create the implicit assumption of feasibly marrying rural development and biodiversity conservation goals, sometimes in the face of weak empirical evidence regarding the likelihood of achieving both outcomes in a given place and time (Adams and Hulme, 2001). As the cases in this volume demonstrate, policy narratives continue to play an important role in framing negotiations and debates over resource rights and tenure throughout east and southern Africa.

One point which should be highlighted is that the interests of influential actors, and popular narratives or discourses, can be either mutually reinforcing or contradictory. For example, decentralization is often widely promoted in formal policy discourse, while the informal political interests of policy-makers contrastingly drive the consolidation of central authority over resources. Policy 'narratives' can be used to mask the more instrumentally-determined directions of policy and legislative changes, both from foreign donor supporters and domestic constituents.

In order to most clearly diagnose the key regional institutional trends concerning the governance of natural resources, the chapters in this volume focus on studying the distribution of rights rather than the content of policy. It is important to recognize that, particularly in sub-Saharan Africa, the two are by no means synonymous. Often policy changes are espoused but not implemented. Legislative changes may reflect policy-makers' key strategic interests whereas policy is used, like broader discursive narratives, to shroud the actual direction of institutional change. Thus we place less emphasis on policy (cf. Keeley and Scoones, 2003) and focus more on the distribution of rights, power and institutional accountability (cf. Agrawal and Ribot, 1999). Even formal rights expressed in law, however, do not necessarily translate into exercisable authority, and the cases attempt to focus on rights as they exist in practice rather than as they may be legislatively defined.

The volume is divided into four sections. The first section is introductory, setting the regional and conceptual context for the case studies. Following this introductory chapter, James Murombedzi frames the evolution of community-based natural resource management regimes in southern Africa through a review of key historical and political-economic forces influencing agrarian relations in the region. He highlights the way that CBNRM has generally failed to address the root causes of inequality and marginalization in southern Africa's communal tenure regimes, and the need for more transformative approaches to natural resource governance reform.

The second section focuses on the political economy of natural resource governance at the national level, with case studies drawn from Kenya, Namibia, Tanzania and Botswana. These cases draw largely on experiences with wildlife governance reforms in the region's savannah landscapes, with the Tanzania case also providing a detailed comparison between institutional reforms in the wildlife and forestry sectors. All four cases focus on contemporary national struggles over wildlife governance, but also frame these struggles within a longer historic set of institutional developments and evolutions. Important contrasts emerge from the cases, with Namibia providing the strongest, and rather aberrant, case of devolving significant rights over wildlife to the local level, while neighbouring Botswana has recently witnessed a considerable re-centralization of its CBNRM programme. In Tanzania, wildlife governance has been recentralized during the past decade, in sharp contrast to a narrative of devolutionary policy reform and also in contrast to tangible institutional changes supporting localized management regimes in the country's own forestry sector.

The third section takes the analysis closer to the grass-roots level, examining local governance dynamics and institutional linkages across multiple scales in Zambia, Mozambique, Zimbabwe, Botswana, South Africa and Tanzania. These cases examine linkages between macro and micro natural resource governance and local strategies for influencing institutional changes. The cases highlight the non-linear pattern of institutional change across the region; apparently successful local models of community-based management can collapse due to higher-scale political changes and processes (e.g. Zambia, Zimbabwe), yet at the same time communities frequently demonstrate resilience in their ability to organize to engage with higher-scale developments. The cases all highlight the constant, iterative nature of local negotiations over resources in contexts influenced by both local and non-local factors.

The final section is synthetic and forward-looking, attempting to distil the key patterns of institutional change across the region, and, in the case of climate change, to anticipate the influence of important new dynamics which may drive substantial change in the near future.

The volume aims to contribute towards the development of more effective approaches to natural resource reform, community empowerment and sustainable use of natural resources in east and southern Africa, and potentially beyond. The material presented here can also be looked at through the lens of broader struggles over governance, which not only influence the ways that natural resources are used, but which also are in turn shaped by ongoing contests over resource rights, tenure and local resource governance. Just as a range of development and conservation practitioners seek more accountable and decentralized arrangements for managing the environment and natural resources, African citizens as well as external interests such as foreign donors continue to search for measures to strengthen democratic governance across the region. Struggles over natural resource use are an important arena of action in this search for more accountable governance. Democracy and sustainability are two sides of the same coin with respect to natural resource governance; this does not mean that democratic governance guarantees sustainable use, but rather that the search for democracy and sustainable institutional arrangements for natural resource use are fundamentally intertwined.

References

Acemoglu, D. and Robinson, J. A. (2006) *Economic Origins of Dictatorship and Democracy*, Cambridge University Press, Cambridge

Adams, W. (2004) *Against Extinction: The Story of Conservation*, Earthscan, London

Adams, W. and Hulme, D. (2001) 'Changing narratives, policy and practices in African conservation', in D. Hulme and M. W. Murphree (eds) *African Wildlife and Livelihoods: The Promise and Performance of Community Conservation*, James Currey, Oxford

Agrawal, A. (2007) 'Forests, governance, and sustainability: Common property theory and its contributions', *International Journal of the Commons*, vol 1, no 1, pp111–136

Agrawal, A. and Ribot, J. C. (1999) 'Accountability in decentralization: A framework with South Asian and West African cases', *The Journal of Developing Areas*, vol 33, pp473–502

Ake, C. (1996) *Development and Democracy in Africa*, Brookings Institute, Washington, DC

Alcorn, J., Kajuni, A. and Winterbottom, B. (2002) *Assessment of CBNRM Best Practices in Tanzania*, Final Report for USAID/Tanzania and USAID/Africa Bureau – Office of Sustainable Development, Dar es Salaam and Washington, DC, www.cbnrm.net/pdf/ usaid_007_tanzania_assessment2002.pdf Accessed 22 August 2009

Alden Wily, L. (2008a) *Whose Land is it? Commons and Conflict States, Why the Ownership of the Commons Matters in Making and Keeping Peace*, Rights and Resources Initiative, Washington, DC

Alden Wily, L. (2008b) 'Custom and commonage in Africa rethinking the orthodoxies', *Land Use Policy*, vol 25, pp43–52

Alden Wily, L. (2006) *Land Rights Reform and Governance in Africa: How to Make it Work in the 21st Century?* Discussion Paper, Drylands Development Center and Oslo Governance Centre, Nairobi and Oslo, Kenya and Norway

Alden Wily, L. and Mbaya, S. (2001) *Land People and Forests in Eastern and Southern Africa at the Beginning of the 21st Century: The Impact of Land Relations on the Role of Communities in Forest Future*, IUCN-EARO, Nairobi, Kenya

Anderson, D. and Grove, R. (1987) *Conservation in Africa: People, Policies, and Practice*, Cambridge University Press, Cambridge

Anstey, S. (2005) 'Governance, natural resources and complex adaptive systems: A CBNRM study of communities and resources in northern Mozambique', in V. Dzingirai and C. Breen (eds) *Confronting the Crisis in Community Conservation: Case Studies from Southern Africa*, University of KwaZulu-Natal, Pietermaritzburg, South Africa

Barnes, J.I. and de Jager, J.L.V. (1995) *Economic and Financial Incentives for Wildlife Use on Private Land in Namibia and the Implications for Policy*, Research Discussion Paper No. 8, Ministry of Environment and Tourism, Windhoek, Namibia

Barrow, E., Gichohi, H. and Infield, M. (2000) *Rhetoric or Reality? A review of community conservation policy and practice in East Africa*, Evaluating Eden Series No. 5, International Institute for Environment and Development and the World Conservation Union, London and Nairobi

Bates, R.H. (1981) *Markets and States in Tropical Africa*, University of California Press, Berkeley and Los Angeles, CA

Batterbury, S.P.J. and Fernando, J.L. (2006) 'Rescaling governance and the impacts of political and environmental decentralization: An introduction', *World Development*, vol 34, no 11, pp1851–1863

Bayart, J.F., Ellis, S. and Hibou, B. (1999) *The Criminalization of the African State*, Indiana University Press, Bloomington, IN

Blaikie, P. (2006) 'Is small really beautiful? Community-based natural resource management in Malawi and Botswana', *World Development*, vol 34, no 11, pp1942–1957

Blomley, T., Pfliegner, K., Isango, J., Zahabu, E., Ahrends, A. and Burgess, N. (2008) 'Seeing the wood for the trees: Towards an objective assessment of the impact of participatory forest management on forest condition in Tanzania', *Oryx*, vol 42, no 3, pp380–391

Bond, I., Child, B., de la Harpe, D., Jones, B., Barnes, J. and Anderson, H. (2004) 'Private land contribution to conservation in South Africa', in B. Child (ed) *Parks in Transition: Biodiversity, Rural Development and the Bottom Line*, Earthscan, London

Boone, C. (2003) *Political Topographies of the African State: Territorial Authority and Institutional Choice*, Cambridge University Press, Cambridge

Bratton, M. and van de Walle, N. (1997) *Democratic Experiments in Africa: Regime Transitions in Comparative Perspective*, Cambridge University Press, Cambridge

Brockington, D., Duffy, R. and Igoe, J. (2008) *Nature Unbound: Conservation, Capitalism and the Future of Protected Areas*, Earthscan, London

Chabal, P. and Daloz, J.P. (1999) *Africa Works: Disorder as Political Instrument*, James Currey, Oxford

Chhatre, A. (2008) 'Political articulation and accountability in decentralization: Theory and evidence from India', *Conservation and Society*, vol 6, no 1, pp12–23

Collier, P. (1997) 'The failure of conditionality', in C. Gwyn and J. Nelson (eds) *Perspectives on Aid and Development*, Overseas Development Council, Washington, DC

Cooksey, B. (2003) 'Marketing reform? The rise and fall of agricultural liberalisation in Tanzania', *Development Policy Review*, vol 21, no 1, pp67–91

Costello, C., Gaines, S.D. and Lynham, J. (2008) 'Can catch shares prevent fisheries collapse?', *Science*, vol 321, pp1678–1681

Cotula, L., Vermeulen, S., Leonard, R. and Keeley, J. (2009) *Land Grab or Development Opportunity? Agricultural Investment and International Land Deals in Africa*, FAO/IIED/IFAD, Rome and London

Cotula, L., Dyer, N. and Vermeulen, S. (2008) *Fueling Exclusion? The Biofuels Boom and Poor People's Access to Land*, FAO/IIED, Rome and London

Devarajan, S., Dollar, D.R. and Holmgren, T. (2001) *Aid and Reform in Africa*, The World Bank, Washington, DC

Dietz, T., Ostrom, E. and Stern, P.C. (2003) 'The struggle to govern the commons', *Science*, vol 302, pp1907–1912

Duffy, R. (2006) 'The potential and pitfalls of global environmental governance: The politics of transfrontier conservation areas in Southern Africa', *Political Geography*, vol 25, pp89–112

Edwards, M. and Hulme, D. (1996) 'Too close for comfort? The impact of official aid on nongovernmental organizations', *World Development*, vol 24, no 6, pp961–973

Fabricius, C., Koch, E., Magome, H. and Turner, S. (2004) *Rights, Resources, & Rural Development: Community-based Natural Resource Management in Southern Africa*, Earthscan, London

FAOSTAT (FAO Statistics Division). (2009) Available at: http://faostat.fao.org/site/377/DesktopDefault.aspx?PageID=377#ancor Accessed 23 January 2009

Ferguson, J. (2006) *Global Shadows: Africa in the Neoliberal World Order*, Duke University Press, Durham, NC

Ferguson, J. (1994) *The Anti-politics Machine: 'Development', Depoliticization, and Bureaucracy in Lesotho*, University of Minnesota Press, Minneapolis, MN

Frost, P.G.H. and Bond, I. (2008) 'The CAMPFIRE programme in Zimbabwe: Payments for wildlife services', *Ecological Economics*, vol 65, pp776–787

Gibson, C.C. (1999) *Politicians and Poachers: The Political Economy of Wildlife Policy in Africa*, Cambridge University Press, Cambridge

Gibson, C.C., Andersson, K., Ostrom, E. and Shivakumar, S. (2005) *The Samaritan's Dilemma: The Political Economy of Development Aid*, Oxford University Press, Oxford

Hardin, G. (1968) 'The tragedy of the commons', *Science*, vol 162, pp1243–1248

Hayes, T.M. (2006) 'Parks, people, and forest protection: An institutional assessment of the effectiveness of protected areas', *World Development*, vol 34, no 12, pp2064–2075

Hesse, C. and MacGregor, J. (2006) *Pastoralism: Drylands' Invisible Asset? Developing a Framework for Assessing the Value of Pastoralism in East Africa*, Drylands Issue Paper No. 142, International Institute for Environment and Development, London

Hulme, D. and Murphree, M.W. (2001) *African Wildlife and Livelihoods: The Promise and Performance of Community Conservation*, James Currey, Oxford

Hutton, J., Adams, W. M. and Murombedzi, J. (2005) 'Back to the barriers? Changing narratives in biodiversity conservation', *Forum for Development Studies*, vol 2, pp341–370

Hyden, G. (2008) *Institutions, Power and Policy Outcomes in Africa*, Discussion Paper No. 2, Africa Power and Politics Programme, Overseas Development Institute, London

Ihonvbere, J.O. (2006) 'Where is the third wave? A critical evaluation of Africa's non-transition to democracy', in J.M. Mbaku and J.O. Ihonvbere (eds) *Multiparty Democracy and Political Change: Constraints to Democratization in Africa*, Africa World Press, Trenton, NJ, and Asmara, Eritrea

IIED (International Institute for Environment and Development) (1994) *Whose Eden? An Overview of Community Approaches to Wildlife Management*, International Institute for Environment and Development, London

Jones, B.T.B. (2004) *Synthesis of the Current Status of CBNRM Policy and Legislation in Botswana, Malawi, Mozambique, Namibia, Zambia, and Zimbabwe*, Report prepared for WWF SARPO, Harare, Zimbabwe

Jones, B.T.B. and Murphree, M.W. (2004) 'Community-based natural resource management as a conservation mechanism: Lessons and directions', in B. Child (ed) *Parks in Transition: Biodiversity, Rural Development, and the Bottom Line*, Earthscan, London

Keeley, J. and Scoones, I. (2003) *Understanding Environmental Policy Processes: Cases from Africa*, Earthscan, London

Kelsall, T. (2008) 'Going with the grain in African development?', *Development Policy Review*, vol 26, no 6, pp627–655

Leach, M. and Mearns, R. (1996) *The Lie of the Land: Challenging Received Wisdom on the African Environment*, Heinemann, Portsmouth, NH

Lund, J.F. and Treue, T. (2008) 'Are we getting there? Evidence of decentralized forest management from Tanzania's Miombo woodlands', *World Development*, vol 36, no 12, pp2780–2800

Mamdani, M. (1996) *Citizen and Subject: Contemporary Africa and the Legacy of Late Colonialism,* Princeton University Press, Princeton, NJ

Manor, J. (1999) *The Political Economy of Democratic Decentralization*, The World Bank, Washington, DC

Martens, B, Mummert, U., Murrell, P. and Seabright, P. (2002) *The Institutional Economics of Foreign Aid*, Cambridge University Press, Cambridge

Martin, R.B. (1986) *Communal Areas Management Programme for Indigenous Resources*, Department of National Parks and Wildlife Management, Harare, Zimbabwe

Milledge, S.A.H., Gelvas, I.K. and Ahrends, A. (2007) *Forestry, Governance and National Development: Lessons Learned from a Logging Boom in Southern Tanzania,* TRAFFIC East/ Southern Africa/Tanzania Development Partners Group/Ministry of Natural Resources and Tourism, Dar es Salaam, Tanzania

Moore, B. (1966) *Social Origins of Dictatorship and Democracy: Lord and Peasant in the Making of the Modern World*, Beacon Press, Boston, MA

Murombedzi, J. (2001) 'Committees, rights, costs and benefits: Natural resource stewardship and community benefits in Zimbabwe's CAMPFIRE programme', in D. Hulme and M.W. Murphree (eds) *African Wildlife and Livelihoods: The Promise and Performance of Community Conservation*, James Currey, Oxford

Murphree, M.W. (2005) 'Congruent objectives, competing interests, and strategic compromise: Concept and process in the evolution of Zimbabwe's CAMPFIRE, 1984–1996', in J.P. Brosius, A.L. Tsing and C. Zerner (eds) *Communities and Conservation: Histories and Politics of Community-based Natural Resource Management*, AltaMira Press, Walnut Creek, CA

Murphree, M.W. (2004) 'Communal approaches to natural resource management in Africa: From whence and to where?', *Journal of International Wildlife Law and Policy*, vol 7, pp203–216

Murphree, M.W. (2002) 'Protected areas and the commons', *The Common Property Resource Digest*, no 60, pp1–3

Murphree, M.W. (2000) *Boundaries and borders; the question of scale in the theory and practice of common property management*, Paper presented at the Eighth Biennial Conference of the International Association of Common Property (IASCP), Bloomington, IN

NACSO (Namibian Association of CBNRM Support Organizations) (2008) *Namibia's Communal Conservancies: A Review of Progress in 2007*, NACSO, Windhoek, Namibia

Nasi, R., Brown, D., Wilkie, D., Bennett, E., Tutin, C., van Tol, G. and Christophersen, T. (2008) *Conservation and Use of Wildlife-based Resources: The Bushmeat Crisis*, Technical Series No. 33, Secretariat of the Convention on Biological Diversity, Montreal, and Centre on International Forestry Research, Bogor, Indonesia

Nelson, F. (2009) 'Conservation and aid: Designing more effective investments in natural resource governance reform', *Conservation Biology*, vol 23, no 5, pp1102–1108

Nelson, F. (2008) 'Are large mammal declines inevitable?', *African Journal of Ecology*, vol 46, no 1, pp3–4

Nelson, F. and Agrawal, A. (2008) 'Patronage or participation? Community-based natural resource management reform in sub-Saharan Africa', *Development and Change*, vol 39, no 4, pp557–585

North, D.C. (1990) *Institutions, Institutional Change and Economic Performance*, Cambridge University Press, Cambridge

Ostrom, E. (1990) *Governing the Commons: The Evolution of Institutions for Collective Action*, Cambridge University Press, Cambridge

Ostrom, E. and Nagendra, H. (2006) 'Insights on linking forests, trees, and people from the air, on the ground, and in the laboratory', *Proceedings of the National Academy of Sciences of the United States of America*, vol 103, pp19224–19231

Oyono, P.R. (2004) 'One step forward, two steps back? Paradoxes of natural resource decentralization in Cameroon', *Journal of Modern African Studies*, vol 42, no 1, pp91–111

Oyono, P.R., Ribot, J. and Larson, A. (2006) *Green and Black Gold in Rural Cameroon: Natural Resources for Local Governance, Justice, and Sustainability*, Environmental Governance in Africa Working Paper No. 22, World Resources Institute, Washington, DC

Peluso, N.L. and Watts, M. (2001) *Violent Environments*, Cornell University Press, Ithaca, NY

Ribot, J.C. (2008) *Authority over Forests: Negotiating Democratic Decentralization in Senegal*, Working Paper 36, Representation, Equity, and Environment Working Paper Series, World Resources Institute, Washington, DC

Ribot, J.C. (2004) *Waiting for Democracy: The Politics of Choice in Natural Resource Decentralization*, World Resources Institute, Washington, DC

Ribot, J.C., Agrawal, A. and Larson, A.M. (2006) 'Recentralizing while decentralizing: How national governments reappropriate forest resources', *World Development*, vol 34, no 11, pp1864–1886

Roe, D. (2008) *Trading Nature: A Report, with Case Studies, on the Contribution of Wildlife Trade Management to Sustainable Livelihoods and the Millennium Development Goals*, TRAFFIC International, Cambridge, UK and WWF International, Gland, Switzerland

Roe, E. (1991) 'Development narratives or making the best of blueprint development', *World Development*, vol 19, no 4, pp287–300

Sachedina, H. (2008) 'Wildlife is our oil: Conservation, livelihoods and NGOs in the Tarangire Ecosystem, Tanzania', PhD thesis, University of Oxford

Scholfield, K. and Brockington, D. (2008) *Non-governmental Organisations and African Wildlife Conservation: A Preliminary Analysis*, University of Manchester, Manchester

Shackleton, S. and Shackleton, C. (2004) 'Everyday resources are valuable enough for community-based natural resource management programme support: Evidence from South Africa', in C. Fabricius, E. Koch, H. Magome and S. Turner (eds) *Rights, Resources, & Rural Development: Community-based Natural Resource Management in Southern Africa*, Earthscan, London

Shackleton, S., Campbell, B., Wollenberg, E. and Edmunds, D. (2002) 'Devolution and community-based natural resource management: Creating space for local people to participate and benefit?', *Natural Resource Perspectives*, No. 76, Overseas Development Institute, London

Shivji, I.G. (1998) *Not Yet Democracy: Reforming Land Tenure in Tanzania*, IIED/HAKIARDHI/ Faculty of Law, University of Dar es Salaam, Dar es Salaam and London, Tanzania and UK

Shyamsundar, P., Araral, E. and Weerarante, S. (2005) *Devolution of Resource Rights, Poverty, and Natural Resource Management: A Review*, Environmental Economics Series Paper No. 104, The World Bank, Washington, DC

Suich, H., Child, B. and Spenceley, A. (2008) *Evolution and Innovation in Wildlife Conservation: Parks and Game Ranches to Transfrontier Conservation Areas*, Earthscan, London

Sunderlin, W.D., Hatcher, J. and Liddle, M. (2008) *From Exclusion to Ownership? Challenges and Opportunities in Advancing Forest Tenure Reform*, Rights and Resources Initiative, Washington, DC

Szeftel, M. (1998) 'Misunderstanding African politics: Corruption and the governance agenda', *Review of African Political Economy*, no 76, pp221–240

Toulmin, C. and Quan, J. (2000) *Evolving Land Rights, Policy and Tenure in Africa*, International Institute for Environment and Development, London

UNCTAD (United Nations Conference on Trade and Development) (2008) *World Investment Report: Transnational Corporations and the Infrastructure Challenge*, United Nations, New York and Geneva

Vallely, P. (2009) 'Wish you weren't here: The devastating effects of the new colonialists', *The Independent*, 9 August 2009, www.independent.co.uk/environment/nature/wish-you-werent-here-the-devastating-effects-of-the-new-colonialists-1767725.html Accessed 22 August 2009

VonDoepp, P. and Villalón, L.A. (2005) 'Elites, institutions and the varied trajectories of Africa's third wave democracies', in L.A. Villalón and P. VonDoepp (eds) *The Fate of Africa's Democratic Experiments: Elites and Institutions*, Indiana University Press, Bloomington, IN

van de Walle, N. (2001) *African Economies and the Politics of Permanent Crisis, 1979–1999*, Cambridge University Press, Cambridge

Western, D. (1994) 'Ecosystem conservation and rural development: The case of Amboseli', in D. Western, R.M. Wright and S.C. Strum (eds) *Natural Connections: Perspectives in Community-based Conservation*, Island Press, Washington, DC

World Bank (2008) *Putting Tanzania's Hidden Economy to Work*, World Bank, Washington, DC

World Bank (2006) *Tourism: An Opportunity to Unleash Shared Growth in Africa*, Note No. 16, World Bank, Washington, DC

Wrong, M. (2009) *It's Our Turn to Eat: The Story of a Kenyan Whistleblower*, Fourth Estate, London

2

Agrarian Social Change and Post-Colonial Natural Resource Management Interventions in Southern Africa's 'Communal Tenure' Regimes

James C. Murombedzi

Southern Africa has been hailed as a leading innovator in designing and implementing community-based natural resource management (CBNRM) programmes that devolve rights over natural resources to local communities. Most of the region's CBNRM programmes have been based on the legal devolution of narrowly delimited rights over specific resources from state agencies to local authorities or some representative body of the 'local community' (Steiner and Rihoy, 1995; Hulme and Murphree, 2001). Within the regional CBNRM movement, there is a growing realization that most initiatives have fallen short of providing significant rights over resources to local communities (Murombedzi, 2001); that typically the principal benefits accruing to communities are relatively limited revenues from resource use and exploitation by others rather than real rights to the resources (Bond, 1993; Murombedzi, 2001); and that in most cases the revenues are invested in collective social services or 'petty projects of municipal socialism' (Shopo, 1985; Murombedzi, 1994).

As the shortcomings of CBNRM policies and practices have become more apparent, the viability of CBNRM as a strategy for achieving both conservation and development objectives has come under increasing scrutiny. Calls for a reversion to centrist natural resource management regimes have emerged (Redford and Taber, 2000). Referred to by some as the 'back to the barriers counter-narrative' (Hutton et al, 2005), these calls are based on the view that despite some positive social impacts, CBNRM has not sufficiently improved the status of wildlife or forest resources and that evidence suggests that centralized management of natural resources is more efficient.

Consequently, the regional CBNRM discourse has focused on refining its policies and practices in order to support improved conditions of resource tenure for local communities by perfecting the devolutionary process itself (i.e. amending legislation, devolving more control and rights to communities than to local governments, and so on). In addition to this 'flawed devolution' discourse in CBNRM there have also been calls for the extension of CBNRM to other resources beyond the traditional southern African focus on wildlife (Dzingirai, 1995; Madzudzo, 1996). But even these calls have focused on resources that can attract commercial capitalist interests such as forest resources (including timber and now carbon) and water. Although CBNRM initiatives in some places have generated benefits for participating communities, including revenues and greater institutional capacity, in general the reforms carried out to date have been peripheral to the land and resource rights contestations of greatest salience to the beneficiary communities.

CBNRM initiatives are implemented in the context of southern Africa's communal tenure regimes, typically without problematizing the nature and dynamics of these so-called 'customary' tenure systems and their associated governance and power structures. Many authors have highlighted the central role that the formation of customary tenure regimes played in the development of the colonial state in Africa (e.g. Mamdani, 1996; Amanor, 1999; Peters, 2004). Communal tenure in post-colonial southern Africa is maintained to the extent that it privileges a small political élite and enables them to stay in power (Amanor, 1999), and continues to be applied in ways that typically create space to maintain a high level of bureaucratic intervention in local economies. CBNRM efforts have tended to reinforce this state–local relationship, and to further opportunities for the state to define and control local land use. Furthermore, CBNRM often extends the reach of private capital into communal areas, resulting in further land and resource expropriations (Hughes, 2006).

Throughout sub-Saharan Africa, and much of the developing world, evidence abounds of intensifying competition and conflict over land and natural resources, accompanied by deepening social differentiation (Peters, 2004). These processes have their origins in commodity production in the form of export crops, and a subsequent fall in crop prices in the 1930s; colonial constraints on African trading and land markets; oscillating patterns of migration; tenure reforms associated with the post-World War II push to develop a 'yeoman' farmer class in many British territories; rising debt and declining prices for primary commodities which led to the Structural Adjustment Programmes of the 1980s and 1990s (Ibid). The resultant widespread inability of rural producers to maintain earlier levels of farming, coupled with Structural Adjustment Programmes' induced retrenchments of civil servants and other losses of formal employment, all provided impetus for the diversification of rural incomes. In the face of limited opportunities, family land has increasingly come to constitute the most significant source of cash and food (Ibid). The increasing importance of land contributes to the increasing intensity of land conflicts both within communities, and also between communities and outsiders.

Other causes of land conflicts in many southern African contexts are immigration between communities (Dzingirai, 1995; Murombedzi, 1995; Nyambara, 2001); alienation of land for 'development' projects such as the recent growth in biofuel plantations; and land set aside for conservation programmes. These land alienations put pressure on available arable land and pastures (Peters,

2004), and lead to increased land use competition and conflicts. In Peters' (2004, p291) words:

>...*rural groups seek to intensify commodity production and food production, while retrenched members of a downsized salariat look for land to improve food income options; states demarcate forestry and other reserves, and identify areas worthy of conservation (often under pressure from donors and international lobbying groups)...and valuable resources both on and under the land (timber, oil, gold, other minerals) attract intensifying exploitation by agents from the most local...to transnational networks...*

Because conventional CBNRM initiatives do not confront these complex agrarian political economic realities, such initiatives may be attractive to southern African governments as an opportunity to implement development initiatives that do not challenge existing land tenure arrangements and tenure regimes. In some cases CBNRM actually increases the state's reach into rural communities (Alexander and McGregor, 2001), and allows for greater intervention and control of local land use, usually through the mechanism of local government authorities (Murombedzi, 1994). CBNRM also appeals to foreign governments' aid agencies to the extent that it conforms with approaches to development that build on existing systems of land and resource tenure rather than seeking to transform them.

In southern Africa, communities today are actively demanding land and property rights. These demands take many different forms, and social movements are coalescing around the issue of land tenure and property rights, as they did during colonial liberation struggles (Moyo and Yeros, 2005). However, communities encounter legal, policy and power obstacles in this pursuit. By placing the evolution of CBNRM initiatives in the historical agrarian context of southern Africa, this chapter attempts to explain the complex ways in which the managerial project of the region's CBNRM initiatives has resulted in a parochial focus on a few commercially valuable natural resources (Murombedzi, 1994), avoidance of agrarian politics and 'political ecology' (Abel and Blaikie, 1986), and an inherent inability to engage with prominent issues surrounding the fundamental transformation of agrarian relations in the region's communal tenure regimes (Dzingirai, 1994; Murombedzi, 2001; Moyo and Yeros, 2005).

With few exceptions (Murphree, 1993; 1995; Dzingirai, 1994; Adams and Mulligan, 2003), studies of CBNRM in southern Africa rarely contextualize the evolution of these policies and programmes. The historical and material context in which these policies and programmes evolved is frequently reduced to a benevolent technocratic response by the policy-makers to the realization that communities are more efficient managers of communal resources than the central state. Communities are perceived to be more efficient managers than the state because they are closer to the resource in question, can more efficiently internalize the costs of resource management, and it is their 'natural right' (Parker, 1993). However, the historical claims that communities have to the resources in question, the ongoing struggles to resolve the land question (of which resource tenure is a part), and the politics of rural land and resource use are not the determinants of these policies and practices.[1]

One of the most enduring outcomes of colonialism in southern Africa is the creation of the 'customary' or 'communal' land tenure system and its attendant systems of local government and administration. Both of these are key issues in the evolution, focus and nature of CBNRM programmes in the region and serve to frame ongoing struggles over resource rights, tenure and access. It is thus necessary to preface this discussion with an exploration of the historical trajectory of colonialism in the region, and place the evolution of CBNRM within this historical context.

The colonial agrarian order

Post-colonial states in southern Africa are confronted with the challenges of resolving the impacts of long-term exploitation of its labour force by colonial capital (the 'labour question'); integrating the indigenous population into the citizenry of the post-colonial state (the 'native question'); and transforming the state itself in order to create the basis for post-colonial development (the 'national question'). In resolving this national question, perhaps the most important policy issue in post-colonial sub-Saharan Africa is the issue of agrarian reform. In southern Africa, agrarian transformation is dominated by the land question (Amin, 1976; Mamdani, 1996; Moyo and Yeros, 2005). This is particularly true in the post-settler colonial states of Namibia, Mozambique, South Africa and Zimbabwe, but also applies to post-colonial transformation in the rest of southern Africa.

It is not easy to generalize the complex colonial and environmental histories of the southern African region. However, there are certain commonalities that have had generally similar implications for post-colonial transformations in the different countries of the region. First, a defining feature of sub-Saharan Africa's history is the relatively late establishment of colonial rule. As former Tanzanian President Julius Nyerere once remarked, 'For Lenin imperialism was the last stage of capitalism, but for Africa it was the first' (quoted in Woodhouse et al, 2000, p3). The principal European powers that established vast colonial territories in Africa (Britain and France) were industrialized countries and their 'second industrial revolution' generated a massive growth of demand for agricultural and mineral raw materials which were to be supplied by colonial economies in an expanding and shifting international division of labour. Southern Africa was an important region for the supply of both agricultural and mineral raw materials, and the colonial economies of the region were progressively structured to this end. Settler colonialism in parts of the region also contributed to the late decolonization of the region in comparison to other parts of Africa.

Second, in Africa colonialism encountered a vast range of social formations, habitats and modes of livelihood, on which colonial administrations attempted to impose their own structures, first through pacification, and then through various forms of social engineering. Many of the features of these social formations survived colonial social engineering and persisted into the post-colonial era, and continue to exert significant influence on state–society relationships and interactions.

Amin (1976) distinguished three macro-regions of sub-Saharan Africa through a broad typology of their colonial formations. West Africa was characterized by agricultural export production by peasant farmers, and in some cases by large-scale indigenous producers. It did not entail widespread dispossession and its patterns of commoditization of the rural economy proceeded without the institution of private property rights and markets in land. In many cases commoditization was realized through movement into and clearing of new areas to farm cocoa, oil palm (in the forest belt), and cotton and groundnuts (in the savannah). These remain the four classic export crops of West Africa.

Second, the 'labour reserve' colonies stretching through parts of central to southern Africa in which there was widespread land alienation to European settlers. The rationale for dispossessing Africans and concentrating them in 'native reserves' was two-fold: to provide land for settlers and commercial farming, and to create regular supplies of labour to these large farms and plantations, as well as to the mining complexes of North and South Rhodesia (Zambia and Zimbabwe, respectively) and of South Africa.

The third category is the 'Africa of concessionary companies' found in the region of the Congo River basin. The concessionary companies were granted vast territories for exploitation, with serious consequences for both their inhabitants and natural resources. Generally, however, they were unable to establish the conditions of systematic and sustained capitalist agriculture that came to prevail in east and southern Africa. The actual trajectories of Africa's modern history are inevitably less clear-cut than explained by Amin's broad schema. In West African colonies, for instance, land was often expropriated for extractive industries (mining, timber, rubber), if not for purposes of European settlement (as in the Gold Coast/Ghana). Some countries combined elements of all three types of colonial economy, notably Mozambique and Angola under Portuguese rule. At the same time, peasant commodity production (and its associated class differentiation) was never completely extinguished in the labour reserve/settler colonies, even within the severe constraints imposed by colonial authorities. Moreover, over time the colonial economy shifted towards a greater weight of peasant commodity production which was actively promoted in the latter colonial period. In most of sub-Saharan Africa, with the exception of the territories featuring extensive (white) settlement (Kenya, Southern Rhodesia, South Africa), peasant farmers (including pastoralists) were not dispossessed but encouraged, through economic and extra-economic forms of coercion, to enter the commodity-based economy as producers of agricultural commodities and/or labour power.

Indirect rule and the colonial construction of customary authority

At the same time as colonial African economies were being organized to produce tropical agricultural products and mineral ores for export, these activities were also expected to yield the revenues to pay for European colonial administration. The formation and operation of colonial states were based on indirect rule in British colonies, 'association' in French colonies, or segregation (later apartheid) in South Africa, which were all in effect similar responses to the common challenge of establishing and maintaining 'native' subjugation and to exercise political domination at low cost to the colonial authorities (Amin, 1976; Berry, 1993; Mamdani, 1996; Bernstein, 2005). Berry (1993) refers to this phenomenon as 'hegemony on a shoestring'.

Under indirect rule, the lower tiers of state administration in the countryside were allocated to the authority of local chiefs and headmen governing through the ostensive 'customary law' of particular 'tribes', to which rural people were subject on the basis of their 'tribal' identity as perceived and legislated by colonial rulers (Mamdani, 1996). While the powers of the chiefs were completely subordinated to those of the colonial state in relation to key functions such as tax collection and labour recruitment, they were often greatly increased in relation to their local subjects. This colonial refashioning of chieftaincy in effect fused executive, legislative and judicial powers of customary authority in the countryside, and was not so much an embrace of local 'traditional' institutions but rather the construction of new forms of local political authority that were inherently tied to the colonial project. Mamdani (1996) refers to these local governance systems as the 'decentralized despotism' of indirect rule.

Indirect rule had potent and enduring effects for rural land tenure and resource use practices and institutions, as for local governance more generally. As a key foundation of indirect rule and chiefly authority, 'customary' or 'communal' land tenure functioned in part to maintain rural stability, and in part to prevent, limit or otherwise manage the dynamics of class formation (e.g. by returning migrant workers to their 'tribal communities' and the benign patriarchal authority of their chiefs) (Bernstein, 2005). Through the institution of indirect rule, the 'customary' in Africa in relation to land, as well as political authority, was refashioned or even reinvented. To ensure the success of this project, colonial authorities suppressed the commoditization of land, including the development of land markets, which might have led to greater social and economic mobility in rural areas. Communal land tenure was fashioned in this context as part of a package of economic and extra-economic measures to limit the agricultural and other resource use potential of the native populations, thereby coercing them into wage labour and other forms of political and economic dependence (Bernstein, 2005; Moyo and Yeros, 2005).

Constructions and legacies of communal tenure

The ways in which 'communal' or 'customary' land on the one hand, and state land on the other hand, were defined and contested retain a powerful resonance in many parts of Africa today. This resonance is amplified by widespread rural poverty and growing inequality. Land expropriation and the colonial reconstruction of 'communal' tenure combined to undermine rural livelihoods in the region. Partly as a result of the overcrowding and resultant unregulated or 'open access' resource use, most natural resources in the communal lands were degraded in the years immediately following their creation. This contributed to driving the populations of the reserves into wage labour, and years later provided fertile recruiting ground for the region's liberation wars. Landlessness and land hunger were the principal drivers of those liberation wars.

An important feature of colonialism in the 1930s that has ongoing repercussions for the land and native questions is so-called 'Fabian colonialism' (Cowen and Shenton, 1991). This refers to the set of ideas and practices in which the central motif of colonialism was notionally to protect the natives from the costs of capitalism while gradually allowing them to share in its benefits. 'Protection' of the natives required the prevention (or indefinite postponement) of such features of bourgeois civilization as private property rights in land and ease of access to commercial credit for African entrepreneurs (Bernstein, 2005; Moyo and Yeros, 2005). This phase was characterized by the introduction of a wide range of community development projects, social clubs and other local initiatives which were designed to 'advance' the native populations in various respects (Murapa, 1977). This notional advancement of Africans was expressed in a number of areas of economic and social policy including land use planning, environmental conservation, welfare and development, hygiene and so on (Burke, 1996).

Some analysts have concluded that 'Fabian colonialism' did function to effectively halt the further advance of colonial capital into the native reserves, and thereby retain enclaves that would become important areas of investment for indigenous capital in the post-colonial era (Hughes, 2006). However, studies of the expansion of commodification in the reserves suggest otherwise. Burke (1996) makes the case for both the hegemonic practices of colonial and capitalist interests and the efforts made by native actors to participate in and resist these practices in the development of merchant capital and manufacturing in Southern Rhodesia. An array of laws, practices, incentives and disincentives combined to limit native merchant capital and restrict class formation in the reserves. Moreover, even when there were some disincentives for colonial capitalist expansion into the native reserves, where high-value resources existed in sufficient quantity, capital expansion was never restricted. This was indeed the experience with mining, as well as with other natural resource-based investments such as safari hunting following the 1960s boom in the safari industry. In Zimbabwe, for instance, most of the safari hunting was undertaken outside the conservation estate on freehold lands or in the native reserves themselves.

Starting in the late colonial era after World War II, when some African colonies were being prepared for independence through various governance reform measures, and continuing through the post-independence period, indirect rule through customary authority began to be partially replaced by efforts to institute representative local government in the form of municipal townships and rural councils. These councils were endowed with legislative powers to discharge specific functions, to raise part or much of their revenue, and to recruit and manage staff. This often added new layers of complexity and tension to those of indirect rule, and the claims and counter-claims of chiefly authority, which was challenged by these new elective structures rather than necessarily being extinguished. The challenge of raising revenues for the newly established local authorities in the native reserves meant that from the outset, these authorities encouraged all manner of commercial investment, and also sought to control revenues in order to finance their own recurrent expenditures. These pressures were to increase starting with the 1970s' financial and economic crises and continuing with Structural Adjustment Programmes (SAPs) in the 1980s, which gave added impetus to the local authorities' preference for privileging the commercialization of 'communal' resources by private capital and thereby restricting local capitalist expansion. Local government continued to function as an instrument of policy implementation rather than formulation.

In addition to the racialized landholding structure, colonial land expropriation resulted in a tripartite division of land, between black, white and land set aside for wildlife (Mackenzie, 1988). As with land expropriated for the establishment of capitalist white agriculture, the colonial conservation estate was created on land taken from local communities. Local communities not only lost access to lands and wildlife resources but now also incurred significant ongoing costs from wild-life predation and destruction of property. Expropriatory conservation initiatives were characterized by European ideological conceptions of nature which perceived native populations as the ultimate threat to sustainable resource use (Anderson and Grove, 1987). Conservation concerns in this legal context ultimately became a significant element of 'native policy' (Bernstein, 2005) and led to more state intervention in the communal lands, resulting in the substitution of state regula-tions in place of local resource management institutions (Murombedzi, 1994). Thus in addition to racialized agrarian structures, nature conservation was a key component in the disempowerment of local communities in southern Africa.

Land tenure reform and the evolution of CBNRM in contemporary southern Africa

Southern Africa today is thus characterized by grossly unequal and racialized agrarian relations, particularly in the former settler colonies of South Africa, Mozambique, Namibia and Zimbabwe. The colonial landowning classes histori-cally held up to 80 per cent of the best agricultural lands, with the bulk of the indigenous populations confined not only to arid and semi-arid zones, but also burdened with 'customary' land tenure and onerous land use regulations, 'tradi-tional' authority systems and restrictions on their movement.

The central legacy of settler colonialism in southern Africa is the land question. Except for Zimbabwe, this question remains largely unresolved within Southern Africa. Even in Zimbabwe, fast-track land reform since 2000 has redistributed significant amounts of land (Mamdani, 2009), but has not adequately addressed the congestion in communal lands; nor have appropriate reforms for communal land tenure been developed. With the possible exception of Zimbabwe, the histor-ical structure of tenure dualism and grossly unequal land holdings inherited from the colonial state has generally continued largely unchanged in the post-independ-ence era. But even as Zimbabwe has developed a more complex and less polarized agrarian structure, numerous issues remain unresolved, especially pertaining to land and natural resource tenure (Moyo and Yeros, 2005).

A land tenure system cannot be understood except in relation to the economic, political and social systems which produce it and which it influences (Bruce, 1988). Land tenure is fundamental to political structures and relationships in sub-Saharan Africa; as Boone (2007, p566) notes, 'the terms of land access remain the hard core of the social contract between the post-colonial state and rural popu-lations.' Extant land tenure systems in southern Africa are the outcome of the establishment of sustained capitalist agriculture in the regions. The principal characteristics of the agrarian structure of the colonial economies were tenure dualism (i.e. the dichotomy between communal and freehold lands) and bimodalism (meaning landholding patterns characterized by the concentration of land in a few large estates with the majority of farmers consigned to very small holdings), and with 'communal' tenure dominating the smallholder sector. This agrarian structure has continued in the post-independence era, even despite numerous land reform policies and initiatives. In this context, communal tenure continues to represent patterns of legally guaranteed land and resource use, rather than constituting a form of land ownership (Bruce, 1988).

Without exception, the post-independence political settlements of southern Africa were designed to guarantee colonial land rights through constitutional limitations on the expropriatory powers of the new governments, as well as through market-based land reform programmes which protected the interests of the landowners and resulted in limited land transfers to the landless or land-poor majorities. At the same time, the new governments did not implement any comprehensive reforms of the prevailing communal land tenure and associated local government systems. The result was that demands for land and tenure reform have remained high among the rural poor, while the legitimacy of traditional authorities has been challenged, at times by the state and at times by the communities themselves throughout the region.

Communal tenure in most of east and southern Africa remains insecure. In law, convention and practice, the communal lands of the region generally remain state property, with local government bodies exercising legal authority over most land and natural resources. The communal tenure regimes of these regions are characterized by high levels of state intervention and interference with local and private land use, ranging from land use planning to collectivization and other settlement reorganization schemes and programmes (e.g. see Scott, 1998). But tenure is also insecure in two other respects. First, there are few incentives to invest in either individually held land parcels or communally held rangelands, forests and other land types. Second, there are no land markets in the communal tenure regimes. Land sales and transfers do occur, frequently disguised as sales of permanent improvements to the land (Bourdillon, 1987), and such transactions also extend access to communal resources to the purchasers, but there are no markets in land titles.

With a few notable exceptions such as Botswana and Lesotho, the agrarian structure characteristic of most southern African countries tends to be bimodal. But even in unimodal systems such as in Botswana, there are distinctive patterns of access to customary lands which indicate that the wealthy and powerful have access to more land and natural resources than the poor (Peters, 2004).

The imposition of Structural Adjustment Programmes throughout the region in the 1980s and 1990s (except South Africa, which was then going through the throes of decolonization) exacerbated rural poverty, accelerated land demands and led to increased tensions and sometimes open conflicts over land between the landless and the landowners (Moyo, 2000). Structural adjustment resolutely submerged the land question, but did not stem popular demand for land reform and contestation between the market-based land reforms and land occupations

(Moyo and Yeros, 2005). As in the numerous land occupations which occurred in Zimbabwe during this period, the state continued to protect the property rights of the landed classes and to repress the demands of the rural poor. This had the effect of channelling land demands into other less densely populated communal lands, such as state lands devoted to wildlife conservation (Murombedzi, 1994).

Contested rural lands and the emergence of CBNRM in Zimbabwe

In Zimbabwe, one of the most significant of these rural mass movements of peasants occurred in the Zambezi valley, in communal lands that had earlier been cleared of tsetse fly. Tsetse fly eradication in the Zambezi valley, coupled with the expansion of settlements mainly into communal and state lands in that region in direct response to limited land redistribution opportunities elsewhere in Zimbabwe, resulted in massive influxes of immigrants starting in the early 1980s, and culminating in formal large-scale resettlement schemes in the early 1990s.

It was in this context that CBNRM emerged as a policy response to ongoing challenges related to the dominant patterns of rural capital accumulation within the natural resources sector. The emergence of the CBNRM agenda in the 1980s coincided with and indeed fit very well into the structural adjustment approach which effectively replaced industrialization with export agriculture and tourism as the principal engines of economic development. Marginalized communal areas with wildlife resources offered an economic opportunity to be exploited, and indeed were attractive to commercial enterprises in that the new CBNRM programmes protected investments from extant challenges by the local communities. By and large, these challenges have taken the forms of struggles to create new forms of resource rights by local communities, through the expansion of agriculture into wilderness and other hunting concession areas (Murombedzi, 1994), poaching, or settlement and other destructions of wildlife habitat (Dzingirai, 1995). In Zimbabwe, the genesis of the CBNRM policies and programme was stimulated in part by large-scale and unprecedented settlements in previously marginal, remote and relatively inaccessible communal lands. Because of their remoteness, and especially because of the limitations placed on agricultural expansion by human and livestock diseases as well as by the inaccessibility of markets due to limited infrastructure, these 'marginal' communal lands had for decades been managed as safari hunting areas with very low population densities and higher wildlife (especially large mammal) densities.

Because they are the legal custodians of all wildlife resources throughout the region through the operation of the 'King's Game' notion in the prevailing Roman Dutch jurisprudence, which holds that the state is effectively the owner/trustee of all wildlife, state wildlife authorities generally exercise a high level of intervention in communal areas that have significant and commercially valuable wildlife resources. Similarly, forestry authorities have legal authority over valuable indigenous trees in communal areas, even where these trees grow outside formally designated forest reserves. In such areas, concessions for the use and benefit of wildlife/trees are given by those authorities, and until recently, without the participation of local resident communities.

The innovation of many CBNRM initiatives has been to ostensibly involve communities, through their local government representatives, in natural resource management decisions. Because most 'communities' in southern Africa are not landholding entities and thus not clearly defined legal entities, they consequently cannot enter into binding agreements regarding the use and exploitation of resources, for example the allocation of hunting or tourism concessions. For example, district authorities in Zimbabwe manage communal lands through centrally-delegated powers and thus have the legal authority to contract for such uses. By creating new yet limited rights to natural resources in essentially unchanged communal tenure regimes, with no reference to the wider issues of land rights or regulation of access to high-value natural resources, credit markets and changes in the local administrative structures, CBNRM in southern Africa generally constitutes highly limited resource tenure reform.

CBNRM and private capital

As a consequence of the post-adjustment neo-liberal agenda supported by governments and aid agencies, CBNRM initiatives throughout the region tend to support private sector ecotourism and commercial wildlife utilization interests rather than local resource proprietorship. Through CBNRM, the private sector is able to expand its geographic operations beyond the leasehold and freehold tenure regimes into the communal areas, while at the same time mobilizing state support to ensure the security of this expanded access to natural resources. Hughes (2001, p575) demonstrates how ecotourism is undermining black smallholders' entitlements to land in Zimbabwe:

> *Based on economic and ecological arguments, CAMPFIRE has redefined the black entitlement as merely a claim competing with those of other 'stakeholders'. No guarantees exist for residents and cultivators. Indeed, government and NGOs are fast transforming the lowland reserves into privileged and subsidized investment zones. Held in check for a century, a new kind of settler colonialism is sweeping down from the highlands.*

The principal objective of many CBNRM initiatives, at least in practice if not always in theory, is to create financial incentives for sustainable use of natural resources. Often this is equivalent to establishing a more stable environment for greater capital investments in wildlife in the agriculturally marginal communal lands. This places high emphasis on so-called joint venture partnerships between the private sector (i.e. private capital operating the safari industries), and the communities whose putative wildlife resources are made available for investment and exploitation. However, the power imbalances between the communities and their private sector partners, and the absence of clear or strong community rights to the resources in question, frequently are not raised. CBNRM is thus in practice often more a vehicle for advancing private capital interests rather than rural land and resource tenure and governance priorities.

One of Zimbabwe's initial pre-independence efforts to enhance local involvement with wildlife conservation was a scheme developed by the Parks and Wildlife

Department designed to redistribute some of the safari hunting revenues to African District Councils adjacent to safari hunting areas in communal lands. The rationale was that because wildlife is a fugitive resource, its mobility led to the residents of communal lands neighbouring parks and reserves incurring costs of wildlife predation and crop destruction. To manage the resultant conflicts, it was necessary to extend some benefits of wildlife management to those who bore the brunt of these costs. Known as WINDFALL (Wildlife Industries New Development for All), this initiative did not however propose new tenure arrangements regarding the wildlife resources, and shared the financial revenues from safari hunting with district authorities and not their constituent village-level communities.

The links between 'wilderness capital' and the freehold capitalist settlers of the region is an important component of the history of CBNRM. The safari hunting industry was given impetus by legislative reforms which extended property rights in wildlife to landowners in Zimbabwe in the 1970s (see Chapter 1, this volume). The same landowners subsequently converted vast quantities of land in marginal ecosystems to wildlife and other tourism uses, and as the industry grew and the demand for the safari experience expanded, the investment demands also transcended the limitations of extant wilderness and wildlife assets contained in state and freehold lands.

As the safari hunting industry expanded, so too did the need to expand the hunting areas into new and secure territories. However, since the communal lands did not enjoy the same tenure status as the private and leasehold lands, a device was developed to enable safari operators to negotiate concessions directly with the local authorities, circumventing the inertia of central government bureaucracy, and at the same time providing incentives for local authorities to regulate interactions between their constituencies and the wildlife industries. This legal device, called 'Appropriate Authority' in the Zimbabwean context (see Murphree, 1993; Dzingirai, 1994), is a limited reform of the wildlife laws which transfers to local authorities the right to enter into wildlife use agreements and benefit directly from wildlife use on communal lands. The revenues accruing to local authorities are typically a percentage of the total revenues generated from concession and hunting fees from hunting concessions on communal lands.

'Appropriate Authority' was the legal basis for the Communal Areas Management Programme for Indigenous Resources (CAMPFIRE) CBNRM programme that developed in Zimbabwe in the 1980s and subsequently influenced CBNRM throughout the rest of southern Africa. Thus CBNRM initiatives across the region originated in central government policies, supported by an array of international donors and national and international NGOs, and driven by private (usually white) capital investments. This state–capital alliance functions to protect existing property rights and helps deflect attention away from the struggles of rural communities for land and property rights by providing limited access to financial benefits from resource use (Murombedzi, 2001).

Because of limited rights to land and natural resources under many regional CBNRM programmes, communities have little discretion to determine actual resource uses and only rights to revenues generated from natural resource exploitation by external interests, and often cannot participate in that exploitation themselves (Murombedzi, 2001). Such limitations are a function of CBNRM initiatives' failure adequately to address or reform extant communal tenure regimes in southern Africa. These limitations are recognized by some new initiatives, such as recent tourism joint venture models being developed in South Africa that are based on enabling communities to gain equity at all the levels of the game lodge tourism industry, on the basis of secure rights to the land on which game lodges are developed (Massyn, 2004).

CBNRM and the politics of land reform in southern Africa

CBNRM programmes tend to narrowly focus on the devolution of property rights in wildlife and other natural resources, typically those with high exchange values and therefore high external commercial interests. CBNRM initiatives generally do not engage with broader issues concerning land reform, understood to mean 'the redistribution of landholdings and changes in the agrarian structure' (Bruce, 1998), nor confront the historical legacies of 'indirect rule' in relation to local government structures. Alliances of international and local capital combine to support certain forms of community participation, and limited rights and economic benefits, and thus regional framings of CBNRM. This framing involves the co-optation of local community élites (Dzingirai, 1995), local government and other policy élites (Murombedzi, 1994)) into the CBNRM project, shifting attention away from the peasantry's redistributive agenda (Magome and Murombedzi, 2003), and in the process guaranteeing commercial rights of access to valuable natural resources in agriculturally marginal communal areas without necessarily improving the livelihoods of the communities themselves (Bond, 1993; Murombedzi, 2001).

CBNRM programmes and the associated discourse in much of southern Africa are decidedly apolitical. The struggles of the participating communities for land and resource rights are glossed over in two important ways in the prevalent discourse. First, rural peasants are generically treated as 'communities', thus imputing the absence of internal class divisions and antagonisms. This also implies that the different strategies employed by the different strata within these communities to fight against or collaborate with capital are typically unrecognizable in the discourse. By failing to recognize and understand ongoing rural struggles for resource rights in the communal tenure regimes of the region, CBNRM remains incapable of addressing local rural tenure reform demands, let alone engaging the broader land reform challenges of the agrarian context in which it is firmly situated. To be sure, there have been calls for tenure reform within the CBNRM discourse, but these have largely focused on devolving greater rights over wildlife or trees to communities rather than local government authorities. Such calls do not perceive municipal governments as currently structured to be part of the governance dynamic of an imperfect communal tenure system. Consequently, this discourse does not call for an overhaul of the land tenure system and its attendant authority structures, but is limited to lobbying for the devolution of greater rights to benefit from the use of resources under state control, and managed through local governments. This allows the CBNRM discourse to avoid confronting the land and resource endowment inequalities characteristic of the bimodal agrarian structures of the region.

By addressing only tenure reform issues and ignoring the historical structural asymmetries in land ownership in the bimodal agrarian structures of most of east and southern Africa, the discourse surrounding CBNRM (and 'community conservation' or 'community-based conservation') has also failed to identify the struggles of the rural populations in these regions for greater equity in land owner-ship and participation in local governance. Only insignificant attempts have been made to engage the land reform programmes of the region.

Land and land tenure reform has been a development priority at various times in both colonial and post-colonial Africa. The impetus for these reforms origi-nated in the need to extend state control over the countryside, commodification of land for export crop production, and alienation of land by the state for agri-business and other large-scale investments in ecotourism and other resource-based enterprises (Amanor, 1999; Peters, 2004; Hughes, 2006). The focus of these reforms has thus changed at various moments in history, and in response to the changing priorities of governments and foreign aid agencies, from the creation of communal tenure systems (early colonial times), privatization (late colonialism), the 'abolition' of colonial communal tenures and replacement with various forms of state control over the countryside (immediate post-independ-ence period), and more recently, the reorganization of communal tenures after the failures of individualization, collectivization and other forms of state control. All of these interventions have, in turn, generated various reactions within the rural populations. The impact of these reforms and responses is that the label 'traditional' rarely reflects existing land relations in rural Africa. In general, the impact of the various tenure reforms has been to provide new means of élite appropriation of land and natural resources, and CBNRM initiatives often have functioned as another such avenue.

To take one regional example, land tenure struggles have proliferated in Mozambique since independence in 1975. These struggles have given rise to a very sophisticated civic movement which has represented the rural poor (successfully at times) in the conceptualization and implementation of various land reforms, notably the policy and legal reforms of the mid-1990s. Yet this movement, which has emerged and grown out of concerns with land and resource rights, has gener-ally not bought into the CBNRM agenda. The União Nacional de Camponese (National Peasants Union) (UNAC) of Mozambique is perhaps the largest organ-ized peasant movement in the region. Founded to establish and defend peasant land rights, the union has continued to engage with national policy in the imple-mentation of the country's reformed land laws, as well as to assist members with food security, water rights and related issues. However, the Union has not been involved in the CBNRM movement, and appears not to consider the CBNRM movement to be essential to the evolving context of land rights in the country (D. Nhampossa, pers. comm.). In addition, although national CBNRM policies have been developed, only a few CBNRM initiatives are being implemented despite the obvious potential in Mozambique. Despite the elaboration of provisions for local natural resource governance in forestry and wildlife policy and legislation, CBNRM programmes are being implemented only in the Tete province (Tchuma Tchato), Maputo Province and in Niassa Province (Chipanje Chetu) in northern Mozambique (Anstey, 2001).

The South African government recently decided not to honour any further land claims in the Kruger National Park because of their potential implications for the national conservation estate (Whande, this volume). Significantly, this decision was celebrated by the tourism industry and many conservation organizations. By refusing to recognize the historical rights of communities to lands in the conservation estate, and in direct contravention of its own policies (trumpeted globally through for example the Makuleke land claim), the South African government in fact demonstrated that land claims would only succeed when they are relatively uncomplicated and pose little threat to existing property relations between capital, the state and local communities. As the claims become more complex, so too does the likelihood that they will be resolved in favour of the state and/or commercial interests.

Although Zimbabwe's private freehold wildlife conservancies have been presented as creating increased financial opportunities for wildlife-based land uses (de la Harpe, 1994), they are also a stark example of how wildlife conservation has become a mechanism to consolidate landholdings and thus change the dynamics of land contestations. The establishment of wildlife conservancies entailed the creation of private companies to hold and manage groups of farms as single consolidated units, and thus attract financial investment to capitalize large expenses of land with more wildlife, tourist infrastructure and basic machinery and equipment. They thus became a focus of attracting national, regional and international capital in the tourist sector (Mombeshora, 2005). In essence, conservancies remove the visibility of the human face of individual land ownership from the struggles over land and shift these to abstract legal entities of ubiquitous domicile (Moyo, 2000).

Given the limited power exerted by local communities in current manifestations of CBNRM in the region, it seems unlikely that these provide communities with sufficient motivation and organization to resist or negotiate accelerating land use changes in the near future. Such changes are driven by international agribusinesses' search for cheap investment destinations in Africa, and supported by national governments. An example of these is the complex interplay within the Great Limpopo Transfrontier Conservation Area (TFCA) between Mozambique, South Africa and Zimbabwe, and the proposed ProCana investment in a 30,000-hectare bio-ethanol sugar cane plantation in the Mozambique part of the TFCA, which is threatening the very existence of the region's largest and most heralded TFCA.

The contested terrain of 'CBNRM'

The experiences and lessons of CBNRM could certainly be applied to developing appropriate, secure and more dynamic systems of communal land and resource tenure which transcend the limits of the region's extant systems. To do this, however, CBNRM would need to transcend its own managerial preoccupation with 'projectizable' natural resource management systems that are based on creating conditions for capital expansion into communal lands. This is unlikely to happen if CBNRM continues to be championed by the current alliances of international conservation NGOs, private tourism interests, government wildlife departments and foreign donors which have been the dominant CBNRM actors in southern Africa to date.

These groups have had clear historical and political reasons not to include broader objectives related to agrarian social transformation and land tenure reform in the CBNRM agenda. CBNRM has thus been shaped according to these dominant players' interests, rather than those of rural peasantries. These allied interests may continue to work against the transformation of the CBNRM agenda.

Without exception, all the CBNRM programmes in the region are top-down initiatives. Many of them originate in wildlife and forestry departments, and are closely linked to conservation and protected areas management agendas. While governments put in place the policies for devolution, NGOs have become the main drivers of CBNRM in southern Africa. Many of the programmes and policies are developed by donors and NGOs with the collaboration and support of central government. Many of the demands for policy reform to facilitate CBNRM are made by NGOs, with donor funding, rather than by the local communities that would benefit from the implementation of these programmes.

To be sure, some communities have attempted, unsuccessfully, to resist CBNRM in their areas because they perceive the programmes as extending the interventionist strategies of the state rather than supporting their land and resource tenure contestations (Dzingirai, 1995; see also Ngoitiko et al, this volume). There have been many instances of local resistance to this increased interventionism, in the form of immigration and settlement in designated conservation and concession areas (Murombedzi, 1994; Dzingirai, 1995) and investment in agricultural intensification, which in many cases conflicts with wildlife conservation (Murombedzi, 2001). However, unlike smallholders in leasehold and freehold tenure regimes who can choose not to participate in CBNRM initiatives, communities in southern African communal tenure regimes are not allowed to exercise this option because land use decisions are largely outside their control. In this regard, CBNRM constitutes an imposition, and in some cases an entrenchment, of externally determined land use decisions and an extension of the states' interventionist strategies in communal tenure regimes throughout the region.

Where individuals have more secure tenure rights, they have in fact been able to resist CBNRM programmes. Yet little has been made of their struggles in the regional CBNRM discourse to date. For instance, attempts to implement CAMPFIRE in a range of formal resettlement areas during the market-based land reform era in Zimbabwe failed to take off, yet these failures have remained largely unanalysed. It would appear, however, that in such instances the costs of CBNRM were locally perceived as being greater than the benefits, and thus because of their stronger tenurial position those smallholders had the option of refusing to participate in CBNRM programmes.

Conclusion

Dualistic land tenure structures continue to define agrarian relations in contemporary southern Africa. Communal tenure in this system provides very little control over land to local communities, who can only exercise rights of usufruct and limited discretionary control over land use. Rural transformation will depend heavily on an organized and functioning peasantry, with strong and enforceable rights to land and natural resources, with enhanced influence over political and policy processes. Thus far, CBNRM efforts across the region have focused principally on developing usufruct rights to exchange access to natural resources for financial benefits, although the local ability to regulate this exchange is often limited in practice. The actual land use decision-making process remains in whole or in part under the control of the central state, through land use and other land management plans which guarantee wildlife management, usually on increasing land areas, while at the same time criminalizing or otherwise restricting the expansion of peasant agriculture and other locally controlled land uses into designated tourism concession, wildlife conservation or game management areas. The parochial focus on wildlife user rights has restricted the capacity of regional CBNRM programmes to respond to or support the land and property rights of the communities that are co-opted into CBNRM, and in many cases function to actually demobilize – at least for certain sections of those communities – those land and property rights contestations. Further, by creating hunting and other wildlife concession areas, typically with only token consultation with the communities (who in any case have limited means to refuse), CBNRM further constitutes a form of land alienation, especially since the opportunity costs of land use change associated with CBNRM – particularly for the poorer members of communities who are more dependent on various strategies of accessing multiple natural resources – are often higher than the undifferentiated benefits generated from CBNRM.

Because of this parochial focus, CBNRM has not been a critical factor in the transformation of agrarian relations in the region, but has rather constituted an extension of capital penetration into new landscapes and an entrenchment of élite interests in natural resources in communal tenure regimes. Broader agrarian transformation has generally not been on the formal regional CBNRM agenda, and CBNRM initiatives were not designed and have never functioned to respond to the tenure dualism characteristic of post-colonial southern Africa. Because of its origins in a non-redistributive agenda, CBNRM generally does not provide target communities with new opportunities to organize against the existing limitations of 'communal' tenure in post-colonial southern Africa. At the same time, communities do understand that 'communal tenure' in the dualistic tenure context in fact constitutes one of the main structural causes of their enduring poverty.

Contemporary CBNRM discourse in the region generally fails to analyse local socio-economic stratification in local communities. Yet it is clear that internal contradictions and conflicts and specific class interests play an important role in community organization and dynamics in the CBNRM programmes. In many cases the peasantries of the region are relatively well-organized and highly mobilized as an outcome of the liberation struggles of many countries of the region, as in the rural-based liberation movements of Zimbabwe, Mozambique and Angola.

CBNRM discourse needs to develop a more nuanced understanding of environmental and conservation policy, through the location of policy processes in national and global political economy. In addition to more detailed investigation of local government and local institutional arrangements for resource tenure and management, critical evaluation of 'communal' tenure and the search for more enduring forms of resource ownership that coincide with the changing aspirations of rural populations as conditioned by the material conditions of reproduction in post-colonial southern Africa is required. This calls for pro-active engagement with land and agrarian reform processes, movements and scholarship.

Note

1   To be sure, natural resource tenure is an important consideration in the southern African CBNRM narrative (e.g. Murombedzi, 1992; Rihoy, 1995). However, community tenure and rights to natural resources tend to be completely divorced from the broader land distribution and tenure context of the post-colonial transformation agendas of the region's countries.

References

Abel, N. and Blaikie, P. (1986) 'Elephants, people, parks and development: The case of the Luangwa Valley, Zambia', *Environmental Management*, vol 10, no 6, pp735–751

Adams, W.M. and Mulligan, M. (2003) *Decolonizing Nature: Strategies for Conservation in a Post-colonial Era*, Earthscan, London

Alexander, J. and McGregor, J. (2001) 'Elections, land and the politics of opposition in Matabeleland', *Journal of Agrarian Change* vol 1, no 4, pp510–33

Amanor, K.S. (1999) *Global Restructuring and Land Rights in Ghana: Forest Food Chains, Timber and Rural Livelihoods*, Nordiska Afrikainstitutet Research Report no. 108, Uppsala, Sweden

Amin, S. (1976) *Unequal Development: An Essay on the Social Formations of Peripheral Capitalism*, Monthly Review Press, New York

Anderson, D. and Grove, R. (1987) *Conservation in Africa: People, Policies and Practice*, Cambridge University Press, Cambridge

Anstey, S. (2001) 'A bottle of Coke at the end of the world: Modernist and customary institutions in natural resource governance in northern Mozambique', *Commons Southern Africa*, vol 3, no 2, pp11–13

Bernstein, H. (2005) 'Rural land and land conflicts in sub-Saharan Africa', in S. Moyo and P. Yeros (eds), *Reclaiming the Land*: The Resurgence of Rural Movements in Africa, Asia and Latin America, Zed Books, London

Berry, S.S. (1993) *No Condition is Permanent: The Social Dynamics of Agrarian Change in Sub-Saharan Africa*, University of Wisconsin Press, Madison, WI

Bond, I. (1993) *The Economics of Wildlife and Land Use in Zimbabwe: An Examination of Current Knowledge and Issues*, WWF Multispecies Animal Production Systems Project Paper No. 36, WWF, Harare, Zimbabwe

Boone, C. (2007) 'Property and constitutional order: Land tenure reform and the future of the African state', *African Affairs*, vol 106, pp557–586

Bourdillon, M.F.C (1987) *The Shona Peoples*, Mambo Press, Gweru, Zimbabwe

Bruce, J.W. (1988). 'A perspective on indigenous land tenure systems and land concentration', in R.E. Downs and S.P. Reyna (eds) *Land and Society in Contemporary Africa*, University Press of New England, Hanover, NH

Burke, T. (1996). *Lifebuoy Men, Lux Women: Commodification, Consumption and Cleanliness in Modern Zimbabwe*, Duke University Press, Durham, NC

Cowen, M. and Shenton, R. (1991), 'The origins and course of Fabian colonialism in Africa", *Journal of Historical Sociology*, vol 4, no 2, pp143–174

De La Harpe, D.A. (1994) *The Lowland Conservancies: New Opportunities for Productive and Sustainable Land Use*, Price Waterhouse, Harare, Zimbabwe

Dzingirai, V. (1994) *Politics and Ideology in Human Settlement: Getting Settled in the Sokomena Area of Chief Dobola*, CASS Working Paper, University of Zimbabwe, Harare, Zimbabwe

Dzingirai, V. (1995) *'Take Back Your CAMPFIRE': A Study of Local level Perceptions to Electric Fencing in the Framework of Binga's CAMPFIRE Programme*, CASS, University of Zimbabwe, Harare, Zimbabwe

Hughes, D.M. (2001) 'Rezoned for business: How ecotourism unlocked black farmland in eastern Zimbabwe', *Journal of Agrarian Change*, vol 1, no 4, pp575–99

Hughes, D.M. (2006) *From Enslavement to Environmentalism: Politics on a Southern African Frontier*, University of Washington Press in association with Weaver Press, Harare, Zimbabwe

Hulme, D. and Murphree, M.W. (2001) *African Wildlife and Livelihoods: The Promise and Performance of Community Conservation*, James Currey, Oxford

Hutton, J., Adams, W.M and Murombedzi, J.C. (2005) 'Back to the barriers? Changing narratives in biodiversity conservation', *Forum for Development Studies* vol 2, pp342–370.

Mackenzie, J.M. (1988) *The Empire of Nature: Hunting, Conservation and British Imperialism*, Manchester University Press, Manchester

Madzudzo, E. (1996) *Producer Communities in a Community Based Wildlife Management Programme: a Case Study of Bulilimamangwe and Tsholotsho Districts*, CASS, University of Zimbabwe, Harare, Zimbabawe

Magome, H. and Murombedzi, J. (2003) 'Sharing South African National Parks: Community land and conservation in a democratic South Africa', in W.M. Adams and M. Mulligan (eds) *Decolonizing Nature: Strategies for Conservation in a Post-Colonial Era*, Earthscan, London

Mamdani, M. (2009) 'Lessons of Zimbabwe: Mugabe in context', *ACAS Bulletin*, no 82, pp3–13

Mamdani, M. (1996) *Citizen and Subject: Contemporary Africa and the Legacy of Late Colonialism*, Princeton University Press, Princeton, NJ

Massyn, P.J. (2004) *Safari Lodges and Rural Incomes: Some Key Southern African Trends*, Unpublished paper

Mombeshora, S. and Le Bel, S. (2009) 'Parks–people conflicts: The case of Gonarezhou National Park and Chitsa community in south-east Zimbabwe', *Biodiversity & Conservation*, vol 18, no 10, pp2601–2623.

Mombeshora, S. (2005) *Collaborative Partnerships in Transboundary Wildlife Management: A Review of Southern African Experiences*, Unpublished paper for IUCN ROSA, Harare, Zimbabwe

Moore, D. (1996) 'Marxism, Culture, and Political Ecology: Environmental struggles in Zimbabwe's eastern highlands', in R. Peet and M. Watts (eds) *Liberation Ecologies: Environment, Development, Social Movements*, Routledge, New York

Moyo, S. (2000) *Land Reform Under Structural Adjustment in Zimbabwe: Land Use Change in the Mashonaland Provinces*, Nordiska Afrikainstitutet, Uppsala, Sweden

Moyo, S. and P. Yeros (2005). 'The Resurgence of Rural Movements Under Neoliberalism', in S. Moyo, and P. Yeros (eds) *Reclaiming the Land: The Resurgence of Rural Movements in Africa, Asia and Latin America*, Zed Books, London

Murapa, R. (1977) *Geography, Race, Class and Power in Rhodesia*, Paper presented at the Conference on the Special Problems of Landlocked and Least Developed Countries in Africa, University of Zambia, Lusaka, 27–31 July 1977

Murombedzi, J.C. (1992) *Decentralization or Recentralization? Implementing CAMPFIRE in the Omay Communal lands of Nyaminyami District*, CASS Working Paper, Centre for Applied Social Sciences, University of Zimbabwe, Harare, Zimbabwe

Murombedzi, J.C. (1994) 'The dynamics of conflict in environmental management policy in the context of the Communal Areas Management Programme for Indigenous Resources', PhD thesis, University of Zimbabwe, Zimbabwe

Murombedzi, J.C. (1995) *Zimbabwe's CAMPFIRE Programme: Using Natural Resources for Rural Development*, Mimeo, University of Zimbabwe, Centre for Applied Social Sciences, Harare, Zimbabwe

Murombedzi, J.C. (2001) 'Committees, rights, costs and benefits', in D. Hulme and M.W. Murphree (eds) *African Wildlife and African Livelihoods: The Promise and Performance of Community Conservation*, James Currey, Oxford

Murphree, M.W. (1993) 'Decentralizing proprietorship of wildlife resources in Zimbabwe's communal lands', in D. Lewis and N. Carter (eds) *Voices from Africa: Local Perspectives on Conservation*, World Wildlife Fund, Washington DC

Murphree, M.W. (1995) 'Optimal principles and pragmatic strategies: Creating an enabling politico-legal environment for community based natural resource management (CBNRM)', in E.C. Rihoy (ed) *The Commons Without the Tragedy? Strategies for Community Based Natural Resources Management in Southern Africa*, SADC Wildlife Technical Cooperation Unit, Lilongwe, Malawi

Nyambara, P.S. (2001) 'The closing frontier: Agrarian change, immigrants and the "squatter menace" in Gokwe, 1980–1990s', *Journal of Agrarian Change*, vol 1, no 4, pp534–549

Parker, I. (1993) 'Natural justice, ownership and the CAMPFIRE programme', unpublished paper at the CASS Library, University of Zimbabwe, Harare, Zimbabwe

Peters, P.E. (2004) 'Inequality and social conflict over land in Africa', *Journal of Agrarian Change*, vol 4, no 3, pp269–314

Redford, K.H. and Taber, A. (2000) 'Writing the wrongs: Developing a safe-fail culture in conservation', *Conservation Biology*, vol 14, no 6, pp1567–1568

Scott, J.C. (1998) *Seeing Like a State: How Certain Schemes to Improve the Human Condition have Failed*, Yale University Press, New Haven, CT

Steiner, A. and Rihoy, E. (1995) 'The commons without the tragedy', in E.C. Rihoy (ed) *The Commons Without the Tragedy? Strategies for Community Based Natural Resources Management in Southern Africa*, SADC Wildlife Technical Cooperation Unit, Lilongwe, Malawi

Woodhouse, P., Bernstein, H. and Hulme, D. (2000) *African Enclosures? The Social Dynamics of Wetlands in Drylands*, James Currey, Oxford

Part 2

Political Economies of Natural Resource Governance

3

The Politics of Community-Based Natural Resource Management in Botswana

Liz Rihoy and Brian Maguranyanga

Introduction

Botswana is widely known as the African 'exception', which refers to its unmatched record of internal peace, economic growth and democratic governance since independence in 1966 (Good, 1992; Samatar, 1999; Molutsi, 2005). The country recorded the highest per capita GDP growth rates in the world in the 1980s and now has a per capita Gross National Income of US$5,680, more than six times the sub-Saharan African average (World Bank, 2009). With a geography dominated by the Kalahari Desert in the centre and south of the country, and the unique inland Okavango Delta in the north, the economy is dominated by mining, which constitutes roughly 30 per cent of GDP and 90 per cent of exports as well as tourism and livestock production. Transparency International's Corruption Perception Index (2008) ranks Botswana as the least corrupt country in sub-Saharan Africa, and also places it ahead of industrialized non-African nations including South Korea and the Czech Republic.

Wildlife remains widespread, particularly in the Okavango Delta which supports most of Botswana's approximately 150,000 elephants, constituting over a quarter of the total estimated population for sub-Saharan Africa (Blanc et al, 2007). During the past two decades, Botswana has used its wildlife to successfully compete with more well-established wildlife safari destinations such as Kenya; by 2005 tourism generated US$568 million in total income (WTO, 2007). Starting in the late 1980s, Botswana began to develop approaches for increasing benefits from wildlife to rural communities through a national community-based natural resource management (CBNRM) programme, drawing on parallel efforts in neighbouring Zimbabwe and Namibia.

An examination of CBNRM in Botswana reveals the extent to which policy processes and management outcomes are determined by political contestation.

A focus on CBNRM policy highlights the importance of political choices in natural resource management, demonstrating that policy-making is not a rational, linear process guided by scientific knowledge but rather a political process where ideology and individuals' and groups' interests interact. This chapter explores the policy-making process because it represents the interaction of different, sometimes competing, interests, and at the same time rationalizes them through narratives used to advance particular interests. We examine the politics of CBNRM policy and governance in relation to changes in local governance and macro-institutional factors. The linkage between the local and macro levels is an important intersection because it sheds light on the opportunities and shortcomings of CBNRM in changing power relations, strengthening democratic space, creating accountable local governance institutions, and empowering communities to direct their destiny and livelihoods.

CBNRM is premised on empowering local people so that they may leverage existing social and natural resource capital in ways that enhance economic opportunities from resources such as wildlife. By changing the status quo in terms of access to natural resources, CBNRM inevitably has implications for empowerment and broader political processes. To assume that these empowerment objectives are inevitably welcomed by governments and the political élite is to ignore the reality that governments are not necessarily committed to the economic and political empowerment of rural communities, for a variety of reasons. The findings presented here demonstrate that even in Botswana, which is upheld by many analysts as sub-Saharan Africa's foremost example of stable multiparty democracy, such an assumption is far from safe. CBNRM is socially and politically contested in Botswana, with resource rights and benefits subjected to struggles amongst local communities and political economic élites.

Central factors in these struggles include processes of resource accumulation – particularly land and livestock – and privatization in rural Botswana and particularly amongst the country's élites; the contested nature of wildlife as a local versus a national resource; and a resurgent 'protectionist' wildlife management paradigm championed by key political figures, notably the country's current President, Ian Khama. Within Botswana, critics of localizing wildlife benefits argue that it contradicts the fundamental nation-building ideals of the country and the tenets upon which the Constitution of Botswana is based, which treat all natural resources – and most importantly, diamonds – as 'national resources'. In confronting these challenges, advocates of CBNRM, which include local communities as well as foreign donors, have been limited by the lack of a strong and diverse domestic political constituency that can contest the centre's attempts to reconsolidate control over wildlife and tourism revenues. This roll-back of local benefits has also been enabled in part by unaccountable local governance structures for CBNRM at the community level, which have led to frequent charges of mismanagement of revenues, and lent a technocratic justification for recentralization on the grounds of insufficient local capacity. Thus a complex and evolving set of factors from local to central scales of government, and incorporating important external influences, comprise the political contestation of CBNRM in Botswana.

Methods

The material presented in this chapter is based on a qualitative study (Rihoy and Maguranyanga, 2007; Rihoy, forthcoming) involving ethnographic-style semi-structured interviews with approximately 150 individuals, including key government officials (politicians and bureaucrats at national and local levels), NGO staff, CBNRM experts and academics, community leaders and general community members, donors and journalists covering CBNRM issues; as well as analysis of official government and NGO documents, correspondence, newspaper articles and academic publications. The research was carried out in Botswana during three two-month periods from 2005 to 2008. The core analytical framework informing this work is the policy process framework (Keeley and Scoones, 2003; see Chapter 1), which captures the dynamic interplay of forces shaping CBNRM policy in Botswana as 'a product of ongoing negotiations and bargaining between multiple actors over time' (Rihoy and Maguranyanga, 2007, p3). We explore these processes in the context of Botswana using three overlapping approaches to understand policy change: structured political interests, the agency of actors involved in the policy-making process and power–knowledge relations that discursively shape practice in particular ways. This analytical framework attempts to capture the interaction between political interests, discourse and networks of multiple actors in shaping the landscape of CBNRM and affecting devolution and democratization of natural resource governance in Botswana.

The emergence of CBNRM in Botswana

Botswana officially embraced CBNRM in 1989, and the Department of Wildlife and National Parks (DWNP) became the government implementing agency working with other relevant government ministries and NGOs. DWNP received substantial funding through the USAID-funded Natural Resource Management Program (NRMP), which ran from 1989 to 1999. The NRMP was underpinned by the scientific rationale of sustainable use and political ideals of 'small government' and devolution. Botswana's stable socio-political and economic climate appeared to be an ideal context for successful implementation (Rihoy and Maguranyanga, 2007). Programme designers regarded wildlife management as an ecologically and economically viable land use option in a country with a limited range of alternatives, with only 5 per cent of its land suitable for productive agriculture, abundant and high-value wildlife populations, and a low human population of approximately 1.5 million people with an average density of 2.4 per square kilometre (Whiteside, 1995; UNDP, 2005; Rihoy and Maguranyanga, 2007).

The small population size and relative ethnic homogeneity of Botswana's rural communities were also considered ideal for CBNRM initiatives. The Botswana government's record of democratic governance, commitment to citizen empowerment, and policies promoting sustainable development, sustainable use of natural resources, economic diversification and decentralization all provided additional impetus for implementation (Rihoy and Maguranyanga, 2007).

Within this national context, the basic institutional framework developed for CBNRM in Botswana involves the creation of local trusts or 'community-based organizations' (CBOs), since communities in rural Botswana have no pre-existing corporate identity. Once they form a CBO, communities are able to apply to DWNP for user rights to wildlife, in the form of a quota, and, at least until recently, were entitled to keep 100 per cent of revenue from wildlife utilization. In addition, if communities wish to develop commercial ventures on their land, such as tourism enterprises, the CBO must obtain a land lease from District Land Boards. Leases are granted on 15-year terms and enable the CBO to enter into third-party access agreements or 'joint ventures'.

By 2003, there were 67 registered CBOs, which included 120 villages and 103,000 people (Swatuk, 2005). Some CBOs, particularly those located in Ngamiland, which is situated in the Okavango Delta, were earning up to several hundred thousand US dollars annually from commercial hunting and tourism ventures by this time. Wildlife numbers were generally stable across Botswana in the 1990s, with CBNRM given credit for creating more favourable incentives for conservation in rural areas (Arntzen et al, 2003). Thus on economic and ecological fronts, many have pointed to Botswana as an emblematic southern African example of CBNRM, along with its neighbours Zimbabwe and Namibia. Despite this record of progress, implementation of CBNRM in Botswana has proven extremely problematic and the policy and political context ultimately highly constraining to the principles of sustainable use and devolved resource management that CBNRM is premised on.

Challenges to CBNRM in Botswana

'Foreign-grown' CBNRM

CBNRM implementation during the past two decades has been constrained by multiple factors, many of which can be traced to the conditions of emergence of CBNRM in Botswana. CBNRM emerged in Botswana as a 'foreign import' and expatriate-driven programme. When USAID funding for the NRMP came to an end in 1999, the World Conservation Union (IUCN) and Netherlands Development Organization (SNV) teamed to initiate a CBNRM Support Program. CBNRM activities were later also funded by the European Union-funded Wildlife Conservation and Management Program (2002–2007). The DWNP worked with donor agencies and expatriate personnel in managing these programmes. The high visibility and dominance of expatriate staff reinforced the perception that CBNRM represented a foreign environmental management paradigm. This perception compromised the relevance and local legitimacy of CBNRM. Such founding circumstances stripped Botswana's CBNRM programme of its national identity since it was perceived to lack indigenous conceptualization and development (Rihoy and Maguranyanga, 2007).

The result is a lack of cultural understanding, relationships, identities and connection of CBNRM to social and political networks in Botswana, arising from difficulties associated with embedding foreigners in the local institutional and social landscape. In the absence of such connectivity, the CBNRM approaches did not develop to reflect the unique social and political realities of Botswana (Jones and Murphree, 2001; Rihoy and Maguranyanga, 2007). This foreign dominance is reflected in the term informally used to describe CBNRM within the DWNP: '*Dilo tsa Makgoa*' which translates as 'something for the white people'. The following quote succinctly illustrates this commonly held view:

> *CBNRM is just one more approach introduced by well-meaning donors who are following fashions. The history of development here is full of them and like those it will fade away when all the donors and foreign experts have gone.*[1]

This historical dominance of expatriates in these donor-supported CBNRM support programmes inhibited the emergence of a strong, supportive national 'actor network' and key individuals who would act as advocates for CBNRM. Even at the local level, CBNRM was perceived as externally imposed, with the imposers being the DWNP and various NGOs. As one Member of Parliament comments:

> *In theory, CBNRM is a great idea and just what we need. It promotes self-reliance and self-sufficiency and makes people value and conserve resources. But it is being imposed on people. The participatory elements are being ignored as they're too difficult to implement. And this destroys the whole purpose.*[2]

Such perceptions de-legitimized the national and local authenticity of CBNRM. Whilst a viable political constituency of national advocates and 'policy entrepreneurs' briefly emerged in 2000 in response to the activities of the IUCN/SNV support programme and was able to provide critical leverage for the programme by building a case for its support among political leadership at the national level, this too proved dependent on foreign support and financing, and as such was not sustainable. Without any 'politically salient constituency' (Murphree, 1995) at either the local or national levels which could anchor CBNRM in national political discourse and policy-making arenas, the approach became subject to interests which were not necessarily supportive of CBNRM at both national and local levels. In particular, CBNRM became vulnerable to capture or reversal by the political economic élite whose interests are not served by this approach.

Realities of constituency-building in Botswana

Compounding the reliance of CBNRM on foreign influences and the lack of a national-level support network is the challenge posed by Botswana's relatively weak and disorganized civil society. Civic organizations in Botswana have capacity challenges in terms of financial and human resources, skills and specialization (Molutsi and Holm, 1990), and their dependence on government funding after donors withdrew from Botswana in 2003[3] further weakened their ability to oppose government's positions and preferences. Many NGOs actively court government favour by seeking representation of government officials or senior political figures in their governance structures. For example, President Ian Khama is patron of all remaining environmental NGOs operating at the national level in Botswana. By embracing senior political figures within their governance structures, civil society organizations weaken their ability to fashion and represent independent, alternative perspectives.

The absence of a vibrant civil society and dearth of effective national champions and an influential actor-network rendered CBNRM vulnerable once the government shifted its political support and donors withdrew financial support, which both have occurred progressively since 2000, following the first decade of CBNRM development. Donor withdrawal in 2003 significantly impacted the programme and undermined the donor-dependent NGOs supporting CBNRM. Cracks appeared in the CBNRM programme as funding dried up, and traditionally CBNRM-focused NGOs refocused their activities on more general rural development activities. For example, the CBNRM Support Program lost SNV funding, whilst BOCOBONET – the national umbrella and networking organization for all CBNRM-related CBOs – has since 2003 refocused on general rural development activities.[4] Some NGOs active in CBNRM, such as the Forestry Association of Botswana, collapsed and others such as the Agency for Cooperation and Research in Development (ACORD) withdrew from the country. The outcomes of this dwindling support network included an even more depleted CBNRM constituency, as well as increased problems of accountability within local CBOs due to lack of institutional support and capacity building.

Recentralizing control

When the NRMP terminated in 1999, it became apparent that the sustainability of CBNRM was questionable. USAID determined that there was a need to ensure continuity and develop broader support for CBNRM through the creation of a national-level organization capable of representing the interests of the growing number of local CBOs, and consequently played an instrumental role in the creation of the national CBO umbrella organization, BOCOBONET (Botswana Community-Based Organizations Network). Subsequent donor support to CBNRM made concerted efforts to develop an influential constituency and well-organized stakeholder group between 1999 and 2003 in order to overcome CBNRM's political isolation. The IUCN/SNV CBNRM Support Program invested in the development of a local interest group, the National CBNRM Forum, representing all stakeholders including local communities. This Forum initially grew rapidly, with the membership of 35 organizations in 1999 (IUCN/ SNV, 2000) expanding to 161 in 2003 (National CBNRM Forum, 2004).

The significant political influence of the CBNRM Forum was clearly demonstrated in terms of its ability to shape policy when it effectively blocked the Ministry of Local Government's 'Savingram'[5] of 2001 which sought to divert revenues from CBNRM activities to District Councils instead of local CBOs. A national CBNRM review concluded that:

> *Through the efforts of BOCOBONET and the CBNRM Forum structures, a significant proportion of wildlife-based CBOs have participated in the policy dialogue and have played an active role in lobbying and advocacy on issues of importance to CBNRM. Stakeholders have become a movement with different interests but a common goal.*
>
> (Arntzen et al, 2003, p12)

The 2001 Savingram represented the government's first overt attempts to reduce local rights to wildlife benefits under the CBNRM framework on the grounds of restraining problems of local corruption and mismanagement in CBOs, and also demonstrated government opposition to the devolutionary processes under-pinning CBNRM. However, the National CBNRM Forum steering committee and BOCOBONET's swift and well-orchestrated response of opposition to the Ministry's directive led to the eventual withdrawal of the Savingram.

The political influence that the stakeholder group wielded proved to be short-lived, as government's response to a similar effort by the group to another Savingram in 2005 clearly demonstrates. Several events began to undermine the stakeholder group's ability to function as a lobbying/advocacy entity. While the government had agreed to the National CBNRM Forum providing input into the finalization of CBNRM policy in 2001, its position shifted drastically in 2005 as the Permanent Secretary of the Ministry of Environment, Wildlife and Tourism explicitly stated that policy-making was government's prerogative:

> *It must be understood that policy is developed by government, taking the views of all stakeholders into consideration not just of a special interest group such as the National CBNRM Forum might represent.*

> (Gakale, 2005)

The Permanent Secretary's response to the May 2005 National CBNRM Forum's submission reflects government's growing unwillingness to accept civil society inputs into the policy-making process and the corresponding closing of space for non-governmental influence. The shift in response over the four-year period reflects changes in the policy environment and shifts in the balance of power during this period. In essence, it was about clipping the National CBNRM Forum's wings and marginalizing it in the policy-making arena. Central authorities became more determined to control policy processes.

This process of reasserting central control over wildlife benefits culminated in the CBNRM Policy released in 2008. This policy reversed the past gains by commu-nities whereby they had received 100 per cent of revenues from wildlife-based enterprises on their lands. The new policy indicated that CBOs may keep only 35 per cent from the sale of natural resource concessions and quotas for their use and Trust operations, while up to 65 per cent of the funds could go to the National Environmental Fund (NEF) for financing community projects nationwide.[6]

Undermined from above: CBNRM and political leadership

Whilst all the trappings and institutions of a liberal democracy are in place in Botswana (Obeng, 2001; Rotberg, 2007), Good and Taylor (2005) demonstrate how these are manipulated by the ruling élites, both through the Constitution and through contemporary practices of the ruling party, based on the inherited political culture.[7] Swatuk (2005, p12) comments:

> *Politics in Botswana resembles African village democracy, where the* kgotla *(public gathering) allows for the illusion of inclusion and open (though limited) expression*

of opinion by the citizenry, but where the agenda is set and key decisions are taken by the ruling class.

Such settings do not lend themselves to increasing public participation in the policy-making process and public debate. This has shrunk the policy space for consultation, transparency, dialogue, accountability and public engagement in policy-making debates (Rihoy and Maguranyanga, 2007). In previous sections, we highlighted the weakening of civil society's influence and ability to create independent, alternative perspectives to government. The government also made clear its intolerance of the National CBNRM Forum's expectations to have strong input into the policy-making process (Rihoy and Maguranyanga, 2007) and its penetration of official policy-making structures. Without a voice and forms of political leverage, civil society organizations' influence on CBNRM policy outcomes is limited.

President Ian Khama's dominance and influence in contemporary Botswana politics extends into many social and economic areas. Not only is he President, he is also Paramount Chief of the Bamangwato[8] and eldest son of the nationally revered Sir Seretse Khama, securer of independence and first President of Botswana. Thus to paraphrase from Mamdani (1996), Khama is simultaneously the representative power in civil society whilst also the despotic power over native authorities. An understanding of his role is best summed up in the words of a senior government official.

...to understand what's going on you have to understand about Khama and the effect his name has on people. He is feared like a lion. No Batswana will contradict him. Now that he has made his position known everyone, whether they agree or not, will fall in line.[9]

Whilst this statement may be exaggerated, there is little doubting the influence that President Khama wields within the conservation sector where is he widely upheld and revered as the 'Father of Conservation in Botswana', in which role films have been made (e.g. *Wildlife Warriors*) and much media space devoted to him. This dominance of one individual on conservation throughout the country is unique to Botswana within the southern African region. Khama's reputation stems from his days as Commander of the Botswana Defence Force when he deployed military personnel on anti-poaching missions to curb poaching of species such as elephants. For this act he received international awards and acclaim. This included mass recognition and accolades from private sector tourism operators, the vast majority of whom independently recognize President Khama on their websites as 'the unsung hero of conservation' (a significant serenade for one who is ostensibly unsung).

Today President Khama is the dominant figure behind all significant conservation-oriented organizations and initiatives within Botswana (Rihoy and Maguranyanga, 2007). He is on the board of one of the world's most well-financed NGOs, Conservation International (CI), which is also one of the few international conservation NGOs operating in Botswana, and active within the board of the Peace Parks Foundation. He is widely rumoured to have interests in a leading tourism company and has personal relationships with many of the larger tourism operators, all of whom make their opposition to some of the principles underlying CBNRM, notably sustainable use (i.e. hunting), well known (Rihoy, forthcoming). President Khama's open adoption of coercive conservation tactics in using the army to engage in anti-poaching activities, and public anti-hunting statements that he has made subsequently, leave little doubt as to his belief in a protectionist conservation paradigm. The conservation organizations with which he is associated adopt a 'protectionist' approach to conservation and it is these influences and networks with which he interacts as a result of his relationships with CI, Peace Parks and the tourism industry (Rihoy, forthcoming). As one ex-senior government DWNP official notes:

> *Khama will probably get another international conservation award if he undermines sustainable use in Botswana, including CBNRM, and returns us to exclusively protectionist conservation. He's working towards that.*[10]

Khama's allegiance to a protectionist conservation paradigm and the tendency that he has already demonstrated (Rihoy, forthcoming) to personally dictate conservation policy in Botswana will lead to further shrinkage of policy space. His political dominance and influence throughout the country ensure that his conservation ideals permeate policy and have facilitated recent policy changes towards recentralization and 'nationalization' of wildlife revenues.

The 'diamond debate'

CBNRM has generated recent debate in Botswana focusing on the status of wildlife as a 'local' as opposed to a 'national' resource. This question has far-reaching political ramifications for the manner in which the government manages other natural resources, particularly the revenue from diamonds that accounted for 33 per cent of the country's GDP in 2007 (World Bank, 2009) and as such draws CBNRM into the midst of one of the most controversial political issues in the country. This debate has significant implications for the nation-building approach upon which the ruling party, the Botswana Democratic Party (BDP), has based its political strategies since independence (Poteete, 2007).

The Constitution of Botswana states that all natural resources are national assets, and the proceeds from their exploitation should be managed centrally through national coffers to ensure transparent and equitable distribution. CBNRM principles call for wildlife resources and benefits to be localized, with local communities being the primary beneficiaries since they bear the cost of living with wildlife. By delineating resource rights locally, CBNRM activities contradict the constitutionally implied 'national citizenship' that entitles all citizens to benefit from minerals, land and other natural resources. Therefore, CBNRM appears to undermine the principle that all natural resources be national resources. As a result, CBNRM represents a divergent strategy which is politically controversial as it reinforces local political identities through its localization of benefits, thus undermining one of the cornerstones upon which the Botswana state was established (Poteete, 2007).

Politicians and communities from diamond-rich areas have seized upon the precedent of localization set by CBNRM and have argued for exemption from the constitutional rule that all natural resources are national resources so that their locales may benefit directly from diamonds in the same manner that CBNRM communities are benefiting from wildlife. As a matter of principle, they argue, their communities should have similar rights to benefits accorded wildlife-rich communities involved in CBNRM. This 'diamond debate' has brought to the fore politically contested claims to resource management in the country. The government has been forced to re-examine the implications of devolution of wildlife resources and benefits as regards decentralization and/or recentralization of CBNRM benefits in line with the principle of all natural resources being 'national resources'.

The diamond debate brings into sharp relief the policy contradiction that CBNRM represents in the Botswana context. It makes a politically compelling case that all revenues from natural resources should be pooled in a national coffer and then redistributed for community development nationwide as well as to cross-subsidize communities living in resource-poor areas. The distributional struggles that emerge in the 'diamond debate' have to be understood in terms of their political implications, and the political stance of the ruling party. The BDP government's call for centrally managing CBNRM funds is an attempt to address questions raised about its coalition-building strategy (Poteete, 2007) and discrepancy in the treatment of mineral and wildlife resources. It has used the diamond debate to recentralize CBNRM benefits and dictate the future of CBNRM based on its political agenda. This dynamic was a central element of the 2008 CBNRM Policy's provisions for reaffirming central control by allocating up to 65 per cent of the revenue generated by local wildlife-based enterprises and joint ventures to a National Environmental Fund which would ensure at community projects nationwide are financed. Under the leadership of President Khama, the BDP government seems to have succeeded in nationalizing wildlife-derived revenues in ways that address the diamond debate, making all natural resources benefit the nation rather than the 'local.'

This recentralization of wildlife revenues fails to recognize that wildlife and minerals present different management challenges. Recentralizing wildlife benefits removes the incentives for local communities to sustainably manage their natural resources. Minerals do not impose the same types of costs on rural communities as wild animals do, and therefore do not represent the same management challenges. As others in Botswana have noted, 'diamonds don't eat goats' (Mmegi, 2002).

Livestock and land use policy

Another important constraint on CBNRM efforts in Botswana is the country's political economic élites' bias towards livestock production, which is the dominant form of land use in Botswana. Approximately 80 per cent of the rural population's livelihoods are dependent on livestock farming, and it provides one-third of the country's foreign currency earnings (White, 1998). As such, livestock producers' interests intersect with development policy, resource use policy and national politics. Livestock commands a central cultural role, and reflects the health of the agro-pastoral community and the power of its dominant members (IIED,

2004). Its centrality in society has led to the privatization of grazing lands, the shrinking of communal lands as fenced ranches and exclusive use of boreholes on rangelands expand (Taylor, 2000). This policy approach has been partially driven by the belief within the Ministry of Agriculture that communal rangelands were degraded by overgrazing as a result of open access (the classic 'Tragedy of the Commons' scenario) linked to communal land ownership. Consequently, privatization was considered a viable solution (IIED, 2004), and the Ministry of Agriculture used the 'Tragedy of the Commons' narrative to advance privatization within communal areas (Alden Wily, 2003). According to Peters (1994, p218), 'there is no doubt that some highly placed members of the government and party [ruling Botswana Democratic Party] who promote the policy benefit directly as wealthy cattle and borehole owners.' They promote subsidies and policies that create strong incentives for the livestock farming sector as well as encouraging land accumulation for cattle pasturage. This policy bias makes livestock farming artificially more attractive than wildlife or other land use options (Alden Wily, 2003; IIED, 2004). Government has focused on the livestock sector at the expense of wildlife and tourism despite the rhetorical commitment in national development plans to diversify the economy. Ultimately the social and economic interests of Botswana's political élite do not fit comfortably with the principles of common property management, wildlife management and sustainable use which underpin CBNRM, focused as the former are on cattle ranching and rangelands privatization.

Institutional shortcomings of CBNRM implementation

Until April 2008, CBNRM in Botswana was implemented without an officially existing policy or legislative framework. It was informed by a draft CBNRM policy, but local-level implementation outpaced policy-making and legislation for more than 15 years.

CBNRM had been implemented in a fragmented institutional context, and depended on a variety of policies associated with wildlife to guide its operation and implementation. The fragmented pieces of policy included the 1986 Wildlife Conservation Policy, 1990 Tourism Policy, revised 2002 Rural Development Policy, and 2004 draft CBNRM Policy. Such fragmentation opened up CBNRM to manipulation, incoherence in application and accountability problems. Without an overarching favourable policy framework, conflict and competition between ministries and government departments involved in CBNRM activities undermined the development of coherent CBNRM implementation. The mandates of some ministries and departments, such as the powerful Ministry of Agriculture, contradicted the spirit and method of CBNRM (Rihoy and Maguranyanga, 2007). In addition, implementation was subject to the changing whims of different administrative systems, and local resource governance practices could be undermined easily since CBNRM rights were not entrenched in legislation. In essence, CBNRM lacked specific legal provisions, and was at the mercy of senior politicians and bureaucrats.

Notwithstanding this fragmentation, DWNP has been the lead agency for CBNRM policy development and implementation, and other government departments and ministries, notably the Agricultural Resource Board, Land Boards and District Councils have been formally limited to roles on the district-level Technical Advisory Boards. This compartmentalized approach to implementation has resulted in the failure of implementers to engage and integrate CBNRM initiatives with relevant sector initiatives of other departments or ministries (Taylor, 2000; Arntzen et al, 2003; Jones, 2004).

The decision to limit District Councils to a marginal role was deliberately taken in an effort to avoid what where perceived to be the pitfalls of Zimbabwe's CAMPFIRE programme (see Murombedzi, this volume). As noted by the former head of the USAID-funded NRMP:

> *Decentralizing to councils, as in Zimbabwe, was seen by us as using wildlife to provide a subsidy to local government which then passed on a percentage, under imposed terms and conditions, to communities.*
>
> (N. Winer, pers. comm.)

This decision has subsequently been recognized as a tactical error (National CBNRM Forum, 2004). In the context of Botswana, where District Councils have a long and credible history of effective and representative local governance, district authorities could have been important vehicles for empowering local communities to shape local governance and democratize resource management. Greater involvement on their behalf would have significantly improved the capacity for technical implementation at the local level; provided checks and balances to prevent the capture of benefits by local political élites and provided neutral arbitration services when community polarization stalls momentum; whilst ensuring that the politically influential District Councils provided political support to CBNRM and facilitated interaction with national policy-making structures and processes.

Enterprise and accountability: Problems with local governance

Effective devolution of powers to local institutions has to be matched by accountability and representation at the local level (Murphree, 2000; Ribot, 2002). In Botswana, CBOs are marked by low levels of accountability and poor representation of local constituencies' interests (Arntzen et al, 2003; Habarad, 2003; Zuze, 2004; Thakadu, 2005), and hence constituent accountability is frequently lacking.

This section briefly examines CBNRM dynamics at the local level, and highlights the challenges of constituent accountability in CBOs with concessionary joint venture partnerships (JVPs) in relation to corruption, mismanagement of funds and poor governance (Habarad, 2003; Thakadu, 2005). As the cases presented below demonstrate, weak accountability has frequently enabled local élites to capture CBNRM benefits in Botswana. Arntzen et al (2003, p19) argues that because of these accountability challenges, 'real empowerment is yet to be achieved. The transfer of power has by and large been to the Boards or governance structures of organization.' Given the substantial amount of money generated by CBOs through JVPs, the stakes are high, and flawed accountability mechanisms increase exposure to corruption. In Table 3.1 we offer an overview of account-ability challenges in six CBOs engaged in wildlife-related JVPs in Ngamiland and provide a more detailed analysis with the two case studies of the Okavango Community Trust and Khwai Development Trust. The period covered in this table is that from inception of each CBO until 2007.

Table 3.1 *CBOs with joint venture partnerships in Ngamiland*

Name of Trust	Population	Income (pula)	Accountability of CBO	Comments
Cgaecgae Tlhabololo Trust	372	1,497,281	Yes	Accountable trust ensures participation; no reports of financial irregularities. However, CBO unable to work with private sector, and is no longer able to market its quota, resulting in no income.
Khwai Development Trust	395	5,500,728	No	Mismanagement of funds (over P2,000,000 unaccounted for); no community benefit; lack of planning and priority setting.
Okavango Community Trust	6,431	8,589,766	No	Co-option by élites; unconfirmed misappropriation of P430,000; no community involvement or benefit; high administrative overheads; lack of planning and priority setting.
Okavango Kopano Mokoro Community Trust	2,000 (est.)	6,486,568	No	Misappropriation of P12,500 in 2002; limited community participation and benefit; high administrative overheads; lack of planning and priority setting.
Sankuyo Tshwaragano Management Trust	372	4,966,666	No 1995–2003 Yes 2003–2005	Misappropriation of P20,000 in 2002; limited community participation or benefit prior to this. Since 2002 the new leadership and a new constitution have improved the situation. Ongoing controversy with JVP.
Mababe Zokotsama Community Trust	157	3,305,263	No 1998–2003 Yes 2003–2005	P99,461 misappropriated in 2002; limited community benefit or participation prior to this. Since 2002 the new leadership has improved the situation.

Note: One pula was equivalent to approximately US$0.15 throughout this period.

Source: Rihoy and Maguranyanga, 2007

Okavango Community Trust (OCT)

In March 1995, the OCT was the first CBO in Ngamiland to be registered, representing the five villages granted rights over the established hunting and tourism concession areas (ACORD, 2002) in the north of the Okavango Delta. The establishment of OCT was politically motivated, and as a result community participation was marginalized from the start in order to expedite the registration process (ACORD, 2002). The Member of Parliament (MP) for Okavango North, in collaboration with a local safari operator, approached the DWNP with a demand that CBNRM projects be established in his area. The DWNP directed NRMP staff to proceed immediately and undertake community briefing and mobilization meetings (O. Thakadu and N. Winer, pers. comm.). A month later, on returning to the area to complete the process prior to the registration of OCT, the NRMP staff learnt that OCT had already signed a contract entering into a joint venture with a safari operator, and a constitution had been drawn up for OCT by a lawyer in consultation with the MP (Hartly, 1995). The community had not been consulted on these processes. This set a weak foundation upon which to build a community-driven organization. ACORD (2002, p9) states:

> *...it was, as it were, driven to them...locals did not readily accept the trust as theirs, neither were they fully aware of its functions, nor did they participate in its activities.*

The project itself emerged as an imposition and external initiative driven by political interests and expediency:

> *...the establishment of the OCT was for two purposes and driven by two individuals. The purposes were to gain votes for the MP while lining his pocket because of the favourable terms of the agreement with the operator – it never even went out to tender – and not surprisingly the individuals pushing it were the MP and the operator, who got on board a few powerful local residents. Local participation and needs had nothing to do with it.[11]*

The OCT was effectively established by the local MP, the safari operator and a lawyer. The OCT became the owner of wildlife resources in its jurisdictional area, and its natural resource management activity has involved subleasing its hunting quota to the same operator who was involved in establishing the Trust. This raises questions about transparency and favouritism in OCT's deals. According to a DWNP (2000, p3) report:

> *...there is apparently strong private sector and political influences over the board activities and decisions and in the process of establishing this, members have been excluded from any meaning[ful] participation in the trust's activities.*

In view of these problems, ACORD, in partnership with the government bodies DWNP and the Tawana Land Board, undertook initiatives in 2001 to institutionally strengthen the OCT and raise general community awareness. Increasing awareness of the communities' rights was necessary to enable communities to demand accountability and question decisions of the OCT board members. This resulted in a delegation of disgruntled community representatives approaching the District Commissioner to express dissatisfaction with the way things were run (ACORD, 2002). The delegation was dissatisfied with the Trust's decision to renew the joint venture agreement with the existing safari operator without going through an open tender, a procedure which the broader community preferred. The District Commissioner sought the support of the Minister of Commerce and Industry, who issued a directive to OCT to have an open tender. Acting upon its lawyer's advice, the OCT then invoked its legal rights to make decisions on behalf of the community as stipulated in its constitution (ACORD, 2002). The Minister withdrew her directive in face of this legal interpretation of the Trust's constitution. The OCT remained in full control of the local concessionary process.

The district authorities did not directly intervene, and became resigned to the extant situation and process. Local village representatives had approached district authorities as their legitimate, democratic representatives with the objective of seeking resolution on problems of non-accountability of the Trust.[12] District Council staff, in collaboration with local DWNP officers, had undertaken a comprehensive consultative process and negotiations in five villages over several months (ACORD, 2002). They sought the Minister's support in addressing the problem but were rebuffed on legal grounds since they had no formal right to intervene (Rihoy and Maguranyanga, 2007).

Meanwhile the appropriation of funds by the OCT Executive Committee has continued unabated as of 2008. The income from OWS that accrues to OCT every year is Pula 2.5 million (~US$400,000). Of this amount P166,000 is paid on a monthly basis and P508,000 as a lump sum.[13] Of this, the general running costs of the trust average P160,000–170,000 per month in 2008 – the first year in which such figures have been available – or 80 per cent of the income from concession fees (OCT, 2008). The most significant expenditure items include salaries for the 54 staff equaling approximately P80,000 per month, vehicle running costs of approximately P50,000 and costs associated with Village Trust Committees (VTC) and OCT meetings.[14] Financial mismanagement is rife within the OCT. The year 2006 provides a typical example. According to the draft auditor's report, P1,595,768 (~US$255,000), or over 65 per cent of total income, could not be accounted for (DSVG, 2007).

The total income for OCT between 1995 and 2007 is estimated at approximately P13,500,000 (~US$2.16 million). From this, P6,000 has been disbursed to each VTC on two occasions, totalling only P30,000 (~US$4,800) over 12 years. Funds have, however, also been used to support various village-level projects, although these have not proved sustainable. These include projects requiring significant capital expenditures, such as 'supermarkets' in each village, boats for transport and construction of a funeral parlour. However, the majority of such projects were abandoned midway through construction and none remained operational as of June 2008. In early 2008 the board decided to disburse P100,000 annually to each village. This has been achieved by issuing the chairperson of each VTC with a personal cheque for P100,000. In the three case study villages, these funds still remained with the VTC chairperson as of June 2008.

This brief review of the financial situation makes it clear that OCT has been characterized by mismanagement and personal appropriation of funds and that significant financial benefits have accrued to a few powerful individuals within the villages and their external allies. The institutional factors and relationships underlying this situation are succinctly stated:

> *Members of the OCT trust are in alliance with national politicians and local councillors and have formed a power block. They are in control and able to circumvent any procedures. They've shown they can beat the minister and tell her to stay out of their affairs, so all government personnel now stay away. The same operator has recently renewed the contract, although now there are new problems. We just had another delegation from the community, but we can't do anything. We are only allowed to advise through our role on the TAC [Technical Advisory Committee]. If the trust chooses to ignore our advice they can do so.*[15]

Mvimi et al (2003) conducted research in two OCT villages to explore communities' perceptions and understanding of CBNRM projects. In 2002, when this research was conducted, five villages of OCT with a total population of 6,431 had received approximately P7 million (approximately US$1,000,000) from CBNRM initiatives. At this time, 86 per cent of respondents indicated that they had heard about CBNRM in the consultation meetings but had lost track of matters as the clashes between the DC, MP and lawyer advanced. Only 14 per cent indicated having any relationship with the project since its inception. Results showed that 32 per cent felt that the community had benefited from the project, and only 2 per cent felt that it had benefited in terms of social services or infrastructural development. These findings question the trickle down effect of CBNRM benefits and the extent to which they have permeated into the community. It is therefore not surprising that in 2008 approximately 90 per cent of respondents interviewed regarding their expectations of CBNRM indicated that they had not been met, blaming mismanagement and poor leadership for problems (Rihoy, forthcoming).

We have presented the OCT case study to illustrate the local accountability and governance challenges in CBNRM enterprises in Botswana. These problems were not confined to OCT, with other CBOs experiencing similar challenges but on a different scale.

Khwai Development Trust (KDT)

Khwai village consists of 395 people of the Babukakhwae or 'River Bushmen' ethnic group. It is situated next to the Moremi Game Reserve in the Okavango Delta. The Khwai village was among the first villages encouraged to participate in CBNRM in the early 1990s but it was among the last to implement it. The delays resulted from the villagers wanting a concession for the Babukakhwae only, which the government considered unacceptable and discriminatory. As a result, the Khwai Development Trust (KDT) was not registered until 2000.

The KDT's natural resource management activities include marketing hunts, subsistence hunting on part of their quota, grass and crafts marketing, and community campsites. Between 2000 and 2003, KDT generated over P3,000,000 from commercial wildlife-based joint ventures. However, problems emerged in managing such large CBNRM funds (National CBNRM Forum, 2004), and huge sums of money were not accounted for. Mismanagement was pervasive, and over P2,000,000 remained unaccounted for in 2003.

When the KDT failed in 2003 to present its audited annual financial accounts to DWNP for the third year in a row, the DWNP withheld the 2004 quota pending an investigation (National CBNRM Forum, 2004). The KDT's initial appeal was denied but the course of events changed with the oncoming national elections. In July 2004, just a month before the national elections, the Minister of Environment and Tourism and the new BDP parliamentary candidate for Kasane District (in which Khwai is situated) held a political rally in Khwai. At the political rally, the BDP candidate MP produced the quota and 'returned' it to the people. Political influences prevailed, and the candidate MP successfully won his bid for the Kasane seat. Notable is that the Khwai community had in the previous 15 years supported the opposition Botswana Alliance Movement, and somehow switched its support to the BDP in this particular election. While there might not be definitive causal links, the story highlights overt tactics used by politicians to manipulate wildlife resources for political gain. The politicians used the wildlife quota to dispense patronage to a local political clientele. As a consequence, the Khwai community and MP are beholden to each other at the local level whereas at the national level the MP would have a sense of obligation and loyalty towards senior level politicians who delivered the quota to the MP (Rihoy and Maguranyanga, 2007). In this case, the lifeline of CBNRM was connected to electoral politics and the ability of politicians to extract political mileage from it. The politicians used their political clout to 'bring' back the quota despite KDT's failure to meet the technical, bureaucratic requirements of DWNP.

The gross financial mismanagement and abuse of earlier years have been brought under control with the election of new KDT trustees and introduction of an external accountant. However, limited financial abuses and mismanagement of resources still exist, and the clean-up has impacted the community:

> *I can't speak for the people of Khwai, but I spend a lot of time there and in my experience the majority of those within Khwai who aren't on the board of trustees would tell you that CBNRM should be scrapped. It's brought nothing but trouble, fighting and arguments within what was previously a cohesive community; now their sons and daughters face jail and public disgrace, and in return for all this they have nothing.*

> (I. Hancock, pers. comm.)

Despite management shortcomings, the Khwai village of 395 people has had CBNRM income exceeding P4,000,000 for the period 2000 to 2004, which represents a potential per capita income of P10,126 (~US$1,519).

Cgaecgae Tlhabololo Trust (CTT)

The Cgaecgae Tlhabololo Trust (CTT) offers a positive example of a CBO that evaded problems of mismanagement or financial accountability controversies (see Table 3.1). The majority of community members indicated that they had benefited from the CTT projects and were involved in decision-making (Mvimi et al, 2003;

Rihoy and Maguranyanga, 2007). Instead of using the traditional *kgotla* forum for consultation, CTT avoided it because of concerns for democratic participation and effective decision-making (Mvimi et al, 2003). It was felt that the *kgotla* meetings would marginalize segments of the community, and often were poorly attended. Therefore, they did not serve as democratic decision-making institutions (Taylor, 2000; Habarad, 2003). However, the DWNP equated the representation and accountability of CBOs with elections conducted in *kgotla* meetings, which were deemed 'transparent and democratic' (Thakadu, 2005, p203).

The CTT has generated relatively low annual income of P342,262, which is considerably less than those of other CBOs. Rihoy and Maguranyanga (2007) argue that the low financial performance of CTT activities could be explained by the paucity of its wildlife resource base. Such a wildlife resource base has been shunned by operators who often are unwilling to enter into commercial agreement with CTT. As a result, CTT fails to realize the value of its quota. In 2000, CTT earned P342,262 but has had no income since 2003.

Central responses to local mismanagement

The Botswana government drew attention to problems of local CBOs' mismanagement to justify the return to a more centralized wildlife management system. Previously, the DWNP had not increased its staff and resource commitments to enhance the organizational capacity and monitoring of CBOs but rather focused its effort in mobilizing communities to form trusts so that they could acquire quotas and enter into joint ventures with the private sector for photographic tourism and safari hunting (Rihoy and Maguranyanga, 2007). According to Rozemeijer and Van der Jagt (2000, p6):

> *DWNP does not have the resources for long-term facilitation and at times endorses the establishment of a trust with a quota knowing that it will not be able to provide the necessary follow-up, leaving behind a resource-rich but institutionally puzzled community.*

The government effectively blamed the CBOs which they had established without initially building their organizational capacity. In this way, the CBOs were set up for failure given the limited attention paid in addressing low local organizational capacity. It is unrealistic to expect communities without organizational capacity to meet the management and technical bureaucratic requirements of complex contracts and financial accountability associated with CBO activities. These institutional design flaws of CBNRM in Botswana contributed to CBO mismanagement and accountability shortcomings. Unfortunately, such shortcomings provided the central government with reasons to recentralize management of revenue and 'transform wildlife into a national resource, and thus redistribute wildlife benefits' rather than 'to solve problems of institutional design or local capacity' (Poteete, 2007, p11). We would suggest that CBO problems were a 'blessing in disguise' from the central perspective since they legitimized government's re-centralization of wildlife revenue in line with Botswana's constitutional principle of natural resources as national resources (Poteete, 2007; Rihoy and Maguranyanga, 2007).

Conclusion: Revisiting the politics of CBNRM policy in Botswana

Natural resource policy and governance depends on the relative political influence of different interest groups; this relative influence shifts over time. In Botswana, we argue that the dearth of a vibrant civil society and influential actor network has prevented the development of CBNRM policy supportive of grass-roots interests and CBNRM ideals related to localized resource tenure. We also explained the implications of the overwhelmingly influential President Ian Khama's preferences for a 'protectionist' conservation paradigm and his reservations on the concept of sustainable use. The 'diamond debate' over national versus local control over natural resource revenues has provided a powerful political argument for recentralizing wildlife-derived revenues and to roll back earlier measures to devolve rights to the local level. The perceived foreign origins of CBNRM helped undermine its legitimacy or acceptability since CBNRM did not manage to develop an indigenous identity supported by a strong politically-salient constituency in the country. In the absence of these conditions, central government actors were able to drive policy in a way that ultimately reversed the gains of the previous 15 years as well as undermining CBNRM ideals. The 2008 CBNRM Policy emerged in the context of limited resistance since the government has succeeded in restricting the democratic space for rural communities and civil society to participate in the policy-making process.

At the local level, unaccountable governance structures have facilitated concentration of benefits in the hands of local élites and inhibited local attempts to address mismanagement of revenues. These problems of accountability and mismanagement have been used by some national politicians and bureaucrats to justify the re-centralization of wildlife revenues. It should be pointed out that rather than focusing on the problems and using visible stories of fraud, mismanagement and abuse of CBO funds to recentralize those funds, it would have been plausible to build the organizational capacity of CBOs as well as investing institutionally in accountability and governance structures. The 2008 CBNRM Policy recentralized control over revenue as an ostensive response to local corruption and mismanagement; however, this does not deal with the organizational capacity deficit and poor governance mechanisms on the part of CBOs. Politics prevailed and favoured the transfer of financial power to the centre, thereby contradicting the aspirational CBNRM principle of devolving financial benefits to the local 'producer communities'. While it is a plausible argument that, as Ribot (2002, p3) contends, 'transferring power without accountable representation has proven dangerous', the problems of mismanagement of CBO funds have to be understood within the context of CBO organizational incapacity and institutional design flaws which facilitate élite predation. The politicized nature of CBNRM implementation ensures that such teething challenges receive scrutiny from national politicians and élites opposed to the concepts of sustainable use and devolution.

Initial advocates of CBNRM did not pay close attention to the political dimensions of natural resource policy-making processes. We argue that inattention to socio-political processes of empowerment and the potential of CBNRM to alter levers of power proved costly to CBNRM. CBNRM strengthens social empowerment, capital and community development, which could be leveraged into political capital. The Khwai and OCT case studies reveal how politics intersect with CBNRM at the local level and interact with outcomes of electoral politics. The 'diamond debate' invoked political questions and contradictory impulses of CBNRM and nation-building or national development. Natural resource politics permeates policy, making it imperative that CBNRM implementers and policy advocates understand the power dynamics and levers that shape natural resource governance.

In southern Africa, CBNRM practitioners and policy-makers have sought to create strong feedback between local investments in wildlife management and benefit capture through devolved institutional arrangements. As noted earlier, one of the main lessons regional practitioners took from Zimbabwe's CAMPFIRE programme was that insufficient devolution of property rights over wildlife to local communities, as opposed to upwardly accountable District Councils, undermined local incentives and economic returns from natural resources. Murphree captures this perspective which frames 'decentralization' as effectively a mechanism for states to maintain control over valuable resources, in contrast to 'devolution' as the desired means of local empowerment:

> *States, even when they grasp the importance of local management and steward-ship, thus prefer decentralisation to devolution. This tendency, more than any other factor, is responsible for the failure of programmes ostensibly designed to create local natural resource management jurisdictions.*
>
> (2000, p6)

In Botswana, such concerns contributed to a focus on devolving control over wildlife benefits and led to the marginalization of District Councils in CBNRM implementation. With the benefit of hindsight, this was a tactical error since District Councils could have bridged the gulf between local communities and central government, and also could have brought natural resource governance closer to democratically-elected local government structures. Instead, district authorities viewed CBOs as rival single-purpose authorities, and such perceptions undermined opportunities for collaboration between CBOs and district governments to challenge national political interests. This prevented local CBOs and other CBNRM advocates from bringing district governments into collaborative efforts to contest national government's preferred policy directions as reflected in the 2008 CBNRM Policy. With central authorities currently having prevailed in the struggle over wildlife governance and benefits in Botswana, the future ability of locally-based natural resource governance regimes to contribute to conservation and rural development goals will depend largely on the ability to construct more influential constituencies for CBNRM.

Notes

1 Interview with Senior DWNP official, Gabarone, February 2005.
2 Interview with P. Buteti, Gabarone, February 2005.
3 In 2003, Botswana was formally reclassified by the World Bank and International Monetary Fund as a 'middle-income' country, resulting in the withdrawal of many donors from the country.
4 Interview with A. Mabei, CEO of BOCOBONET, Gabarone, February 2005.
5 A Savingram is a directive issued by the Government of Botswana. See Savingram (2001) 'Management of funds realised from the Community Based Natural Resources Management Project', Ministry of Local Government, 30 January 2001, Ref: LG/3/6/2/1 IV (46).
6 However, how this will play out at the local level is as yet unclear. Implementation guidelines have yet to be developed, leaving local-level technical staff unclear on how to proceed.
7 They identify the shortcomings of the state of democracy in Botswana as the centralization of constitutional and political power in the Office of the President; the lack of free speech and curtailment of the freedom of the media; the pervasiveness of secrecy in government decision-making; and the inability of government to accept or engage with criticism.
8 Wylie (1990) writes persuasively about the 'God-like' status of a Tswana chief in the 20th century.
9 Interview with Senior DWNP official, Gaborone, February, 2005
10 Interview with ex-DWNP official, Gaborone, February, 2005.
11 Interview with former DWNP/NRMP field officer, Maun, February 2005.
12 Interview with Ngamiland District Council Officer, Maun, February 2005.
13 Interview with OCT accountant, Seronga, June 2008.
14 These include sitting allowances of P900 per person for each of the four mandatory OCT meetings per year, P400pp for each of the mandatory 4 VTC meetings per year and P100pp for each of the 4–5 special meetings by VTCs held each month and related food and accommodation costs. To put these sitting allowances into some perspective, full-time unskilled District Council personnel, such as cleaners, earn P800 per month. Such expenditures can amount to P30,000 per month. Additionally Executive Committee members make monthly all-expense-paid trips to Maun, costs for which amount to several thousand Pula (see OCT, 2008).
15 Interview with Senior District Council Officer, June 2008.

References

ACORD (Agency for Cooperation and Research in Development) (2002) 'Through our Eyes: ACORD's Experiences in CBNRM', Okavango Community Trust, Unpublished report, ACORD, Gaborone, Botswana

Alden Wily, L. (2003) *Governance and Land Relations: A Review of Decentralization of Land Administration and Management in Africa*, International Institute for Environment and Development, London

Arntzen, J., Molokomme D., Terry, N., Molele, N., Tshosa, O. and Mazambani, D. (2003) *Final Report of the Review of Community-based Natural Resource Management in Botswana*, Report prepared by the Centre for Applied Research for the National CBNRM Forum, Gaborone, Botswana

Blanc, J.J., Barnes, R.F.W., Craig, G.C., Dublin, H.T., Thouless, C.R., Douglas-Hamilton, I. and Hart, J.A. (2007) *African Elephant Status Report 2007: An Update from the African Elephant Database*, IUCN, Gland

DSVG (2007) 'The Okavango Community Trust: Financial Statements for the Year Ended 31 December 2006', Unpublished DSVG Certified Public Accountants Report to the members of the OCT, April 2007, Gaborone, Botswana

DWNP (Department of Wildlife and National Parks) (2000) *CBNRM Progress Report*, Gaborone, Botswana

Gakale, J. (2005) 'Response to CBNRM Forum Commentary on CBNRM Policy', Unpublished letter from PS Dr J. Gakale, Ministry of Environment, Wildlife and Tourism to Ms M. Madzwamuse, Secretariat CBNRM National Forum; 28 June 2005: Gaborone, Botswana

Good, K. (1992) 'Interpreting the exceptionality of Botswana', *The Journal of Modern African Studies* vol 30, no 1, pp69–95

Good, K. and Taylor, I. (2005) *Presidential Succession in Botswana: No Model for Africa*, Paper presented to a politics seminar, 25 February 2005, University of Botswana, Gaborone

Habarad, H. (2003) 'CBNRM, community politics and the village elite', Unpublished paper

Habarad, J., Dikobe, L. and Gaboiphiwe, J. (1995) 'Understanding community dynamics: PRA and other tools for social analysis', in E. Rihoy (ed) *The Commons without the Tragedy? Strategies for Community-based Natural Resources Management in Southern Africa*, Southern African Development Community (SADC) Wildlife Technical Coordinating Unit, Lilongwe, Malawi

Hartly, R. (1995) 'Trip Report – Kgotla Meetings in Okavango Community CHA's', Unpublished Natural Resources Management Project internal document, 9 January 1995

IIED (International Institute for Environment and Development) (2004) 'Winners and Losers: Privatizing the Commons in Botswana', Unpublished briefing paper prepared for RECONCILE, IIED, London

IUCN/SNV (The World Conservation Union/Netherlands Development Organization) (2000) *Proceedings of the First National CBNRM Forum Meeting in Botswana, 30–31 May and CBNRM Status Report 1999/2000*, National CBNRM Forum, Gaborone, Botswana

Jones, B.T.B. (2004) *Synthesis of the Current Status of CBNRM Policy and Legislation in Botswana, Malawi, Mozambique, Namibia, Zambia, and Zimbabwe*, Report prepared for WWF SARPO. WWF, Harare, Zimbabwe

Jones, B. and Murphree, M.W. (2001) 'The evolution of policy on community conservation in Namibia and Zimbabwe', in D. Hulme and M.W. Murphree (eds) *African Wildlife and Livelihoods: The Promise and Performance of Community Conservation*, James Currey, Oxford

Keeley, J. and Scoones, I. (2003) *Understanding Environmental Policy Processes: Cases from Africa*, Earthscan, London

Mamdani, M. (1996) *Citizen and Subject: Contemporary Africa and the Legacy of Late Colonialism*, Princeton University Press, Princeton, NJ

Mbaiwa, J. (2004) 'The success and sustainability of community-based natural resource management in the Okavango Delta, Botswana', *South African Geographical Journal*, vol 86, no 1, pp44–53

Mmegi (2002) 'Diamonds do not eat goats', *The Mmegi* 22–27 November 2002, Mmegi Publishing House, Gaborone, Botswana

Molutsi, P. (2005) 'Botswana's democracy in a southern African regional perspective: Progress or decline', in Z. Maudeni (ed), *40 Years of Democracy in Botswana: 1965–2005*, Mmegi Publishing House, Gaborone, Botswana

Molutsi, P. and Holm, J. (1990) 'Developing democracy when the civil society is weak: The case of Botswana', *African Affairs*, vol 89, pp323–348

Murphree, M.W. (2004) 'Communal approaches to natural resource management in Africa: From whence and to where?', *Journal of International Wildlife Law and Policy*, vol 7, pp203–216

Murphree, M.W (2000) 'Boundaries and borders: The question of scale in the theory and practice of common property management' Paper presented at the International Association for the Study of Common Property (IASCP) conference on 'Constituting the commons: Crafting sustainable commons in the new millennium', Bloomington, Indiana, May 31–June 4

Murphree, M.W. (1995) 'Optimal principles and pragmatic strategies: Creating an enabling politico-legal environment for Community-based Natural Resources Management (CBNRM)', in E. Rihoy (ed) *The Commons without the Tragedy? Strategies for Community-based Natural Resources Management in Southern Africa*, Southern African Development Community (SADC) Wildlife Technical Coordinating Unit, Lilongwe, Malawi

Mvimi, E., Othusitse, B. and Navrud, S. (2003) *Community-based wildlife management: A comparative multiple success criteria assessment*, in Conference Proceedings of the Botswana Institutional Co-operation and Capacity Building Project (BONIC), Department of Wildlife and National Parks, Gaborone, Botswana

National CBNRM Forum Botswana. (2004) *Proceedings of the Third National CBNRM Conference in Botswana and the CBNRM Status Report, 25–26 November 2003*, Printing and Publishing Company, Gaborone, Botswana

Obeng, K. (2001) *Botswana: Institutions of Democracy and Governance of Botswana*, Associated Printers, Gabarone, Botswana

OCT (Okavango Community Trust) (2008) 'Report: Okavango Community Trust Income Statement January to March 2008', Unpublished report from OCT accountant to Board of Trustees, 11 April 2008, Seronga, Botswana

Peters, P. (1994) *Dividing the Commons: Politics, Policy and Culture in Botswana*, University of Virginia Press, Charlottesville, VA

Poteete, A.R. (2007) 'Resources for the Nation or for Community? Interactions between Mineral Rights, Wildlife Policies and Political Coalitions in Botswana', Paper presented at the 2007 Annual Meeting of the American Political Science Association, August 30 – September 2, 2007, Chicago, IL

Ribot, J.C. (2002) *Democratic Decentralization of Natural Resources: Institutionalizing Popular Participation*, World Resources Institute, Washington, DC

Rihoy, E. (forthcoming) 'Devolution and democratisation: Policy processes and community-based natural resource management in Southern Africa', Unpublished PhD Thesis for submission (November 2009) to Programme for Land and Agrarian Studies (PLASS), University of Western Cape, South Africa

Rihoy, E. and Maguranyanga, B. (2007) *Devolution and Democratization of Natural Resource Management in Southern Africa: A Comparative Analysis of CBNRM Policy Processes in Botswana and Zimbabwe*, CASS/PLASS Occasional Paper Series No. 18. Programme for Land and Agrarian Studies, University of Western Cape, Cape Town, South Africa

Rotberg, R (2007) *Africa's Successes: Evaluating Accomplishment*, Belfer-WPF Report 43, Programme on Interstate Conflict, Cambridge, MA

Rozemeijer, N. and Van der Jagt, C. (2000) *Community Based Natural Resource Management (CBNRM) in Botswana: How Community Based is CBNRM in Botswana?*, Paper prepared for the research project 'Community-based natural resource management: Where does the power really lie?' Institute for Environmental Studies, University of Sussex, Brighton

Samatar, A. (1999) *An African Miracle: State and Class Leadership and Colonial Legacy in Botswana Development*, Heinemann Press, Portsmouth

Swatuk, L. (2005) 'From "project" to "context": Community based natural resource management in Botswana', *Global Environmental Politics*, vol 5, no 3, pp 95–124

Taylor, M. (2000) 'Life, land and power: Contesting development in northern Botswana', PhD thesis', University of Edinburgh, UK

Thakadu, O. (2005) 'Success factors in community based natural resources management projects mobilization in northern Botswana: Lessons from practice', *Natural Resources Forum*, vol 29, no 3, pp199–212

Transparency International (2008) '2008 Corruption perceptions index', www.transparency.org/news_room/in_focus/2008/cpi2008/cpi_2008_table Accessed 25 June 2009

UNDP (United Nations Development Programme) (2005) *Human Development Report – International Cooperation at a Crossroads: Aid, Trade and Security in an Unequal World*, United Nations Development Programme, New York

White, R. (1998) 'Land Issues and Land Reform in Botswana', in Zimbabwe Environmental Research Organisation, *Enhancing Land Reforms in Southern Africa: Review of Land Reform Strategies and CBNRM*, Zimbabwe Environmental Research Organisation, Harare, Zimbabwe

Whiteside, M. (1995) *Literature Reviews and Fieldwork Plans for South Africa, Namibia, Botswana, Zimbabwe, Zambia, Malawi Agricultural Services Reform in Southern Africa*, Phase 1 Working Papers, Environment and Development Consultancy Ltd., Stroud, UK

The World Bank (2009) *The Little Data Book on Africa 2008*, The World Bank, Washington, DC

WTO (World Tourism Organization) (2007) Tourism highlights: 2007 edition. Available at: www.unwto.org/facts/eng/pdf/highlights/highlights_07_eng_lr.pdf Accessed 21 August 2009

Zuze C. (2004) 'Community based natural resources management projects', Unpublished report by the Community Extension and Outreach Division, Ngamiland District, for the Director, Department of Wildlife and National Parks (DWNP), Gaborone, Botswana

4

Peasants' Forests and the King's Game? Institutional Divergence and Convergence in Tanzania's Forestry and Wildlife Sectors

Fred Nelson and Tom Blomley

Introduction

Tanzania is one of Africa's most richly endowed nations in terms of natural resources. The country's economy and the livelihoods of its 38 million citizens are heavily reliant on natural resources and ecological services. Because of the importance of natural resources to local livelihoods and national economic activity, debates revolving around the use, control and management of these resources are central to issues of governance and political accountability in Tanzania. Natural resource management has been heavily centralized during the colonial and post-colonial periods, but the economic crisis of the 1980s contributed to the promotion of more locally-based, decentralized approaches to the management of natural resources such as forests and wildlife. With central government agencies facing greater resource pressures in an uncertain and changing national fiscal and political context, foreign donors and entrepreneurial individuals were able to influence reforms, as reflected in new wildlife and forestry policies released in 1998 that called for a much greater level of direct involvement in natural resource management by local communities.

Since the late 1990s, institutional changes have continued in both wildlife and forestry sectors, but not necessarily in ways forecast or intended by donors or local proponents of reform. Formalized local rights over community forests, managed by elected Village Councils, have expanded rapidly, supported by reformed national forest legislation and continued strong support from an array of European donor agencies and local and international NGOs. By contrast, wildlife sector reforms have been much more curtailed, with limited opportunities for communities to secure legal rights to manage and benefit from wildlife. New wildlife legislation drafted in 2008 and passed by Parliament in early 2009 virtually reproduces the established centralized regulatory and management framework, and even expands it in some notable respects.

Thus Tanzania's wildlife and forestry sectors, which underwent parallel reform processes during the 1990s, appear to have diverged onto very different institutional tracks since 1998. Despite this divergence, however, certain commonalities persist. Despite the success of forestry reforms in fostering the emergence of locally-managed forests, and providing a relatively clear and supportive policy and legal framework for community-based forest management, little progress has been made in enabling local communities to add value to these forests through timber harvesting or other commercial activities. By contrast, much of the value of Tanzania's booming timber trade in recent years, driven by surging demand from Asia, has been controlled by networks of traders operating informally or illegally, and often through links to public officials (Milledge et al, 2007). Tanzanian communities have seemingly secured rights over their forests but captured few of the economic benefits derived from 'their' resources, which calls into question the impact and sustainability of the national community-based forestry reform effort. Thus in forestry, as is more self-evidently the case with the overtly centralized wildlife sector, Tanzanian villagers effectively continue to be excluded from capturing the economic values of the resources on their lands.

This chapter examines the key factors that have driven institutional change in the management of Tanzania's forests and wildlife during the past 20 years. We seek to account for the nature of policy change in both sectors in the 1990s, the reasons for divergence between forestry and wildlife reform patterns since 1998, and the political economic factors that continue to exclude local communities from capturing more of forests' and wildlife's economic values. This comparison highlights the importance of commercial patterns of natural resource use in shaping the interests, choices and levels of influence of key actors such as central government policy-makers, foreign donors and local communities, as well as the importance of the macro-political context in shaping natural resource reforms. We conclude with some recommendations for future natural resource reform efforts based on the Tanzanian experience.

Tanzania's political economy: From socialism to liberalization

Tanzania's first two decades after independence in 1961 were characterized by the consolidation and extension of the state's control over the economy and the lives of its citizens as the country embarked on a project of socialist development and nation-building. Political authority was monopolized by the ruling party (the Tanganyika African National Union prior to 1977 and the *Chama cha Mapinduzi* or CCM thereafter) and alternative forms of social organization such as trade unions and co-operative societies were either prohibited or incorporated into state/party structures (Coulson, 1982). The party, through its national executive committee and central committee, effectively centralized decision-making and policed internal dissent. As Mallya notes (2006, p51), 'public policy making, particularly policy debates, ceased to be "public"'.

By the early 1980s the country was in a period of economic collapse and fiscal crisis brought on by economic mismanagement, particularly of the parastatal corporations which had become the proprietors of much productive activity during the previous decade, as well as the 1978–79 war with Uganda and external shocks in oil and commodity prices. The structural adjustment policies which were accepted as the condition for the donor rescue package agreed to in the mid-1980s were themselves a considerable socio-economic shock and forced a radical break with the policies of the prior 20 years. The new liberalization discourse promoted foreign direct investment, privatization of parastatal corporations, a reduction in government provision of social services, civil service reform, and a shift from central economic planning to promotion of market-based forces (Campbell and Stein, 1991). These economic reforms also led to a return to political pluralism after nearly 30 years of formal single-party rule.

In terms of changing national governance dynamics, the post-structural adjustment era in Tanzania is best understood by two largely contradictory trends (Kelsall, 2002). On the one hand, political space has expanded substantially with the re-introduction of pluralist politics and the proliferation of non-governmental forms of social organization. An independent media was allowed from 1988 and the number of NGOs has grown rapidly since the early 1990s, with important implications for associational life and the flow of information to citizens, including those in rural areas. With the return to pluralist politics, government institutions from local to national level are no longer formally fused with the structures and membership of the ruling party, as they had been during the socialist era.

Simultaneously, the loss of the state monopoly on decision-making power and the deterioration of governmental patronage resources, such as a downscaled civil service, have created both opportunities and incentives for the spread of private accumulative behaviours within government:

> *Generally speaking, economic liberalisation increased the desire and ability of members of the political elite to enrich themselves…lucrative areas were to be found in land grabbing, urban real estate, and the exploitation of tax loopholes. Divestiture of parastatals also introduced a spoils character into Tanzanian politics, as politicians positioned themselves to receive kickbacks or to become part-owners of the newly privatised companies.*
>
> (Kelsall, 2002, p610)

While the one-party state of the 1970s enjoyed a high degree of popular legitimacy, by the late 1980s the state 'began to resemble a racket for the protection of corrupt and acquisitive public officials' (Kelsall 2003, p56). Following the replacement of Tanzania's home-grown socialist policies with a liberalization discourse that has generally had limited local legitimacy or popular support, governance processes have increasingly come to revolve around these acquisitive interests. Tanzanian governing élites have sought to shape institutional reforms in ways that maintain or expand key discretionary powers and rent-seeking opportunities. For example, Cooksey (2003) describes how narratives portraying the liberalization of controls over key export crops contrast with administrative and regulatory measures that have expanded discretionary authority over this agricultural trade. Despite over

20 years of nominal reforms, the country's political institutions remain heavily centralized with power strongly concentrated in the hands of the executive (Lawson and Rakner, 2005). As Tanzania's public institutions have been colonized by private commercial interests and activities, various forms of corruption have spread and become institutionalized (URT, 2005).

The local institutional context

In 1975, at the height of Tanzania's collectivist *ujamaa* villagization project, the government passed legislation providing for the creation of Village Assemblies, which comprise all the adults in a registered village, and Village Councils, which are elected bodies of up to 25 representatives headed by a Village Chairman. Village Councils are corporate bodies capable of owning property and entering into legal contracts with other parties. Initially, these village-level institutions were intended mainly as mechanisms for modernizing rural populations according to the transformative objectives of *ujamaa*, such as by transmitting central development plans to the grass roots (Shivji and Peter, 2000). The establishment of these village institutions helped to extend the ruling party's reach to the grass roots, and the Village Council Chairman was by definition the village party Chairman. At the district level, elected District Councils were abolished in 1972, and central government functions were decentralized to administrators at the district level. In 1982, local government reforms were passed that reintroduced elected District Councils and strengthened the corporate powers of elected Village Councils. These reforms also empowered Village Councils to propagate their own bylaws, subject to approval by the District Council.

The importance of village governance institutions is enhanced through their legal responsibility for management of customary village lands according to the 1999 Land Act and Village Land Act. Village Councils manage land on behalf of, and subject to approval for most transactions by, the Village Assembly, and this includes demarcating land that is to be allocated to individuals and land which will remain statutorily collective in its use and management (Alden Wily, 2003). The result of this local governance and land tenure structure is that the *boundaries* of common property regimes both with respect to the community, as defined by the membership of the Village Assembly, and the physical resource base as defined by the area of a given village's lands, are relatively clearly delineated in rural Tanzania. Consequently, Tanzania is considered to have one of the strongest local institutional frameworks for community-based natural resource management in sub-Saharan Africa (Alden Wily and Mbaya, 2001).

The evolution and impacts of community-based forest management

Tanzania contains an estimated 34.6 million hectares of forests and woodlands. The main forest types are the extensive *miombo* woodlands that cover the central and southern parts of the country, the *Acacia* woodlands in the northern regions, the coastal forest mosaic in the east, mangrove forests along the Indian Ocean, and closed canopy forests on the ancient mountains of the Eastern Arc, along

Lake Tanganyika in the west, and on the younger volcanic mountains in the north (White, 1983). Of these various forest types, 14.3 million hectares are found within gazetted Forest Reserves, and the remaining 15.8 million hectares of forest lie on village and general (or unowned) land (Akida and Blomley, 2006).

In 1998, Tanzania released a National Forestry Policy, the first new forest policy since the colonial era, which promotes substantial change in the way forests are managed (MNRT, 1998a). The policy aims to promote community-based forest management (CBFM) through the establishment of Village Land Forest Reserves (VLFRs), where communities are both managers and owners of forests, as well as through Joint Forest Management (JFM), where local communities co-manage forests with the designated authorities of National or Local Government Forest Reserves.

The policy is being implemented through the Forest Act of 2002, which provides the basis in law for communities to own, manage or co-manage forests under a wide range of conditions. The Forest Act embraces the principle of subsidiarity, stating as its aim 'to delegate responsibility for the management of forest resources to the lowest possible level of local management consistent with the furtherance of national policies' (URT, 2002, p1170). The Forest Act allows village governments to declare and gazette their own Village Land Forest Reserves or Community Forest Reserves. Several key points about the policy and legal framework for CBFM in Tanzania bear emphasizing. First, policy-makers have been explicit in the devolutionary intent of these reforms, and the importance of granting local communities secure rights to use, manage and own forests on village lands. Guidelines for CBFM published by the Forestry and Beekeeping Division (FBD) in 2001, and revised in 2006/07, state as follows:

> **CBFM is a power-sharing strategy.** *It builds upon the national policy to enable local participation in forest management and the real need to bring control and management to more practical local levels. It aims to secure forests through sharing the right to control and manage them, not just the right to use or benefit from them. Therefore CBFM targets communities not as passive beneficiaries but as forest* **managers.**
>
> (MNRT, 2007, p2, emphasis in original)

Second, local rights to forests and forests' economic values are secured within the law, not merely advocated by policy. The Forest Act secures statutory rights to forest benefits for local communities that establish VLFRs by including the following specific legal provisions (see URT, 2002).

- Waiving official royalty fees on forest products. This means that villages do not have to follow government timber fee schedules but can sell their produce at prices of their own choosing.
- Exemption from benefit-sharing arrangements. As forest managers, Village Councils may retain all of the income from the sale of forest produce from VLFRs.
- Levying and retaining fines and proceeds from confiscated timber and equipment. Fines imposed on violations occurring in VLFRs are retained by the village.

- Exemption from the 'reserved tree species list'. The Forest Act protects commercially important or endangered tree species (reserved tree species) on general land, and places their management with the District Forestry Officer. Once under village management, decisions about harvesting of these species in VLFRs are controlled by the village government.

A third important characteristic of the CBFM framework established by the Forest Act is that the procedures for communities to establish VLFRs are relatively straightforward and build on existing village government institutions and land tenure arrangements. Villages must only form a natural resource or environment committee under the Village Council, demarcate the boundary of the proposed VLFR, and draft village bylaws and a basic management plan for the forest, including different use and user zones. Then the VLFR is declared by the Village Assembly, which formalizes the forest's status under the Forest Act. Policymakers in the forestry sector sought to produce a framework for CBFM which did not duplicate local governance structures but rather builds upon and takes advantage of the existing village governance framework (MNRT, 2007, p3).

CBFM implementation progress to date

CBFM has spread quite rapidly since the initial experiments with different models of local forest management were piloted in northern Tanzania starting in the early 1990s. A national survey undertaken in 2008 established that over 2.2 million hectares were within established VLFRs and that 1,448 villages were participating (Table 4.1).

CBFM tends to be concentrated in the *miombo* woodlands, much of which lie outside government forest reserves and on village land. Montane evergreen and mangrove forests show a disproportionately small coverage under CBFM as the total area under these forest types is smaller and the majority are classified as central government forest reserves due to their higher economic or biodiversity values.

Table 4.1 *Current coverage of CBFM across Tanzania*

Area of forest under CBFM	2.27 million ha	11.6% of unprotected forest estate
Forest types covered by CBFM	Miombo woodlands	68% of total area covered
	Coastal forests	15% of total area covered
	Acacia woodlands	16% of total area covered
	Mangrove	0% of total area covered
	Montane forests	1% of total area covered
Number of declared or gazetted village land forest reserves	383	
Number of villages engaged in CBFM	1,448	13.8% of villages in the country
Number of districts engaged in CBFM	65	68% of rural districts in the country

Source: MNRT, 2008

Where forests have been formalized under community management, signs from available data are that forest condition is improving. In a study (Blomley et al, 2008) that compared growth characteristics of 13 forest areas under varying management regimes, forest condition appears to be better in those areas managed either wholly or jointly by communities (as evidenced by higher basal areas, mean annual incremental growth and stems per hectare), than areas under exclusive state control or under open access regimes. This study, supported by other recent assessments (Pfliegner and Moshi, 2007; Persha and Blomley, 2009) would suggest that by providing incentives for local communities to enforce rules governing forest use, VLFR establishment is able to reduce levels of exploitation, thus reversing processes of forest degradation in these areas.

Thus the impacts of CBFM during the decade that has passed since the release of the 1998 forest policy include the rapidly spreading establishment of VLFRs, securing and formalizing local collective rights over 2.2 million hectares of forests and woodlands, and in many instances spurring the recovery of these forests in terms of their biophysical condition. We now take a step back to examine the historical and institutional roots of CBFM in Tanzania, in order to understand what factors led to these changes in Tanzanian forest governance.

Drivers of reform

Up until the 1970s, forestry in Tanzania remained rooted in colonial era institutions and a technocratic belief in scientific management, with government efforts principally focused on industrial timber production. This involved investing in government parastatal operations, such as sawmills, in order to meet growing demand for timber and increase production. The industrial forestry model was strongly supported by foreign donors, with aid constituting 90 per cent of the non-recurring government forestry budget by the late 1970s (Hurst, 2004).

The economic crisis of the early 1980s was a key driver of institutional change in the forestry sector, as with Tanzanian economic policies more broadly. Deteriorating fiscal circumstances forced foresters to cope with reduced resources and new challenges to their established professional and bureaucratic role as managers of natural resources and landscapes. The industrial forestry model underwent a financial collapse, casting doubt upon the future role of state forestry authorities as parastatals such as sawmills were divested and civil service reforms initiated.

Simultaneously, growing international interest in the biodiversity values of Tanzania's forests, particularly the Eastern Arc range, led to pressure to reduce or cease timber harvesting in these forests and concomitantly improve their protection for conservation purposes. This pressure had external origins, being rooted in global environmental values ascendant during the 1980s, and influenced the foreign donors that were financing Tanzania's forestry sector during this time of fiscal crisis (Hurst, 2004). These values were also given organizational form and agency within Tanzania, as one of the country's first domestic conservation NGOs, the Tanzania Forest Conservation Group (TFCG), was established in 1984 in order to campaign for conservation of the Eastern Arc forests. TFCG played a major role in this and later forest conservation campaigns.

In 1985, following initial proposals from TFCG and supported by international conservation organizations (such as WWF) and donor agencies, the government agreed to establish the first forest-based national park in Tanzania in the Udzungwa Mountains. This move transferred one of the country's largest highland forests from the FBD to Tanzania National Parks (TANAPA). This represented a tangible threat to government foresters that they would lose their lands, role and influence unless they became more aligned with the aims of the growing global biodiversity conservation movement (Hurst, 2004).

These trends, coupled with the collapse of industrial timber production, established a strategic and instrumental basis for the FBD to re-position itself as the guardian of Tanzania's high-biodiversity forests (Hurst, 2004). A ban on logging in highland catchment forests was introduced in the mid-1980s. By the mid-1990s the FBD was increasingly focused on protecting the national forest estate, and its commercial functions had significantly contracted. Indeed, today Tanzania has very few formal timber concessions, compared to other African nations with high levels of forest cover (Table 4.2). For example, neighbouring Mozambique, which also has mostly *miombo* woodlands making up its forest estate, has more than seven times as much land under timber concessions as compared with Tanzania (Sunderlin et al, 2008). Forestry officials in the central FBD bureaucracy are not the overseers of any large-scale centralized system of forest exploitation.

Table 4.2 *Area of forest land under timber concessions in select African countries*

Country	Central African Republic	Cameroon	Gabon	Mozambique	Tanzania
Area of forest lands under timber concession (millons of hectares)	3.40	4.95	6.98	4.55	0.61

Source: Sunderlin et al, 2008

It was in this changing context that CBFM emerged in the early 1990s. In the late 1980s the FBD had attempted to create several new forest reserves in degraded *miombo* woodland in northern Tanzania (Alden Wily et al, 2000; Hurst, 2004). Government officials cleared and demarcated the boundaries of these forests, prompting villagers to protest and to accelerate clearing of the forest so as to secure their lands before the new reserves were gazetted. As this transpired, a combination of district foresters and donor-paid technical specialists[1] developed a counter-proposal to place the forests under improved local management rather than gazetting a central reserve. Donors also had to be convinced, initially, that community-based management was a viable option (L. Alden Wily, pers. comm.), but eventually the Swedish International Development Cooperation Agency (SIDA) and other northern European donors became influential advocates of this new approach. Sweden provided Tanzania with a total of $227 million in forestry sector support from 1973 to 1998 – over 50 per cent of foreign aid to forestry in Tanzania – and thus had a substantial influence over policy decisions (Hurst, 2004, p91). SIDA was supporting a Land Management Project (LAMP) in Babati and Singida Districts that played the key role in developing CBFM pilot initiatives, and thereby later provided the basis for crafting CBFM rules and procedures in the new forest policy and law.

Importantly, the initial CBFM pilot initiatives occurred in forests which were relatively dry and degraded *miombo* woodlands, and thus not particularly valuable forests from a commercial perspective. The FBD's motivation in trying to establish forest reserves in those areas was primarily rehabilitative, seeking to bolster protection and enforcement. There was little or no fiscal rationale for the government to establish its own direct control over those areas.

An additional factor in the adoption of CBFM during the 1990s was the role played by certain individuals, both within government and on the part of donors. The director of the FBD during the 1970s and 1980s was strongly supportive of community participation in forestry, which partly stemmed from his belief in the national socialist development ideology of the time (Hurst, 2004). From 1992 to 1996, a new director of FBD assumed power who considered community-based forestry an abridgement of the technical responsibilities and mandate of government foresters, and who worked to counter the earlier steps towards greater local involvement (Ibid.). His removal, following strong pressure from donors and internal departmental tensions, brought in as director Professor Said Iddi, an academic who was a strong supporter of CBFM and ultimately oversaw propagation of both the new forestry policy and the Act.

In summary then, we can identify a fairly complex set of interacting factors that collectively account for the adoption of Tanzania's strong policy and legal framework for CBFM.

- The fiscal crisis of the 1980s, which greatly enhanced the influence of donor agencies and limited the options of bureaucratic decision-makers, as well as greatly curtailing central capacity for direct forest management in rural areas
- Growing international awareness of the importance of biodiversity in Tanzania's highland forests and international pressure to stop logging in these areas and adopt more preservationist management strategies
- Linked to the above two factors, a shift within the forestry sector from industrial modes of forest management to a much greater focus on protection of biodiversity values and ecosystem services
- Local resistance to expansion of state protected forests in the early 1990s which, in concert with increased donor influence and declining state capacity, catalysed the first experiments with CBFM
- Low commercial values of degraded forests, particularly *miombo* woodlands, which were the site of early CBFM experiments on community lands
- Key individuals working both for government and donors who promoted CBFM and devolution as a new paradigm for forest management, and who ensured that the initial field experiments were effectively translated into sweeping revisions of Tanzanian forestry policy and legislation
- Lastly, the existence of a pre-existing framework for local governance and ownership of common pool resources, in the form of Tanzania's elected village

governments, was a key factor in enabling early CBFM experiments to take place without having to create new institutions or change local government or land tenure legislation.

Rights but not revenues? Institutional struggles over forest use

Despite the general success of CBFM in Tanzania in terms of enabling communities to secure rights over a considerable area of forested land under a clear and simple set of institutional arrangements, recently CBFM outcomes have come under greater scrutiny as it is increasingly apparent that communities have not been able to capture the full range of economic values from the forests over which they ostensibly have legal control (Blomley et al, 2009). Even while community revenues from VLFRs have been very limited, a boom in Tanzania's timber trade has greatly increased the commercial value of forests, including previously marginal timber species from *miombo* woodlands. Despite the existence of a forestry and land tenure framework that gives villages clear opportunities to control and benefit from forest uses on their lands, commercial forest exploitation has largely by-passed rural communities thus far.

Local communities that have established VLFRs are legally entitled to capture a wide range of local products from their forests, including building materials and fuelwood from trees, food, traditional medicines, livestock forage and sources of water. Local benefits from these subsistence uses can be significant. For example, a study of forest products utilization across 377,000ha of community-managed forests in Shinyanga Region estimates the total per household monthly value of these products at the equivalent of US$14, in comparison to average per household monthly expenditures across Tanzania of US$8.50 (Monela et al, 2005).

In addition to these important but largely subsistence uses, forest resources on village lands hold substantial potential for commercial timber production. As noted above, there is no centralized concessionary system for commercial timber harvesting on village lands in Tanzania. Timber harvesting licences are sold by District Forestry Officers, with a proportion of royalty payments accruing back to FBD; once VLFRs are established, districts may not authorize harvesting in those areas. Table 4.3 provides an illustration of a sample of four areas with significant potential for local revenue generation from timber harvesting which are currently under village management.

Despite the scale of potential from many VLFRs and as-yet unprotected forests on village lands, and the growth of the Tanzanian timber trade during the past five years, very few communities are currently harvesting timber from their VLFRs as a source of collective income. The only VLFRs engaged in commercial forest products utilization are several in Iringa Region which earn income from the sale of charcoal and some very limited timber sales, amounting to around US$720 per village as of 2005 (Lund, 2007).

Table 4.3 *Selected areas of forest under village management and their revenue generation potential*

Forest name and location	Size (ha)	Status	Estimated annual revenue from sustainable harvesting	Number of villages managing forest	Potential revenue per village/ annum (US$)
Angai Forest, Liwale District	141,000	VLFR	US$784,000	13	60,300
Suledo Forest, Kiteto District	164,000	VLFR	US$213,000	9	23,700
Mtanza Msona Forest, Rufiji District	10,713	VLFR	US$57,900	2	28,950
Ipole Wildlife Management Area, Sikonge District	247,500	Wildlife Management Area	US$730,000	4	182,500

Source: IUCN, 2004; Mellenthien, 2005; Mustahalti, 2007; Nelson and Blomley, 2007

Until recently the country's extensive *miombo* woodlands had limited commercial value save for a few highly prized species, but this is rapidly changing. China has emerged as the fastest growing importer of hardwoods from Tanzania, representing a major shift in trade dynamics when compared to the 1980s, when the vast majority of sawn hardwood exports were destined for Western Europe. This increase in demand has coincided with improved road networks – such as the opening of the Mkapa Bridge over the Rufiji River – which greatly increased access to southeastern Tanzania. This part of the country is characterized by high levels of poverty but it possesses some of the largest areas of unutilized coastal forests and *miombo* woodlands in Tanzania. Lindi Region, for example, is one of Tanzania's poorest rural areas and has an estimated 3.75 million hectares of unreserved forests, virtually all of which falls on village lands (Milledge et al, 2007).

Tanzania's growing timber trade is almost entirely informal; Milledge et al (2007) estimate that in recent years over 95 per cent of the trade has been carried out illegally, for example depriving the state of an estimated $58 million in lost taxes and fees in 2003. This research also documents how this trade is carried out along a value chain involving public officials within local and national government institutions, village leaders, logging operators and political élites (Milledge et al, 2007; Mustahalti, 2007). Arising quickly in an institutional context characterized by government resource shortages and lack of effective controls, this timber trade became very profitable and many people entered the business with a view to exporting round-wood to lucrative overseas markets (Milledge et al, 2007). Local communities which should legally be able to exclude outsiders from harvesting on their lands have, in practice, little knowledge of the actual market values of forest products and equally limited awareness, in many places, of their legal rights to manage forest resources. Without external support, villagers in forested rural areas are unable to carry out the relatively simple set of steps required to close access to forests through declaration of a VLFR. In addition, some village leaders, having become involved in illegal timber harvesting, possess disincentives to channelling forest revenues to the collective community or to enabling formation of a VLFR. As a result, communities that are the legal proprietors of many of the forests on village lands are only capturing about 1 per cent of the value of the timber trade (up until the point of export) in southeastern Tanzania (Milledge et al, 2007). The system of informal trade based on patronage relationships between private traders and public officials, having been established, creates strong profit-based incentives for its own perpetuation and the continued marginalization of local communities. The existing informal system of commerce thus creates incentives at a number of different institutional scales that work against local communities capturing a greater share of the value of forests on village lands.

The role, capacity, and interests of district governments are also relevant because CBFM generally relies on district-level forestry officers to facilitate the process. Despite significant decentralization and local government reforms over the past two decades, many districts are still highly constrained by human and operational resources, which restrict them from effectively implementing forest laws and policies at the local level. In addition to capacity constraints, district governments, both individual officials and District Councils as a whole, may also possess disincentives to enabling village-level formalization of rights over forests. For District Councils administering large land areas with significant areas of unreserved forest, forest revenues, levies and taxes constitute an important source of local income which can be used without the conditions attached to much central government funding. For example, the Kilwa District Council collected 33 million Tshs (~US$30,000) in 2003, which comprised about 18 per cent of its total local revenue receipts (DANIDA, 2004). The transfer of large areas of unreserved forest to village management may undermine higher level goals to boost district level revenue generation.

In addition, the conversion and transfer of effectively 'open access' forests on village lands to forests managed by mandated village governance institutions with clear roles and responsibilities may undermine some of the corrupt networks that perpetuate illegal logging, also leading to declining benefit flows to those higher up the chain, which often includes district-level forestry officials. In such cases, district staff and councillors often find that they face a clear conflict of interest – over the continued benefits they enjoy from illegal harvesting in unreserved forests, but also their responsibilities to assist communities in securing tenure and forest management rights under CBFM (Persha and Blomley, 2009). This conflict of interest often manifests itself through the slowing down (and often halting) of key stages in the legal process of CBFM establishment, such as District Council approval of village bylaws and management plans (Mustahalti, 2007).

Capacity at the community level plays a pivotal role in how actors at district and national governmental levels, as well as amongst the private sector, influence CBFM outcomes. Where communities are aware of their rights and the returns available under CBFM, experience suggests that they are ready and able to defend them, through active patrolling of forest areas, arresting and fining of illegal forest users, and the confiscation and sale of forest produce and equipment. Similarly, attempts by government staff at higher levels to capture and monopolize forest benefits are more strongly resisted in areas with higher levels of legal literacy as villagers are more able to appreciate and defend their rights (Blomley, 2006).

Wildlife sector reform

Tanzania's wildlife populations represent perhaps the most extraordinary assemblage of terrestrial large mammals left on the planet. These animals support a tourism industry worth over $1 billion in annual revenue and which has been one of the most important sources of national economic growth during the past 20 years.

Tanzania's wildlife sector was progressively centralized through establishment of regulations governing hunting and state protected areas during the colonial era and into the post-independence period (Nelson et al, 2007). By the 1980s the wildlife sector faced a state of crisis, as Tanzanian civil servants' wages had declined by over 90 per cent in real terms since 1970 (van de Walle, 2001), and the dramatic reduction in state law enforcement capacity facilitated a boom in illegal use. As ivory and rhino horn prices soared and commercial poaching intensified, the country lost half of its elephants and nearly all of its black rhinos (WSRTF, 1995).

These crises drove a range of changes, as donor involvement increased markedly and the traditional protectionist management discourse lost much of its legitimacy. New donor-government partnerships were forged to increase investment in the wildlife sector and to address rampant illegal wildlife use and management shortfalls. An important partnership between the German and Tanzanian governments, the Selous Conservation Programme, arose in the late 1980s and soon became a lead mechanism for promoting community involvement in wildlife management (Baldus et al, 2003). A range of other local projects seeking to improve local participation and benefit-sharing in wildlife management emerged, nearly all supported by foreign donors (Leader-Williams et al, 1996). TANAPA began a formal programme of sharing revenues from parks with surrounding communities as a way to improve relations and enlist local support in stopping poaching (Bergin, 2001). All of these programmes reflected the greatly enhanced influence of foreign donors in Tanzania in the 1990s, as well as the emerging enthusiasm amongst donor agencies for projects combining natural resource conservation and rural development goals.

The government and its donor supporters initiated a review of the country's wildlife management policies and institutions in order to develop a policy that would address existing challenges and adapt to Tanzania's changing political and economic environment. This process resulted in adoption of a new wildlife policy in 1998 which gave community wildlife management a prominent role. Although this policy stated clearly that the central government would maintain ownership of wildlife, and that National Parks and Game Reserves, as the 'core protected areas', would continue to be the foundation of conservation efforts, it called for a new approach on village lands. The policy aimed to allow rural communities to manage wildlife on their land for increased local benefits (MNRT, 1998b). The policy described community-managed Wildlife Management Areas (WMAs) as the mechanism for implementing these reformist aims: 'The Government will facilitate the establishment of a new category of PA [protected area] known as WMA, where local people will have full mandate of managing and benefiting from their conservation efforts' (MNRT, 1998b, p31).

In the years following the issuance of the 1998 policy, very limited actual devolution of rights to manage wildlife and capture the resource's economic value has occurred. Rural communities have invested substantial resources in establishing the WMAs, in some instances spending nearly two decades prior to establishing a gazetted WMA, and have set aside an estimated 16,000km² of village land as WMAs. At least ten WMAs have been gazetted and some of them are now receiving revenues shared out by the Wildlife Division.

The institutional design of WMAs has limited implementation of the initial reformist policy aims. The basic conceptual framework for WMAs that was developed in the 1990s involved villages zoning a portion of their land as a wildlife conservation area where agriculture and settlement, and perhaps livestock grazing as well, would be excluded (Leader-Williams et al, 1996). The rules governing WMAs would be enforced through locally-appropriate village land use plans and bylaws. In return, the Wildlife Division would grant a wildlife utilization quota which the communities could either hunt themselves or alternatively sell to a tourist hunting operator. The economic potential of tourist hunting played a central role in the logic of this framework, by providing the revenues that would translate into incentives for local conservation measures in these rural areas.

The regulations that define how WMAs will actually operate were released in December 2002, nearly five years after the policy was produced. These and subsequently modified regulations have two salient features (see MNRT, 2002). First, they statutorily establish a long set of prerequisite conditions which communities must fulfil in order to create a WMA. In order to form a WMA and start earning revenue from wildlife uses therein, the communities are required to fulfil at least a dozen procedural requirements (Nelson, 2007). These include preparing a strategic plan, village land use plans and a general management or zoning plan as prerequisites to applying for WMA gazettement. After the WMA is gazetted, the communities still must request the Director of Wildlife to designate a tourist hunting block in the WMA (if they wish to earn revenue from tourist hunting activities), develop an investment plan and investment agreements and have Environmental Impact Assessments carried out on the proposed investments.

Second, the regulations do not devolve secure or long-term wildlife use rights to communities that are able to establish a WMA. The regulations do not allow the communities to allocate their hunting block to hunting outfitters, but rather retain hunting concession allocation authority at the ministerial level. The user rights to wildlife granted commensurate with WMA gazettement are short-term, limited to renewable three-year periods, and are revocable. Of critical importance, the WMA regulations do not specify what proportion of the revenues generated by commercial activities in the WMA will be retained by the local community; this has been one of the most problematic provisions of these regulations in terms of clarifying the rights that WMA establishment confers at the local level (Nelson, 2007).

A final issue that has affected the implementation of WMAs is that rather than empowering existing village governance organs, WMA formation requires the creation of a new supra-village organization to manage wildlife. Because WMAs are envisioned as comprising multiple adjacent villages, the regulations require communities to establish a community-based organization (CBO), which becomes the legal holder of wildlife user rights and the manager of the WMA. While the CBO is supposed to report to the Village Councils, its governing membership is distinct from the Village Council and Village Assembly structures. Village governance institutions are given the role of holding the CBO accountable but are no longer directly involved in managing the resources placed within the WMA. In this way, the WMA framework creates an additional layer of governance institutions for natural resources on village lands, rather than building on existing structures as forestry measures have done.

Some local communities have actively resisted implementation of WMAs promoted by central and district government officials, foreign donors and the international conservation NGOs that have been given the role of WMA facilitation in most areas (see Nelson and Ole Makko, 2005; Igoe and Croucher, 2007; Sachedina, 2008). The main reasons for this resistance have been local concerns about allocating large areas of village land in return for the unspecified benefits and weak levels of local control defined in the WMA regulations. Village leaders in Vilima Vitatu village, one of seven villages in the Burunge WMA, were threatening to pull out of the WMA two years after it was formally gazetted, alleging that the process for establishing it was top-down and not participatory (Luhwago, 2008; see also Igoe and Croucher, 2007). In many of these locales historical tensions between communities and protected area managers present a barrier to effective collaboration, and the top-down WMA framework provides a poor mechanism for building trust and overcoming local concerns (see Nelson and Ole Makko, 2005).

In addition, a number of the communities that have rejected WMAs as the formal state-sanctioned form of community wildlife management had already developed their own independent means of capturing economic benefits from wildlife. In the early 1990s, tourism operators in northern Tanzania initiated several joint venture agreements with local villages through contracts with the Village Council. These operator-village contracts have spread widely in northern Tanzania, with revenue to villages increasing over the past decade as tourism numbers and investment have increased (Nelson, 2004). For example, seven villages in Loliondo Division adjacent to Serengeti National Park earned more than US$300,000 in total in 2007 (Ngoitiko et al, this volume). Some of these contractual agreements have been in place for nearly 20 years, surviving repeated renegotiations of pricing and terms between operators and villages. However, for the past ten years these ventures have faced a fairly constant state of conflict with centrally-issued tourist hunting concessions situated in the same areas on village land but issued at the ministerial level. Villages have sought to maintain their incomes from tourism, while central government has sought to ensure its ability to lease community lands out as fairly lucrative commercial hunting concessions, as we describe further below.

In sum, rather than devolving authority for wildlife to the local level as called for in the 1998 policy, institutional reforms over the past decade represent a general expansion of centralized authority over wildlife use and management (Nelson et al, 2007), as characterized by the following developments.

- In 2000 the Ministry released regulations for tourist hunting management which declared that any tourism activities occurring in any hunting blocks without the express permission of the Director of Wildlife are illegal (MNRT, 2000). Because about half of all hunting concessions in Tanzania are located on village lands, these regulations represented the first time that the Wildlife Division had claimed explicit jurisdiction over non-consumptive tourism activities being carried out on village lands and according to village agreements with tourism operators. Because local government legislation and land legislation effectively provide local communities with jurisdiction over access to land, and the rights to enter into contracts with commercial entities, local communities and civic activists argued that the Wildlife Division lacks the regulatory power to control these agreements (e.g. Nshala, 2002). This conflict of jurisdictional authority has persisted in a functional stalemate since 2000, with numerous local conflicts emerging, some community-tour operator ventures being restricted or eliminated, but no legal clarity emerging to resolve the issue.
- In 2007 the Ministry released regulations under the Wildlife Conservation Act of 1974 to regulate non-consumptive tourism, both inside Game Reserves and in unprotected areas or village lands. These regulations contain a fee structure that will displace much of the revenue earned locally from tourism ventures by forcing operators to pay the Wildlife Division, effectively taxing (at a rate of over 50 per cent) the direct local income from tourism that villagers had been earning from these ventures. These regulations have once again caused tensions between villagers and state authorities to rise, and their implementation is currently being debated and negotiated (TNRF, 2008).
- In 2008 a new overarching Wildlife Bill was released for comment and then tabled in Parliament by the Ministry of Natural Resources and Tourism. The main changes made by this Bill, in comparison with the extant 1974 Wildlife Conservation Act, involve creating new types of protected areas to regulate local land use on community or private lands, such as 'corridors' and 'dispersal areas', and placing a range of restrictions on village land uses in areas where wildlife is found. The Bill includes provisions for establishing WMAs, but does not secure any rights to benefits from wildlife in those WMAs or provide clarity on key issues, or otherwise grant communities any new rights to manage and benefit from wildlife. Local communities widely criticized the Bill in public meetings with government officials (e.g. Ihucha, 2008).

Institutional change in Tanzania's wildlife sector over the past two decades is thus characterized by the contrasting trajectories of the devolutionary policy reform process of the 1990s and subsequent regulatory and legislative measures that serve to consolidate and reinforce centralized control and authority over wildlife on village lands. This pattern of nominal decentralization followed by re-assertion of bureaucratic control has been described in Tanzania for other sectors such as agriculture (Cooksey, 2003) as well as the regulation of civil liberties such as freedom of association (Lissu, 2000). In the wildlife sector, the observed patterns of institutional change have been critically influenced by the political economy of commercial wildlife utilization, particularly the country's lucrative tourist hunting industry.

The wildlife sector reforms of the 1990s were spurred by similar factors to those that drove change in the forestry sector: the fiscal implications of economic crisis and structural adjustment in relation to bureaucratic capacity; the greatly expanded influence of foreign donors within that fiscal context; and new neo-liberal discourses based on decentralization and market-based incentives.

All wildlife outside national parks[2] and the unique Ngorongoro Conservation Area falls under the jurisdiction of the Wildlife Division of the Ministry of Natural Resources and Tourism. The main functions of the Wildlife Division are:

- to oversee and implement general wildlife policy; and
- to manage all forms of wildlife utilization.

The most commercially important form of wildlife utilization administered by the Wildlife Division is tourist hunting, which occurs both inside Game Reserves, in which people are not allowed to reside, and outside state protected areas on village lands, where much wildlife in Tanzania persists. Today there are about 140 hunting concessions and over 40 different hunting companies holding them, with the total area used for hunting about 250,000km[2] (Baldus and Cauldwell, 2004).

Tourist hunting was originally organized under a system of centrally managed concessions in the 1950s. From 1973 to 1978 all hunting was banned, and when hunting was re-opened it was controlled directly and monopolistically by the parastatal Tanzania Wildlife Corporation. In 1988, the hunting industry was opened up to other operators, and administrative responsibility for hunting concessions was placed with the Wildlife Division. Since the industry's liberalization, the total annual value of hunting concessions has increased dramatically. Direct government income increased from about US$1.5 million in 1988 to over US$10 million by 2001 (Baldus and Cauldwell, 2004; Barnett and Patterson, 2006). Government figures for 2006 estimate revenue earned by wildlife utilization at about Tshs 15.2 billion, or around US$14 million, with most of this coming from tourist hunting activities (URT, 2006).

Tourist hunting concessions are allocated administratively; Tanzania is one of the few countries in southern Africa which does not employ any competi-tive tendering or auction procedures in the management of its hunting industry (Barnett and Patterson, 2006). As a result, Tanzania's hunting industry has long been characterized by low levels of transparency, in terms of public access to infor-mation, and very little external oversight. Local communities have no formal role in determining which companies hunt on the village lands that Village Councils administer. The amount of money involved in the growing tourist hunting industry, the lack of mechanisms for public transparency or accountability, and the strong discretionary authority central bureaucrats have over concessions all create substantial opportunities for rent-seeking and private–public collusion in the process of hunting concession allocation. These opportunities are further enhanced by hunting concession prices and fees which have been kept artificially low, reducing government income by an estimated US$7 million annually and leading to allegedly widespread albeit nominally illegal sub-leasing of conces-sion blocks (Baldus and Cauldwell, 2004; World Bank, 2008). More recently, public debate over allegedly 'institutionalized corruption' in the wildlife sector has increased calls for reform of wildlife sector governance and tourist hunting administration (e.g. ThisDay, 2007).

Transferring authority over wildlife and hunting revenues to the village level, as called for by the 1998 policy, presents clear conflicts with the instrumental interests of government policy-makers, including both well-placed individuals and bureaucratic institutions at the ministerial level as a whole. Wildlife is a valuable resource to these key actors for rent-seeking and the construction of patronage relationships. These hunting revenues are far easier for officials to 'privatize' than donor project funds, and have provided the financial leverage for policy-makers to marginalize the reformist policy adopted in the 1990s and to resist pressure from donors to carry out more far-reaching changes during the past decade.

This changing balance of power between foreign donors and the wildlife bureaucracy was readily apparent by 2003–2005. During this period, the GTZ community wildlife advisor, who had played a key role in design of the WMA framework and adoption of the 1998 policy, became increasingly critical of what was perceived as government refusal to devolve greater powers to local communities (Baldus and Cauldwell, 2004). By 2005, these disagreements led to the end of 17 years of GTZ support to the Tanzanian Wildlife Division, with the advisor in question concluding in frustration that 'the government does not intend to share' wildlife benefits with local communities (Baldus, 2006). Other wildlife sector donors active during the 1990s, such as the Norwegians and the British (DfID), had already phased out support to community wildlife management projects, leaving USAID as the only significant long-term supporter of the Wildlife Division.

Divergence or convergence? Commercial values, governance choices, and local rights

The trajectories of institutional reforms in the wildlife and forestry sectors in Tanzania demonstrate how different sectoral contexts, particularly political economic patterns of resource exploitation, can contribute to divergent patterns of reform even within the same Ministry. In both sectors, reforms emerged following Tanzania's economic crisis in the early 1980s and the loss of resources and capacity within the central bureaucracy. Policy-makers were forced to adapt to the changes brought on by this period of fiscal crisis and sweeping policy change, including the collapse of the socialist state and its ideological underpinnings. Bureaucratic officials needed to attract resources from foreign donors, who consequently came to play a much more prominent role in policy formulation. The process of formulating new policies in the wildlife and forestry sectors during the 1990s was dominated by a handful of donor and NGO technical advisors and their government counterparts within the Ministry of Natural Resources and Tourism. Both policies reflect the neo-liberal global development discourse of the time, promoting a reduced role of the state in productive economic activities and an emphasis on decentralization and privatization.

From the late 1990s, however, the institutional paths of forestry and wildlife reforms diverged considerably, as illustrated by the differences between WMAs and VLFRs summarized in Table 4.4.

Table 4.4 *A comparison of key aspects of the governance frameworks for community-based management of wildlife (WMAs) and forests (VLFRs) in Tanzania*

	Wildlife	Forestry
Management Authority	Community-based organization (CBO)	Village Natural Resource Committee of the Village Council
Benefit Sharing	Revenue divided between CBO and government; proportions never formally defined to date.	Villages may retain 100% of revenue earned.
Utilization Rights	User rights limited to 3 year terms Government grants hunting concession allocations	Utilization of all forest products according to village management plans and bylaws.
Resource Tenure	State	Village

Source: Nelson, 2007

The two sectors' divergence since 1998 is largely a function of institutional incentives linked to bureaucrats' discretionary authority over commercial resource values, but is also influenced by historical factors and the agency of individual leadership. By the 1980s, Tanzania's forestry sector was sharply reducing its involvement in industrial forest production. The most valuable highland forests were set aside for strict biodiversity preservation at that time, and other commercial enterprises were either closed down or privatized. Some commercial utilization continued through licensed harvesting of valuable hardwoods found in *miombo* woodlands, but these areas are relatively vast, licence fees were low, and, unlike in most forest-rich African nations, harvesting was not organized into any formal centralized concession system. It is telling that even as of 2004, the FBD's expenditures exceeded its revenues by more than 30 per cent, and those revenues were 40 per cent less than annual earnings in both the Wildlife and Fisheries Divisions (World Bank, 2008).

When initial CBFM projects emerged in the late 1980s, they did so primarily in relatively low-value *miombo* woodlands. Although the FBD had initially sought to gazette these areas as reserves, when foresters encountered local resistance and donor pressure it was relatively costless to adopt an alternative locally-based management approach, and in fact served the bureaucracy's interests. Individuals such as SIDA advisor Liz Alden Wily and the Director of FBD, Said Iddi, played key roles in catalysing the initial pilot projects and translating them into fairly radical policy and legislative changes. Hurst (2004) argues that, rather than threatening bureaucratic interests, the establishment of VLFRs as a statutory mechanism for communities to gazette their own forest reserves served to expand the protected forest estate, formally vested locals with responsibility for the costs of forest protection, and enabled central officials to leverage critical new forms of donor support as external investment in Tanzanian CBFM grew rapidly. Forestry officials have thus lost little and gained much through their adoption and support of CBFM during the past 20 years.

While the FBD had greatly scaled down its commercial forestry activities by the late 1980s, the Wildlife Division only became the overseer of a centralized tourist hunting concession system in 1988. Since then, direct government revenues from tourist hunting have increased about ten-fold. While the area under centralized timber concessions in Tanzania is much less than in comparable nations (Table 4.2), Tanzania has the largest land area used for tourist hunting of any African country, with about half of this area falling on community lands (Lindsey et al, 2007). The tourist hunting concession system has few checks on administrative discretionary power, and no competitive pricing or tendering procedures, and thus presents wide rent-seeking opportunities which have expanded in line with the growing value of the tourist hunting industry. By keeping concession prices lower than their market value, Tanzania's system of wildlife management has created what Bates (1981) terms 'administratively derived rents', which in sum are estimated at about US$7 million annually in terms of the difference between the real market value and the administrative pricing of Tanzania's hunting concessions. Because so little documentation exists on these informal value chains, however, the real value of these rents may be considerably higher. The devolutionary changes called for by the 1998 wildlife policy conflict directly with the interests of key policy-makers, given the value of the numerous hunting concessions that overlay village lands. Policy-makers have consequently maintained discretionary central control over tourist hunting, limiting the devolutionary content of the WMA regulations, and simultaneously expanded control over other forms of wildlife utilization such as community joint venture tourism agreements on village lands.

The variant political economies of the wildlife and forestry sectors also account for the relative ability of other actors to influence institutional processes. Foreign donors have been strong and sustained supporters of reform in both sectors. In forestry, donors have had a great deal of leverage as a result of the FBD's lack of alternative sources of political and financial capital and hence patronage resources.[3] In the wildlife sector, by contrast, the rents from tourist hunting have provided policy-makers with financial assets that have effectively enabled officials to deflect donor pressure for reform. Donors have consequently had very little influence over the past decade and the recent trend has been for foreign agencies to exit involvement in Tanzania's wildlife sector as a result of their inability to bring about the reforms required for wildlife to have a more positive direct impact on rural livelihoods.

Despite the considerable differences in formal legislative and regulatory reforms exhibited by the forestry and wildlife sectors, there are nevertheless some important points of convergence. Even though communities have greater opportunities to secure rights over forests on village lands, translating these rights into collective income from forest products such as timber has generally proven elusive. Informal timber harvesting networks in Tanzania, often operating through various forms of private–public collusion, have in recent years proliferated and dominated the timber trade. While rent-seeking in the wildlife sector is effectively institutional-ized, corruption in the forestry sector is more disorganized and decentralized, and not solely the province of the forestry bureaucracy. In the wildlife sector, the entire reform process has been shaped and largely undermined by informal political economic interests in controlling wildlife use. In forestry, despite the much greater

impact of formal reform processes in restructuring legal rights, those formal measures have increasingly been subverted by prevalent patterns of informal trade,
which have in turn influenced the actions of forestry officials at local and national
levels. Ultimately, in both sectors powerful public and private actors are effectively
able to capture the vast majority of resource rents and to exclude local communities from lucrative economic value chains.

Reforming natural resource governance in Tanzania: Future trends and strategic directions

Natural resource governance reform processes in Tanzania during the past 20
years have been dominated by central government agencies and foreign donors,
and in some cases international NGOs that effectively serve as the agents of
those donors (Sachedina, 2008). In contrast to widespread notions regarding
the overwhelming influence of foreign donors and their neo-liberal narratives in
shaping policy processes in Tanzania and other sub-Saharan African countries,
our analysis demonstrates that the leverage of these foreign actors depends on
the alternative resources that bureaucrats possess, and the distribution of costs
and benefits they face in adopting a given set of reforms. In the case of forestry,
donors have had a great deal of leverage where the costs of reforms to policy-
makers was relatively low, but in the wildlife sector donors have had limited
influence as a result of the high costs of reforms to bureaucratic interests and
the availability of alternative sources of financial resources from hunting revenues. In both sectors, donors have had limited success in influencing patterns
of implementation and greater local control over economic benefits, which are
largely captured within highly informal value chains or 'hidden' economies (see
World Bank, 2008).

In Tanzania, the influence of centralized bureaucratic policy-makers is enhanced
by historical factors such as the concentration of power in the executive branch,
the dominance of a single political party and the weakness of the media and
civil society organizations. These are all macro-political factors which enhance
the ability of bureaucratic actors to maintain control over and extract rents from
valuable natural resources. Donors appear to be relatively influential in Tanzania
largely because political power in the country has been so heavily concentrated
in state and party organs, and alternative voices in society from rural communities, organized labour, the private sector or civil society organizations have all
been marginal at best for most of the time since independence. With the lack of
domestic challenges to political élites, foreign influence has been the main source
of non-state influence within the policy-making realm. But as we have shown, this
foreign influence is conditionally limited and has had limited success in promoting
locally accountable forms for natural resource governance. The emergence of
more democratic systems of resource governance in Tanzania requires change on
the domestic front.

It is therefore of great significance that Tanzania's political environment is
currently undergoing a process of significant political change. Over the last
several years there has been marked increase in public demands for more

accountability and transparency on the part of government. Public scandals have come to light involving the alleged large-scale embezzlement of public assets, highlighting the long-simmering economic gap between the political and economic élites and the rest of the population (e.g. Parliament of Tanzania, 2008). Importantly, the ruling party discipline that has characterized Tanzanian politics since the return to pluralism in 1992 has become fissured, with parliamentary debates as much between ruling party members as between ruling and opposition party members. The opposition, however, while still small numerically, shows a higher degree of unity, coordination and sophistication than it has during its fractious past. This public discourse is also being catalysed by an enhanced role of the media and civil society organizations. Tanzania appears to be reaching a threshold in its contemporary political evolution whereby the monopoly on power by a small group of ruling party élites is giving way to more pluralist forces. In contrast to the reformist period of the late 1980s and early 1990s, change today is not driven by sudden formal institutional changes, but rather by changes in the behaviour and power of different actors within the existing institutional environment.

The increasingly open public policy debates in contemporary Tanzania often focus on natural resource management. Mining has become a particularly prominent subject of debate, with the focus on the terms and procedures for granting state mining concessions to commercial firms. Forestry and wildlife management issues are raised in newspaper headlines and in parliamentary debate with increasing frequency as well. Publication of a major report on illegal logging in southern Tanzania (Milledge et al, 2007) has brought new public prominence to forestry issues, and the institutionalized corruption in the tourist hunting industry has been described in the media with increasing openness (e.g. ThisDay, 2007).

There is emerging evidence of this changing political environment affecting important policy decisions. After several years of public debate, in late 2007 the President eventually removed the long-serving Director of Wildlife from office. This individual had been the subject of long-running and increasingly acrimonious debate in parliament and in the media. Another notable recent change was a decision in the 2007/08 budget, made by the Ministry of Natural Resources and Tourism, to substantially raise the fees paid to the government by private outfitters for hunting concession leases. This decision did not devolve any authority to local communities – by contrast, it sought to raise central government income from hunting – but by raising the fees payable for long-underpriced concessions, it does have the impact of potentially reducing the value of rent-seeking opportunities within the concession allocation process. This, in turn, may substantially alter the value of maintaining centralized control over wildlife and make future reform efforts more acceptable.

A significant factor in the changing tenor of policy discourse in Tanzania is the growing influence of the media and civic organizations. With growing public space for debate and public demands for accountability, the importance of these civic organizations in producing accurate and timely information, and working to build the knowledge and capacity of local communities, becomes critical to shaping public debate and taking advantages of new opportunities to influence policy. For example, the Tanzania Natural Resource Forum, a coalition of various organizations, local communities and private companies, which was formalized only in 2006 and aims to improve the governance of natural resources in the country, has recently initiated a collaborative campaign to improve forest governance based on the recommendations made by Milledge et al (2007) in their widely cited report. This aims at changing the relative bargaining power of local communities in coastal forest areas by increasing their awareness of their rights and legal opportunities to capture the benefits of forests and to exclude outside exploitation (TFWG, 2007). Such public campaigns targeting forest governance issues have become a conventional part of civil society activities in other parts of Africa, but are unprecedented in contemporary Tanzania.

The expansion of public debate around natural resource management issues and the increasing capacity of media and civil society organizations are essential in terms of increasing the political space for wider participation in policy formulation in Tanzania. By reducing the ability of central actors to monopolize power in order to pursue accumulative interests, these broad political changes provide new opportunities for local communities and civic activists to challenge existing practices and promote alternative institutional arrangements. The growth of this political space is fundamental to enabling institutional changes in natural resource management, and will need to be a central strategic element in how reformist efforts are supported in the future.

Acknowledgements

We are grateful to Liz Alden Wily, Tor Benjaminsen and Geir Sundet for reading earlier drafts of this chapter and providing numerous helpful comments and insights. An earlier version of this paper was presented at the eighth biennial global conference of the International Association for the Study of the Commons, held in Cheltenham, UK, with support to attend the meeting to F. Nelson provided by the International Forestry Resources and Institutions programme.

Notes

1   Key among these was Liz Alden Wily, an expatriate expert on land tenure and advisor to these local SIDA forestry projects. Wily played a key role in promoting CBFM during the 1990s, including in the drafting of the 1998 National Forestry Policy and 2001 CBFM guidelines.
2   National Parks in Tanzania are managed by a semi-autonomous parastatal agency, Tanzania National Parks (TANAPA), and the sole use of wildlife is through non-consumptive (eco-) tourism. These areas have driven Tanzania's tourism boom.
3   However, donor influence in the forestry sector has been far from absolute. The FBD has successfully resisted donor initiatives for improving revenue collection systems and transformation of the Division into an autonomous parastatal authority (Tanzania Forest Service).

References

Akida, A. and Blomley, R. (2006) 'Trends in forest ownership, forest resources tenure and institutional arrangements: Are they contributing to better forest management and poverty reduction? Case study from Tanzania, prepared for the FAO Rome', Unpublished report, Food and Agriculture Organisation of the United Nations, Rome

Alden Wily, L. (2003) *Community-based Land Tenure Management: Questions and Answers about Tanzania's New Village Land Act, 1999*, Drylands Issue Paper No. 120, International Institute for Environment and Development, London

Alden Wily, L. and S. Mbaya. (2001) *Land, People and Forests in Eastern and Southern Africa at the Beginning of the 21st Century: The Impact of Land Relations on the Role of Communities in Forest Future*, IUCN-EARO, Nairobi, Kenya

Alden Wily, L., Akida, A., Haule, O., Haulle, H., Hozza, S., Kavishe, C., Luono, S., Mamkwe, P., Massawe, E., Mawe, S., Ringo, D., Makiya, M., Minja, M. and Rwiza, A. (2000) 'Community management of forests in Tanzania: A status report at the beginning of the 21st century', *Forest, Trees and People Newsletter*, vol 42, pp36–45

Baldus, R. (2006) *Case study: The crucial role of governance in ecosystem management – results and conclusions of the Selous Conservation Programme, 1987–2003*, Paper presented to the Serengeti Conference, Seronera, Tanzania. Available at: www.wildlife-baldus.com/download/Governance%20in%20Tanzania%20Wildlife%20 Conservation.pdf Accessed 19 August 2009

Baldus, R.D. and Cauldwell, A.E. (2004) *Tourist hunting and its role in development of wild-life management areas in Tanzania*, Paper presented to the Sixth International Game Ranching Symposium, Paris, July 6–9, 2004

Baldus, R., Kibonde, B. and Siege, L. (2003) 'Seeking conservation partnerships in the Selous Game Reserve, Tanzania', *Parks*, vol 13, no 1, pp50–61

Barnett, R. and Patterson, C. (2006) *Sport Hunting in the Southern African Development Community (SADC) Region: An Overview*, TRAFFIC East/Southern Africa, Johannesburg, South Africa

Bates, R.H. (1981) *Markets and States in Tropical Africa*, University of California Press, Berkeley and Los Angeles, CA

Bergin, P. (2001) 'Accommodating new narratives in a conservation bureaucracy: TANAPA and community conservation', in D. Hulme and M.W. Murphree (eds) *African Wildlife and Livelihoods: The Promise and Performance of Community Conservation*, James Currey, Oxford

Blomley, T. (2006) *Mainstreaming Participatory Forestry within the Local Government Reform Process in Tanzania*, Gatekeeper Series No. 128, International Institute for Environment and Development, London

Blomley, T., Ramadhani, H., Mkwizu, Y. and Böhringer, A. (2009) 'Hidden harvest: Unlocking the economic potential of community based forest management in Tanzania', in L. German, A. Karsenty and A.M. Tiani (eds) *Governing Africa's Forests in a Globalized World*, Earthscan, London

Blomley, T., Pfliegner, K., Isango, J., Zahabu E., Ahrends, A., and Burgess, N. (2008) 'Seeing the wood for the trees: Towards an objective assessment of the impact of Participatory Forest Management on forest condition in Tanzania', *Oryx*, vol 42, no 2, pp1–12

Campbell, H. and Stein, H. (1991) *The IMF and Tanzania*, SAPES Trust, Harare, Zimbabwe

Cooksey, B. (2003) 'Marketing reform? The rise and fall of agricultural liberalisation in Tanzania', *Development Policy Review*, vol 21, no 1, pp67–91

Coulson, A. (1982) *The Political Economy of Tanzania*, Clarendon Press, Oxford

DANIDA (Danish International Development Agency) (2004) 'Review of the Present Royalty and Revenue Collection System for Forest Products in Lindi Region', Final Report, PEM Consult Ltd, East Africa

Hurst, A. (2004) 'Not yet out of the woods: A political ecology of state forest policy and practice in mainland Tanzania, 1961–1998', PhD thesis, Oxford University

Igoe, J. and Croucher, B. (2007) 'Conservation, commerce, and communities: The story of community-based wildlife management in Tanzania's northern tourist circuit', *Conservation and Society*, vol 5, no 4, pp534–561

Ihucha, A. (2008) 'Wildebeests will vote for you in 2010', *IPP Media*, www.ippmedia.com/ipp/guardian/2008/10/22/124905.html Accessed 30 October 2008

IUCN (2004) *Mtanza-Msona Village. Our Village Environmental Management Plan – An Account of How We Drew It Up and are Implementing It*, IUCN–EARO, Nairobi, Kenya

Kelsall, T. (2003) 'Governance, democracy and recent political struggles in mainland Tanzania', *Commonwealth & Comparative Politics*, vol 41, no 2, pp55–82

Kelsall, T. (2002) 'Shop windows and smoke-filled rooms: Governance and the re-politicisation of Tanzania', *Journal of Modern African Studies*, vol 40, no 4, pp597–619

Lawson, A. and Rakner, L. (2005) *Understanding Patterns of Accountability in Tanzania*, Final Synthesis Report, Oxford Policy Management, Chr. Michelsen Institute, and REPOA, Oxford

Leader-Williams, N., Kayera, J.A. and Overton, G.L. (1996) *Community-based Conservation in Tanzania*, Occasional Paper of the IUCN Species Survival Commission No. 15, IUCN, Gland, Switzerland and Cambridge

Lindsey, P.A., Roulet, P.A., and Romañach, S.S. (2007) 'Economic and conservation significance of the trophy hunting industry in sub-Saharan Africa', *Biological Conservation*, vol 134, pp455–469

Lissu, T.A. (2000) *Repackaging Authoritarianism: Freedeom of Association and Expression and the Right to Organize Under the Proposed NGO Policy for Tanzania*, Lawyers' Environmental Action Team, Dar es Salaam, Tanzania

Luhwago, R. (2008) 'Two villages want out of Burunge wildlife area', *The Citizen*, Available at: www.thecitizen.co.tz/newz.php?id=5763 Accessed 13 June 2008

Lund, J.F. (2007) 'Money talks: CBFM and village revenue collection in Iringa District', *The Arc Journal*, vol 21, pp14–16

Mallya, E.E. (2006) 'Civil society and the land question in Tanzania', in A.S. Kiondo and J.E. Nyang'oro (eds), *Civil Society and Democratic Development in Tanzania*, MWENGO, Harare, Zimbabwe

Mellenthien, J. (2005) 'Timber Utilisation in Suledo Village Land Forest Reserve Kiteto District', Unpublished report for ORGUT Consulting AB, Dar es Salaam, Tanzania

Milledge, S.A.H., Gelvas, I.K. and Ahrends, A. (2007) *Forestry, Governance and National Development: Lessons Learned from a Logging Boom in Southern Tanzania*, TRAFFIC East/Southern Africa/Tanzania Development Partners Group/Ministry of Natural Resources and Tourism, Dar es Salaam, Tanzania

MNRT (Ministry of Natural Resources and Tourism) (2008) *Participatory Forest Management in Tanzania: Facts and Figures*, Forestry and Beekeeping Division, Dar es Salaam, Tanzania

MNRT (Ministry of Natural Resources and Tourism) (2002) *The Wildlife Conservation (Wildlife Management Areas) Regulations*, Government Printer, Dar es Salaam, Tanzania

MNRT (Ministry of Natural Resources and Tourism) (2007) *Community-based Forest Management Guidelines*, Forestry and Beekeeping Division, Dar es Salaam, Tanzania

MNRT (Ministry of Natural Resources and Tourism) (2000) *Wildlife Conservation (Tourist Hunting) Regulations*, Government Printer, Dar es Salaam, Tanzania

MNRT (Ministry of Natural Resources and Tourism) (1998a) *The National Forest Policy*, Government Printer, Dar es Salaam, Tanzania

MNRT (Ministry of Natural Resources and Tourism) (1998b) *The Wildlife Policy of Tanzania*, Government Printer, Dar es Salaam, Tanzania

Monela, G.C., Chamshama, S.A.O., Mwaipopo, R. and Gamassa, D.M. (2005) *A study on the social, economic, and environmental impacts of forest landscape restoration in Shinyanga Region, Tanzania. Nairobi and Dar es Salaam*, IUCN-EARO and Ministry of Natural Resources and Tourism, Dar es Salaam, Tanzania

Mustalahti, I. (2007) 'Msitu wa Angai: Haraka, haraka, haina baraka! Why does handing over the Angai forest to local villages proceed so slowly?', in J. Gould, and L. Siitonen (eds), *Anomalies of Aid: A Festschrift for Juhani Koponen*, Institute of Development Studies (Interkont Books 15), Helsinki, Finland

Nelson, F. (2007) *Emergent or Illusory? Community Wildlife Management in Tanzania*, Drylands Issue Paper No. 146, International Institute for Environment and Development, London

Nelson, F. (2004) *The Evolution and Impacts of Community-based Ecotourism in Northern Tanzania*, Drylands Issue Paper No. 131, International Institute for Environment and Development, London

Nelson, F. and Ole Makko, S. (2005) 'Communities, conservation, and conflict in the Tanzanian Serengeti', in B. Child and M.W. Lyman (eds) *Natural Resources as Community Assets: Lessons from Two Continents*, Sand County Foundation and The Aspen Institute, Madison, WI, and Washington, DC

Nelson, F. and Blomley, T. (2007) 'Eating from the same plate: Integrating community-based wildlife and forest management,' *The Arc Journal*, vol 21, pp11–13

Nelson, F., Nshala, R. and Rodgers, W.A. (2007) 'The evolution and reform of Tanzanian wildlife management', *Conservation and Society*, vol 5, no 2, pp232–261

Nshala, R. (2002) 'Village rights relating to land management, tourism, and tourist hunting', Unpublished report by Lawyers' Environmental Action Team, Dar es Salaam, Tanzania

Nshala, R. (1999) *Granting Hunting Blocks in Tanzania: The Need for Reform*, Policy Brief No. 5, Lawyers' Environmental Action Team, Dar es Salaam, Tanzania

Parliament of Tanzania (2008) *Richmond report*, Available at: www.parliament.go.tz/bunge/docs/richmond%20final.pdf Accessed 28 April 2008

Persha, L. and Blomley, T. (2009) 'Management decentralization and montane forest conditions in Tanzania', *Conservation Biology*, vol 23, no 6, pp1485–1496

Pfliegner, K. and Moshi, E. (2007) 'Is joint forest management viable in protection forest reserves? Experiences from Morogoro Region', *The Arc Journal*, vol 21, pp17–20

Sachedina, H. (2008) 'Wildlife is our oil: Conservation, livelihoods and NGOs in the Tarangire Ecosystem, Tanzania', PhD thesis, University of Oxford

Shivji, I.G. and Peter, C.M. (2000) *The Village Democracy Initiative: A Review of the Legal and Institutional Framework of Governance at Sub-District Level in the Context of Local Government Reform Programme*, Report for Ministry of Regional Administration and Local Government and the United Nations Development Programme, University of Dar es Salaam, Dar es Salaam, Tanzania

Sunderlin, W.D., Hatcher, J. and Liddle, M. (2008) *From Exclusion to Ownership? Challenges and Opportunities in Advancing Forest Tenure Reform*, Rights and Resources Initiative, Washington, DC

TFWG (Tanzania Forestry Working Group) (2007) *'Mama Misitu' Forestry, Governance, and National Development: An Advocacy and Public Awareness Campaign. A Proposal*, TFWG, Dar es Salaam, Tanzania

TNRF (Tanzania Natural Resource Forum) (2008) *Wildlife for all Tanzanians: Stopping the Loss, Nurturing the Resource and Widening the Benefits. An Information Pack and Policy Recommendations*, TNRF, Arusha, Tanzania

ThisDay (2007) 'Govt set to plug holes in tourist hunting sector', 12 June 2007. Available at: www.thisday.co.tz/News/2136.html Accessed 13 June 2008

URT (United Republic of Tanzania) (2006) 'The economic survey 2006', Available at: www.tanzania.go.tz/economicsurveyf.html Accessed 6 April 2008

URT (United Republic of Tanzania) (2005) *State of the Public Service Report 2004*, President's Office- Public Service Management, Dar es Salaam, Tanzania

URT (United Republic of Tanzania) (2002) *The Forest Act*, Government Printer, Dar es Salaam, Tanzania

van de Walle, N. (2001) *African Economies and the Politics of Permanent Crisis, 1979–1999*, Cambridge University Press, Cambridge

White, F. (1983) *The Vegetation of Africa. A Descriptive Memoir to Accompany the UNESCO/ AETFAT/UNSO Vegetation Map of Africa*, UNESCO, Paris

World Bank (2008) *Putting Tanzania's Hidden Economy to Work: Reform, Management and Protection of its Natural Resource Sector*, The World Bank, Washington, DC

WSRTF (Wildlife Sector Review Task Force) (1995) *A Review of the Wildlife Sector in Tanzania. Volume 2: Possible Future Options*, Ministry of Tourism, Natural Resources and Environment, Dar es Salaam, Tanzania

5

The Evolution of Namibia's Communal Conservancies

Brian Jones

Introduction

Namibia's communal 'conservancy' programme is widely considered the leading example in southern Africa of community-based natural resource management (CBNRM) (Roe et al, 2009). Legislation enacted in 1996 enables rural communities to apply to government to gain rights over the use of wildlife and tourism on communal land. In order to gain these rights the community must form a 'conservancy' – a local common property resource management institution which has a defined membership, defined area of land and a governing constitution. Since the registration by government of the first three conservancies in 1998, the conservancy programme has grown considerably. In 2007, 50 registered conservancies together earned a total of N$20,582,789 (~US$2.9 million) in direct cash income from various sources including different types of hunting and photographic tourism (NACSO, 2008). The value of other forms of non-cash benefits to the conservancies such as meat from hunting and culling of game was approximately US$1 million. The conservancies included a total of about 220,600 residents. Since 2007, five more conservancies have been registered, bringing the total to 55 and now covering close to 15 per cent of Namibia's total land area, which is about equal to that covered by state protected areas. This chapter describes the political processes that led to the development of Namibia's communal conservancy policy and legislation and examines why the Namibian government has gone further than others in the region in devolving rights over wildlife to local communities.

The Namibian political context

Namibia, a former German colony, was placed under South African administration as a League of Nations Mandate Territory after the First World War. South Africa increasingly ruled Namibia as in effect a fifth province, ignoring United Nations resolutions calling for South Africa to lead Namibia to independence according to the terms of its mandate. During the 1960s South Africa introduced an apartheid-style system of ethnic 'homelands' that formalized the division of the country into white-owned freehold land (43 per cent of the land), black communal land (about 41 per cent), protected areas for conservation and other state land. It was not until 1990, due to increased international pressure and the economic drain of a liberation war, that South Africa granted Namibian independence.

Since independence, the wider Namibian governance context has been broadly democratic, with regular multi-party elections. The ruling party is the South West Africa People's Organisation (SWAPO) which led the liberation war and was elected in the country's first elections with an overwhelming majority, which it still retains 20 years after independence. However, Namibia's emerging democracy appears to be fragile. SWAPO has reacted nervously to the emergence of new parties from within its own ranks and meetings of these parties have been violently disrupted. A new 'Spy Bill' under consideration in the National Assembly would reportedly provide government with wide-ranging powers to spy on private email and internet traffic.

The overall approach to policy development is characterized by openness and transparency, and recent policy changes have been accompanied by extensive stakeholder consultation as part of an overall commitment by government to transparency and democracy. However, within the ruling party and within the higher echelons of the civil service there are competing ideological tendencies representing, on the one hand, liberal democracy and decentralization, and on the other, command and control through centralization and the dominance of party ideology throughout all branches of government. Policy outcomes, and the extent to which public participation in the policy process is achieved, often depend upon the prevailing ideological tendencies within a particular ministry at a particular time and the influence of individual ministers or senior civil servants.

Post-independence policy change in the wildlife sector

In 1996 the Namibian National Assembly passed legislation that gave rights over wildlife and tourism to local communities on communal land. The Nature Conservation Amendment Act provides for communities to acquire these rights through the formation of a common property resource management institution called a conservancy. According to the Act, any group of persons residing on communal land may apply to the Minister of Environment and Tourism to have the area they inhabit declared a conservancy. The Minister will declare a conservancy in the government gazette if (see Long and Jones, 2004):

- The community applying has elected a representative committee;
- The community has agreed on a legal constitution which provides for the sustainable management and utilization of game in the conservancy;
- The conservancy committee has the ability to manage funds;
- The conservancy committee has a method for the equitable distribution of income from the sustainable use of wildlife and from tourism;

- The community has a defined membership;
- The conservancy has defined boundaries agreed by neighbouring communities;
- The area concerned is not subject to any lease or is not a proclaimed game reserve or nature reserve.

Once a conservancy has been declared in the government gazette, in terms of the legislation it automatically acquires rights to use wildlife and to conduct commercial tourism activities on its land. These rights are the same as those conferred by pre-independence legislation passed first in 1967/68 that applies solely to white freehold farmers. In the case of freehold farmers, the use rights are conditional on adequate fencing of a farm so that game animals are contained within the farm. In the case of communal farmers, the condition is the formation of the conservancy and fencing is not required.

Through the 1996 legal reforms, conservancies that are gazetted gain 'ownership' over what the legislation calls 'huntable game' species (oryx, springbok, greater kudu, warthog, buffalo and bushpig). Ownership means that the conservancy can use these species for its own purposes (e.g. subsistence hunting and consumption) without permits, quotas or hunting seasons being imposed by government authorities. In addition, the conservancy can carry out trophy hunting based on government approved quotas, can apply for permits for the use of protected and specially protected species, and buy and sell game animals. The legislation enables communal conservancies to carry out commercial tourism activities within the conservancy and, if the conservancy wishes, to enter into contracts with private companies for the development of commercial tourism activities. The legislation enables conservancies to earn income directly from their own use of wildlife and their own tourism activities, to retain all of this income and to decide how to spend the income.

An important feature of Namibia's institutional framework for the communal conservancies is that local rights over wildlife and tourism are entrenched in legislation and are not administrative privileges that can be arbitrarily removed. Once a conservancy is declared in the government gazette it acquires rights clearly defined in legislation which can be defended in the law courts. This is one of the main differences between the Namibian approach and the approach of other southern African countries where in some cases there is a written policy but no legislation that provides clear rights (e.g. Botswana); where legislation provides vague and undefined management rights (e.g. Zambia); or where legislation provides for rights at decentralized district government level but not directly to local communities (e.g. Zimbabwe).

The enabling conditions for institutional change

A number of factors created a set of enabling political conditions that favoured the changes in wildlife governance on communal lands described above. These include the existence of a coalition or network of like-minded individuals in NGOs and government; the policy space opened up by Namibian independence; and the low commercial value attached to wildlife resources on communal lands at the time.

A network of like-minded influential actors

At independence there existed in Namibia a general consensus around sustainable use as a legitimate wildlife management strategy. The pre-independence government and conservation authorities had in the late 1960s and early 1970s provided consumptive use rights over wildlife to white freehold farmers. However, the pre-independence apartheid government did not countenance giving the same rights to black communal farmers. A crucial change in approach that came after independence was to extend the ambit of sustainable use of wildlife to include black communal farmers. Newsham (2007) draws attention to the importance of a network of like-minded actors in Namibian conservation at the time of independence that was able to drive policy reform. He links the development of the discourse around sustainable use in Namibia to the emergence of international debates about sustainable development and the role of local communities in conservation (Newsham, 2007, p145):

> *The increasing credibility invested, at the global level, in the concept of sustainability led to changes in thinking on conservation and development in Namibia from the 1970s onwards. The notions of using natural resources carefully as a way of conserving, of seeing all manner of people as capable of conserving biodiversity, of tackling the question of sufficient incentive for conservation outside the protected areas are all found ... in global debates about sustainability. They underscore policy and legislation for the conservancy programme, from the mid-1970s onwards on private land and the mid-1990s in Namibia's communal areas. Communal land inhabitants, from being viewed as incapable and excluded from conservation efforts therein, are now seen as actors of vital importance...*

The Namibian 'actor network' drew inspiration from the changes in thinking internationally that challenged what has been called the narrative of 'fortress conservation' – meaning conservation based on game reserves and national parks protected by paramilitary guards and emphasizing the exclusion of people from these areas and a separation of people and nature (Adams and Hulme, 2001). The development of 'community conservation' as a counter-narrative linked conservation with the notion of sustainable development and provided conservationists concerned with human and social aspects of conservation with a framework within which to explore these links.

In addition, the Namibian actor network was influenced by emerging thinking in common property resource management that suggested there was empirical evidence for successful collective sustainable management of natural resources based on certain design principles (e.g. Berkes, 1989; Ostrom, 1990). The influence of this emergent global scholarship is seen in the institutional form for conservancies adopted in the 1996 legislative reforms.

The Namibian actor network was also part of a wider network of conservationists within southern Africa experimenting with community-based approaches in Zambia (the Administrative Management Design for Game Management Areas: ADMADE), Zimbabwe (the Communal Areas Management Programme for Indigenous Resources or CAMPFIRE) and Botswana (the Natural

Resources Management Programme or NRMP). The most influential of these programmes was CAMPFIRE which was underpinned by a considerable body of research and analysis on common property resources management theory and practice based within the Centre for Applied Social Sciences of the University of Zimbabwe and led by Professor Marshall Murphree. Indeed, Murphree applied common property resource management theory specifically to wildlife management on communal lands in southern Africa and developed a set of principles for collective wildlife management (Murphree, 1993) which also significantly influenced the development of the Namibian conservancy policy and legislation.

This actor network that promoted these changes in Namibia consisted of government officials in the then Ministry of Wildlife, Conservation and Tourism (MWCT) and the Directors of the Namibian NGO, Integrated Rural Development and Nature Conservation (IRDNC). In some respects this network can be thought of as including the first SWAPO Minister of Wildlife, Conservation and Tourism, Niko Bessinger, and the Ministry's first post-independence Permanent Secretary, Hanno Rumpf. Officials and others approached Bessinger and Rumpf to explain their vision for a new inclusive form of conservation in Namibia based on sustainable development principles and including black communal farmers. This vision drew partly on the positive results of work carried out by IRDNC in the northwest of the country. IRDNC had helped local communities establish a network of community 'game guards' and established a pilot project to bring tourism revenue to a local community as an incentive for conservation of local wildlife. Further, the vision drew on the early experiences of CAMPFIRE and the NRMP in Botswana.

The ideas suggested to them provided Bessinger and Rumpf with a concrete platform for reform within the fledgling Ministry. It was useful to be able to demonstrate to the new Permanent Secretary and Minister the empirical evidence based on devolved wildlife user rights on freehold land, which had led to a widespread recovery of game species on those private lands, as well as from the early work of IRDNC with Namibian communities, that incentive-based approaches to conservation could work. In addition it was important to be able to demonstrate that other independent, neighbouring states had developed similar approaches.

The first opportunity for this actor network to put its ideas into practice as part of a formal government programme came with the withdrawal of the South African Defence Force (SADF) from the Caprivi Game Reserve in northeastern Namibia prior to independence in 1990. Conservation officials working with NGOs carried out a 'socio-ecological survey' which investigated the status of plant and animal biodiversity in the park as well as the development aspirations and attitudes to conservation of the 3,000–4,000 inhabitants of the area who were mostly San people, many of whom had worked for the SADF as soldiers or civilians. The survey led to the identification of problems and issues shared by the people and the conservation authority, identification of joint solutions and a pilot project to integrate community aspirations with conservation objectives, elaborated in a strategic community-based environment and development plan (Brown and Jones, 1994).

The participatory processes, akin to participatory rural appraisal, used during the socio-ecological survey in the Caprivi Game Reserve were used in several other surveys in Namibian communal areas over the next four years. The surveys confirmed two things. First, Namibian communities in northern Namibia did not want to see wildlife disappear, although they wanted something done about predators that killed livestock and elephants that ate crops or destroyed water installations. Second, the black communal farmers wanted the same rights over wildlife as had been given to white freehold farmers. The communal farmers were aware that the white farmers were able to use wildlife and earn income from it and wanted to benefit in the same way. Essentially this meant that in Namibian communal areas there was a political constituency that was interested in wildlife as a form of land use that could contribute to local development. The result was that officials, backed by Minister Bessinger and Permanent Secretary Rumpf, began working on a new conservation policy for communal areas that would ultimately lead to the 1996 legislation.

The process of policy formulation began in 1992, and by 1993 the Namibian CBNRM initiatives were being supported by donor funding from the United States Agency for International Development (USAID) through the Living in a Finite Environment (LIFE) Programme. LIFE was implemented by World Wildlife Fund (WWF)-US, which provided grants and technical assistance to Namibian NGOs working with local communities.

LIFE was expected by USAID to engage in policy reform to create an enabling environment for CBNRM in Namibia. However, the WWF Chief of Party realized that such reform was being led by government officials and that a more strategic approach would be to support the officials in the reform process. LIFE therefore supported the CBNRM actor network in developing a specific set of activities to help create a positive political climate for the policy to be accepted (Jones, 2000). An extensive media campaign highlighted the problems faced by local communities living with wildlife and the existing attempts to promote CBNRM. Policy briefs were developed for politicians. A large amount of economic data was collected and the benefits of community-based approaches to natural resources management to the national economy were demonstrated. Opportunities were taken by officials to feed this information into speeches made by politicians including the President. A video was made and presented at a cocktail party for directors and Permanent Secretaries of key government departments. Opportunistic use was made of a theatre production designed by the Southern African Sustainable Use Specialist Group (SASUSG) for performances at international venues portraying the conservation issues faced by local communities and the costs they bear from living with wildlife. A gala performance was provided for Cabinet Ministers, Permanent Secretaries and donor representatives, including a speech by the President promoting CBNRM. Presentations were given to the Parliamentary Standing Committee on Land and Natural Resources and the Chair of this committee attended a regional CBNRM conference, gaining exposure to a wide range of issues. The same conference was attended by a prominent Regional Councillor whose approach to CBNRM and conservancies changed as a result of the conference.

This early information and publicity campaign in support of policy reform helped lay the foundation for the development of a Namibian CBNRM narrative which has helped CBNRM gain acceptance beyond the original actor network that first promoted it. This narrative has been supported by ongoing monitoring and presentation of data that provides empirical evidence of success (e.g. NACSO, 2008), resulting in CBNRM being included as a government strategy in National Development Plans and Namibia's Vision 2030 development strategy. The number of conservancies formed is formally used as an indicator for National Millennium Goal 7 (Environmental Sustainability). In addition, CBNRM has been included in the curriculum for the Nature Conservation Diploma at the country's Polytechnic. For the young conservation officials studying the diploma, CBNRM is therefore presented as the way conservation in rural areas is carried out. Indeed CBNRM has been accepted as a major component of the current Ministry of Environment and Tourism Strategic Plan. The current struggles are no longer about whether CBNRM should be implemented, but how (see sub-section below on policy implementation).

Independence and policy space

Importantly, independence in 1990 provided the policy space for the Namibian actor network to promote community conservation. There was a policy environment favourable to reform as part of Namibia's transformation from apartheid under what was effectively South African colonial rule. This new environment allowed space for new and innovative ideas to be introduced in natural resource management that resonated with the politics of transformation (Jones, 2000). The new SWAPO government moved quickly after being elected to repeal race-based legislation and remove institutional discrimination based on race. A National Land Conference provided the foundation for developing policies aimed at redistributing land from whites to blacks. The country's new Constitution provided for basic human rights and outlawed racial discrimination.

Members of the actor network described previously had been instrumental in working with SWAPO to include a clause in the Constitution that committed the government to the maintenance of essential ecological processes and biodiversity as well as the sustainable use of natural resources for the benefit of citizens. In these circumstances, it was possible to introduce policies and legislation promoting greater community involvement in decision-making and greater community control over local resources as these could be seen as redressing inequalities of the past. This window of opportunity existed for perhaps five or six years, after which the government moved into a phase of consolidation in which the focus was on implementing the transformative new policies and legislation.

Indeed the policy document that preceded the 1996 conservancy legislation and which served to formally articulate the conservancy concept was specifically framed as reforming apartheid conservation policies. This policy document on 'Wildlife Management, Utilisation and Tourism in Communal Areas' states as one of its objectives:

To redress past discriminatory policies and practices which gave substantial rights over wildlife to commercial[1] farmers, but which ignored communal farmers.

(MET, 1995, p2)

The document goes on to state that although commercial farmers had been given rights over wildlife leading to an increase in wildlife and the development of a multi-million Namibian-dollar wildlife industry, such a system had not been applied to communal lands. State control of wildlife resources on communal land had alienated people from wildlife, resulting in poaching, a severe decline in wildlife numbers in some areas and political pressure for land proclaimed as game reserves to be returned to the people for grazing. The document noted that local benefits from wildlife were marginal with minimal spin-offs from tourism activities on communal land, none of which were run or controlled by local residents. A central conclusion of the policy document was that:

> *The discrimination of the past needs to be redressed, and people living on communal land need to be afforded the same rights as were conferred on commercial farmers.*
> (MET, 1995, p5)

These sentiments clearly fitted the agenda of the post-independence Namibian government. The reformist conservation agenda being proposed by certain officials was adopted by the MWCT Minister Bessinger and Permanent Secretary Rumpf, who then championed it within government. The political legitimacy of the approach was enhanced by evidence from the socio-ecological surveys that communal area residents were themselves demanding the same rights over wildlife as enjoyed by white freehold farmers.

The commitment of the Minister and Permanent Secretary in this process was crucial because there was no consensus in the Ministry among officials that providing rights over wildlife to black communal farmers was an appropriate policy. The push for reform was being driven by a small policy and planning directorate within the Ministry established by Bessinger. However, many officials in the parks and wildlife directorate did not think that black rural farmers could manage wildlife successfully and believed that law enforcement should be the primary conservation mechanism in rural areas (Jones and Murphree, 2001). Officials were also reluctant to give up control over wildlife. This was not because they would lose control over the allocation of access to a valuable resource as has been suggested for other community conservation programmes in the region (e.g. in Zambia as related by Gibson, 1999). It was rather because of the natural bureaucratic impulse to hold on to power and authority (Murphree, 1991; Jones, 2000) and a belief that without their active intervention wildlife could not be protected and conserved.

The development of a new conservation policy formed part of a broader reform process within the Ministry led by Minister Bessinger. A series of internal Ministry meetings chaired by the Minister led to restructuring of the Ministry and the production of a series of new policies on biodiversity conservation and land use planning, all of which emphasized inclusion of local communities in planning and decision-making and the provision of economic incentives for sustainable use of land and natural resources. In order to develop the new conservancy policy, Bessinger chaired a large national-level meeting of community leaders and traditional authorities to confirm some of the results of the socio-ecological surveys and to hear directly how people viewed wildlife and conservation. Prior to Cabinet approval of the conservancy policy document in 1995, Permanent Secretary Rumpf and Deputy Minister, Ben Ulenga, accompanied by officials, embarked on an extensive tour of northwestern and northern Namibia to promote the conservancy approach among local leaders in communal areas, against the backdrop of a government election campaign.

This level of political support at the top level of the Ministry made it difficult for dissenting government officials to openly oppose the new approach. It would be too easy, however, to cast the events at the time as a simple contest between reformists backed by the new Minister and conservatives wedded to the old regime. Analysis that posts individuals into 'interest groups' and then interprets all their actions as representing the interests of that group is simplistically one-dimensional. Individuals often belong to different interest groups at the same time and strategically switch allegiance between them. Within the Ministry, there was a group that was ideologically led in its opposition to giving rights over wildlife to black people on racial grounds. At the same time, however, there were officials who had been working in the field in communal areas and who favoured reform. There were others who saw and understood the logic behind the new approach but were unsure how to implement it. And as indicated above, there was an underlying reluctance on the part of some officials to give up power and what they saw as their mandate to protect wildlife. Whatever their motivations, a number of senior officials in the parks and wildlife directorate worked with the planning and policy directorate to develop new legislation once Cabinet had approved the conservancy policy in 1995.

The fiscal dimension: Low centrally captured revenues from wildlife use

Nelson and Agrawal (2008) argue that key factors enabling the conservancy reforms in Namibia included relatively low levels of institutional corruption coupled with relatively low centrally captured revenues from wildlife use on communal lands. As a result there was little financial incentive for officials to hold on to control of wildlife resources in order to fund Ministry budgets or in order to retain the power of patronage with a view to possible rent-seeking.

At the time of independence in 1990, most income from consumptive use of wildlife went to freehold farmers and there were a limited number of trophy hunting concessions on communal land that generated relatively low income for the state. For example in Kunene Region trophy fees to government amounted to the equivalent of roughly US$45,260, in Caprivi they were about US$203,050 and in the former Bushmanland about US$51,770, while the MWCT budget for 1993 was N$18 million (~US$5,580,000) (Yaron et al, 1993). In addition, all trophy fees went directly to the central revenue fund and there was no link between the fees generated and the Ministry budget. Strict government tender procedures were adhered to in the auction of trophy hunting concessions. There was therefore little income going to the state from consumptive use of wildlife in general and in particular from the concessions on communal land over which the state had allocative authority. Further, there was little opportunity for corruption in the allocation of hunting concessions. This situation is in stark contrast to the post-independence wildlife sector in Zambia described by Gibson (1999). He provides evidence that the more valuable wildlife resources were increasingly used by government officials and ruling party members to reward their friends and supporters, and as a result wildlife policy was shaped partly by the need of officials and politicians to retain distributive powers of patronage (see also Nelson and Agrawal, 2008).

The role of donor support in the Namibian CBNRM programme

Large-scale donor projects such as the USAID-supported LIFE Programme in Namibia have in other settings elicited considerable criticism. In some cases, such as the Botswana NRMP, the project activities have been largely externally imposed and have not been taken up by a strong national actor network (see Rihoy and Maguranyanga, this volume). Policy is often developed by donor-funded consultants and not adopted by the host government, while projects are often driven by donor interests, agendas and time frames. The introduction of USAID support to the Namibian CBNRM programme in 1993 had the potential to lead to similar outcomes. However, the national CBNRM actor network was successful in managing the USAID support and avoiding many of the negative results seen elsewhere.

Local management of the LIFE Programme was facilitated by the nature of the relationship between USAID and WWF-US, which was governed by a Cooperative Agreement (CA). In contrast to a contract, the CA provided WWF with much more autonomy in its decision-making and implementation approach, partly because under the CA it was also providing a substantial proportion of the funding for the programme. This higher level of discretion could have resulted in WWF pressing its own organizational agenda in the implementation of CBNRM in Namibia. However, the LIFE Chief of Party saw the need to work in partnership with the Namibian NGOs in the CBNRM sector. As a result WWF effectively became co-opted as part of the broader Namibian CBNRM actor network.

Management of LIFE was guided by a steering committee that was composed of a majority of Namibian organizations, including the Ministry of Environment and Tourism (MET) as chair, as well as USAID and WWF. Decision-making was by consensus, or by voting if consensus could not be reached. USAID and the MET retained a veto right on any issue that contravened their own government's policies or laws. In all other respects USAID as a donor and MET had the same level of power on the committee as any other member.

The structure and membership of the steering committee and its decision-making processes promoted accountability of WWF and USAID to a Namibian-driven implementation agenda (LIFE, 2000). This Namibian agenda had a longer time horizon than that of the project phases, and the steering committee was used by Namibians to ensure that the project did not pursue short-term 'successes' that would not be sustainable. The importance of this longer-term vision was demonstrated during Phase 1 of LIFE when the emerging Nyae Nyae conservancy was experiencing problems. The USAID Mission Director advocated strongly for the redirection of funds from Nyae Nyae to another community to speed up their conservancy formation process. A MET official, a WWF technical assistant and Namibian NGO personnel carried out a survey in the Nyae Nyae area among local residents. The survey team recommended to the LIFE steering committee that support should continue, despite the misgivings of the Mission Director (Jones, 1996). The committee accepted this recommendation and Nyae Nyae became the first conservancy to be registered by the Namibian government.

At this stage of development of the Namibian CBNRM programme, the MET played an important coordinating role through an official in the Directorate of Environmental Affairs specifically tasked with programme coordination. The MET CBNRM coordinator attended weekly meetings of LIFE Project implementing partners, was vice chair of the steering committee and had regular liaison with LIFE personnel, including joint field activities.

In addition, LIFE actively supported the expansion of the Namibian CBNRM actor network. When the USAID support to CBNRM in Namibia began, the actor network called itself a 'collaborative group' modelled on the CAMPFIRE collaborative group in Zimbabwe comprising government officials, NGOs and academics that guided the implementation of CAMPFIRE (Murphree, 2005). With the establishment of the LIFE steering committee, the Namibian collaborative group tended to meet less often, because the same people were part of the steering committee. However, with the growth and geographical spread of CBNRM, there was a need to re-establish a national coordination forum with a separate identity to LIFE. WWF was also keen to ensure that appropriate coordination at national level would take place once the project came to an end. These considerations led to the formation of the CBNRM Association of Namibia (CAN) which was later re-named the Namibian Association of CBNRM Support Organisations (NACSO). LIFE funded the NACSO secretariat, supported the establishment of NACSO thematic working groups and handed over its grant-making activities to a Namibian NGO, the Namibia Nature Foundation, which was a NACSO member. NACSO now includes 13 Namibian NGOs and provides the major forum for coordination of Namibian CBNRM activities.

The USAID-funded LIFE Programme therefore avoided many of the pitfalls of similar large-scale donor projects elsewhere in the region. It was designed to support existing Namibian activities. The implementing agency, WWF, was accountable to a steering committee composed of a majority of Namibian organizations and which had decision-making authority. The steering committee provided the mechanism for Namibians to actively manage the LIFE Project and ensure that it was implemented in the interests of CBNRM in Namibia. Further, WWF had a small implementation role and focused mainly on support to existing Namibian organizations that implemented policy and legislation developed by the Namibian government. The problem of local 'ownership' of a donor project was never at issue. The Namibian CBNRM actor network, of which WWF became a part, succeeded in managing the USAID donor influence.

Implementing conservancy policy: Contesting institutional change

Adams and Hulme (2001) suggest that government agencies and officials have wide discretion in the interpretation of policy so that the link between policy and action can take many different forms. In addition they note that past practice exerts considerable influence over future changes. In Namibia there have been considerable gaps between the implementation of policy and the original intent of the policy-makers. By and large the way in which policy has been implemented reflects an inherent distrust by officials that communities will use wildlife sustainably.

Corbett and Jones (2000) note several gaps between the conservancy policy's intention and implementation. While the intent was for communal area conservancies to receive the same rights over wildlife as freehold farmers, the Ministry of Environment and Tourism (which had replaced the MWCT formed after independence) placed additional administrative restrictions on communal conservancies. For example, officials insisted that the conservancies have approved quotas and obtain permits for their own use of huntable game. In addition the conservancies are supposed to have a management plan before a quota for trophy hunting or own use would be approved. In essence the officials administratively contested the fuller devolution of ownership of huntable game by the conservancies envisioned by the policy and provided for in the legislation. An internal Ministry memo of July 2000 stated that because conservancies do not own land (or lease it from government) they cannot have ownership of the huntable game on such land. Due to pressure from conservancies and the actor network that had driven the development of the reforms, the officials sought a ruling from the Office of the Attorney General on this issue. The resulting legal opinion was very clear. The Office of the Attorney General in its response wrote that the crux of the matter was whether or not game on an area declared as a conservancy belonged to the state. Quoting sections of the legislation, the opinion went on to state:

> *The above-mentioned provisions are not open for ambiguous interpretation and it is clear that conservancy committees do in fact have ownership of huntable game in that conservancy.*

Despite this ruling, the MET continues to insist on approving quotas for own use by conservancies of huntable game even while there is no legal provision on which this is based. In general, however, this administrative insistence on quotas has not significantly hindered the activities of conservancies but illustrates the way in which officials try to maintain control over wildlife use.

The years since the conservancy legislation was passed in 1996 and the establishment of the first conservancies in 1998 reflect several contradictions in the way that MET has implemented the legislation. Again, it would be easy to depict the events since 1996 as a struggle between MET officials trying to hold on to control and power over wildlife and communities trying to wrest more control from MET. On the one hand MET has indeed tried to restrict the powers of conservancies under the legislation as noted above, suggesting that officials do not trust conservancies with the management of wildlife. On the other hand, MET has embarked on an official programme of re-introducing wildlife to many conservancies, often with wildlife being donated by the state from protected areas. MET has a custodianship programme where state-owned black rhino are provided to freehold farmers deemed to be able to provide security for the rhino. This programme has been extended to communal area conservancies, several of which have been trusted by MET with re-introduced black rhino.

MET has over the past few years been carrying out a review and revision of existing policy and legislation. Some headquarters officials have blocked the development of new policy and legislation that promotes co-management of protected areas between MET and local communities. Yet in fact MET officials in the field are already implementing the very activities the headquarters officials are blocking. In the Caprivi region, protected area officials cooperate with local communities in joint antipoaching patrols, game counts and fire management in an area known as the Mudumu North Complex, consisting of part of the Bwabwata National Park, the Mudumu National Park and neighbouring conservancies and community forests. Wildlife has been reintroduced by MET to the conservancies in the Mudumu North Complex.

Government agencies are not monolithic organizations with a consistent and unified set of interests pursued by all officials. In the same way that communities consist of different interest groups, often competing for control over natural resources, so government agencies can consist of individuals with different ideologies and factions based on ideology or even ethnicity. Governance outcomes often depend upon the ascendancy of individuals or such factions within government agencies, particularly in the absence of clear policy directives from above. In contrast to the situation at independence, there is currently an absence of policy direction from the Minister. As a result, policy revision and development of new legislation take place through competition between individuals and factions within the Ministry. This results in stalemate, evidenced by the fact that new legislation to replace the pre-independence conservation law has been in the development stage for the past ten years with little sign that it will reach the National Assembly, at least as of 2009.

In recent years there have been more indications that wildlife was being perceived by elements of the ruling élite to have significant economic value. The MET is awarding new concessions in protected areas and individual politicians and even the youth wing of the ruling party, the SWAPO Youth League, are reported to be interested in gaining access to these concessions. The Namibian conservancy approach will be severely tested if Ministry officials bow to external pressure regarding the allocation of concessions and interfere in the choosing of joint venture partners by conservancies.

There are also signs, however, that conservancies themselves form an important political constituency which has some power to protect its own interests. In 2004 the Namibian Cabinet decided that a national park should be established consisting of three tourism concessions on communal land in the northwestern Kunene Region. Due to initial resistance by conservancy leaders and traditional authorities, government began negotiations with the communities neighbouring the concessions. The conservancies and traditional leaders set a number of conditions for their acceptance of the proposed park. These conditions included the stipulation that the protected area should be established not by government proc-lamation under existing legislation but by contract between the communities and the government in terms of new legislation being developed. The conservancies and traditional leaders have sought their own legal advice and are determined to retain some control over their land, in contrast to the proclamation of protected areas in the past which deprived people of access to land and resources. This process helps to illustrate that conservancies are institutions whose legitimacy regarding land and resources issues has been recognized by government and which have developed sufficient strength and resilience to stand up to new challenges that could potentially undermine their interests.

Conclusion

Namibia's conservancy programme has become a global model for CBNRM and devolved wildlife management based on sustainable use. The origins of Namibia's communal conservancies lie in a range of historic, political and socio-economic patterns and trends. Namibia's unusual history involving earlier devolution of wildlife use rights, early community conservation experiments in the 1980s, and the need to redress inequalities between freehold and communal lands, and black and white citizens, in the post-apartheid era all played a central role in shaping the reforms adopted in the 1990s. At the global level, ideas related to communal resource management and the integration of conservation and development through sustain-able use played a formative role. CBNRM initiatives elsewhere in the region, partic-ularly Zimbabwe's CAMPFIRE programme, also were an important influence on the evolution of ideas in Namibia and the emergence of an actor network of govern-ment officials and conservationists committed to devolving rights to manage wildlife to residents of communal lands. These factors have all shaped a national CBNRM narrative that places devolved institutional arrangements based on sustainable use at the centre of rural conservation and development practices and policies.

Note

1 Euphemism at the time for white freehold farmers.

References

Adams, W. and Hulme, D. (2001) 'Changing narratives, policy and practices in African conservation', in D. Hulme and M.W. Murphree (eds) *African Wildlife and Livelihoods: The Promise and Performance of Community Conservation*, James Currey, Oxford
Berkes, F. (1989) *Common Property Resources: Ecology and Community-based Sustainable Development*, Belhaven Press, London
Brown, C. J. and Jones, B.T.B. (1994) *Results of a Socio-ecological Survey of the West Caprivi Strip, Namibia: A Strategic Community-based Environment and Development Plan*, Directorate of Environmental Affairs, Ministry of Wildlife, Conservation and Tourism, Windhoek, Namibia

Corbett, A. and Jones, B.T.B. (2000) 'The legal aspects of Governance in CBNRM in Namibia', Paper delivered at the CASS/PLAAS Second Regional Meeting on the legal aspects of governance in CBNRM. University of the Western Cape, 16–17 October 2000, Cape Town, South Africa

Gibson, C.C. (1999) *Politicians and Poachers: The Political Economy of Wildlife Policy in Africa*, Cambridge University Press, Cambridge

Jones, B. (2000) *Case Study on Information Support to Natural Resource Management Policy in Namibia*, Technical Centre for Agricultural and Rural Cooperation, Wageningen, The Netherlands

Jones, B.T.B. (1996) *Institutional Relationships, Capacity and Sustainability: Lessons Learned from a Community-based Conservation Project, Eastern Tsumkwe District, Namibia, 1991–1996*, Research Discussion Paper No. 11, Directorate of Environmental Affairs, Windhoek, Namibia

Jones, B.T.B. and Murphree, M.W. (2001) 'The evolution of policy on community conservation in Namibia and Zimbabwe', in D. Hulme and M.W. Murphree (eds) *African Wildlife and Livelihoods: The Promise and Performance of Community Conservation*, James Currey, Oxford

LIFE (Living in a Finite Environment) (2000) *End of Project Report Phase I for the Period May 7, 2003–June 30, 2000*, WWF LIFE Project, Windhoek, Namibia

Long, S.A. and Jones, B.T.B. (2004) 'Contextualising CBNRM in Namibia', in S.A. Long (ed) *Livelihoods and CBNRM in Namibia: the Findings of the WILD Project*, Final Technical Report of the Wildlife Integration for Livelihood Diversification Project (WILD), prepared for the Directorates of Environmental Affairs and Parks and Wildlife Management, Ministry of Environment and Tourism, Windhoek, Namibia

MET (Ministry of Environment and Tourism) (1995) *Wildlife Management, Utilisation and Tourism in Communal Areas*, Policy document, Ministry of Environment and Tourism, Windhoek, Namibia

Murphree, M.W. (2005) 'Congruent objectives, competing interests, and strategic compromise: Concept and process in the evolution of Zimbabwe's CAMPFIRE, 1984–1996', in J.P. Brosius, A.L. Tsing, and C. Zerner (eds) *Communities and Conservation: Histories and Politics of Community-based Natural Resource Management*, AltaMira Press, Walnut Creek, CA

Murphree, M. W. (1993) *Communities as Resource Management Institutions*, Gatekeeper Series No. 36, International Institute for Environment and Development, London

Murphree, M. W. (1991) 'Research on the institutional contexts of wildlife utilisation in communal areas of eastern and southern Africa', in J.G. Grootenhuis, S.G. Njuguna and P.W. Kat. (eds) *Wildlife Research for Sustainable Development*, National Museums of Kenya, Nairobi, Kenya

NACSO (Namibian Association of CBNRM Support Organizations) (2008) *Namibia's Communal Conservancies: A Review of Progress in 2007*, NACSO, Windhoek, Namibia

Nelson, F. and Agrawal, A. (2008) 'Patronage or participation? Community-based natural resource management reform in sub-Saharan Africa', *Development and Change*, vol 39, no 4, pp557–585

Newsham, A. (2007) 'Knowing and deciding: Participation in conservation and development initiatives in Namibia and Argentina', PhD Thesis, Centre of African Studies, University of Edinburgh

Ostrom, E. (1990) *Governing the Commons: The Evolution of Institutions for Collective Action*, Cambridge University Press, Cambridge

Roe, D., Nelson, F. and Sandbrook, C. (2009) *Community Management of Natural Resources in Africa: Impacts, Experiences and Future Directions*, IIED Natural Resource Issues No. 18, International Institute for Environment and Development, London

Yaron, G., Healy, T. and Tapscott, C. (1993) *The Economics of Living with Wildlife in Namibia*, The World Bank, Washington, DC

6

Historic and Contemporary Struggles for a Local Wildlife Governance Regime in Kenya

Ngeta Kabiri

Introduction

The governance of natural resources should ideally be based on efficient and sustainable production. In Africa, though, natural resource management institutions are largely shaped by political processes that reflect the interests of competing actors. Within this context, the question of how institutional change occurs cannot be approached as if it is a technical issue. This chapter describes both longer-term historical and more recent contests amongst different actors with divergent interests and claims in Kenya's wildlife sector. The history of wildlife governance in Kenya suggests that institutional change needs to be considered within the context of the balance of power in a society. In Kenya, dynamics surrounding institutional change in wildlife governance are also related to the interests and influence of external actors with leverage over those who exercise public authority.

The influence of external interests in Kenya's wildlife policy arena does not negate the agency of local communities, but highlights elements of competition between local, national and transnational actors and forces. Local communities have long endeavoured to advance their interests in spite of various structural and institutional barriers. But local groups' influence has always been limited, partly because their antagonists benefit from a war of attrition between them and the locals on the biodiversity that the bureaucracy presides over. The failure by the bureaucracy to share public authority over wildlife with local communities, in spite of the adverse implications this failure has had for biodiversity conservation, has to be conceptualized within the broad framework of the crisis of governance in Africa, and is not specific to the wildlife sector. Rather, these governance issues run like a pervasive thread through the entire gamut of Kenyan society amidst a ruling clique prepared to pursue power for power's sake.[1] The nature of governance in Africa prior to the 1990s, and limited tendencies towards democratization since then, was such that pursuit of narrow private interests was the principal motive of African leaders (Ake, 1996). To a large extent, decisions on economic policies and programmes were not driven by technocratic (efficiency) imperatives but by political pressures (e.g. Krueger, 1990). This chapter explores the way that different actors' powers and influence over wildlife governance in Kenya have changed during different periods of time from the colonial era to the present. Although the dynamics of wildlife policy formulation have changed radically, barriers to increased local control over wildlife have persisted and evolved in a complex manner.

The material presented here draws on both primary and secondary data; the former was collected during dissertation field-work carried out in the 2002–2004 period (Kabiri, 2007). Such data involved collecting published and unpublished reports of both governmental and non-governmental organizations, attendance of seminars and meetings held by various groups and networks, and interviews with individuals from local to national level involved in the conservation sector.

On public authority in Africa, and Kenya in particular

Public authority is not a contract resultant from circumstances like those to be found in market settings; it is imposed on the losers by winners, and losers may have their say but not their way and must largely live with the imposed authority of the winners (Moe, 1990; 2005). Nowhere is this characterization more apparent than in the case of governance in post-colonial Africa. A key to understanding institutional change is the question of what drives the formulation of public policy (and specifically natural resources policy).

Three forces are central to an understanding of the context in which public policy is constructed in African countries. There is the tendency towards rent-seeking informed by a rentier psychology,[2] which has taken root because of the evolution of an 'imperial' presidency operating within a political economy of underdevelopment. A rentier psychology, imperial presidency and socio-economic underdevelopment interact to create a dysfunctional public policy environment that accounts for the failed natural resources governance regimes which are now the subject of reform efforts. In Kenya, for example, this dysfunction is evident in the lopsided distribution of land starting from the colonial era to the present. The post-independence political élite accumulated lands acquired from the departing British colonial landholders and lands that had been Crown lands (Odinga, 1967). In subsequent years, forest reserves were excised and doled out as patronage goods (KFWG, 2006; Agutu, 2009). With respect to wildlife, during the peak of wildlife decimation in Kenya during the 1970s and 1980s, it was difficult for conservation actors to arrest the situation because the prime movers of poaching had strong links to the central state (Gibson, 1999).

The tendency of public office holders to enrich themselves using opportunities provided by proximity to state power demonstrates how, at least to those exercising this power, the state was conceptualized and used not as an arena to render public service but as a tool to appropriate state largesse at the earliest opportunity.

Sometimes such appropriation was so crude that it assumed the dimension of a roving bandit unconcerned about the merit of reproducing the state (on the general question of institutions and economic performance, see for example, North, 1981; 1990; Olson, 2000). For these actors, apart from selling public service to the highest bidder, appropriating natural resources was considered a matter of course. In this pursuit, they were enabled by institutional arrangements that vested overwhelming powers in the presidency.

Through a process of revising the negotiated independence Constitution that some say was a fairly good Constitution for the emerging nation, the presidency came to control all three branches of government such that both the legislature and the judiciary were as demobilized as the executive of which the President was supposed to be in charge. The President, for example, appointed the head of the judiciary and could initiate his dismissal without recourse to, for example, Parliament. A belief was popularized to the effect that holders of public office do so at the pleasure of the President. On the other hand, the President held constitutional powers to dissolve the legislative assembly even before its term expired. The popular approach, however, was to invoke his powers to consign to detention without trial individuals considered to be a threat to state security; in this case recalcitrant members of the legislature could be controlled (see for example Nyong'o, 1987; Widner, 1993)

While public actors are notionally accountable to society, such accountability is a function of the way a society's institutions distribute authority. Public officials may conceptualize their professional loyalty in terms of the appointing authority instead of fidelity to public service. In such instances, public officials serve either their personal interests or those of the appointing authority. The concentration of public authority in the hands of the presidency facilitates this orientation in public service. Even when a group of bureaucrats embody an esprit de corps, policies adopted and/or implemented are those sponsored by agents enjoying a close proximity to State House. In practice, the presidency becomes synonymous with policy. In Kenya, the doctrine of separation of powers that in advanced democratic polities constrains the executive from acting unilaterally has for the most part been merely a nominal construct.[3] However, despite the fact that the presidency is the repository of public authority, it is not invariably the case that the presidency can obtain its desires even when its power is not being overtly contested. There is always the possibility that implementing agents can decide to interpret policy in their own ways.[4] Thus the principal–agent problem implies that even if the presidency intends good public policies, the entire environment within which public policy evolves does not guarantee sound public policy-making or implementation. This state of affairs, particularly in the context of natural resources, is compounded by the challenges of the political economy of underdevelopment, especially its balance of payment dimensions.

Fiscal constraints and policy implications

The balance of payments circumstances typical of underdeveloped countries put immense pressure on natural resources in diverse ways. Capital deficits, interacting with the rent-seeking orientation of public officials, expose public institutions, and by extension, public policy formulation and implementation, to manipulation by vested interests. Consequently, interest groups find it easier to influence what is finally pronounced as policy.[5] This influence may take diverse forms, such as annexation of resource flows, or emasculating departments responsible for managing these resources, not necessarily for material gains but to serve partisan ideological preferences. In cases where these departments are often cash-strapped, their benefactors can have undue influence in the way bureaucratic agencies conduct business. The objectives of dominant interest groups do not always converge with the public good, resulting in a situation where natural resources management ends up serving narrow interests. Under circumstances where local communities are not well-organized, they are unable to present a credible force that would enable them to emerge as an influential pressure group (Bates, 1989). Consequently, their interests in natural resources are marginalized. This is the context within which struggles for institutional reforms in natural resource governance in Kenya occur.

Historical roots of centralized wildlife policy: The colonial era

The restructuring of local communities' relationship with natural resources, and especially with respect to wildlife, began with the intervention of British imperial rule in Kenya in the late 19th century. During that time, the Imperial British East African Company (IBEAC), imposed a licence on ivory hunters, but initially this regulation only affected the white hunters (Kelly, 1978, p93). This imposition is one of the earliest manifestations of centralized institutional control over wildlife in Kenya. In 1893, the IBEAC also prohibited the killing of female elephants in an endeavour to provide for the replenishing of the depleted herds. It is significant to note that the impetus to these new institutional dynamics dates back to as early as the 1870s, when fears of the extermination of elephants in the East African Protectorate were being voiced, particularly by hunters who were interested in the preservation of species for sport hunting (Kelly, 1978; Maforo, 1979).[6]

The protectorate government also had vested interests in imposing regulations governing wildlife use for at least two other reasons. First, decimation of game, particularly elephants, would deprive the state of a steady source of income given that the government saw the ivory trade as one easy way of securing the revenue needed to administer the protectorate (Meinertzhagen, 1957; Kelly, 1978). Second, centralizing control over wildlife was tied to controlling the influx of guns into the protectorate. This was because some ivory traders were giving their porters guns to hunt elephants and yet some of these porters were prone to desertion, meaning that from the administration's perspective, weapons of violence were falling into African hands at a time when the protectorate sought to tilt the balance of military power against the natives (Kelly, 1978).

In 1896, Lord Salisbury instructed the protectorate chief, Hardinge, to impose a closed season, quotas, fees and reserves for the purposes of checking the imminent decline of big game in the protectorate (Kelly, 1978). This initial centralization of authority over wildlife did not, however, affect the Africans. As Hardinge's reports (1897/8) show, Africans were excluded from the game laws because it was difficult to enforce the law among them and also because their use of rudimentary hunting tools meant that they were less destructive than the white hunters who used guns (Ibid.). By 1900, though, hunting by Africans was brought under the control of district officers (Ibid.). Thus, while initially Africans had space for manoeuvre in their access to wildlife, even though not for commercial use, their counterparts among the white communities were beginning to face what would develop into a struggle over wildlife governance institutions and local rights.

Early wildlife governance regulations, exemplified in prohibitions on shooting game without a licence, were felt more directly by Kenya's white settler community. The settlers complained of damage done to farms by wildlife, and in addition to this, they had grievances against the setting up of the initial game reserves. The latter were viewed as limiting access to fertile land needed for agriculture. Within this context, a debate over landholder compensation for wildlife damage to agricultural crops found its way into the wildlife governance discourse. The settlers called for compensation for damage done by wildlife to settler property but the colonial state refused. Explaining the fear that the state had with regard to compensation claims, the acting Game Warden in 1935 argued that acknowledging any liability by government would be dangerous because claims from Europeans, Indians and natives would occur at the rate of thousands per week and it would be impossible to investigate them (Kelly, 1978). It is against this background that the state's initial moves towards devolution of authority over wildlife to the local level began to take shape, soon after or simultaneously with the initial imposition of central regulations.

In an attempt to mollify settler grievances, the state ceded some authority over wildlife to the settler community. In a 1909 ordinance, for example, the state introduced a traveller's licence that allowed the holder to shoot game on private lands with the permission of the landowner. The settlers sold shooting rights and also charged fees to shoot certain species (Kelly, 1978; Maforo, 1979). Thus the settlers were able to extract concessions for some authority over wildlife on the basis of the costs wildlife imposed on them at a time when the state lacked the fiscal capacity to compensate them. The state was therefore being forced to balance central claims of wildlife ownership with its production costs.

Settler representation at the legislative council level also accounts for the success of settlers in securing limited rights to manage wildlife. This can be inferred from the fact that other groups in colonial Kenya, such as Africans and Indians, who also staked some claims to wildlife, did not get the same rights as did the European settlers. It was not until the 1950s that African interests began to be addressed by wildlife governance institutions. Thus, macro-political dynamics in terms of proximity to political (legislative) authority determined that white settlers got limited rights to manage wildlife earlier than other social groups, even though all shared the same grievances related to wildlife. Similarly, changes in the structure of wildlife governance institutions to accommodate African interests evolved simultaneously with African representation in the legislative council as well as the rise of African nationalism. Thus even though the state had economic interests in wildlife which would have made it prefer to retain exclusive control, proximity to political power by contending non-state actors led to equivocated forms of devolution.

For example, the 1945 National Parks Ordinance provided for consultation with Africans when their land was to be affected by establishment of protected areas. While it would be a stretch to call this requirement for consultation devolution of authority, it was certainly a shift in the governance regime given the context of a colonial administration in which native interests were secondary to those of the state and settler communities. The 1900 East African Game Regulations had earlier provided that the Commissioner (of the protectorate) could, with the approval of the Secretary of State, declare any area a game reserve and could also alter any boundaries. The 1945 Ordinance thus brought local-level actors (Africans) closer to the orbit of natural resources governance institutions as the colonial state was beginning to be more sensitive to African grievances as the tide of nationalism took shape, thereby reducing the imperial distance between the governors and the governed.

By 1957, tangible reforms were becoming more evident. The 1957 Wild Animals and Park Ordinance amendment brought game fees in African District Councils' land units into par with government charges and created Controlled Areas in African land units in which African District Councils had powers to pass bylaws (Maforo, 1979). The culmination of these reforms occurred in 1961, only two years before independence, when both Amboseli and Maasai Mara were removed from the control of the National Parks Trustees and handed over to the Kajiado and Narok District Councils, respectively (Lindsay, 1987). The impetus for this radical step was the need to appease the local populations so that they might be more amenable to the conservation of wildlife. However, this measure was not uncontested. The colonial Governor appears to have acted behind the back of the National Parks Trustees and the latter were horrified by the move, and so were the conservation lobby groups who had all along opposed Maasai access to Amboseli (Ibid.).

It thus appears that proximity to decision-making authority, interacting with the estimation of those in power as to the weight of local grievances against the extant natural resources governance institutions, was a critical determinant of the way reforms were carried out. In the case of decentralizing governance of Amboseli to the Kajiado African District Council, for example, the authorities sought to placate the Maasai who had contended that they would continue conserving wildlife if they could benefit from it (Ofcansky, 2002). Given that this approach was being pursued in the twilight of colonial rule, the authorities perhaps sought to secure Amboseli as a wildlife reserve by giving it to the local District Council because the departing authorities feared that the incoming independent regime might not be sympathetic to wildlife conservation (Western, 1997). Such fears were not unfounded given that the nationalist movement had mobilized against, among other things, the supposedly harsh colonial wildlife laws. The departing colonial authorities actually seemed to have resigned themselves to this fate as seen in the position of the 1959/60 Game Policy. That policy observed that the future of wildlife in Kenya would depend on the attitude of the people of Kenya towards it. To this extent, the policy underscored the need to have economic incentives for game preservation on the part of local people (Colony, 1959/60, pp4–5). In retrospect, it is now clear that the nationalist vanguard, both in Kenya and elsewhere in Africa, never intended to overturn the colonial wildlife governance regime (see for example Gibson, 1999; Ofcansky, 2002). To the contrary, as successors to the departing colonial edifice, the post-independence government proved to be more Catholic than the Pope. This disposition was imposed, as we see below, by the political realities of economic underdevelopment and a constitutional dispensation that denied the public space to assert their claims over their leaders.

The colonial era can thus be summed up as a period when both state and non-state actors competed for a (re)structuring of wildlife governance regimes. The form that these regimes took reflected the balance of power at the macro-political level. The dynamics of this balance of power were negotiated within the institutions crafted by the colonial state, but these institutions were in turn re-shaped by events at the local level. Two narratives about wildlife appear to have provided the context within which these negotiations were played out. There was the presentation of wildlife as a renewable resource that needed the proprietary role of the state if depletion and subsequent extinction were to be avoided. But within state circles, there was also a parallel narrative that informed centralized control over wildlife by depicting wildlife as an invaluable resource in a cash-strapped emerging colonial state whose imperial guardian had sounded the warning that it had to fend for itself. In contrast, non-state actors pursued a 'liability' narrative that depicted wildlife as a candidate for extinction unless it was made to mitigate its costs at the local level. Underwriting this liability narrative is the institution of private property that wildlife was conceived as threatening. The discriminatory recognition of property rights by the colonial state largely accounts for the variance in the incorporation of the non-state actors in the wildlife governance regime. Thus, the European settlers precede Africans in this area, not because of race, but because of the property relations between the state, settlers and Africans.

The post-colonial state and wildlife governance

The post-colonial state was equally informed by the considerations that drove its colonial predecessor's approach to natural resource governance. The nascent Kenyan state sought to appropriate wildlife as an economic resource and, to this extent, centralizing, not decentralizing, control over wildlife institutions was deemed appropriate to achieve this objective. Government's sessional papers and parliamentary legislation were deployed to give legal force to this objective (RoK, 1965; RoK, 1975). The 1965 Sessional Paper, for example, was clear that devolution, especially in its privatization dimension, was out of the question as far as wildlife resources were concerned. Indeed, it spelt out clearly that the participation of the people, hence local actors, was to follow a government script (RoK, 1965, pp11, 57). During this period of change, wildlife governance institutions continued to be shaped by macro-political exigencies, namely the desire to use wildlife to swell up national coffers, rather than the interests of local-level actors living with wildlife.

There were, however, some notable variations to this general pattern with respect to certain aspects of wildlife utilization. The Wildlife Conservation Act of 1976 (RoK, 1977) allowed landowners some leeway in the management of the sport hunting industry. Landowners controlled commercial hunting on private land and were entitled to payments for game hunted on their land. Nevertheless, this arrangement did not translate into devolution of authority in the sense that landowners cannot be understood to have had power over wildlife on their lands. The question of whether they reserved the power to consent on whether a hunter could hunt or not is quite tenuous (RoK, 1977, s.29). Nevertheless, even the indeterminate authority they may have had was extinguished in 1977 when the state banned sport hunting as a form of wildlife utilization. This had the effect of removing even the indefinite veneer of local-level control over wildlife that may have existed, even if nominally.

The 1977 ban on consumptive utilization

In 1977, the government banned sport hunting following an outcry over perceived declines in wildlife numbers which were attributed to uncontrolled hunting. It was also thought that sport hunting facilitated illegal poaching. Animal rights groups (whose influence in post-colonial Kenya was specifically referred to in the sessional paper on wildlife) and the tourism industry are said to have been at the centre of calling for this ban. Because the latter rely on wildlife abundance for their trade, it is credible to assume that there may have been a marked decline in wildlife numbers or that there was something about sport hunting that was perceived to damage their industry. The legacy of this ban has weighed down heavily on subsequent attempts to devolve authority over wildlife to local communities because it is often presented as a constraint the wildlife regulatory authority has in holding devolved levels accountable in their management of wildlife. Thus, a narrative of regulatory failure shapes the debate on sport hunting and, by extension, devolution of wildlife to local actors.

Critics of devolution argue that the factors that led to the failure of sport hunting in the pre-1977 period remain relevant to Kenya's situation and hence, it would be premature to devolve authority again as that would amount to treading an already beaten path. Proponents of devolution, however, contest this interpretation of the 1977 hunting ban. They contend that the ban should not be misconstrued as an indictment of the ability of local-level actors to husband natural resources because it was not aimed at them, but rather, at governmental wildlife authorities. It was government authorities, they argue, who were the culprits because they would issue permits in bulk to the dealers.[7] To the proponents of devolution, the sport hunters could not have been a problem, otherwise there would be evidence of prosecution of hunters for malpractices. The ban on sport hunting was followed by a ban on sales of animal products such as skins. In the latter case, the government revoked wildlife dealers' licences so that nobody could trade in wildlife products in Kenya. What this meant was that even when a wildlife cropping experiment was introduced in the 1990s, landowners could not process hides and skins but had to export them to Tanzania and South Africa, and then re-import the finished products back to Kenya. To local groups, this did not make sense and it showed the extent to which the establishment was insensitive to their right to utilize their lands economically. Yet, in addition to this deprivation, the state still went ahead to impose an additional burden on communities living with wildlife by abdicating responsibility for compensation for wildlife damage.

Devolving costs of wildlife production: The 1989 Wildlife (Management and Conservation) Amendment Bill

Analysis of the debate over the 1989 Wildlife Bill in Parliament represents a study of the absurd. The Bill sought to remove compensation for property damaged by wildlife. At this time, the post-independence state was compensating for the loss of both human and livestock life and physical property damaged by wildlife. The process was, however, so widely abused that by the time of this amendment, cases of non-existent damage had been compensated while genuine ones were still pending. The wildlife-related debt that the state owed landowners was so great that proponents of abolishing compensation for wildlife damage to property (other than human life) argued that paying the debt would bankrupt the wildlife agency. Most of the parliamentarians who contributed to the debate commended the Minister for introducing the Bill, on the basis that under the new law people would be compensated and thus live harmoniously with wildlife. In fact, the Bill intended to do the exact opposite. While it is standard practice for the relevant Minister or the Attorney General to inform the parliamentarians if they are misinterpreting a Bill (in this case thinking that there would be greater compensation) in this instance the MPs were left to wallow in their utter confusion.

What is of interest is that those MPs who seem to have read and realized that the amendment was removing compensation argued against it, but still ended up supporting the Bill. For example, one MP condemned the drafters of the amendment and said that it would be committing a crime against God to support a Bill that is against the people.[8] Yet in the end he supported the Bill. On the other hand, the Minister responsible for wildlife, and the key mover of the Bill, represented a constituency that was at the epicentre of human–wildlife conflict. There were very few MPs who pegged their support of the amendment to the deletion of the clause on abolition of compensation for wildlife damage but politicians known to be strongly pro-establishment came out openly to support the Bill. As a result, the Bill was adopted and compensation for wildlife damage thereby abolished (although provisions for compensation were subsequently reinstated). What explains such a radical institutional change which served to abdicate governmental responsibility for wildlife damage yet excluded local actors from control over the resource, at a time when central regulation and protection of wildlife in Kenya were plagued by problems?

The explanation for these legislative dynamics lies in the emasculation of Kenyan governance institutions as power became increasingly monopolized by the presidency in the late 1980s and political repression intensified. The 1988 national elections that produced this Parliament were arguably the most abused electoral contest in Kenyan history. It was ingrained in the national electoral psyche that if the executive and the only political party (by then the two had become quite indistinct) was determined to rig a politician out of politics, the demise of the political career of such a candidate was a foregone conclusion (see for example Widner, 1993). Opposition to those in power was equated with political subversion and was deemed actionable. During this period, all the proponents of legislative proposals needed was support from the presidency, and they would be almost certain of getting their preferred outcome by portraying their opponents as pursuing subversive activities detrimental to the interests of the state. Indeed, one MP known for his avid support of the regime overtly stated that the Wildlife Bill had to be passed because the President wishes it to be so.[9] Thus, the power wielded by the executive branch in Kenya at the time dominated patterns of institutional change and wildlife governance.

In this particular episode, actors in the wildlife sector within the establishment were concerned that the claims for wildlife damage pending action before the wildlife authority were so huge that the agency would have to ground all other activities for it to be able to even approximate paying the claims. Within this context, the state decided to repudiate its responsibility for wildlife damage. Thus, the institutional change of this era is largely accounted for by an authoritarian political dispensation which had disabled the electorate as principals of the legislature and was consequently able to emasculate the latter into handing the executive a blank slate in which it could author its wishes into law. It was against this background that widespread agitation for reform took place in the 1990s including the re-introduction of pluralist politics. The climax of this agitation was realized after the then-ruling party (Kenya African National Union, KANU) lost power in the 2002 general elections, leading to a more open political environment that paved the way for a more diverse range of civic actors to agitate overtly for wildlife sector reforms.

Reform efforts since the 1990s

The study of contemporary institutional reforms in Kenya's wildlife sector is a continuing story of the obstacles posed by macro-political factors to improving natural resource governance. This is the case even when such reforms were sponsored by the Kenya Wildlife Service (KWS) itself, the country's national wildlife authority. Prior to 1989, the wildlife sector was organized in two departments: the Game Department and National Parks. The former was in charge of wildlife outside of the protected areas, while the latter took charge of national parks. The 1989 Wildlife Amendment Act merged these two into the parastatal Kenya Wildlife Service (KWS). Popular opinion now holds that the previous wildlife organizations were mismanaged, and wildlife decline was the norm. The key signifiers of this decline included poaching that had gone out of control and poor relations between the wildlife sector and communities living with wildlife. Indicative of the former, wildlife populations across Kenya declined by about 30 per cent from 1977 to 1994, and the country's elephant population crashed as a result of poaching (DRSRS, 1995; Leakey, 2001). Thus, the new outfit was charged with, among other things, bringing poaching to an end as well as improving relations between the wildlife bureaucracy and communities living alongside wildlife.

In the early 1990s, KWS undertook several internal initiatives to reform the wildlife sector. KWS was perhaps aware of the smouldering discontent among communities living with wildlife, and that the opportunity of falling back on the security provided by state organs was waning in light of the new democratic dispensation provided by the onset of multiparty politics. KWS may have thought it preferable to placate the communities before they rebelled in one form or another against extant arrangements. Thus macro-political changes contributed to new efforts to restructure wildlife governance in a way that took greater account of local economic interests.

In 1990–1991, KWS undertook a comprehensive wildlife sector review, resulting in a document dubbed the Zebra Book, which set out the sector's policy framework and development plans. With respect to institutional reforms, fairly progressive observations were made that pointed towards devolving greater authority to local actors. For example, the Zebra Book stated:

> *KWS policy is that landowners should retain all the revenue that they derive from wildlife on their lands, as they do for competing land uses. KWS will aim to cover its supervision and administrative costs…Landowners will certainly not be obliged to seek wildlife use rights in order to develop tourism on their land.*
>
> (KWS, 1990, pp46–47)

Such targets were, however, not followed through, even as KWS subsequently moved to help communities hosting wildlife to organize themselves in a National Wildlife Forum so as to present a unified body that KWS could work with. There was an attempt, led at this time by KWS, at reintroducing consumptive wildlife utilization as a way to expand the returns from wildlife on private lands. In addition, KWS began a community service scheme that sought to share wildlife benefits with communities neighbouring national parks, but, as Table 6.1 shows, its funding relative to other budgetary provisions was minimal.

Table 6.1 *KWS expenditures, 1998–2003 (figures in thousands of KShs)*

	1998/99	1999/2000	2000/01	2001/02	2002/03
Wages	690,875	677,533	697,532	833,534	808,478
Operating Expenses	372,118	453,173	525,719	725,538	536,867
Community Services	11,281	18,450	10,133	34,523	11,318

Source: adapted from Wachira, 2004

The National Wildlife Forum, comprised of landholder and community representatives from Kenya's wildlife-rich districts, was formed around 1994, through the initiative of KWS under David Western's directorship. It was, however, beset with problems even as it was being conceived. The registrar of societies had reservations about the forum. The problem, according to him, was that some national political functionaries were apprehensive about the rise of an organization supposedly representing the people; they argued that elected political leaders were already representing the people (see Kabiri, 2007). This reservation by the politicians should be understood as reflecting less an analysis of what is good governance in the wildlife sector, but more as turf wars in regions where such an organization might have a significant political impact. But even when conservation-specific considerations came to the fore, obstacles to reform from interest groups were the norm as the case of sport hunting demonstrates.

In 1994 KWS commissioned a review group to study the wildlife sector and give recommendations on the way forward. The review group recommended, among other things, the re-introduction of sport hunting as a way of increasing wildlife's economic value to local communities and private landholders (KWS, 1996). This recommendation became controversial not only in the national public arena, but also because some members of the team are said to have disowned the recommendation, claiming that it was smuggled into the report without their knowledge (Opanga, 1997). In a public meeting held to discuss the report, the KWS director was part of the coalition supporting the re-introduction of hunting. He was enjoying the support of the emerging National Wildlife Forum while the opposition to lifting the ban was spearheaded by Kenyan conservation NGOs such as the David Sheldrick Wildlife Trust and personages from the Kenya Association of Tour Operators (Coffman, 2001). The former can be said to represent animal welfare persuasions opposed to hunting on ideological grounds while the latter argues that sport hunting is detrimental to Kenya's overall tourism industry. It was this combination of interests that stalled the bid to reopen sport hunting in the mid-1990s, despite the support of KWS. This shows the extent to which even KWS itself is not necessarily the driving force behind wildlife governance institutions in Kenya.[10] It is merely an actor within a broader struggle for the control of the sector at different levels of government and society. The obstacles to reform lie in the differential and often incompatible interests of those multiple actors.

The last major reform initiative of the mid-1990s involving KWS was the attempt to review national wildlife legislation. In 1996 KWS, with financial support from the United States Agency for International Development (USAID), produced a draft Wildlife Bill that sought to devolve some power to local authorities, but the initiative never materialized. There are conflicting opinions as to what happened to the Bill. Some observers, including KWS officers, claim that it was returned to the Ministry by the Cabinet because it was not consultative enough.[11] Other observers claim that the Bill was either withdrawn from the Cabinet paper trail or disappeared before reaching the Cabinet for discussion.[12] The point is that there is no clear evidence about what the position of the state was in the 1990s regarding wildlife sector institutional reform, especially with regards to devolving greater power to the local level. The only evidence of a state perspective on this issue is the 1999 Sessional Paper on environment and development.

The 1999 Sessional Paper No. 6 on Environment and Development, in contrast to the 1975 Sessional Paper on Wildlife Conservation, marked the first attempt by the state to recognize the need to involve communities as effective actors in biodiversity conservation (RoK, 1999). It recognized that there are inadequate incentives to stimulate local community participation in biodiversity conservation and proposed greater involvement of local communities in wildlife conservation and management. But apart from stating that it will develop mechanisms to allow communities to benefit from wildlife, there is no clear expression of an intention to devolve governance of wildlife to local-level actors as was the case with, for example, neighbouring Tanzania's 1998 Wildlife Policy (Nelson and Blomley, this volume). It was this void that the communities hosting wildlife in their lands sought to address in subsequent reform initiatives which were enabled by macro-political changes that gave political pluralism some effective meaning following the 2002 presidential transition.

The 2004 'GG Bill'

Up until this time, locally-driven responses to wildlife governance were haphazard, given the failure of the national wildlife movement to take place. In Amboseli, there were well-established mechanisms for KWS to share revenue from Amboseli National Park with local communities. This arrangement was negotiated through the group ranches as the locus of community interest in land matters in Kenyan pastoralist areas. In Maasai Mara, the Narok County Council was in charge of the reserve, and since it is assumed that the county council belongs to the local community, for some time community interests were seen as being addressed by the council. During the 1990s, however, due to the failure of communities to get what they considered a fair share of the proceeds from the reserve, communities began to organize themselves around group ranches and the council was forced to channel a certain percentage of the reserve proceeds to the communities (Homewood, 2009). In other areas of Kenya, there was little attempt to have local communities share the proceeds from the wildlife estate, except where the same is designated as a National Reserve, in which case the proceeds go to the local authority instead of KWS. Such proceeds involved are, however, limited to non-consumptive utilization. As such, the failure to have some of these local authorities utilize wildlife in all its possible aspects drove these communities into joining those who were receiving nothing in the agitation for institutional reforms.

These concerns around local benefits from wildlife led to the development of the 'GG Bill' (RoK, 2004),[13] which played out as the most contentious recent episode in Kenya's long-running political struggles over the transformation of wildlife management institutions. By this time, communities had effectively lost faith in other (bureaucratic) avenues for securing greater property rights in wildlife. Community and landholder representatives thus formed a forum, the Kenya Wildlife Working Group (KWWG)[14] through which they set to lobby for review of the wildlife legislation. They sought to do so through a Private Members' Parliamentary Bill, which after a series of lobbying efforts for and against, was passed by Parliament. In the end it failed to become law as it did not secure presidential assent. Among the highlights of the Bill were the restructuring of the balance of power in the KWS board whereby landowners would have more input in the management of wildlife, there was provision of high rates of compensation for wildlife damage, and legalization of consumptive utilization (hunting). While the micro-political conditions for securing a transformation in the institutions of wildlife management were favourable, given the rise of an organization representing local landholders' interests, the macro-level conditions were not yet ripe to fully support such a change, the opening of national democratic space notwithstanding.

The reformist strategy

KWWG pursued a two-pronged approach to reform. It sought to work within the establishment and hence pursued dialogue with KWS and the Minister in charge of wildlife. When this failed, it went directly to Parliament to secure the support of legislators so that the bill would be passed once tabled in Parliament. With respect to KWS, KWWG hoped that they could influence the wildlife policy from within, banking on the fact that a new government had been instituted in Kenya[15] which was proving to be more receptive to public participation in the management of public affairs. In this setting, the popular opinion on the ground in Kenya was that policy-makers and policy implementers could now make decisions without having to wait for directives from the powerbrokers in State House as was the case with previous regimes. At first, it seemed as though this strategy could work. Initial encounters with the Minister in charge of wildlife were promising, but soon the doors began to close and KWWG's letters to the Minister went unanswered.[16]

The failure to strike a rapport with the Ministry's top brass does not seem to have had anything to do with the personalities there. Between the beginning of the GG Bill initiative and its enactment into law by Parliament, KWWG dealt with three different Ministers in charge of wildlife. The pattern was the same with all three: initial favourable response followed relatively quickly by a blackout. This suggested to KWWG that there were antagonistic forces which were not only active but were also gaining an upper hand in alienating the top brass in the Ministry from forging a relationship with KWWG. Consequently, KWWG shifted its efforts towards Parliament.

KWWG first moved into Parliament through the window presented by the Pastoralists Parliamentary Forum. This is an informal grouping of MPs from pastoralist areas that is used to rally support for pastoralist interests in and outside Parliament. Almost all pastoralist areas are endowed with wildlife and thus most of these MPs were perceived as sympathetic to wildlife-based issues. KWWG also had the advantage of access to then-Speaker of the National Assembly, Francis Ole Kaparo, by virtue of his hailing from Laikipia District and thus being one of their own as a landowner from a wildlife-rich pastoralist area. The linkage with the Speaker proved a good anchor to the group's ability to forge links with Members of Parliament and even the Minister in charge of wildlife.[17] The immediate outcome of these efforts was the formation of an informal parliamentary committee on wildlife.[18] The aim was to sensitize MPs on the need for legal reform within the wildlife sector.[19] KWWG held several meetings with this group in 2003 and 2004.

These meetings took the form of brief luncheons or retreats where KWWG had technical experts take the MPs through the key issues that needed to be addressed. After one luncheon that was held in Nairobi, KWWG came out exuding confidence on the progress they were making in their lobbying activities as reported in the subsequent monthly meeting:

Members noted that the luncheon was a big success as pertains sensitizing MPs on the proposed wildlife policy and drawing their input into the document, as well as winning their support to lobby for speedy revival of the national wildlife policy review process. It was noted that due to effective media coverage of the event, and the on-going human wildlife conflicts…MPs and other stakeholders' interest and support for KWWG activities had been aroused.[20]

KWWG lobbying also took legislators and other wildlife sector actors on trips to southern African countries practising consumptive utilization so that the legislators could have an empirical view of the wildlife industry in those countries. The tours included Ministry officials, KWS staff, MPs and KWWG trustees. The tours worked well for KWWG because MPs involved largely agreed with the group's proposals regarding the need for reintroducing consumptive utilization. During a seminar organized to receive a report of this tour, one MP claimed that when the GG Bill comes up for debate he would argue that people have to benefit from wildlife through sport hunting, although it should be controlled. Thus KWWG's lobbying efforts were paying dividends. But this success also ignited a strong counter-lobby to the GG Bill and the agenda that KWWG was pursuing.

Opposition to reform

The opposition to the GG Bill was organized by a consortium of NGOs that adopted the name Kenya Coalition for Wildlife Conservation and Management (KCWCM). Central to this consortium was a group of animal rights NGOs, including both local and international organizations, opposed to consumptive wild-life utilization and organized around the Kenya Wildlife Coalition (KWC).[21] The composition of KWC is significant in that their values, as animal rights groups, shed some light on the source of the opposition to the GG Bill.

In opposing the GG Bill, the KCWCM lobbied Kenyan legislators against passing the Bill. For example, they organized a consultative meeting with them in Nairobi in the run-up to the debate of the Bill in Parliament. The letter of invitation to the individual MPs read thus:

The Coalition of Wildlife Conservation Group...has now organized a consulta-tive Meeting with members of parliament to facilitate dialogue and deepen MPs understanding of the impact of the current Amendment Bill so as to realize a more community and human rights responsive legal regime... The meeting will be attended by other members of parliament from affected areas, policy experts and community representatives...[22]

The inclusion of community representatives here may be seen as a tactic to under-mine the claim by the proponents of the GG Bill that they represented the inter-ests of local communities.

The GG Bill was finally adopted by Parliament in 2004, but that did not mean that the opposition ended. The opponents opened a new front where they now targeted the next institutional stage in law-making: the assent by the President. The coalition overtly staged a demonstration against the GG Bill once it was passed by Parliament. The demonstration was aimed at appealing to the President not to assent to the Bill. During the demonstration, the coalition issued a press release in which they appealed to the President for his intervention in the GG Bill by not assenting to the Bill. They cited reasons for their opposition and the fact that:

...the local communities will be the major losers if this bill is enacted; ...we hereby appeal to His Excellency the President to refer this Bill back to parliament to allow due constitutional process and appropriate all inclusive amendments thereof.[23]

Given this turn of events, the proponents of the Bill had two possible strate-gies (which were not necessarily mutually exclusive). They could likewise make inroads to the Presidency to influence his decision as their antagonists were doing, or they could stick to Parliament and raise a two-thirds support of legisla-tors who would over-rule a presidential veto on the bill. Neither of these possi-bilities worked in their favour.[24] So, when the President failed to assent to the bill, their efforts to entrench their interests through transformation of wildlife management institutions failed with it. How is the conflict over the GG Bill to be accounted for and how is the triumph of one camp over the other to be explained?

The eye of the storm:The animal welfare lobby and the politics of sport hunting in Kenya

As noted earlier, hunting was banned in 1977, but elements of it were re-introduced in the early 1990s as a pilot wildlife cropping scheme. Sport and/or recreational hunting was, however, not re-introduced, in spite of several KWS administrative initiatives favouring its re-introduction (KWS, 1990; KWS, 1994; Wanjala and Kibwana, 1996). The anti-hunting lobby has somehow been able to sell its case to the government and, to a significant degree, to the public. One element of this success has been the anti-hunting lobby's ability to prey on the fears of the state with respect to the tourism industry. As far back as 1975, for example, the govern-ment issued a policy paper on wildlife in which it argued in a way similar to that of the hoteliers and tour operators. As if allaying the antipathy towards hunting, the government appealed to the West to be sympathetic to the country's pursuit of sport hunting as a management tool:

> *Overseas public education activities are extremely important, from the standpoint of the future economic value of wildlife. Potential donors must be informed of the difference between simple preservation and conservation, so that donations do not dry up due to misunderstandings. Even more important, we must ensure that the potentially large and secure export market, for the products of consumptive wildlife utilization (sports hunting, sales of meat, skins and other trophies), are not fore-closed through ignorant 'preservationist' pressure on overseas Governments and firms. Already there is some evidence to suggest that prices of some skins have fallen due to such pressure. If wildlife are to 'pay their way' over large parts of Kenya, such development as this must be reversed – and quickly.*
>
> (RoK, 1975, p35)

The government was, and still is, thus sensitive to two issues related to sport hunting. First, the enterprises that are based on the wildlife sector (especially photographic tourism and the hotel industry), and second, the externally-derived donations to the wildlife sector. Opponents of sport hunting advanced the argu-ment that if the government lifted the ban, the outcome would be that tourists would shun Kenya in favour of other destinations.[25] At a time when the economy was heavily reliant on tourism, it is not difficult to see why the government would be unwilling to experiment with the wildlife sector. As Table 6.2 shows, tourism earn-ings have been growing and in terms of its contribution to the national economy, the tourism sector has increasingly moved to the forefront, competing for the lead position with tea and horticulture. In 2006, for example, tourism contributed 12 per cent of Kenya's Gross Domestic Product (RoK, 2007). Hence, the state can be expected to treat wildlife-related issues with caution, thereby giving actors claiming to represent tourism interests preferential treatment in the clamour for state attention.

Table 6.2 *Tourism earnings in Kenya, 2000–2007*

Year	Amount
2000	283
2003	347
2005	579
2007	934

Note: 2007 figures provisional; figures in millions of US$.

Source: RoK, 2007; Honey, 2008, p299

Moreover, the tourism industry and the animal welfare lobby against sport hunting are well-organized, not to mention that many of those in decision-making echelons of the state are themselves shareholders at one level or another in the tourism industry. The clout of the anti-hunting lobby stands in contradistinction to the local communities living with wildlife, who for the most part have been beset with collective action problems with respect to influencing government policy formulation (see for example Yeager and Miller, 1986).

The anti-hunting lobby, therefore, was able to advance its interests without necessarily saying they were doing so because they had personal or instrumental objections to wildlife hunting. Their narrative is founded on the economy of the country (and hence national welfare) plus the health of wildlife populations. Opponents of sport hunting argue that the reasons that led to the banning of hunting in 1977 are still valid and that until institutions able to check abuse are put in place, it would be a grave error for the state to lift the ban. In addition to the recourse to conservationist arguments, opponents also appeal to nationalist sentiments. Sport hunting was depicted as a race and class issue that eluded the indigenous poor Kenyans who bear the brunt of supporting the wildlife estate. One commentary claimed that when a former Attorney General was in charge 'of the Board and [Richard] Leakey the vice-chairman, KWS danced to the whims of game ranchers and to the detriment of Kenya's conservation goals' (Mbaria, 2003). Nevertheless, KWWG and the proponents of consumptive utilization saw their opponents' position in a different way. They crafted a counter-narrative that argued that the opposition to hunting is based on preservationist ideologies that oppose killing of wildlife for recreational purposes. The key question then is how to explain the success of one side over the other in achieving their preferred outcome.

The answer may lie partly in the interaction of a well-resourced global animal welfare movement that is strongly committed to its ideology, and the fiscal constraints besetting KWS as the lead state wildlife authority. This is thus an argument based on the politics of underdevelopment. KWS faces a significant shortfall in its annual operating budget (Table 6.3), which it seeks to fill through external sources of funding.

Table 6.3 *KWS income and expenditure, 1998–2004*

Year	1998/99	1999/2000	2000/01	2001/02	2002/03	2003/04
Operating Deficit	619,799	396,514	322,613	790,041	492,290	958,942
External (non-treasury) Grants	523,599	274,802	273,416	373,882	274,077	93,770
Net Operating Balance (Deficit)	(46,200)	(121,712)	(49,197)	(416,159)	(218,213)	(865,171)

Note: Figures in thousands of Kshs.

Source: Adapted from Wachira, 2004

Consequently, interest groups that can mobilize large amounts of revenue as support for KWS may obtain significant leverage over these governmental actors. As Table 6.4 shows, KWS and other local wildlife actors receive substantial contributions from leading animal welfare NGOs such as the International Fund for Animal Welfare (IFAW). These funds are in addition to non-cash donations in the form of training, repairs and housing; occasionally, aircraft are also donated.

Table 6.4 *Contributions by IFAW to various Kenyan organizations in 2005 and 2006*

Recipient	2005	2006
David Sheldrick Wildlife Trust	41,138	19,677
Wildlife Clubs of Kenya	6,152	12,028
Kenya Wildlife Service	519,622	265,562
Bill Woodley Mount Kenya Trust		15, 103
Laikipia Wildlife Forum		110,576
Olare Orok Conservancy		88, 572
Kuku Group Ranch	3,110	
Maasailand Preservation Trust	9,618	
Namunyak Wildlife Conservation Trust	10, 253	
Olpusare Conservation Youth Group	1,951	

Note: Cash only, figures in US$.

Source: IFAW Internal Revenue Service tax returns (publicly available)[26]

Consequently, the clout of the global wildlife and animal rights lobby cannot be underestimated in its ability to influence wildlife policy and governance in Kenya

(Norton-Griffiths, 2007). It is thus easy to sympathize with the verdict of the proponents of sport hunting as to what the causes of their tribulations were. The GG Bill sought to re-introduce consumptive utilization of wildlife[27] and this was the most contentious issue. Other supposed problems in the bill cited by its opponents were mostly diversionary (see Kabiri, 2007). Moreover, the anti-hunting lobby was able to more fully outflank its antagonists in the next round of drafting new wildlife policy and legislation in 2007.

Reform anti-climax

In 2007, a new wildlife policy and Bill was drafted, and the latter was awaiting debate in Parliament at the time of writing (RoK, 2007). What the draft wildlife law promises relative to the question of reforming the wildlife sector is clearly inclined more towards further centralization, not decentralization. Whereas one would have expected to have substantial community representation in the new Bill, given the reference to lack of local representation as a basis for the earlier presidential rejection of the GG Bill, the current draft does not promise greater community clout in wildlife management, in spite of the inclusion of community representatives in the Board of Directors of KWS. This representation is however limited to one-sixth of the total board's composition, meaning that community interests can only prevail at the pleasure of the executive that is more heavily represented. Moreover, community representation is conditioned in the sense that membership of the non-government officers of the board is pegged to academic qualification. This means that communities may not necessarily be represented by those who understand their problems most. The draft Bill has aroused considerable concern within Kenya's conservation community, at least in some quarters, as a result of the perception that it will create further disincentives for local communities to support conservation on their lands.

Conclusion

This chapter has shown how wildlife policy and governance institutions in Kenya have been shaped by a range of political forces and contextual factors from the early colonial period up until recent reform efforts and debates. During the colonial era, white settlers were able to use their representative legislative bodies and claims relating to wildlife damage to private property to gain concessions related to access to benefits from wildlife and limited control over wildlife utilization on private lands. Local District Councils were, in the latter colonial period prior to independence, able similarly to force concessions that resulted in some of Kenya's major wildlife protected areas – namely Amboseli and the Maasai Mara – being transferred from national jurisdiction to district-level control. In the post-colonial era, the evolution of Kenya's highly centralized, neo-patrimonial state led to wildlife governance measures that eventually came to greatly limit any form of local involvement. Widespread private appropriation of public resources in Kenya during this period contributed heavily to the decline of wildlife through illegal use in the 1970s and 1980s.

In recent years debates over wildlife governance have continued, pitting advocates of more locally-based frameworks that enable landholders and rural communities to make decisions about [wildlife] use against the tourism industry and global animal welfare organizations. These latter groups have been more effective at forging alliances with the government wildlife authorities in the form of the chronically indebted KWS. With Kenya having lost over half of its wildlife during the past 30 years while periodic efforts at reform were caught in these interest group conflicts, reform is at once urgently needed yet increasingly unlikely on political grounds. While Kenyan politics has clearly become more open and pluralistic following the adoption of a multi-party system in the early 1990s and again following the landmark 2002 general election, the democratization of wild-life governance institutions has been remarkably limited. This is due both to the difficulties of entrenching democratic governance in Kenya and also to the tactical influence of well-resourced and strategically astute external interests in wildlife policy. The next generation of reform efforts will have to grapple more effectively with these structural political challenges if more sustainable patterns of wildlife governance in Kenya are to be achieved.

Notes

1   It did not matter whether society would collapse or not. Thus, the governance of the wildlife sector should not be understood differently – i.e., one should not be tempted to assume that because a war of attrition with local communities could spell doom to biodiversity, then the relevant actors with public authority over wildlife should be expected to see sense and give in. Giving in to popular pressures was not part of the game in African governance circles for a long time prior to the 1990s (for studies on transition in African governance in the 1990s, see for example, Bratton and van de Walle, 1997). Apparently, even after transition to democracy, the new actors have not yet demonstrated that their pursuit of power is for the transformation of society rather than their own raw pursuit of power; hence the sense of stalled democratic transition currently enveloping Africa (see Ake, 1996)

2   Over the years, a mentality was ingrained among Kenyans that state/public property is a resource that a person (especially holders of public office) may use for personal aggrandizement. The Kiswahili phrase *mali ya umma* (public property) has come to have the allusion of: use it to your advantage without regard to cost because those costs are externalities to be borne by the public. This mentality gained currency under founding President Jomo Kenyatta. Soon, it became common in Kenya to hear comments to the effect that if you occupy a big office and do not make it (that is, move beyond poverty levels), you will be considered a useless person in the eyes of the public who would characterize you thus: you were a high ranking person in society yet you did not help yourself (i.e. use public office to amass personal wealth; the implication being that you can't, therefore, be expected to help others). Thus, these stories, taken together, led to the development of a mindset that today holds society hostage in as far as appropriation of state largesse is concerned. The land sector, state parastatals and wildlife have been prime targets of this mindset. See Wrong (2009) for a recent account of this characteristic of Kenyan public life.

3   See, for example, Zegart (1999) on how in the US, the executive is constrained from unilateralism by the doctrine of separation of powers to the extent that it is sometimes difficult to undertake bold reforms because the legislature and the executive have to trade compromises which sometimes dilute the necessary legislation.

4 This was case in Tanzania during the implementation of *Ujamaa* (villagization) when bureaucrats seemed to impose their version of the project contrary to party policy. This forced President Julius Nyerere to complain of the tendency of some leaders not to listen to the people, but rather only to tell people what to do (Scott, 1998, p236).

5 For the role of interest groups in influencing public policy, see for example Sunstein (1985), Morone (1992) and Crowley (2003).

6 For the influence of the sports-hunting interests in the early institutional dynamics of wildlife management in Africa, see for example Mackenzie (1988).

7 KWWG meeting, 4 April 2003.

8 Hansard Reports of Kenya's National Assembly Debates on Wildlife Conservation (Amendment) Bill, 1989 and 2004, National Assembly, Nairobi, Kenya.

9 Such references to the wishes of the President became a signature strategy in Kenyan political debates of the time (whether or not the President was actually aware of the issue).

10 In terms of the multifaceted way in which forces driving conservation should be conceptualized, this point echoes Gibson's observation regarding the failure by President Kaunda of Zambia to always have his way with respect to his preferences about the wildlife sector (Gibson, 1999).

11 Seminar sponsored by East African Wildlife Society to discuss the GG Bill on Wildlife Conservation and Management (Amendment) Act, 2004, held at Kenya Commercial Bank, Karen, 1 December 2004.

12 KWWG meeting, 2 July 2004.

13 The 2004 Bill to amend the Wildlife Conservation and Management Act was commonly known as the GG Bill because it was tabled in Parliament by the then MP for Laikipia West, G.G. Kariuki.

14 This forum grew out of the regional fora that had developed in the 1990s, in part due to KWS's prompting.

15 Following the 2002 general elections in which the ruling party for the past 40 years, KANU, was dethroned for the first time.

16 For example, in the July 2003 KWWG monthly meeting it was reported: 'The Secretariat confirmed having sent a letter to the Minister of Environment, Natural Resources and Wildlife, seeking an appointment for him to meet a delegation of KWWG of which no feedback had been received....The Secretariat reported having sent a letter to the Chairman of KWS seeking to have a meeting between him and KWWG members of which there has been no feedback.' From 'Minutes of a KWWG Monthly Meeting Held on 4 July 2003 At the EAWLS Boardroom' Nairobi, Kenya (on file with the author).

17 KWWG meeting 4 April 2003; 'Minutes of a KWWG Monthly Meeting Held on 4 April 2003 At the EAWLS Boardroom' Nairobi, Kenya (on file with the author).

18 Parliamentarians from tea, coffee and sugar growing areas have a similar committee.

19 KWWG meeting 24 July 2004; 'Minutes of a KWWG Meeting Held on 24 July 2004,' Nairobi, Kenya (on file with the author).

20 KWWG meeting 4 July 2003; 'Minutes of a KWWG Monthly Meeting Held on 4 July 2003 At the EAWLS Boardroom', Nairobi, Kenya (on file with the author).

21 Prominent among the members of this coalition were the International Fund for Animal Welfare (IFAW), Born Free Foundation, David Sheldrick Wildlife Trust, Kenya Human-Wildlife Conflict Management Network (KHWCM Network) and Youth for Conservation. According to their critics (such as KWWG), the coalition partners had no interest in conserving Kenya's wildlife, rather, tying them together was a combination of animal rightist ideology, turf wars in the struggle for the control of wildlife

agenda at local level and career hunting (in case of the first three, KHWCM Network, and Youth for Conservation, respectively) (see Kabiri, 2006).

22   KCWCM letter of invitation to MPs to attend a meeting on GG Bill (on file with author).

23   KCWCM Press Release urging President not to assent to the GG Bill (on file with author).

24   Raising a two-thirds majority in a multi-party Parliament requires an issue that has, for example, captured the national imagination and wildlife conservation has not reached that stage yet. On the other hand, what happened with respect to State House in case of this Bill remains a black box.

25   Since the demise of the apartheid regime in South Africa, some proponents of sports hunting have held that the argument of Kenya potentially losing tourists because they find sport hunting morally repulsive has been discredited, because Kenya is now operating under the fear of losing its traditional clientele to South Africa, yet the latter widely pursues both consumptive and non-consumptive utilization of wildlife.

26   For 2005 data: http://dynamodata.fdncenter.org/990_pdf_archive/311/311594197/311 594197_200606_990.pdf
    For 2006 data: http://dynamodata.fdncenter.org/990_pdf_archive/311/311594197/311 594197_200706_990.pdf Both accessed 27 September 2009.

27   RoK, 2004, s. 10 (b) (3).

References

Agutu, M. (2009) 'Revealed: Big names given Mau forest land', *Daily Nation*, 2 April 2009 www.nation.co.ke/News/-/1056/556332/-/u3r7pi/-/index.html Accessed 25 September 2009

Ake, C. (1996) *Development and Democracy in Africa*, Brookings Institute, Washington, DC

Bates, R.H. (1989) *Beyond the Miracle of the Market: The Political Economy of Agrarian Development in Kenya*, Cambridge University Press, New York

Bratton, M. and van de Walle, N. (1997) *Democratic Experiments in Africa: Regime Transitions in Comparative Perspective*, Cambridge University Press, New York

Coffman, J.E. (2000) '"Without money, there is no life": Global forces and the invention of wildlife in southern Kenya', PhD Thesis, University of North Carolina, USA

Colony (1959/60) *A Game Policy for Kenya: Sessional Paper No. 1 of 1959/60*, Government Printer, Nairobi, Kenya

Crowley, J.E. (2003) *The Politics of Child Support in America*, Cambridge University Press, New York

DRSRS (Department of Resource Surveys and Remote Sensing) (1995) *Data Summary Report for the Kenyan Rangelands, 1977–1994*, DRSRS, Nairobi, Kenya

Gibson, C.C. (1999) *Politicians and Poachers: The Political Economy of Wildlife Policy in Africa*, Cambridge University Press, Cambridge

Homewood, K. (2009) 'Policy and practice in Kenya rangelands: Impacts on livelihoods and wildlife', in K. Homewood, P. Kristjanson and P.C. Trench (eds) *Staying Maasai? Livelihoods, Conservation, and Development in East African Rangelands*, Springer, New York

Honey, M. (2008) *Ecotourism and Sustainable Development: Who Owns Paradise?* Second edition, Island Press, Washington, DC

Kabiri, N. (2007) 'Global environmental governance and community-based conservation in Kenya and Tanzania', PhD Thesis, University of North Carolina, Chapel Hill, NC

Kabiri, N. (2006) 'Dispersing Environmental Governance Authority in Africa: Are NGOs the New Enemy?', Paper presented at the Eleventh Biennial Conference International Association of the Study of Common Property (IASCP) in Bali, Indonesia June 19–23, 2006

Kelly, N. (1978) 'In wildest Africa: The preservation of game in Kenya, 1895–1933', PhD Thesis, Simon Fraser University, Canada

Kenya Forests Working Group (KFWG) (2006) *Collective Action for Conservation: The Kenya Forests Working Group Story (1995–2005)*, KFWG, Nairobi, Kenya

Krueger, A. (1990) 'Government failures in economic development', *Journal of Economic Perspectives*, vol 4, no 3, pp9–23

KWS (Kenya Wildlife Service) (1996) *Wildlife–Human Conflicts in Kenya: Report of the Five-Person Review Group, December, 1994*, KWS, Nairobi, Kenya

KWS (Kenya Wildlife Service). (1994) *Kenya Wildlife Service Public Briefing Document on Revenue-sharing: 'Let the Money Go Where the Wildlife Goes'*, Annex 3 in *Conservation of Biodiverse Resource Areas (COBRA) Interim Contract Report*, prepared by COBRA Contract Team, 9 May 1994, KWS/USAID, Nairoibi, Kenya

KWS (Kenya Wildlife Service) (1990) *Kenya Wildlife Service: A Policy Framework and Development Programme 1991–96*, Kenya Wildlife Service, Nairobi, Kenya

Leakey, R.E. (2001) *Wildlife Wars: My Fight to Save Africa's Natural Treasures*, St. Martin's Press, New York

Lindsay, W.K. (1987) 'Integrating parks and pastoralists: Some lessons from Amboseli', in D. Anderson and R. Grove (eds) *Conservation in Africa: People, Policies and Practice*, Cambridge University Press, Cambridge

Mackenzie, J.M. (1988) *The Empire of Nature: Hunting, Conservation and British Imperialism*, Manchester University Press, Manchester

Maforo, D.D. (1979) 'Black–white relations in Kenya game policy: A case study of the Coast Province, 1895–1963', PhD Thesis, Syracuse University, USA

Mbaria, J. (2003) 'Wildlife: Only the community has the solutions', *The East African*, August, 2003

Meinertzhagen, R. (1957) *Kenya Diary, 1902–1906*, Oliver and Boyd, Edinburgh

Moe, T. (2005) 'Power and political institutions', *Perspectives on Politics*, vol 3, no 2, pp215–233

Moe, T. (1990) 'The politics of structural choice: Toward a theory of public bureaucracy', in O. Williamson (ed) *Organizational Theory: From Chester Barnard to the Present and Beyond*, Oxford University Press, New York

North, D.C. (1990) *Institutions, Institutional Change, and Economic Performance*, Cambridge University Press, New York

North, D.C. (1981) *Structure and Change in Economic History*, W.W. Norton, New York

Norton-Griffiths, M. (2007) 'Whose wildlife is it anyway?', *New Scientist*, vol 193, issue 2596, p24

Nyong'o, P.A. (1981) 'What the friends of the peasants are and how they pose the question of the peasantry', *Review of African Political Economy*, vol 8, no 20, pp17–26

Odinga, O. (1967) *Not Yet Uhuru*, Hill and Wang, New York

Ofcansky, T. (2002) *Paradise Lost: A History of Game Preservation in East Africa*, West Virginia University Press, Morgantown, WV

Opanga, K. (1997) 'Campaign to lift ban on hunting: What's at stake?', *Daily Nation*, 23 March 1997

RoK (Republic of Kenya) (2007) Ministry of Tourism website, http://www.tourism.go.ke/ministry.nsf/doc/Facts%20&%20figures%202007.pdf/$file/Facts%20&20%figures%20 2007.pdf Accessed 6/30/2009.

RoK (Republic of Kenya) (2004) *The Wildlife (Conservation and Management) (Amendment Bill), 2004*, Government Printer, Nairobi, Kenya

RoK (Republic of Kenya). (1999) *Sessional Paper No. 6 of 1999 on Environment and Development*, Ministry of Environmental Conservation, Nairobi, Kenya

RoK (Republic of Kenya) (1977; revised 1985) *The Wildlife (Conservation and Management) Act*, Government Printer, Nairobi, Kenya

RoK (Republic of Kenya) (1975) *Sessional Paper No. 3 of 1975: Statement on Future Wildlife Management Policy in Kenya*, Government Printer, Nairobi, Kenya

RoK (Republic of Kenya) (1965) *Sessional Paper No. 10 on African Socialism and its Application to Planning in Kenya*, Government Printer, Nairobi, Kenya

Scott, J.C. (1998) *Seeing Like a State: How Certain Schemes to Improve the Human Condition have Failed*, Yale University Press, New Haven, CT

Sunstein, C.R. (1985) 'Interest groups in American public law', *Stanford Law Review*, vol 38, no 1, pp29–87

Wachira, N. (2004) *Kenya Wildlife Sector Assessment – Final Report*, Consultancy report presented to KWS/USAID, Nairobi, Kenya

Wanjala, S. and Kibwana, K. (1996) *Draft Wildlife (Conservation and Management) Bill, 1996*, Kenya Wildlife Service, Nairobi, Kenya

Western, D. (1997) *In the Dust of Kilimanjaro*, Island Press, Washington, DC

Widner, J.A. (1993) *Rise of a Party-State in Kenya: From 'Harambee' to 'Nyayo!'*, University of California Press, Berkeley, CA

Wrong, M. (2009) *It's Our Turn to Eat: The Story of a Kenyan Whistleblower*, Fourth Estate, London

Yeager, R. and Miller, N. (1986) *Wildlife, Wild Death: Land Use and Survival in Eastern Africa*, State University of New York Press, Albany, NY

Zegart, A.B. (1999) *Flawed by Design: The Evolution of the CIA, JCS, and NSC*, Stanford University Press, Palo Alto, CA

Part 3

Local Struggles and Negotiations across Multiple Scales

7

Windows of Opportunity or Exclusion? Local Communities in the Great Limpopo Transfrontier Conservation Area, South Africa

Webster Whande

The last time I saw Endani – frail, half blind and over 100 years old – he repeatedly pointed to the very rudimentary plan he had for a house. The plan, drawn on the ground in the form of trenches for the foundation, had been standing there the entire time I was conducting research along the Madimbo corridor in the far northeast of South Africa. His wish was to live in 'that house' before he died. However, that was not to be, as he died before the house could be built. His one-room house was very basic. It had a single window on one side, located too high for him to sit on his bed and look outside.

During my field-work, Endani described his experiences with state intervention. To me, his descriptions were themselves windows in time, which opened up new perspectives on the past and on the future. His stories provided me with a different understanding of the physical and conceptual windows through which he viewed various interventions. In the village of Bennde Mutale, Endani's companions of similar age, Gakato and Maphukumele, had managed to get their houses, courtesy of the post-apartheid South African government's Reconstruction and Development Programme. Yet they too would always sit at the entrances of their houses, and not by their expansive windows. To me these elders opened windows of their memories as hunters in their youth, and their reliance on a range of natural resources in the area. They spoke of how their relations with the environment were disrupted and of local people's difficult relations with state conservation officials and of life along a frontier zone.

They highlighted their disappointment at how their aspirations had not been met. However, while expressing sadness about some of their experiences in the past, they did not lose sight of the future. The stories they told formed the basis upon which local people's claims to the Madimbo corridor were based, and lay at the heart of a range of post-apartheid policy changes. Their memories served as the maps of the old homesteads, livestock grazing areas and of paths that connected them with social relations across the border in Zimbabwe. The stories, though they spoke of hopes and expectations, serve as windows bequeathed by the elders for the younger generation to contest state interventions that exclude local people from participation and decision-making over their land and natural resources. The early phases of establishing the Great Limpopo Transfrontier Conservation Area appear to be reinventing the exclusion of local people by subverting local mental and lived maps with alternative visions for ordering the landscape, and thus closing windows of exclusion rather than opening windows of opportunity based on the elders' stories and local aspirations. Local communities appear to be standing on one side and unable to contribute to the proper functioning of the windows being constructed by the South African transfrontier conservation initiative, which raises the question of whether transfrontier conservation areas present opportunities or represent enhanced exclusion of local communities along the Madimbo corridor.

Introduction

This chapter explores the dynamics of transfrontier conservation implementation along the Madimbo corridor, a land restitution case in the northeast corner of South Africa bordering Zimbabwe, but also a central cog in the Great Limpopo Transfrontier Conservation Area (GLTFCA). The story of the Madimbo corridor juxtaposes national and regional priorities for transfrontier conservation against local demands for the restitution of land and resource rights, which is the key 'action arena' and window of analysis for this chapter. Windows in terms of opportunities relate to the politics of framing, which is understood to be an outcome of who or what is included or excluded (Apthorpe, 1996), and of material possibilities. In policy terms, windows relate to the convergence of problems, politics and policy in the formation of public policy (Kingdon, 1984); that is, when policy provides solutions to problems at a politically opportune moment for action and implementation. The restitution of land rights as provided for in South African legislation presents a window of opportunity for formalizing the needs and aspirations of people like Endani, by restoring local people's land and resource rights in light of historical dispossessions. However, unequal power dynamics and access to financial and technical resources have emerged as keys to the actual realization of rights in terms of what is formalized in policy terms and implementation processes. This suggests that the convergence of problems, policies and politics can be influenced by different interests which do not necessarily reflect local social concerns in influencing policy evolutions. Local people along the Madimbo corridor are excluded from meaningful participation in both formulating ideas about the future management of their land and physically from the land itself.

Land restitution is post-apartheid South Africa's response to years of systematic dispossession of black people through colonial and apartheid laws. It is provided for through the South African constitution as well as the Land Restitution Act No. 22 of 1994, which allows groups or individuals who were dispossessed of their land through racially motivated laws and practices, since the 1913 Natives Land Act, to claim their lands. Land restitution presents a policy solution to historical injustices in the context of post-apartheid South Africa's political dispensation, which provides the imperative for implementation.

The Madimbo land restitution case is characterized by a complex political matrix involving local and non-local actors, state and non-state agencies, private tourism enterprise developers, national and international NGOs such as the land rights-focused Nkuzi Development Association; the transboundary protected areas facilitator, the South Africa-based Peace Parks Foundation (PPF); and recently NGOs such as ResourceAfrica and Cesvi. They all have various agendas and different capacities to influence the policy formulation and implementation process. The question of local land rights – here used in reference to access to and control over land and other natural resources – in an area of global biodiversity significance, much like in other parts of South Africa (see Kepe, 2008), is subject to a variety of contestations and presents a policy window based on historical experiences of injustice and exclusion. The contestations over land rights involve the local leadership – including chiefs and an elected Vhembe Communal Property Association (CPA) – and occur between local leaders and other external actors, including national and international NGOs, the private sector, and local, provincial and national government. The dynamics along the Madimbo corridor are specifically driven by the politics of inclusion and exclusion in making decisions over land and natural resources, which are further shaped by the specific location of the area along an international geopolitical boundary.

The location of the Madimbo corridor within the GLTFCA adds another layer of contestation to the land restitution process and decision-making over land uses and management. One complication in relation to this physical location is that the land restitution process for the Madimbo corridor is no longer solely the national preserve of South Africa, but is rather tied to the establishment of the GLTFCA. The GLTFCA itself opens another policy window in relation to biodiversity as a global public good to be conserved for future generations, juxtaposed against the restoration of local communities' land rights. The TFCA concept combines objectives of biodiversity conservation, promoting regional peace and stability, and job creation through tourism development (Hanks, 1997). This TFCA image is one of breaking down the boundaries and fences that divide nation states and communities from conservation areas, yet it is also seen as picking up Cecil John Rhodes's colonial empire-building dreams and opening up spaces for private sector investment (Wolmer, 2003) to the exclusion of local communities (see Hughes, 2003; Dzingirai, 2004; Spierenburg and Wels, 2006). Tourism is the central axis around which the success of the TFCAs is organized, as exemplified by the 2005 Southern African Development Community (SADC) Regional Council of Ministers' endorsement to position TFCAs as southern Africa's premier tourist attraction (RETOSA, 2009). Yet major questions remain on the openness of the process to determine land uses such as tourism – including exclusive private sector operations and supposedly community-based tourism initiatives.

The location of the corridor in an area of global and regional biodiversity significance affects the nature of negotiations over land uses, and whether the local community adopts a strategy based on mutual gains (i.e. 'win–win'), or a more confrontational distributive approach (see Fay, 2007). The Land Claims Commission approved the Madimbo land claim in 2004, which signalled the beginning of a new process of negotiation over land use and tenure in the area. Observations from elsewhere indicate that local communities fare badly when matched against seasoned negotiators representing various state departments and well-resourced NGOs, with respect to the attainment of win–win outcomes through co-management arrangements such as Contractual National Parks (CNPs) (see Fay, 2007). Kepe (2008, p319) provides further details on the ambiguity of land restitution negotiations, noting that in most land claims involving state protected areas, decisions have kept land under conservation uses.

A process-related issue concerns ambiguity in both the land restitution process and the establishment of the GLTFCA, both of which continue to frustrate the needs and aspirations of local people along the Madimbo corridor. A source of misunderstanding is that there is a formal agreement for the establishment of the GLTFCA, which there is not. Rather, the GLTFCA implementation in areas such as the Madimbo corridor is based on the treaty signed in 2002 for the establishment of the Great Limpopo Transfrontier Park (GLTP) (Whande and Suich, 2008). The core GLTP is concerned with establishing protected areas, which is quite different from the multiple land use TFCA (Figure 7.1). It is difficult to disentangle policy and administrative decisions made for the GLTP from processes related to the implementation of the GLTFCA. This confusion also affects the hierarchy of the actors involved. Transfrontier protected areas are state-controlled and -managed, leaving the process for the establishment of the GLTFCA confused with regards to the exact role of the state with regard to other stakeholders, particularly local communities, and in the case of the Madimbo corridor, the resolution of land restitution claims.

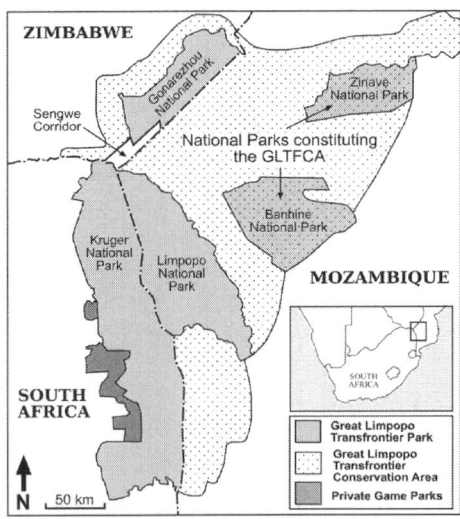

Figure 7.1 *The Great Limpopo Transfrontier Conservation Area and constituent protected areas*

The next section in the chapter discusses debates surrounding local communities and conservation. It is followed by a brief historical overview of the Madimbo corridor, exploring the closure of windows of local engagement in the affairs of the corridor. The macro-political changes of the 1990s, with the demise of apartheid, opened new policy windows for regional cooperation at a national level as well as for re-engagement of local communities such as those along the Madimbo corridor in deciding how their lands and natural resources are governed. This section is followed by a discussion of local contestations of exclusion through legal pursuit of a land restitution claim. The strategies and tactics of state and NGO planners in resisting these local claims are discussed before concluding with a synthesis of key emerging windows of engagement and exclusion.

Framing local communities in transfrontier conservation

The role (or lack thereof) and place of local communities and local land and resource rights in the implementation of conservation initiatives globally, and specifically of transfrontier initiatives in southern Africa, is the subject of intense debate amongst academics, development and conservation practitioners and policy-makers, but consensus is far from being achieved. These debates highlight tensions, differences and synergies on the extent of integration between biodiversity conservation objectives and local development needs, resulting in two predominant frames, albeit fluid and dynamic, through which local communities are viewed. These can best be illustrated by discussing governance and livelihood issues in relation to natural resource management.

The first governance frame is concerned with attaining a balance between centralized state-driven and local, community-based approaches to natural resource management. It is based on the notion that 'governance that starts from the ground up and involves networks and linkages across various levels of organization' (Berkes, 2007, p15188) is key to sustainably managing natural resources and inclusive of a variety of actors. This approach provides windows of opportunity for empowering communities and scaling up community-based natural resource management (CBNRM) initiatives across geopolitical boundaries (Jones and Chonguiça, 2001). Creating viable incentives for local communities' involvement in conservation activities is required for success (Metcalfe and Kepe, 2008), and so is a balance between community-based and state-driven approaches as exemplified by regional debates on democratic decentralization and devolution (see Rihoy and Maguranyanga, this volume). Despite this policy window for local incentives and perspectives, and the widespread acceptance and implementation of CBNRM since the 1980s, global environmental governance is also shifting the scale of decision-making upwards to include TFCA agreements among neighbouring states (Duffy, 2006).

The second governance frame for balancing state–local interactions privileges more centralized approaches based firmly on the role of the state. This represents a continuation of protectionist and exclusionary approaches to conservation as pursued for much of the 20th century. There are also trends to have privately managed protected areas run as business enterprises (Fearnhead, 2008).

Arguments for this approach focus on the status of biodiversity as a public good, which cannot be left to local communities to destroy (see Kabiri on the Kenyan conservation discourse, this volume), even though local communities are as much affected by as they impact on biodiversity loss. It is in this context that TFCAs, while defined as multiple use zones, act as windows of exclusion with the discourse inclined towards protected areas and efforts to implement TFCAs heavily reliant on state actors and processes. In governance terms, the focus of TFCAs on state regulated processes replicates 'a "government" style of governing instead of a "more governance mode", dealing with multiple actors in a flexible way' (Büscher and Dietz, 2005, p11).

Livelihoods comprise 'the capabilities, assets (including both material and social resources) and activities required for a means of living' (Chambers and Conway, 1992, p6) another frame through which communities and their linkages to conservation can be explored. Livelihood strategies are of course facilitated or constrained by the governance models and institutions in place. Communities rely on a range of natural resources for their livelihoods, and Salafsky and Wollenberg (2000) describe three generic categories of conservation–livelihood linkages: no linkage, indirect linkage and direct linkage. 'No linkage' corresponds to the centralized governance approach of viewing local livelihood activities as threats to biodiversity that need to be minimized. The 'indirect linkage' category strives to provide substitutes for local uses of biodiversity, thereby limiting the impact of human uses of natural resources. The 'direct linkage' category is character-ized by livelihood–biodiversity connections functioning as an incentive for long-term conservation by local users. Centralized resource governance systems tend to promote the 'no' and 'indirect' linkages, and often prefer linking local livelihoods to tourism revenues generated in areas where local communities are not allowed to directly harvest natural resources.

In the TFCA context, tourism elicits both strong interest and support on the one hand, and resistance on the other hand. For instance, Hughes (2003, p2) notes an emerging 'Africa for tourists, and community for peasants' trend in the plans espoused for transfrontier conservation and peddled through tourism marketing. The latest initiative associated with tourism marketing and development within transfrontier conservation initiatives is 'Boundless Southern Africa', the motto of which is 'open spaces, unlimited beauty, infinite possibilities'.[1] This underscores the main contention on the part of social scientists that TFCAs 'undermine black peasants' claim to work the landscape within the Great Limpopo's zone' (Hughes, 2003, p3; see also Spierenburg and Wels, 2006). Despite these concerns on the part of some analysts, tourism is clearly one of the major underlying factors behind the rise of the southern African TFCA discourse. Between Mozambique, South Africa and Zimbabwe, the three countries involved in the GLTFCA, estimated tourism revenues are about US$2.45 billion per year (Spenceley, 2005), representing very significant amounts of money and illustrating that tourism is a land use potentially offering livelihood diversification – or a substitute for use of biodiversity – for local communities. However, the revenues generated are not equally shared among the three countries, with the lion's share going to South Africa (see van Ameron and Büscher, 2005) nor are these revenues equally shared between local communities and private investors.

The macro-level importance of tourism to South Africa – contributing 8.5 per cent of GDP in 2008 (Mail & Guardian, 2009) – and in particular to South African National Parks (SANParks) and numerous private investors who generally have more political influence than local communities, is a key dynamic in the outcome of the TFCA enterprise. Largely because of the economic importance of tourism, the preferred settlement of land claims on protected areas is to keep them as conservation land and substitute local livelihood strategies with tourism-supported ones. A challenge, however, is that local livelihoods as a whole may be undermined if one specific form of land use is pursued over others. Additionally, the reliance of tourism on conservation, an approach historically pursued through the forced removals of local communities, leads to suspicions at the local level and even resistance (Whande, 2007). Lastly, tourism revenues are subject to market shocks and changing preferences, the benefits are not evenly distributed and the available local skills are not the same as the skills required by the hospitality industry.

The governance and livelihoods debates that frame the discourse around TFCAs illustrate that policy windows are not absolute but are contested by different interests. The balance between different interests involves debates over centralization and decentralization, and the degree to which conservation activities are directly or indirectly linked to local livelihoods.

Closing windows for local engagement: The creation of the Madimbo corridor

The Madimbo corridor has historical significance that cuts across different objectives of the South African state, including protection of the beef industry, biodiversity conservation and national security and sovereignty. Yet the corridor is a creation of colonial and apartheid South Africa, meant to control local people's movements as well as to provide security to a minority of South Africans in a region increasingly faced with liberation movements from the 1960s onwards (Steenkamp, 2001; Linden, 2004; Whande, 2007). As a physical locale, it presented problems whose policy solution included militarization, conservation, veterinary disease control and exclusion of local people. The early attempts to control local movements of people predate the formation of the corridor, with veterinary disease controls limiting animal movements across the Limpopo River. Some of the fences that traverse the area are a result of this early interest in controlling veterinary diseases and protecting livestock production, which continues today.

Protected area designation, in particular the extension of the Kruger National Park north of the Levhuvhu River in 1969, also heralded a new form of control of local people's movements as well as their exclusion from environmental resources that had been central to their livelihoods (Whande, 2007). Security concerns on the part of apartheid South Africa sealed these control mechanisms, resulting in the outright exclusion of local people from the Madimbo corridor. In short, veterinary, military and conservation actors shaped the reality along and within the Madimbo corridor.

The location of the Madimbo corridor, along an international boundary with Zimbabwe, was strategic for apartheid South Africa's national sovereignty and security, as witnessed by the deployment of soldiers in the area in the late 1960s and early 1970s (Poonan, 1996). What is crucial to note here is the linkages between the military and conservation – the pursuit of their respective and shared interests resulted in displacement and restricting movement of local people. From the 1960s, the then-South African Defence Force (SADF) [2] was deployed to areas along international borders where it acted to prevent illegal immigrants and guer-rilla soldiers from entering South Africa (these areas included two military units in the Kruger National Park assigned to the Mozambique border while the Madimbo unit was for Zimbabwe) (see Mckenzie, 1995). Earlier, during the Anglo-Boer war of 1899–1902, the western section of the corridor at Malala Drift had been a flash point between the Boer-controlled Transvaal region and British-controlled Southern Rhodesia (Burrett, 2002).

Policies do not necessarily provide solutions to everyone's problems; often they exacerbate a certain group's problems but are tailored to provide solutions for another. For local people, the corridor was both a home and source of livelihoods, and they had historically hunted in the area to supplement their diets (Bulpin, 1954). In 1969 the Makuleke clan were moved from the eastern section of the corridor and the Pafuri triangle to their current location at Ntlaveni, 80km to the southwest (Steenkamp, 2001). Various Venda[3] families, under Chiefs Mutele and Tshikundamalema, were moved from the corridor to villages immediately along the edges of the southern boundary of the corridor (Linden, 2004; Whande, 2007). Endani's family was moved, and in the process he lost his headmanship because his royal family was moved into a different jurisdiction. As indicated on the map (see Figure 7.2), he moved to the village of Tshikuyu but some of the people from his area, who were under his leadership, moved to Bennde Mutale village. Some of the villages, such as Madimbo and Gumbu, were moved several times to reflect changing apartheid government concerns. Both the Makuleke and Venda families which moved from the corridor were settled in areas designated according to the apartheid government's policy of Bantustans.[4] The Tsonga Makuleke clan was moved into a Tsonga Bantustan, Gazankulu, while the Venda were moved into the Venda Bantustan.

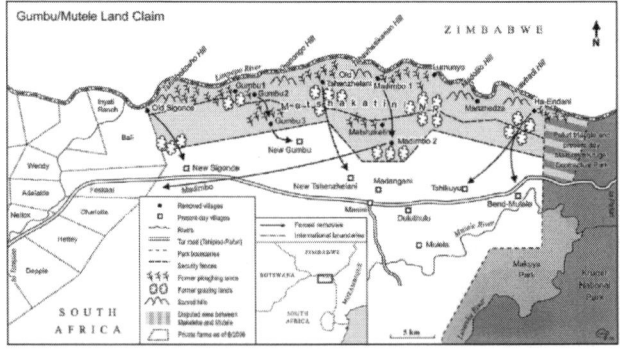

Figure 7.2 *The forced removals from the Madimbo corridor*

The effects of the forced removals were devastating for the communities and include the break-up of families, destruction of houses, settlement in poor agricultural areas, loss of property and of access to natural resources along the Limpopo River (Steenkamp, 2001; Whande, 2007). The legacy of the removals are continuing contestations over who exactly was settled where and has a right to claim which land, as indicated in Figure 7.2, with the area marked disputed between Makuleke and Mutele.[5] The area is also designated as the Matshakatini Nature Reserve because the SADF gazetted a nature reserve in 1992, with the boundaries for the Madimbo corridor and the nature reserve being contiguous.[6] Gazetting military bases into protected areas was not limited to the Madimbo corridor. Mckenzie (1998) notes that the SADF established a nature and environmental conservation unit in the early 1980s, and some military land was managed as conservation land. This general trend within the military to use their training lands for conservation might have motivated the gazetting of the Matshakatini Nature Reserve in 1992, even though it is not clear why this occurred at this stage in the final years of apartheid. A possible reason is that the military was anticipating possible land claims as, by 1995, the newly constituted South African National Defence Force (SANDF) was openly admitting that there were pressures to use military land for other purposes (see Mckenzie, 1995). The effect of this gazettement is that the area has been under multiple state authorities. These include the Department of Public Works, which is the government owner of the land; the SANDF with use rights to the area;[7] and the Limpopo Tourism and Parks Board providing management support to the nature reserve (see Mckenzie, 1998 for comparable situations). However, it should be noted that the Limpopo Tourism and Parks Board never physically established itself in the area in the conventional sense of having game rangers, instead relying on periodic visits from nature conservation officers from Musina Nature Reserve more than 100km away.[8] Given the evolution of transfrontier approaches in the area, it appears that the messy matrix of political and administrative interests will get even more entangled and perhaps more removed from the realm of local communities.[9]

Post-apartheid policy windows for regional cooperation and local resource rights

Understanding the local natural resource governance dynamics along the Madimbo corridor is difficult without first locating them within the regional and national policy context that has emerged since the end of apartheid rule in South Africa. On the one hand, countries in southern Africa hold that there is a central role for local communities in decision-making over land and natural resources, as witnessed by the development of widespread CBNRM initiatives during the last 20 years (see Campbell and Shackleton, 2001) while on the other hand, policies and practices for protected areas retain the centrality of the state in decision-making and implementation (see Metcalfe, 2003). In areas falling along geopolitical boundaries such as the Madimbo corridor, the relationship between the need for community-centred approaches and retention of the state's centrality is often tense, making the fixation of policy windows all the more difficult. In pursuing conservation goals, the balance between the opening of windows of opportunity for local involvement in decision-making and closing those windows in an exclusive fashion is difficult to attain.

Transfrontier conservation approaches and the new South Africa

From their popularization in the mid-1990s, transfrontier conservation approaches were aligned with the demise of apartheid in South Africa in 1994, providing 'images of the continent that emerged after the collapse of the apartheid state in South Africa' that 'were part of a process that sought to shape the future of the continent under entirely new national, regional and global political environment' (Ramutsindela, 2007, p142). Globally, the end of the Cold War opened a policy window for conceptualizations of security other than state militarization (Buzan, 1991). The narrow conceptualization of security in terms of state military intervention was instead encompassed into more nuanced forms of security such as human-concerned, focused on giving voice to the marginalized, and environmental security, which acknowledged the role of degraded environments as sources of conflict. Practically, the conceptual shift in the view of security was through calls to redirect resources spent on militaries to fund natural resource management approaches and development (Steiner, 1993; Cock and Mckenzie, 1998). Transfrontier conservation approaches in southern Africa provide a link between national security concerns, by offering a platform for dialogue and peaceful resolution of conflicts, and concerns for the environment by adopting ecosystem management approaches that transcend fragmented political boundaries (Hanks, 1997). Community-based approaches also offer new interpretations of security in terms of community development needs (Koch, 2004). While the geo-strategic focus on military security and the destabilizing role of South Africa gave way to new forms of regional cooperation, peace and security, this has also led to the strategic expansion of South African economic interests in southern Africa and more broadly on the African continent. In terms of TFCAs, this is playing itself out in terms of tourism revenue, which, in the absence of a clear revenue-sharing structure, is a source of disgruntled voices among South Africa's neighbours (see van Ameron and Büscher, 2005). More broadly, post-Cold War Africa has emerged as a post-apartheid South African export market, with volumes of trade increasing to the advantage of South African exports (Daniel et al, 2003). South Africa dominates in mergers and acquisitions of struggling African companies on the continent in virtually all fields of operations ranging from finance, energy and infrastructure, telecommunications and tourism. South Africa's leadership in the implementation of TFCAs has to be seen within this broad context, particularly in terms of interests in tourism businesses and the role of tourism in TFCAs.

Transboundary approaches to biodiversity conservation and natural resources management are now a prominent feature of inter-state cooperation for managing shared natural resources across political boundaries. The SADC lists 17 regional transfrontier conservation initiatives currently either in the conceptual phase or being implemented.[10] They are supported by the SADC protocol on wildlife, which promotes transfrontier initiatives as inter-state cooperation mechanisms

(SADC, 1999), with the Peace Parks Foundation (PPF) playing the critical role 'to fund and facilitate the development of TFCAs' (Hanks, 1997, pp2–3). South Africa – both in terms of state and non-state actor – has clearly taken leadership of TFCA implementation, nowhere more prominently than in the flagship GLTFCA.

The Great Limpopo Transfrontier Conservation Area

Between Mozambique, South Africa and Zimbabwe, the core Great Limpopo Transfrontier Park (GLTP) covers an estimated 35,000km² incorporating the Kruger National Park and the Makuleke Contractual National Park in South Africa; the recently designated Limpopo National Park in Mozambique; and the Gonarezhou National Park, Manjinji Pan Sanctuary and Malipati Safari Area in Zimbabwe. The overall GLTFCA, encompassing the GLTP, covers an estimated 100,000km², and additionally incorporates Zinave and Banhine National Parks, Massingir and Corumana areas in Mozambique as well as privately and state-owned conservation areas in South Africa and Zimbabwe. The rest of the GLTFCA is made of communal areas in Mozambique and Zimbabwe. The negotiation process for the establishment of the GLTP started in the 1990s, culminating in the signing of a memorandum of understanding (MoU) in 2000, followed by the formal tri-state treaty of 2002 (PPF, 2008).

The signing of the MoU led to the constitution of a Joint Management Board (JMB) for the area, supported in its work by thematic management committees, which were conservation (later changed to conservation and veterinary); safety and security; finance, human resources and legislation; and tourism. In 2004, the management committees were composed of 35 people with a mixed background including veterinary officers, national parks officials, customs officials, the police and one NGO official – the Director of the PPF – but not any community representatives or NGOs concerned with community development or land rights issues. The functions of the management committees are to implement action plans as approved by the JMB. The JMB itself had 12 members responsible for policy interpretation, approving action plans and monitoring implementation, and supporting a three-member Ministerial Committee responsible for overall policy guidance.

The absence of local community representatives in the official structures for the GLTP and GLTFCA underscores the contention that TFCAs exclude the very same beneficiaries to whom they claim to be bringing development. This raises the question of the place of the land restitution process in restoring local land rights and affording landowners the opportunity to determine land uses in the TFCA.

Post-apartheid policy windows for local communities

The major policy problem South Africa inherited from the colonial and apartheid systems is the gross inequalities that characterize the country's social and economic life. This is nowhere more evident than in relation to access to land and natural resources. In a post-apartheid South Africa, the need to redress these inequalities through community-centred approaches is seen in policies and legislation stipulating the restitution of land rights. South Africa has instituted a number of land and natural resource governance reforms aimed at redressing historical and racially motivated land dispossessions. These reforms are especially significant following decades of racial segregation and disenfranchisement of black populations, which after the Natives Land Acts of 1913 and 1936 were eventually restricted to only 13 per cent of land in South Africa, despite constituting the vast majority of the country's population. Additional reforms were aimed at improving local governance after years of abuse by Tribal Authorities, institutionalized by the 1951 Tribal Authorities Act, and which acted as 'decentralized despots' answerable to the colonial and apartheid regimes (Ntsebeza, 2005; see also Murombedzi, this volume). The 1994 Land Restitution Act aims to ensure that communities dispossessed of land since 1913 as a result of racially discriminatory laws receive equitable redress, either in terms of the actual lands they lost or alternative redress. The process is handled through a land claims court and commission established under the 1994 legislation. Other components of the land reform process include land redistribution to the landless and addressing security of tenure for millions of residents.

In relation to protected areas, the redress of historical injustices has thus far been approached through co-management of Contractual National Parks (CNP), which involves formation of legal entities in the form of Communal Property Associations (CPAs) as provided for in the Communal Property Association Act of 1996. That Act enables groups to collectively acquire, hold and manage land under a locally defined and constituted association (Magome and Murombedzi, 2003; Reid et al, 2004; Cousins and Kepe, 2005; Grossman and Holden, 2008).

Co-management is now 'the most popular approach for reconciling land claims and biodiversity conservation in South Africa and beyond' (Kepe, 2008, p311), yet those two societal goals are still characterized by conflict (Kepe et al, 2005). Contractual parks are instituted on land either belonging to the state or groups of people and managed as a national park under joint management agreements between SANParks and the group of people or landowners. CPAs have represented local communities in co-management arrangements involving claimed lands.

The Makuleke/Kruger CNP, adjacent to the Madimbo corridor and a constituent of the GLTP, is frequently portrayed as a South African success story and 'one of the most advanced programmes of community involvement in conservation and wildlife anywhere in the world' (Steenkamp and Uhr, 2000, p2). Robbins and van der Waal (2008, p54) note that this might be because the restitution discourses in South Africa emphasize 'reconciliation, nation building and economic development rather than retributive justice'. The Makuleke community, through its CPA, was from the beginning 'prepared to maintain the conservation status of the land as an integral part of the Kruger National Park' (Steenkamp and Uhr, 2000, p7). Yet it is also possible that conditions set by SANParks influenced the course and nature of the agreement. The option of retaining land uses for conservation is also impacted by the arrangements and agreements between the Ministry of Land Affairs, on the one hand, and the Ministry of Environment and Tourism, on the other hand (Kepe, 2008). Even though the agreement between the two ministries was officially signed in 2008, in practice the negotiations from SANParks were always aimed for a mutual gains outcome at worst. The Mkambati land claim case in the Eastern Cape provides an example of this reluctance on the part of the state to transfer land and allow the new owners freedom of deciding on land uses. In Mkambati, Kepe et al (2005) highlight a constellation of state interests pushing for retaining the area as a protected area as well as for economic development through a Spatial Development Initiative (SDI) that could benefit the land claimants and thereby quell some of the local grievances. Like the GLTP, the grand plan also included expansion of the original protected area's boundaries into Pondoland National Park. A more comparable example, by virtue of location along an international boundary, is the claim by both Khomani San and Mier Transitional Local Council for part of the Kalahari Gemsbok National Park, which has since been included in the Kgalagadi Transfrontier Park with the claimant communities receiving land both within and outside the park. They are, however, 'excluded from management of the transfrontier park since their portion of the park, it is argued, lies geographically outside of the crossborder resource management area' (Kepe et al, 2005, p12). What is important to note, however, is the retention of the land for conservation purposes, assuaging the key interest of SANParks (or the provincial conservation authorities as appropriate) and the 'substitution' of direct use of natural resources with indirect alternative forms of economic development.

Also relevant are recent developments in relation to land claimed within protected areas, which indicate continuing tensions between the need to balance land rights and national objectives of biodiversity conservation. Indications are that SANParks is reluctant to repeat co-management arrangements similar to those in the Makuleke case, especially where land within the Kruger National Park is concerned. In December 2008, the South African Cabinet under former caretaker President Kgalema Motlanthe (who now serves as the Deputy President) approved a plan to settle all land claims within the Kruger National Park through equitable redress as opposed to actual restoration of the rights to land under claim. Whereas restoration of land within the Kruger National Park would have meant similar co-management arrangements between local communities and SANParks, the latest decision means protected area management remains solely the preserve of SANParks. Yet, according to the cabinet, the decision is meant to 'balance rights of claimant communities and the interests of society as a whole' (GCIS, 2009). The rationale for this move reveals the tensions within the post-apartheid government in trying to restore land rights in protected areas and meeting goals of transnational conservation, which converges with the national tourism interests as well as protected areas' managerial preferences for retaining strong centralist and bureaucratic approaches. Under the new President Jacob Zuma, this issue is now being debated in Parliament, with the Land Claims Commission indicating the required 20 billon Rand required to settle these claims is not available and the new Minister responsible for land reform stating that 'it is an issue that needs to be resolved' (Groenewald, 2009).

These developments clearly put paid to the idea that CNPs are a win–win solution for the restoration of land rights and achievement of biodiversity conservation objectives. Previously, land transfers to claimant communities were accompanied with a parallel negotiation for keeping the land as part of national parks through co-management agreements (see Kepe, 2008). It is not yet clear what implications the recent Cabinet notification and ongoing debates within the government will have on the balance between conservation and development initiatives on claimed land that is part of the national parks estate. At the same time, it appears land neighbouring the Kruger National Park is subjected to the same conservation status as core protected areas, with the land restitution claim for the Madimbo corridor having dragged on for years on the basis that it is strategic in relation to transfrontier conservation objectives and national security and sovereignty concerns.

Contesting windows of exclusion: Land rights along the Madimbo corridor

The dynamics along the Madimbo corridor suggest that where policy windows are competing, different interests can appeal to those aspects of policy solutions that advance their cause. The Madimbo corridor is located along the southern banks of the Limpopo River and is about 45km in length and 3–6km wide, adjoining the Makuleke/Kruger CNP which lies to the east. Both the Madimbo corridor and Makuleke/Kruger CNP are of considerable strategic importance to non-local actors, principally the Ministry of Defence, Ministry of Agriculture (veterinary), Ministry of Environment and Tourism, as well as various conservation NGOs. The strategic security importance of the area is evidenced by the long-standing and recurrent presence of fugitives from law at the so-called Crooks Corner.[11] The Makuleke and Madimbo land claims differ in that the Makuleke land has been returned to local communities while the Madimbo corridor is still under negotiation.

Following the Land Restitution Act of 1994, local people along the Madimbo corridor who had been forcibly moved from the corridor claimed the area in 1998. Initially the claim was divided into two, one led by the Gumbu people (from a village by that name, see Figure 7.2) and the other by the Mutele people.[12] However, it was recommended by the Limpopo Regional Land Claims Commission (2004) that it would be better if the two combined, which they subsequently did by forming a joint Gumbu-Mutele CPA, later renamed Vhembe CPA after the local reference to the Limpopo River. The Vhembe CPA was constituted by leaders from both the Gumbu and Mutele areas (past tense as this leadership is currently being disbanded, as apparently it was not properly registered).

Despite the fact that presently different state actors are saying the Vhembe CPA was not properly registered, the Limpopo Regional Land Claims Commission recommended that the Madimbo corridor be transferred to the claimants in August 2004, which paved the way for negotiations on land uses and the actual management and ownership of the land. The transfer of the land held promises of opening up a variety of livelihood-related windows for local residents – irrigated agriculture, possible mining following on diamond prospecting in the mid-1990s, accessing grazing pastures and restoring old settlements along the banks of the Limpopo River. However, from 2004 to date the community has been engaged in protracted negotiations over land uses within the corridor, with, at first, the SANDF taking the lead in claiming that it had to remain in the area for national security purposes as well as conducive training conditions.[13] As it turns out, the transfer of the land was conditional on the SANDF retaining a part of the land for training purposes, the quantity and specific location of which became subject to negotiations. In a meeting in April 2006, the SANDF indicated that they 'needed' half the entire area of claimed land, a demand that did not sit well with the local claimants. Additionally, not only did they want half the land, but this was also seen locally as the most productive land in the eastern side of the corridor, and also strategically located next to the Makuleke/Kruger CNP.

Besides the SANDF, the Vhembe CPA also had to contend with conservation officials as the area had been designated a nature reserve in 1992. What had appeared to be an opening of windows in the post-apartheid reform era soon became as uncertain as it had been in the past.

The ambiguity created by the overlapping interests of multiple state actors has been an effective means to delay the negotiation process and finalization of local land use planning. Essentially there are different layers of negotiation for the restoration of land rights for the Madimbo corridor. The first is between the local community and the different state units with an interest in the Madimbo corridor. The second layer is among the state units themselves and the third is between the state and NGOs such as PPF. The intricacies of this negotiation can be illustrated in the example of the de-proclamation request by the Vhembe CPA.

In April 2006, the Vhembe CPA requested that the Matshakatini Nature Reserve be de-proclaimed and local residents formally allowed to make land use decisions, gain direct access to the corridor for resource use and the rebuilding of settlements.[14] This has not happened even though the SANDF suddenly left the area in early 2009. The departure of the SANDF has not changed anything for local people, however, as the Limpopo Tourism and Parks Board has insisted that the de-proclamation can only be requested by those who set the nature reserve up in the first place (the SANDF) (see Whande 2007).

While negotiations over de-proclamation of the reserve between the CPA and the state are ongoing, locally there are also other manifestations of competition and conflict over authority, a situation that can only weaken the community in its resolve to restore access to land and resources within the Madimbo corridor. The possibility of having a nature reserve divided local people, with the CPA leadership generally in favour of grazing, mining and human settlements in the area while chief Mutele and some of the village headmen along the Madimbo corridor are in favour of conservation-driven tourism. These dynamics mirror broader contestations within the GLTFCA that involve, on the one hand, conservation and tourism interests, and on the other hand land rights and development interests.

Perpetuating local exclusion: The South Africa National Defence Force and the Limpopo Tourism and Parks Board

It has been more than five years since the transfer of the Madimbo corridor to the local claimants was formally approved in 2004. Part of this delay is because the agreement contained a condition that the SANDF should continue using part of the land for training purposes and part is due to the fact that the area is also a nature reserve. It is not clear what is going to happen now since the SANDF quickly packed up and left the corridor in March/April 2009, and were imme-diately replaced by a 'special' policing unit. According to the police, their task is border patrols. This is understandable, as the area is regarded as a major migrant route for Zimbabweans coming to South Africa (Hennop, 2001).

The SANDF noted the unique conditions for military training along the Madimbo corridor (it still retains a small number of troops for 'special' training even after the SANDF moved out of the area). The argument to stay was made in relation to South Africa's peacekeeping obligations and operations on the African continent, with the SANDF officials arguing that the climatic conditions, terrain and vegetation were similar to environmental conditions they encounter on peace-keeping missions in other African countries.[15] The SANDF also argued that they needed half of the corridor for military training purposes, owing to the medium-range missiles they trained with.

However, it is unlikely that the military wanted to stay in the area solely because of similar climatic conditions to the ones encountered on peacekeeping opera-tions. A more plausible reason for the continued presence of the military is directly linked to delaying the finalization of the land claim pursuant to alternative border control arrangements being made. Issues of security, specifically to controlling the influx of Zimbabwean economic refugees (see Hofstater, 2005) are important,[16] even though the discourse surrounding TFCAs suggests otherwise.

While acknowledging wide-ranging changes in international relations in the post-Cold War and post-apartheid era, the South African government still regards certain inter-state activities and conditions as a threat to the South African state. In particular, such threats include underdevelopment, illiteracy and unemployment in neighbouring states, which can result in a flood of refugees which is seen as a threat to South Africa (Government of South Africa, 1995). Until recently, when the soldiers left the Madimbo corridor, criminal activities within the corridor were controlled by the military and not the police.[17] The SANDF apprehended illegal immigrants and smugglers (of gold, cigarettes and meat products) and handed them over to the police.

Hennop (2001) notes the SANDF has a 'filter system' for border controls, with the first filter concerned with deployment of soldiers along the actual border line to raise the alarm concerning illegal immigrants, in this case the Limpopo River. The first ten kilometres forms the second filter while the third filter is 30km from the second, and these two zones are patrolled as immigrants start moving towards major roads, catching taxis and buses. It is therefore more likely that the desire for continued presence along the Madimbo corridor was motivated by concerns focused on illegal immigrants rather than training conditions, and as soon as the police unit was ready to take over operations along the first filter, the SANDF left.

Local residents dismissed the state's rationales for security, arguing that they were the ones suffering the most from the presence of the SANDF. They particu-larly pointed out that the presence of the military and the position of the fence on the South African side meant natural resources within the corridor were available to Zimbabweans and not to them as the new owners of the land. In his presenta-tion about the de-proclamation of the Matshakatini Nature Reserve, the chair-person of the Vhembe CPA argued that livestock from Zimbabwe grazed within the corridor and that local South African residents should also be allowed to access the pastures. In challenging their continued exclusion from the corridor, local residents also alleged that the SANDF was involved in hunting wildlife in the area, an allegation officials from the Limpopo Tourism and Parks Board indicated was widespread wherever nature reserves had been planned on land occupied by the SANDF (see Whande, 2007). According to local people, the continued presence of the SANDF had little to do with national security but rather was intended to keep local people out of the corridor to ease access for pursuing personal hunting interests. The pursuit of national security interests was viewed locally as benefiting individual senior military officials at the expense of local livelihood security and access rights to the corridor.[18]

At the same time, it appears the CPA has often been consumed in conflicts with the Chief and failed to realize certain opportunities to get state actors on their side, even as such opportunities may have meant the continued involvement of the state in the affairs of the Madimbo corridor. In 2007, the Limpopo Tourism and Parks Board proposed using the Madimbo corridor as a hunting concession.[19] While this was suggested as a temporary measure, the CPA refused to apply for a concession, arguing that this would further delay their land claim, while by contrast Chief Mutele supported the proposal. The CPA rejected the proposal, essentially arguing that if the Chief supports it, then it is bad. Leaders of the CPA also argued that the Limpopo Tourism and Parks Board was scripting its own involvement in the future management of the Madimbo corridor, a misread of the situation as the Limpopo Tourism and Parks Board was already involved by virtue of the area having been designated a nature reserve. The CPA leadership was perhaps motivated by the fact that the majority of the Vhembe CPA leadership own cattle – the potential to gain access to grazing pastures might have motivated them to take leadership positions in the land claim – and a hunting concession will potentially be in conflict with their own livelihood interests. It is perhaps imperative to note here that there is diversity of opinions on how to use the Madimbo corridor, as in any group setting with divergent and convergent interests. But more importantly, the CPA's rejection of the hunting concession mirrors a common sentiment among local residents, namely their preference for a redistributive rather than a 'win–win' outcome to the land claim process.

One way for the local residents to gain total control over the Madimbo corridor is through getting the different state actors out of the area and affairs of the corridor. Instead of agreeing to the concession as proposed by the Limpopo Tourism and Parks Board, the CPA pushed to have the area de-proclaimed as a nature reserve, which essentially would have stripped the parks board of any decision-making authority over the corridor. In requesting de-proclamation, the CPA framed its argument in terms of local livelihoods, often pointing out that conservation in the past had contributed little or nothing to their livelihoods. Residents of Bennde Mutale village, who live directly next to the Makuleke Kruger Contractual Park and the Makuya CNP, pointed out that they 'were promised jobs at the beginning' but 'we were surprised that the fences were put up to keep us outside'.[20] The refusal to consider tourism as a livelihood was based on mistrust of conservation officials as people noted that, 'Park people promised us long-term jobs, but, immediately after the fence was done they fired us.'[21] Some of the residents in Bennde

Mutale pointed out that natural resources, such as ilala palms, which they use for making palm wine and sustaining a living, had been fenced inside the parks. They argued that the tourism jobs that had been planned were not forthcoming, and their livelihood situation had deteriorated as a result. This is despite the fact that when parks were established in the area, people worked to put fences up and build houses for game rangers, a situation one of the residents reflects on:

> *When the park was started, some local people were employed there. But the park was the beginning of restrictions for our cattle to graze there. We could not argue against the park, as some people now had jobs.*[22]

The CPA also argued that de-proclamation would allow them to access grazing pastures currently fenced off in the corridor. Applying for a concession, they argued, will just result in the closure of any other livelihood activities. From their arguments, it is clear that obtaining a more direct link between livelihoods and conservation than that proposed by state officials is perceived by locals as their window of opportunity in the land claim process's reformative undertaking.

But the de-proclamation request has taken a long time to resolve since it was officially requested in 2006 and indications are that this is not going to be fully agreed to. In other words, the window of opportunity for direct use of land and natural resources within the Madimbo corridor appears unlikely to be opened, a reality the CPA acknowledges. Recently the government departments assigned to negotiate land uses with the CPA hired an 'independent' consultant[23] to, according to the CPA, put in place a CPA that will agree to tourism as a source of livelihoods. This is possible as the Regional Land Claims Commission, despite having approved the transfer of land in 2004, now says the Vhembe CPA as currently constituted is illegal. The implications of this, of course, is that the CPA as currently constituted cannot proceed with land use planning even if the area is de-proclaimed as a nature reserve. A further hindrance is that officials from the Parks and Tourism Board indicated de-proclamation of the Matshakatini Nature Reserve can only be requested by the SANDF, as they are the ones who established the reserve in the first place.[24] With growing external interest in the land for TFCA conservation purposes, it is unlikely that there is going to be a resolution that responds to the needs and aspirations of the CPA leadership.

Closing windows are forever: Strategies to keep local people out of the Madimbo corridor

While South Africa's post-apartheid national policy changes emphasize co-management and the involvement and rights of local communities, the implementation of the GLTFCA appears to prioritize centralized conservation, tourism investment and security interests. The way this is playing out in the GLTFCA is through the exclusion of local communities from a meaningful contribution towards the evolution of the initiative, both in terms of shaping policy and practical implementation. The role of the Peace Parks Foundation in facilitating the implementation of the GLTP and the GLTFCA is important in understanding these perceptions.

Different groups of stakeholders are differently engaged by the PPF. For instance, Heads of State are invited to be patrons of the PPF, while at an operational level technical experts' salaries are met by the foundation. The PPF to date has not focused on getting local communities involved in the implementation of the GLTP and the GLTFCA; to the contrary, it is actively pushing for the alienation of local communities. Spierenburg and Wels (2006) use the examples of mapping to show how the operations of the PPF are essentially disenfranchising local communities. Mapping is one of the tools deployed by the PPF 'to create ecological and social information systems for the various TFCAs under development' (PPF, 2004). Duffy (2006) notes the use of similar maps by the African Wildlife Foundation in the GLTFCA, which are also not reflective of local realities and livelihood interests.

The maps that PPF produces fulfil a number of objectives. Firstly, they are thematic in that they are used for showing conservation areas within the GLTFCA. They do not indicate, however, the contesting local land use types, such as livestock and crop agriculture, in these areas. Secondly, they are cadastral maps; they denote property boundaries between state land (in this case land allocated for conservation purposes) and other forms of land tenure, specifically communal land. Related to the cadastral maps are the political and administrative aspects, especially where boundaries of municipalities, wards and chiefly territories coincide and overlap. What is significant about the maps, however, is not so much what they show, but what they do not show. In clearly marking the property boundaries, the maps do not show how some of these boundaries are contested and constantly negotiated by local demands for land and natural resources based on historical claims. As a result, the maps are deployed in a way that gives prominence to certain land uses in the GLTFCA while remaining silent on competing and conflicting land use, in particular those that might be preferable for local communities and would create meaningful entry points for local participation.

The main strategy to involve local communities in the constituent communal areas is through tourism development. Tourism is also a major driving force behind the whole initiative even as it is highly susceptible to political disturbances (see Ferreira, 2004). The magical attraction of tourism, similar to the magic of maps that visually simplify highly complex situations, is in the numbers. The PPF (2008) forecasts 61,000 potential jobs in Limpopo National Park (equivalent to more than a third of Mozambique's entire civil service of 167,420 people) as a result of sharing the 1.3 million tourists who visit the Kruger National Park, but this estimate does not actually provide the numbers of people already working in the Kruger National Park. With the estimated population of communal area residents within the GLTFCA at about 500,000, such high employment numbers, if attainable and depending on the nature of the work and remuneration, will have a major impact on livelihoods. These statistics, however, do not indicate anything about the nature of state–local engagement, whether this involves adopting new forms of governance from the ground up or a continuation of the imposition of blueprints from above.

It is clear, however, referring back to Salafsky and Wollenberg's (2000) conceptualization of the linkages between conservation and livelihoods, that the GLTFCA approach is premised on substituting complex local livelihoods with indirect links to conservation and tourism. The implications of the numbers game therefore can be assessed in governance terms, whether local communities have any authority to influence the nature of the linkages between conservation of globally significant biodiversity and their own livelihoods or they are perpetually grateful for jobs which they have limited control over and which can be diverted elsewhere on the slightest indication of political instability. Current tourism planning processes do not do much to suggest that equity and inclusiveness is one of the main priorities. In South Africa and Zimbabwe, the PPF (2008) progress report notes:

> ...the Pafuri Integrated Land-use and Tourism Plan was drafted in order to inte-grate tourism development and conservation in the Pafuri Region. This region includes the northern section of the Limpopo and Kruger National parks, the Makuleke region, areas in South Africa's Limpopo Province that lie to the west of the Kruger National Park and the Makuleke region, and the Sengwe and Tshipise communal areas in Zimbabwe.

> (my own emphasis)

Despite the contested nature of the land restitution along the Madimbo corridor, the PPF report of 2008 as well as some of the maps produced by PPF and Landscape Architects (2006) already portray the area as a link to yet another TFCA to the northwest of South Africa, the Greater Mapungubwe TFCA, and as such already earmarked for tourism development. The point here is not so much that the area is included in the tourism plans but rather that the process of identifying such areas continues the top-down virtual mapping of colonial times, rather than a consultation with the local communities that effectively stand to lose or gain the most.

Local communities are further excluded from the implementation of the GLTFCA on national sovereignty issues. In part this is contributing to the lack of an organic evolution of local transboundary institutions in the management of natural resources. For instance, communities along the Madimbo corridor in South Africa experience high levels of cattle thefts while those in Zimbabwe experience goat theft.[25] It is suspected the livestock is driven across boundaries, yet state controls of human movement continue to hinder meaningful collab-oration in tracking the livestock and putting in place collaborative monitoring arrangements. Interviews with both the military and police force indicate they are unaware (at the local operational level) of the implementation of the GLTFCA and act more as a hindrance to any potential local collaborations than as facilita-tors. The recently constituted Livestock Committee,[26] with a mandate to establish links with Zimbabwean livestock owners, still faces difficulties in moving across national borders.

While local communities present an option in crossborder facilitation of commu-nity-based approaches and balancing the objectives of biodiversity conservation and local development, the governance structures evolving within the GLTFCA, such as the management committees and the Joint Management Board, are slowly resulting in the marginalization of communities in both decision-making and the actual management of land and natural resources. As a result, the focus has shifted drastically to issues of state-led conservation, which quickly is becoming the one-size-fits-all for economic opportunities, local communities' needs and biodiversity conservation. Conservation here is synonymous with exclusive state protected areas, resulting in the designation of a national park on the Mozambique side for 'offloading' elephant populations from the Kruger National Park, although management of elephant populations is not the stated rationale for the Limpopo National Park. As well as an exclusive emphasis on state protected areas as the form of 'conservation' to be pursued, there is also a reluctance to recognize other forms of land use even in areas meant for 'multiple land uses'. As a result, 'conservation', while on paper including the idea of benefits to local communities and development through tourism, is increasingly portrayed as the only measure that will promote regional integration in the context of TFCAs. The focus on conservation indicates a lack of integrated planning and little understanding of the complex land use approaches in the area, and is trending towards putting in place windows for the outright exclusion of local people.

Conclusion

Negotiations over land use and tenure in the Madimbo corridor juxtapose efforts to restore local land and resource rights against national and global interests in transboundary conservation and South African maintenance of national sovereignty and security. Both provide policy windows for dealing with pressing societal problems of inequality and dispossession in the case of land and resource rights and conserving globally significant biodiversity in the case of transfrontier conservation. The policy and legislative reforms of the post-apartheid era, particularly in relation to land restitution and co-management of contractual national parks, provide a window of opportunity to redress historical injustices. However, as this case shows, there continue to be formidable challenges to implementation and powerful forces that keep such windows shut and locals excluded.

The case discussed here suggests that while policy windows are in a continuous state of flux, the interaction of various actors impacts on the outcome of what is actually implemented. This can be seen in the reluctance among national-level actors within the GLTFCA to move from conservation-driven tourism as the only sustainable land use to truly embracing multiple uses of natural resources and exploring more ways of linking conservation and livelihoods in localities such as the Madimbo corridor.

From this case and other examples in South Africa, it appears co-management is increasingly restricting itself towards promoting indirect linkages (through tourism) between livelihoods and conservation, to the exclusion of other livelihood strategies that rely on more direct uses of natural resources. The implications of this in relation to ongoing negotiations over lands and resources is that the state is often relatively intractable when it comes to conservation and that the position of the state is necessarily one oriented towards mutual gains not distributive outcomes (Fay, 2007). In other words, pursuit of retributive justice and a redistributive outcome is counter to current bureaucratic perceptions of nation-building (see Robbins and van der Waal, 2008; Rihoy and Maguranyanga, this volume on the Botswana discourse). The result is that in cases where external interests are high, such as along the Madimbo corridor, in relation to biodiversity conservation, national security and sovereignty, the window of opportunity for restoring local land rights has been turned into a window for continued exclusion.

While the diverse set of actors often acknowledge local communities in their programmes of work, the dynamics along the Madimbo corridor call into question the actual relevance of such references. Additionally, the recent decision by the South African Cabinet not to restore land rights in relation to land claims in the Kruger National Park and the pursuit of co-management even when diverging views exist locally (see Kepe, 2008) raise questions about the perceptions of political leaders with regards to the co-management of CNPs. Local communities, as well as being physically excluded from certain environments deemed important for biodiversity conservation at national and global scales, are also excluded from direct involvement in policy-making processes. However, as lessons from a century of contested implementation of protected areas show, it is unlikely that forced decisions are going to be sustainable in the long run. While the local Madimbo residents have adhered to the legal process as provided in the Restitution Act, they have also previously resorted to illegal hunting within the corridor and at times even within the Makuleke Contractual National Park. Such forms of resistance are likely to be repeated in a context where decisions are enforced from outside, and they highlight local agency against what are perceived as injustices.

An important dimension of the Madimbo corridor is that local communities have not accepted their exclusion from land and natural resource governance. Rather, communities have actively used the provisions of the post-apartheid laws and policies to contest exclusion. This local agency is seen both in using the legislative changes from 1994 to claim lands, but also in pushing for the de-proclamation of the Matshakatini Nature Reserve. The stories told by Endani, Gakato and Maphukumele (as well as countless others who lived and experienced forced removals) are further testimony to local agency. Yet the relationships between local people and other actors can be summed up by referring to maps. While the locally produced map shows details of local people's settlements within the corridor, state and NGO TFCA maps produce a blanket of tourism and wildlife conservation.

Acknowledgements

I thank Bram Büscher, Patience Mutopo and Michael Schoon for comments on a draft version of this paper. The data presented here was part of the multidisciplinary collaborative research project ACACIA (Arid Climate, Adaptation and Cultural Innovation in Africa) at the University of Cologne, funded by the German Research Foundation.

Notes

1   See: http://www.boundlesssa.com/en/
2   Changed to South African National Defence Force (SANDF) at the end of apartheid in 1994 and to reflect the inclusion of Bantustans in the whole of South Africa.

3 The Venda people are located in northern South Africa and south to southwestern Zimbabwe. Linguistically, TshiVenda is related to Shona spoken predominantly in Zimbabwe and Sotho. They also share architectural designs with the Shona as seen in the cities built of stone such as Mapungubwe, Dzata and Great Zimbabwe (see Stayt, 1931).

4 The apartheid government argued that black South Africans were not a homogeneous group and that they could seek self-governance on the basis of culture and language (Bennett, 1996). In reality, however, Bantustans were meant to confine black South Africans to less than adequate land (13 per cent of the entire country) and to control their movement between the Bantustans and commercial and industrial South Africa.

5 A first meeting in 15 years, facilitated by the NGO ResourceAfrica's Community Theatre Outreach, was recently held between the Makuleke and Mutele (Bennde Mutale) people to resolve their differences and explore working together, mostly on tourism-related issues.

6 Administrator's Notice 4 (Provincial Gazette 4799, 1 January 1992).

7 The SANDF left the area in March/April 2009 and it is not clear at the moment what their interest in the area is.

8 Interview with SANDF officers, Polokwane, May 2006.

9 The Limpopo Tourism and Parks Board itself is faced with considerable uncertainty as it is generally left out of the TFCA planning processes.

10 See: www.sadc.int/fanr/naturalresources/transfrontier/.

11 The Crooks Corner is located within the neighbouring Makuleke/Kruger Contractual National Park and is the confluence of the Limpopo and Pafuri Rivers. It draws its name from the fact that in the past fugitives from law escaping from the developing towns and big game hunters came here from where they ran their hunting operations and acted as middlemen for Africans coming en route to seek jobs on diamond and gold mines (see Bulpin, 1954).

12 It is pertinent to note here that Gumbu is a village and as such is constituent to a bigger traditional area under Chief Tshikundamalema. The Mutele, on the other hand, is a collection of villages under Chief Mutele.

13 SANDF presentation at Madimbo base, April 2006.

14 Presentation by Nelson Masikhwa, the former chairperson of the Vhembe CPA at a meeting with various state agencies, April 2006.

15 SANDF presentation, April 2006.

16 Interview, Jack Greefe, Pafuri Gate, March 2006.

17 Interview, Thohoyandou, March 2006.

18 Interviews members of the Vhembe CPA, April 2006; Junior Soldiers at Madimbo corridor, June 2007.

19 Interview, Polokwane October 2007.

20 Focus Group Discussion, Bennde Mutale Village, April 2006.

21 Interview, Bennde Mutale Village, March 2007.

22 Interview, Bennde Mutale Village, October 2005.

23 Some members of the Vhembe CPA pointed out to me in May 2009 that the consultant is not independent as he has been promised an environmental impact assessment job within the corridor if plans for the bridge along the Limpopo River are approved. They alleged he had been hired to 'get rid of them' and put in place people who support Chief Mutele on using the land for conservation purposes (Interview, May 2009).

24 Interview, Polokwane, October 2007.

25 Interviews with local veterinary officials, May 2009.

26 This was formed by local cattle owners in May 2009 to coordinate tracking of stolen cattle.

References

Apthorpe, R. (1996) 'Reading development and policy analysis: On framing, naming, numbering and coding', in R. Apthorpe and D. Gasper (eds) *Arguing Development Policy: Frames and Discourses*, Frank Cass, London

Bennett, T.W. (1996) 'African land: A history of dispossession', in R. Zimmermann and D.P. Visser (eds) *Southern Cross: Civil Law and Common Law in South Africa*, Oxford University Press, Oxford

Berkes, F. (2007) 'Community-based conservation in a globalized world', *Proceedings of the National Academy of Science of the United States of America*, vol 104, no 39, pp15188–15193

Büscher, B. and Dietz, T. (2005) 'Conjunctions of governance: The state and the conservation-development nexus in Southern Africa', *The Journal of Transdisciplinary Environmental Studies*, vol 4, no 2, pp1–15

Bulpin, T.V. (1954) *The Ivory Trail*, Howard B. Timmins, Cape Town, South Africa

Burrett, R. (2002) 'The Anglo-Boer War, 1899–1902: The far northwestern front events in the Tuli area', *Military History Journal*, vol 12, no 3, http://samilitaryhistory.org/vol123rb.html Accessed 25 June 2009

Buzan, B. (1991) 'New patterns of global security in the twenty-first century', *International Affairs*, vol 67, no 3, pp431–451

Campbell, B. and Shackleton, S. (2001) 'The organizational structures for community-based natural resources management in Southern Africa', *African Studies Quarterly*, vol 5, no 3, (online) http://web.africa.ufl.edu/asq/v5/v5i3a6 Accessed 10 July 2009

Chambers, R. and Conway, D. (1992) *Sustainable Rural Livelihoods: Practical Concepts for the 21st Century*, IDS Discussion Paper No 296, Institute for Development Studies, Brighton

Cock, J. and Mckenzie, J. (1998) *From Defence to Development: Redirecting Military Resources in South Africa*, David Philip, Cape Town, South Africa

Cousins, B. and Kepe, T. (2005) 'Decentralisation when land and resource rights are deeply contested: A case study of the Mkambati Eco-Tourism Project on the Wild Coast of South Africa', in J.C. Ribot and A.M. Larson (eds) *Democratic Decentralisation through a Natural Resource Lens*, Routledge, London

Daniel, J., Naidoo, V. and Naidu, S. (2003) 'The South Africans have arrived: Post-apartheid corporate expansion into Africa', in J. Daniel, A. Habib, and R. Southall (eds) *State of the Nation: South Africa 2003–2004*, Human Sciences Research Council, Cape Town, South Africa

Duffy, R. (2006) 'The potential and pitfalls of global environmental governance: The politics of transfrontier conservation areas in Southern Africa', *Political Geography*, vol 25, pp89–112

Dzingirai, V. (2004) *Disenfranchisement at Large: Transfrontier Zones, Conservation and Livelihoods*, IUCN Regional Office for Southern Africa, Harare, Zimbabwe

Fay, D. (2007) 'Mutual gains and distributive ideologies in South Africa: Theorizing negotiations between communities and protected areas', *Human Ecology*, vol 35, no 1, pp81–95

Fearnhead, P. (2008) 'Privately managed protected areas', in H. Suich, B. Child, and A. Spenceley (eds) *Evolution and Innovation in Wildlife Conservation: Parks and Game Ranches to Transfrontier Conservation Areas*, Earthscan, London

Ferreira, S. (2004) 'Problems associated with tourism development in Southern Africa: The case of Transfrontier Conservation Areas', *GeoJournal*, vol 60, no 3, pp301–310

GCIS (Government Communication and Information System) (2009) 'State announces decision on Kruger National Park land claims', 28 January 2009 www.deat.gov.za//NewsMedia/MedStat/2009Jan29/MEDIASTATEMENT28012009.pdf Accessed 10 September 2009

Government of South Africa (1995) Act No. BB of 1995: South African Citizenship Act, Cape Town

Groenewald, Y. (2009) 'Kruger headache returns', *Mail and Guardian Online*, 21 July 2009 www.mg.co.za/article/2009-07-21-kruger-headache-returns Accessed 21 July 2009

Grossman, D. and Holden, P. (2008) 'Towards transformation: Contractual National Parks in South Africa', in H. Suich, B. Child, and A. Spenceley (eds) *Evolution and Innovation in Wildlife Conservation: Parks and Game Ranches to Transfrontier Conservation Areas*, Earthscan, London

Hanks, J. (1997) *Protected Areas During and After Conflict: The Objectives of and Activities of the Peace Parks Foundation*, Paper presented at the Parks for Peace Conference, 16–18 September, Somerset West, South Africa

Hennop, E. (2001) *SANDF Control of the Northern and Eastern Border Areas of South Africa*, ISS Occasional Paper No 52, Institute for Security Studies, Pretoria, South Africa

Hofstater, S. (2005) 'Kruger's crack rangers fight fire with fire', *Farmers Weekly*, 9 September 2005

Hughes, D.M. (2003) *Going Transboundary: Scale-Making and Exclusion in Southern-African Conservation*, Paper presented at the Transboundary Protected Areas Research Initiative Teleconference Seminar, Johannesburg, South Africa, 1 October 2003

Jones, B. and Chonguiça, E. (2001) *Review and Analysis of Specific Transboundary Natural Resources Management Initiatives in the Southern Africa Region*, IUCN ROSA Transboundary Natural Resources Management Series Paper No 2, IUCN Regional Office for Southern Africa, Harare, Zimbabwe

Kepe, T. (2008) 'Land claims and comanagement of protected areas in South Africa: Exploring the challenges', *Environmental Management*, vol 41, no 3, pp311–321

Kepe, T., Wynberg, R. and Ellis, W. (2005) 'Land reform and biodiversity conservation in South Africa: Complementary or in conflict?', *International Journal of Biodiversity Science and Management*, vol 1, no 11, pp3–16

Kingdon, J. (1984) *Agendas, Alternatives and Public Policies*, HarperCollins, New York

Koch, E. (2004) 'Political economy, governance and community-based natural resource management', in C. Fabricius, E. Koch, H. Magome and S. Turner (eds) *Rights, Resources and Rural Development: Community-based Natural Resource Management in Southern Africa*, Earthscan, London

LRLCC (Limpopo Regional Land Claims Commission) (2004) Submission of settlement agreement in terms of SD of the Restitution of Land Rights Act (Act No. 22 of 1994) as amended in the matter of Gumbu/Mutele community land claim over Madimbo corridor, LRLCC, Polokwane

Linden, T. (2004) *Land and Conflict in the Madimbo Corridor*, Paper presented at the Transboundary Protected Areas Research Initiative teleconference, 30 September 2004, South Africa

Mail and Guardian Online (2009) 'More lay-offs as shine comes off tourism industry', www.mg.co.za/article/2009-07-13-more-layoffs-as-shine-comes-off-tourism-industry Accessed 13 July 2009

Magome, H. and Murombedzi, J. (2003) 'Sharing South African National Parks: Community land and conservation in a democratic South Africa', in W.M. Adams and M. Mulligan (eds) *Decolonising Nature: Strategies for Conservation in a Post-colonial Era*, Earthscan, London

Mckenzie, P. (1998) 'Reclaiming the land: A case study of Riemvasmaak', in J. Cock and P. Mckenzie (eds) *From Defence to Development: Redirecting Military Resources in South Africa*, David Philip, Cape Town, South Africa

Mckenzie, P. (1995) 'The SANDF: Conservation or contamination?', *Mail and Guardian*, 22–28 September 1995

Metcalfe, S. and Kepe, T. (2008) '"Your Elephant on our Land": The struggle to manage wildlife mobility on Zambian communal land in the Kavango-Zambezi Transfrontier Conservation Area', *The Journal of Environment and Development*, vol 17, no 2, pp99–117

Metcalfe, S. (2003) *Impacts of Transboundary Protected Areas on Local Communities in Three Southern African Initiatives*, Paper prepared for the workshop on Transboundary Protected Areas in the Governance Stream of the 5th World Parks Congress, Durban, South Africa, 12–13 September 2003

Ntsebeza, L. (2005) *Democracy Compromised: Chiefs and the Politics of the Land in South Africa*, Brill Publishers, Leiden, The Netherlands

PPF (Peace Parks Foundation) (2008) 'Great Limpopo Transfrontier Park Progress Report 1997–2008', www.peaceparks.com/Stories_1180000000_5_0_785_0_785_Great+Limpopo+Progress+Report.htm Accessed 7 July 2009

PPF (Peace Parks Foundation) (2004) 'Communities in TFCAs', www.ppf.org, Accessed 10 August 2007

PPF and Landscape Architects (2006) *Pafuri Region: Integrated Land Use and Tourism Plan*, Prepared for the Governments of Mozambique, South Africa and Zimbabwe

Poonan, U. (1996) 'Land, Animals and Diamonds: A Case Study of the Madimbo Corridor', Unpublished manuscript

Ramutsindela, M. (2007) *Transfrontier Conservation in Africa: At the Confluence of Capital, Politics and Nature*, CABI, Wallingford

Reid, H., Fig, D., Magome, H. and Leader-Williams, N. (2004) 'Co-management of Contractual National Parks in South Africa: Lessons from Australia', *Conservation & Society*, vol 2, no 2, www.conservationandsociety.org/temp/ConservatSoc22377-332491 1_091409.pdf Accessed 31 July 2009

RETOSA (Regional Tourism Organization of Southern Africa) (2009) http://www.retosa. co.za/regional-initiatives/transfrontier-conservation-area Accessed 31 August 2009

Robbins, S. and van der Waal, K. (2008) '"Model tribes" and iconic conservationists? The Makuleke restitution case in Kruger National Park', *Development and Change*, vol 39, no 1, pp53–72

SADC (Southern African Development Community) (1999) SADC Protocol on Wildlife Conservation and Law Enforcement, Signed 18 August 1999, Maputo, Mozambique

Salafsky, N. and Wollenberg, E. (2000) 'Linking livelihoods and conservation: A conceptual framework and scale for assessing the integration of human needs and biodiversity', *World Development*, vol 28, no 8, pp1421–1438

Spenceley, A. (2005) 'Tourism in the Great Limpopo Transfrontier Park', *Development Southern Africa*, vol 23, no 5, pp649–667

Spierenburg, M. and Wels, H. (2006) '"Securing space": Mapping and fencing in transfrontier conservation in Southern Africa', *Space and Culture*, vol 9, no 3, pp294–312

Stayt, H.A. (1931) *The BeVenda*, Oxford University Press, London

Steenkamp, C. (2001) 'The Makuleke land claim: An environmental conflict', PhD Thesis, University of the Witwatersrand, South Africa

Steenkamp, C. and Uhr, J. (2000). *The Makuleke Land Claim: Power Relations and Community-Based Natural Resource Management*, IIED Evaluating Eden Occasional Paper No 18, International Institute for Environment and Development, London

Steiner, A. (1993) 'The peace dividend in southern Africa: Prospects and potentials for redirecting military resources towards natural resource management', paper presented to UNDP Conference on Military and the Environment, Past Mistakes and Future Options, New York

Van Ameron, M. and Büscher, B. (2005) 'Peace Parks in southern Africa. Bringers of an African renaissance?', *Journal of Modern African Studies*, vol 43, no 2, pp159–182

Whande, W. (2007) *Transboundary Natural Resources Management in Southern Africa: Local Historical and Livelihood Realities within the Great Limpopo Transfrontier Conservation Area*, Research Report No. 25, Institute for Poverty, Land and Agrarian Studies, Cape Town, South Africa

Whande, W. and Suich, H. (2008) 'Transfrontier Conservation Initiatives in Southern Africa: Observations from the Great Limpopo Transfrontier Conservation Area', in H. Suich, B. Child, and A. Spenceley (eds) *Evolution and Innovation in Wildlife Conservation: Parks and Game Ranches to Transfrontier Conservation Areas*, Earthscan, London

Wolmer, W. (2003) 'Transboundary conservation: The politics of ecological integrity in the Great Limpopo Transfrontier Park', *Journal of Southern African Studies*, vol 29, no 1, pp261–278

8

'People are Not Happy': Crisis, Adaptation and Resilience in Zimbabwe's CAMPFIRE Programme[1]

Liz Rihoy, Chaka Chirozva and Simon Anstey

Introduction

In the early 1990s Mahenye Ward, located in southeast Zimbabwe, was a leading local reference point for the widely heralded CAMPFIRE Programme (Communal Areas Management Programme for Indigenous Resources), which was in turn a leading influence on wider experimentation with community-based natural resource management (CBNRM) across southern Africa. Regional and international analyses of CAMPFIRE held Mahenye up as a leading functional example of the programme's aspirations to forge new links between local democracy, rural development and wildlife conservation (Peterson, 1991; Murphree, 1995; Borrini-Feyerabend, 1997; Murphree, 2001).

Key factors in the relative success of local people in Mahenye to sustainably manage and derive benefits from their natural resources included 'the insights, ingenuity and commitment of socially dedicated individuals in positions of influence or leadership...which has been balanced in its sources of traditional and popular legitimation'; an 'enlightened private sector'; a capacity for flexibility and acceptance of innovation; and particularly local intra-communal cohesiveness:

> *...in-group solidarity, rooted in history and reinforced by perceptions of external differences...Like any community Mahenye has its internal differentiations but these have been contained by a sense of collective communal interest. The importance of this condition cannot be overstressed...*
>
> (Murphree, 2001, p192)

More recently, and again both reflecting and informing changed national and regional discourse around CBNRM (e.g. Dzingirai and Breen, 2005), the narrative emerging from Mahenye has shifted to one of crisis and collapse and a questioning of the merits of devolving rights over natural resources to the local level (Balint and Mashinya, 2006). Scholars report how local élites have undermined the formerly flourishing CAMPFIRE system and formerly democratic local institutions (Ibid.)

The narratives and counter-narratives[2] about Mahenye and its CBNRM initiative matter not only because of the centrality of natural resources to the people of the Ward, to their survival and their future livelihoods. They also matter because, as in the 1990s, Mahenye has an impact and reach far beyond a peripheral zone of Zimbabwe. The recent narrative of crisis in CAMPFIRE in Mahenye Ward, in questioning the merits of devolution of natural resource governance, in local élite capture of benefits and decision-making, in the strivings for participatory democracy, and in resilience and adaptability all have their reflections and relevance at other scales. These range from academic or policy debates on the 'crisis' in CBNRM in southern Africa (e.g. Dzingirai and Breen, 2005; see also Mapedza, 2007), on the contested evolutions of democracy in Zimbabwe or the region and on natural resource management and human livelihoods more widely.

Methodology

This chapter is based on interviews, primary research and secondary sources. Research in Mahenye was initiated by one of the authors who spent one month living in the Ward in August 2005. He focused on familiarizing himself with the day-to-day lifestyles, concerns, characters and aspirations of the people of Mahenye, holding both informal discussions and formal semi-structured interviews with people living and working there. This was followed by a one-week visit by all the authors in October 2005, during which initial research was verified and further interviews and analysis undertaken. Field-level research was complemented by interviews with relevant government officials, politicians, donors, NGOs, academics and private sector representatives at both district and national level who are currently (or were formerly) involved in CAMPFIRE implementation, analysis and policy development (see also Rihoy, forthcoming).

In total over 100 semi-structured interviews were conducted over a four-month period, including over 50 with people in Mahenye.[3] Attention was paid to ensuring that a representative mix of people was interviewed. These included those who are currently and were formerly involved with the Mahenye CAMPFIRE committee, traditional leaders, others in positions of authority, government employees (e.g. teachers and health workers), employees of the lodges and safari operator, private business people and subsistence farmers.

Background

Evolutions of CAMPFIRE in Zimbabwe

Over the past 20 years the CAMPFIRE programme – like Zimbabwe itself – has seen dramatic fluctuations in its fortunes and in the way in which it has been perceived. CAMPFIRE was initiated in the 1980s by the Department of National

Parks and Wildlife Management. By the 1990s CAMPFIRE was embraced as a holistic approach to environment and development endorsed by the Government of Zimbabwe, local and international NGOs and drawn upon as a source of inspiration for natural resource management regionally (Jones and Murphree, 2001; see Nelson, this volume, Chapter 1).

Since 2000, CAMPFIRE has frequently been portrayed as the archetypal example of CBNRM in southern Africa in crisis (Katerere, 2001; Dzingirai and Breen 2005). It has witnessed the growth, followed by the demise, of a coordinated, multiskilled and expert group of organizations and individuals committed to the implementation of the programme, collectively known as the CAMPFIRE Collaborative Group (CCG) (Rihoy, forthcoming). It has grown from an initiative involving 2–3 districts, to one in which 52 of the country's 57 districts are involved (Child et al, 2003). During the period 1990–2003 it was the recipient of approximately US$30 million in external funding from a variety of international donors (Balint and Mashinya, 2006), all of which have now withdrawn, leaving the programme largely unfunded.

CAMPFIRE has in practice largely been a process of decentralization of legal authority over wildlife to Rural District Councils (RDCs), rather than one of devolution to sub-district level semi-autonomous institutions as was originally conceptualized (Murphree, 2005; see also Nelson, this volume, Chapter 1). Such 'aborted devolution' has repeatedly been identified as the prime challenge for CAMPFIRE and indicative of the need to move on to what Child (2004) calls 'second-generation CBNRM' in which clear authority and responsibility over decision-making is shifted to the smaller scale of producer communities, rather than partially through national or district government agencies.

At the same time, there has also been a growing chorus of voices raising a cautionary note about devolution as panacea. Research from other countries in the region and globally (e.g. Ribot, 2004) contends that management institutions that are not accountable to their constituents (such as those usurped by local élites) can be as serious an impediment to effective community management of natural resources as decentralized control through local government. Murphree (2000), however, points out that devolution is not an exercise in isolationism, but a process of finding local regime inter-dependence within the larger setting of inter-dependence or nested institutions at many scales (see also Ostrom, 1990).

In the CAMPFIRE context these interconnected governance elements include the people of a ward, village or 'producer community' who delegate upwards to a CAMPFIRE committee; the RDC; and national government agencies to tackle jurisdictional, functional or ecological scale aspects; but who retain the right to accountability from this delegation of authority – whether by committee, chair of committee, local or traditional government, RDC or others. Devolution remains the 'cardinal input' (see Murphree and Mazambani, 2002) but a hierarchy of institutions based on delegation from, and accountability to, the producer community provides the cross-scale linkages and democratic process to resolve either local, district or national misappropriation of funds or power. In this sense, CAMPFIRE is fundamentally about experiments in and piloting of democratic governance, lodged in issues of national and local politics, and the people and the scales that they interact within that comprises such politics.

The national context

Zimbabwe has undergone significant and far-reaching political, economic and social upheavals since the mid-1980s when CAMPFIRE was first introduced, and since 2000 has descended into a state of protracted crisis. Its relatively strong economy has been reduced to the weakest in the region (Bauer and Taylor, 2005; Hill, 2005). Once reasonably stable political conditions are now characterized by civil unrest and political repression and a previously well-functioning bureaucracy is in tatters. Respect for basic democratic principles, the rule of law and human rights are limited in their observation (Hammar and Raftopoulos, 2003; Harold-Barry, 2004). Zimbabwe, once a darling of the international donor community, has become a pariah and exhibits many of the attributes of 'disorder as a political instrument' in which political actors and élites seek to maximize their returns from conditions of confusion and uncertainty (Chabal and Daloz, 1999). This decline has had significant impacts on many different elements of the CAMPFIRE programme, including the process of policy-making, the economic benefits available from wildlife and tourism, donor or private investment, governance arrangements and implementation capacities of both NGOs and government agencies.

Economic conditions

The negative macro-economic and political environment in the post-2000 period presents major challenges for local communities to generate revenue from wildlife. Between 2000 and 2003 Zimbabwe's GDP plummeted by 30 per cent and the trend has continued; manufacturing has declined by 51 per cent since 1997 and exports fallen by a half since 2001 (Dell, 2005). Inflation rates reached 1700 per cent by 2005 and near world-record hyperinflation overtook the economy by 2008, rendering the Zimbabwean dollar (Z\$) virtually worthless from one day to the next. Dell (2005) estimates that the proportion of the population living below the official poverty line has more than doubled since the mid-1990s, standing at about 80 per cent as of 2005.

The political and economic turmoil has led to the collapse of the tourism sector. Nemarundwe (2005) highlights the negative impacts of this economic climate on CAMPFIRE, compromising not only its income-generating potential through tourism but also undermining community investment projects. Inflationary changes in prices make a mockery of budgeting, erode financial benefits and value, and given the cycle in which payments of household cash dividends from CAMPFIRE revenue activities takes place six months to a year after activities have occurred, the loses to inflation of cash benefits are massive. Finally, in the absence of many other income or taxable options, the current situation is further increasing the RDCs' dependence on CAMPFIRE wildlife revenue for survival, presenting a disincentive for fiscal or other devolution (see also Taylor and Murphree, 2007).

Political climate

The extreme economic and political problems that now face Zimbabwe can best be analysed and understood in the context of its history (Raftopoulous, 2004). Zimbabwe emerged from almost a century of white rule, following a long and violent liberation war that ended in 1980, fought largely over land. Since 1980, the political priorities of the government have been dominated by reversing decades of racially-biased inequalities in land, resource and asset distribution (Hammar and Raftopoulous, 2004). As the ruling party slogan 'the land is the economy, the economy is the land' implies, struggles over land have been at centre stage throughout the colonial and post-colonial period. This struggle over land and natural resources is central to understanding the political dimensions of natural resource management in Zimbabwe, and explaining why it receives such a high degree of political prominence.

By the late 1990s, due to a range of factors, the political legitimacy of the ruling ZANU-PF party was coming under increasing public scrutiny, culminating in significant and escalating electoral challenges and civil unrest. The response on the part of the party-state was increased authoritarianism, violence and repression of political opposition, leading to the creation of a climate of fear and intolerance (Raftopoulous and Savage, 2005) and a breakdown in the rule of law (Bauer and Taylor, 2005; Hill, 2005). Concerted efforts by the ruling party to consolidate rural support were undertaken, most significantly the Fast Track Land Reform Process (Keeley and Scoones, 2003) but also through the introduction of the Traditional Leaders Act (TLA) in 2001. This restored legal powers and authority to chiefs (a shift from and unclear addition to the previous policy of democratically elected local governance at village and ward level) and is in essence a replica of colonial strategies towards the traditional leadership geared towards co-opting the traditional leadership to ensure political penetration of the state and ruling party into rural landscapes (see Murombedzi, this volume).

In broad political terms Zimbabwe can no longer be described as an ordered political polity (Chabal and Daloz, 1999) in which political opportunities and resources are formally defined and codified by legislation or precedent. Whereas in the 1980s Zimbabwe had a relatively well-functioning bureaucracy, at present informal political relationships have come to play a much greater role in policy formulation and implementation. Powerful ruling party politicians have assumed leading roles within the wildlife management industry in Zimbabwe (see for example Hammer, 2006) and overt political influence on government decision-making is now prevalent.

Civil society

Throughout the 1980s and 1990s, Zimbabwe witnessed the growth of a strong and vibrant civil society. NGOs received generous support from donors and effectively collaborated with many government programmes. CAMPFIRE exemplified this (Duffy, 2000), with the CAMPFIRE Collaborative Group (CCG), a joint facilitating structure of both government agencies, NGOs and academic institutions, playing a key role in implementation until 2000 (Child et al, 2003; Rihoy and Maguranyanga, 2007). However, the shift in the political landscape of Zimbabwe immediately prior to 2000 resulted in major opposition by civil society organizations to a government-led constitutional amendment referendum. From 1999, some segments of civil society began to challenge the government on land, electoral and human rights issues. This challenge was treated as a sign of political defiance warranting the repression of NGOs, and the government introduced the 2005 NGO Bill which considerably curtailed NGO functions and independence.

This volatile political climate translated into a difficult operational environment for civil society, particularly in any area of governance or involvement in rural development (Bauer and Taylor, 2005; Raftopoulous and Savage, 2005).

The impact of this marginalization of civil society on CAMPFIRE has been profound. Members of the CCG formerly played a key role in capacity building at grass-roots level (Child et al, 2003). Members of the CCG also fulfilled a critical role as third-party brokers providing neutral arbitration in instances where community-level polarization stalled progress in programme implementation. As of 2003, because of the political backlash against civil society, NGOs have been prevented from playing any significant role in implementing CAMPFIRE (Rihoy and Maguranyanga, 2007). Compounding this operational marginalization has been the loss of access to funding that has been experienced by NGOs throughout Zimbabwe as a result of donor withdrawal arising from the political situation.

Mahenye: History, people and CBNRM evolutions, 1982–2000

Mahenye Ward is located at the southern end of Chipinge District, bordered on the east by Mozambique and to the west and south by Gonarezhou National Park. It has a low average rainfall of 450–500mm supporting dry land cultivation of grains only in good seasons, but its relatively low human population density has ensured that the low-veldt habitat has remained relatively intact (Booth, 1991).

Many of the current inhabitants of Mahenye were evicted from their traditional lands prior and up to 1966 as these areas became incorporated into the Gonarezhou National Park. Following independence in 1980, strong hopes within the community that their land would be returned to them were soon dashed when the new government indicated its priority was to gain the foreign exchange brought into the country by tourists and the park. This resulted in heightened resentment towards Gonarezhou and wildlife, manifested as increasing incidences of illegal resource use as people sought illicit ways in which to assert their traditional resource rights and livelihoods.

Murphree (2001, p179) notes that one product of the geographic location of Mahenye is its notable 'discreteness and isolation'. Their neighbours to the east are in a different country, to the south is a national park whilst those to the west are in a different province; thus Mahenye retains administrative isolation from those in its immediate vicinity. Perhaps most significant is that within Chipinge District itself, the people of Mahenye are ethnically discrete as they are the only Shangaan-speaking people in a district otherwise made up exclusively of the Shona-Ndau ethnic group. Thus the people of Mahenye are culturally, politically and administratively distinct from their neighbours, which Murphree (2001) concludes led to the development of a strong level of intra-communal cohesiveness – then largely manifested around the institution and individual of the Chief – and a sense of collective communal interest.

Evolution of CBNRM in Mahenye

The granting of Appropriate Authority (AA) status to Gazaland District Council (now Chipinge RDC) in 1991 provided the legal mechanism through which the people of Mahenye were able to benefit from natural resource management activities in their ward, by giving the district user rights over wildlife. At the ward level, in order to ensure effective management of the resource base and an accountable and representative local-level management structure, the Mahenye CAMPFIRE Committee (MCC) was established in the late 1980s. The operations of the MCC are governed by 'bylaws' (commonly referred to locally as 'the Constitution') which were developed following lengthy consultations with the general community, traditional leadership and local CAMPFIRE leadership and are still frequently referred to in CAMPFIRE discussions today. While neither the MCC organization nor the bylaws have formal legal status, they are (or were) strongly legitimized by use, precedent and acceptance by the various CAMPFIRE-related bodies. These bylaws outline the objectives of the organization; specify the roles, responsibilities and terms of the office bearers and general members; and stipulate means through which accountability to the broader membership are to be assured. These, importantly, include:

- the holding of regular Annual General Meetings (AGMs) for transparent disclosure of management and financial activities by the MCC office bearers to the community;
- the holding of annual elections (via secret ballot by Mahenye households) for posts in the Mahenye CAMPFIRE Committee (MCC) such as that of Chairman, Vice-chairman, Finance Manager and others.

The bylaws are a written, widely known and understood representation of the standard to which the MCC should be adhering. They represent an important benchmark against which to measure and exert accountability for the activities of the MCC, its officeholders and the operation of CAMPFIRE at the producer community scale.

Institutional linkages and networks between authorities and across jurisdictional and functional scales also became well-developed during this period. During the early 1980s the primary decision-making institutions in the ward were those of the traditional authority (through the leadership of Chiefs, headmen and *Sabhukus*) working in a closely coordinated relationship with the democratically elected structures such as the Ward Development Committees (WADCOs) and the higher scale of the RDCs. In the 1990s, by virtue of its elected basis and development importance locally, the MCC also became a powerful local institution. The private sector, originally represented by one individual (who had also facilitated early CBNRM evolutions in the ward between the various bodies) also had significant influence (Murphree, 2001). Strong linkages existed between the MCC and a broader national actor network in capacity building and technical wildlife management advice with NGOs, the national CAMPFIRE representative and advocacy body (CAMPFIRE Association) and the state wildlife agency (DNPWM).

Economics of CAMPFIRE in Mahenye

One of Mahenye's progressive attributes during this period, compared to most CAMPFIRE wards, was its diversification in revenue from solely sport hunting income to the ecotourism sector. In the early 1990s the RDC, on behalf of the people of Mahenye, entered into a joint venture arrangement with a private tourism operator for the construction of two lodges – Mahenye Safari Lodge and Chilo Lodge – catering to a high paying tourist market for game viewing and photographic safaris. Under the terms of the 1996 agreement, land was leased by the operator from the RDC for a 10-year period. Initially revenue earned was paid via the RDC, but in 2003/4 a more direct allocation was made to the MCC. In principle this represented a significant step towards fiscal devolution (albeit undertaken in an informal way) but was a decision subsequently reversed at the request of the RDC.

The income potential from these lodges was considerable and by 1997 generated twice the income of sport hunting and was responsible for more than tripling the overall CAMPFIRE income for Mahenye between 1994 and 1997 (Murphree, 2001). However, the downturn in tourism in Zimbabwe post-2000 has meant that the real financial returns have become limited and sport hunting has returned as the largest revenue source. Despite this, the lodges have continued to bring considerable benefits, most notably in the form of employment.[4]

In the early 1990s and again since 2000, the primary form of income generation for the MCC has been from the sport hunting concession in the Mahenye/Mutandahwe area. CAMPFIRE revenue in the period 1992 to 1997 from sport hunting was around US$15–20,000 (largely from elephant hunting) with the total revenues achieved in the late 1990s from both hunting and lodge tourism reaching around US$40,000 (Murphree, 2001). As important as the overall revenue were the actual disbursements to the household level of dividends in the form of cash and the proportion that this represented of the overall CAMPFIRE revenue. On average, in this period the proportion of total revenue allocated to household dividends was consistently around 50 per cent – with around 20 per cent allocated for RDC administration costs (essentially a 'tax'), 2 per cent for the CAMPFIRE Association and the rest roughly equally divided between MCC-managed development projects (e.g. grinding mills) and wildlife management costs (see Murphree, 2001).

The household dividends of around US$15–25 were significant in comparison to other CAMPFIRE areas (median household-level income of US$4.49; see Bond, 2001) and an important incentive for encouraging local support for wildlife management and supporting local household incomes. A number of interviewees from this current research had strong memories of the cash dividends of the late 1990s as being key contributions to the family's ability to purchase goods, food in drought years or enabling the payment of school fees.

CAMPFIRE evolutions in Mahenye, 2000–2005

Institutions, management and local governance

Since 2000 there have been significant shifts of power within and between different actors and institutions in Mahenye, as well as the major shifts in macro-economic and national political context that have occurred in Zimbabwe as a whole. One outcome of these shifts has been the dramatic demise of CAMPFIRE in the view of the overwhelming majority of local inhabitants interviewed, and summed up as follows by one woman: 'CAMPFIRE used to be for all the people, now it's a family business'.

The demise of CAMPFIRE in Mahenye, its core local institution (the MCC) and dramatic falls in the value of household dividends coincide with, and have been strongly influenced by, four related local events:

1   the death of the highly respected old Chief Mahenye in 2001 and replacement by his son, who is the current Chief;
2   on the explicit instructions of the new Chief, the complete change in MCC office bearers following the flawed MCC elections of 2001, including the direct appointment (not election) of the Chief's younger brother as Chairman;
3   the election of a new Councillor for the Ward;
4   the re-tendering of the sport hunting concession which has led to ongoing conflict and the widespread belief among most local stakeholders that the operators are currently un-transparently bidding for the concession and are competing amongst each other in their attempts to illicitly 'buy off' the Chief and MCC to ensure preferential treatment.

These changes have effectively removed the strong local leadership whose commitment and accountability were formerly such a distinctive feature of Mahenye (Murphree, 2001). These included the Chief, headmen and respected elders, the school headmaster and other teachers and an elected leadership including the Ward Councillor and members of the MCC. Collectively these provided a leadership structure that was balanced in its sources of traditional and popular legitimacy.

Local power and authority have shifted away from the delicate balance established between traditional and elected democratic institutions and the leadership of these structures, and concentrated into the hands of a core local élite concentrated within the traditional leadership. 'Honest brokers' in local dynamics, whether of the private sector, NGO, state, RDC or other have become rare, ineffectual or sidelined. As many people in Mahenye said, the result is that they now have their own 'dictator'. An important point in the following discussion is the premise that it is not the institution (rules of the game) of either the MCC or customary authority that is the root source of these governance problems, but the *distortion* of the rules governing both by particular forces since 2000 that have permitted élite capture and perpetuated stalemate, contrary to the past existing delegation and accountability mechanisms.

Management of CAMPFIRE in Mahenye: The situation in 2005

The Mahenye CAMPFIRE Committee, once viewed by the Mahenye people with pride as contributing to the overall development of the community and to the livelihood needs of individual families, is now widely perceived as an institution which mismanages and abuses community funds for the personal enrichment of the Chief and his clan. This has included the use of project vehicles for personal transport, the 'privatization' of the general store, grinding mills and other CAMPFIRE projects, and access to scarce employment opportunities at the lodges being mediated by the Chief's family. Enabling this situation has been the dismantlement of those locally developed and mandated mechanisms that ensured that CAMPFIRE was a participatory process, representative of and accountable to the people of Mahenye.

The demise of democratic procedures

Whilst it has no formal legal basis, the MCC is, according to its Constitution, responsible for carrying out management functions, employing local staff to monitor wildlife and wildlife use, including poaching and the hunting activities of the professional hunter. It sets budgets and is responsible to general community meetings for its activities and planning. Prior to 2000, MCC board members were democratically and transparently elected (once every two years) at open Annual General Meetings (AGMs), and incomes and budgets were openly made and presented with all decisions regarding use of revenues collectively taken at these AGMs.

However, since 2000 only two AGMs have been held, both of which were relatively poorly attended. Elections for committee members have not been held at any AGM since those of 2001. The Chairman (in 2005) was never elected but was given this position by the Chief after his predecessor (who had been elected in the 2001 elections) had left the village after allegedly misappropriating CAMPFIRE funds.

On the rare occasion when AGMs are still held, their function is now very different to the accountability basis outlined in the Constitution. According to the Chairman of the MCC himself:

> ...we use AGMs as a way to tell the community how the committee and traditional leaders have budgeted and spent CAMPFIRE money and other things. It's where we let them know what their leaders are doing for them.

Income and budget transparency has evaporated as the mentality of the leadership has shifted from collective decision-making by and with the people or accounting for actions and decisions (active and inter-active) to informing the people, whose role is now passive.

Shrinking incomes and incentives

The earnings in Mahenye from CAMPFIRE declined dramatically from 2000 to 2005 (Table 8.1), as a result of both local misappropriation and leakages arising from national economic distortions. These leakages primarily result from:

- the loss in value occurring when converting foreign exchange to the massively over-valued Zimbabwe dollar;
- the loss in value resulting from annual inflation rates as high as 650 per cent to over 800 per cent (as of 2004–2005) when revenues remain stored in bank accounts for periods of six months to up to a year before household dividend payments are made.

Table 8.1 *Household dividend payments and proportion of overall revenue in Mahenye, 1996, 1997 and 2004*

	1996	*1997*	*2004*
Household (HH) dividends	Z$183 US$18.67	Z$442 US$27.63	Z$100 (Z$6,100)* US$0.03
Proportion of overall revenues allocated to HH dividends	50%	55%	0.2% (14%)^

Notes:
* The actual HH dividend received by people was Z$100 (US$0.03) after an unclear local 'tax' of Z$6,000 was deducted prior to payouts.
^ In proportion of overall revenues allocated to HH dividends the percentage prior to the' tax' was +/– 14%. The actual cash dividends for the household totalled Z$89,400 (894HH × Z$100) which represents only 0.2% of the Z$40,118,791 noted as total revenues by the RDC records.

Source: 2004: this research and 1990s data adapted from Murphree, 2001. Exchange rates based on Reserve Bank of Zimbabwe data.

Throughout the 1990s annual allocations to household dividends were consistently around 50 per cent of total budgets in Mahenye (Murphree, 2001). Since 2001 there has only been one allocation for household dividends. This took place in May 2004 and was on the basis (according to the official figures submitted by Chipinge RDC) of a total revenue earned (2003) of Z$40,118,791. The household dividend amounted to a cash payment (in principle) of Z$6,100 per household. Of this, each household was first deducted Z$6,000 for a 'district development levy' by the traditional authority, the validity of which has never been verified, resulting in an actual cash dividend 'in hand' of only Z$100 (US$0.03) (see Table 8.1). As a proportion of the overall stated revenues, this sum of 'actual cash in hand' dividend represented less than 1 per cent (0.2 per cent) compared to the 50 per cent averages in the 1990s. As stated by one interviewee:

Z$100 even then wasn't enough to buy one match, and most didn't know about it. I don't know anyone who even went to the [MCC project] office to collect their money.

The most lucrative source of income has been sport hunting and this has been mired in considerable complexity. In 1997 Tshabezi Safaris won the concession for a five-year period. In 2002, the hunting concession was tendered again and once again awarded by the RDC to Tshabezi Safaris. However, no contract has been in place since 2002, one of the causes of the conflict surrounding the hunting concession. The resulting uncertainties and competition between the various stakeholders has been one of the driving forces enabling powerful local-level élite to co-opt the power and resources of the MCC for their own political and personal financial ends.

The simple facts are that the households in Mahenye are getting no meaningful economic dividends from CAMPFIRE, in stark contrast to the 1990s. The outcome of this situation is that there is no longer any independent local body that represents the interests of the people or to which the grievances of the people can be aired. All discussions and decisions now take place at the Chief's *Dare* (assembly meeting). This is the context of changed local governance and economic incentives against which the following section of local narratives are set.

Local narratives and perceptions

Vanhu varwadziwa, havana kwavanochemera
(People are not happy, but they don't know where to complain.)

Given the competing interests at stake it is perhaps not surprising that the narratives surrounding CAMPFIRE in Mahenye differ amongst the various stakeholders and that different scenarios for change are identified by these groups. In very broad terms the stakeholder groups can be identified as follows:

- the traditional leadership and current MCC members;
- general community members;
- external stakeholders such as the RDCs and NGOs such as the CAMPFIRE Association.

However, as the following discussion indicates, this simplistic breakdown of disparate actors hides an overlapping and constantly shifting array of perceptions, alliances and networks. This section relates the stories articulated by each group, highlighting the concerns and issues dominant within each group. Wherever possible this is presented in their own words based on the interviews carried out in 2005.

Traditional leadership

The traditional leadership in Mahenye consists of the Chief, two headmen and 29 kraal heads. Given the thorough co-optation of the MCC by the Chief and his immediate family – in 2005 every member of the 12-person MCC was a relative of the Chief – we combine the traditional leadership and the MCC here as falling within the same stakeholder group, even though there are very clear fault lines developing amongst various individuals and sub-groups. Despite this close association of the Chief with the programme, he claims to have no direct relationship with it, although he is outspoken in his support, noting that:

CAMPFIRE has been here a long time and brought many good things but it needs changes. The main problem is that money from hunting goes to the RDC first, it should come directly to Mahenye; also the RDC want to interfere in who we select as our hunter.

The narrative constructed by both the Chief and the MCC Chairman is one of a successful CAMPFIRE programme that has brought development to Mahenye, whilst protecting the natural resource base and upholding local culture and traditions. They identify some problems with the programme but consider that these are brought about by external agents and technical deficiencies with the implementation process, what they portray as the greed and inefficiency of the current safari operator, coupled with the unwillingness of the RDC to commit to fiscal devolution and local-level decision-making regarding the selection of safari operators.

However, with the exception of these two individuals, the other members of the traditional leadership and MCC interviewed presented a different story by identifying failures in leadership, financial management and governance – including detailing several instances of abuse and misuse of funds and MCC assets by the Chairman – coupled with the technical and administrative problems identified by the Chief and Chair as being the most significant impediment to the programme. As articulated by a senior member of this sub-group:

The situation at the moment is a free for all, soft drinks, sitting allowances, free transport, Christmas parties, nothing like before when things were run properly. It is corruption and bribery (undyire). But those of us with the authority to do something can't because this dispute is in our own clan. Does a son question his father? Someone from outside must step in, either the RDC or CAMPFIRE Association. We made sure an auditor came but now the council (RDC) do nothing, they must remove the culprit, even make arrests. Council are letting us down.

General population

The story told by people in the general community (meaning that they do not belong to the other stakeholder groups) had at its centre disappointment and disillusionment with the current situation, but also a sense that events were still unfolding and that they collectively had at their disposal means to address the current problems. This group unanimously identified poor leadership, governance issues and the misappropriation of power by the MCC as the root cause of their problems but there was also considerable concern and confusion articulated about the private sector tourism operations, the role of NGOs and the role of the RDC.

CAMPFIRE was described as a source of local pride and confidence as well as development for over 10 years. It was considered to have been a genuinely representative process about which the majority of ward residents had considerable information concerning the nature and extent of their rights and technical details relating to wildlife management, and in which they enthusiastically participated and benefited. People articulated trust in and respect for their leaders during that time, who they credited with having brought about this success. Specifically mentioned on many occasions were the (former) Chief, (former) Councillor, (former) MCC members, the private sector partner, as well as NGOs formerly active in the area.

There is universal agreement over the cause of the problems that subsequently emerged:

Our troubles started when the old Chief passed and...[the former MCC Chairman] and the others were pushed out of the committee and...was made Chairman for life.

There was also widespread acknowledgement that there are constraints to what they can do about this because 'people fear to challenge the Chairman, this is challenging the Chief and would result in losing land or even being chased from the area.' A widely anticipated outcome of this is that 'people will go back to poaching because there's no benefit from wildlife otherwise'. There is also a common view that 'the RDC has more power, they should do something'.

However, whilst there is little that people can do overtly, they do have their own covert means of expressing their displeasure and translating this into political statements. Identical versions of the following story were recounted by several different interviewees.

The Chief had been told by the District Administrator that everyone must vote ZANU-PF and then he would get a vehicle. We were told to do so, but everyone here voted MDC to get back at him. He couldn't do anything about that because it was a secret ballot. We hoped that the Chief wouldn't get his vehicle and realize that everyone was aware that he was allowing our CAMPFIRE money to be lost.[5]

Thus there is a remarkable level of agreement on the basic situation and the way to resolve it amongst the majority of those in Mahenye. However, beyond this common understanding the situation is complicated further by the ongoing conflict between the MCC, the safari operators and the RDC over the re-tendering of the hunting quota. There is a strong perception amongst the community members that this conflict is being used by the MCC as a smokescreen to cover for their own misconduct.

Despite large-scale disillusionment with the situation, the majority of interviewees identified a core strategy to solve their problem. This strategy involves appeals to the RDC, as the only institution with the authority, legitimacy and mandate, to intervene and assist in the restoration of local structures that are accountable and representative of the community. Thus the collective local demand is for the RDC to accept its responsibilities as the agency granted Appropriate Authority (AA) for wildlife in the district and act accordingly to ensure that the CAMPFIRE 'Constitution' (the bylaws of the MCC) and democratic local institutions (the MCC under the rules of the bylaws) are in place. Essentially the action demanded was the holding of elections for the posts of the MCC according to the bylaws' procedures, after four years of blatant flouting of these basic rules.

Local people are thus collectively indicating that the RDC has an important function to play in fostering the conditions that will ensure their empowerment by providing a neutral arbitration role in a situation that, for a variety of reasons, cannot at present be addressed locally. People are clear that CAMPFIRE, by providing them with information about their rights and those of the other institutions involved, has provided them with the basis to express demands to the RDC:

> *People are very much aware of their rights and obligations and they know this because the old committee used to bare all things and read the Constitution in public at AGMs and other meetings, we also know from this what the RDC should be doing.*

However, this does not imply that the RDC is viewed entirely favourably in Mahenye and mounting frustration was articulated by many. The RDC is perceived to be primarily concerned with ensuring maximum income from the hunting operations to meet their own financial needs at the expense of the people.

The most striking element of the local community's narrative is the level of agreement on the nature of the problem and how it can potentially be solved through RDC intervention to restore earlier local democratic institutions. Despite considerable problems (and dangers), the people of Mahenye continue to demonstrate the remarkable level of 'intra-communal cohesiveness' and capacity for expressing 'constituency demands' identified in the past (Murphree, 2001).

The Rural District Council (RDC)

The role of the RDC includes formal awarding of the hunting concession following an established process of advertising and competitive tendering. As well as having a legal obligation in this regard, they also have a financial incentive to ensure that the process is efficiently managed as they are recipients of 20–35 per cent of income as an administrative fee or tax. In theory, tenders are evaluated both in terms of financial value and on qualitative considerations, with the expectation that RDCs take into account the views of the wildlife-producing ward. However, an independent Commission of Inquiry undertaken in 2005 at the request of the Chipinge RDC indicates that established procedures and competitive bidding processes have not been adhered to with the result that there is: 'no clear relationship between the value of the resources and the total amount paid by the safari operator in terms of the contract'.

Following a written request from the Mahenye Ward Councillor, backed up by anonymous letters from Mahenye residents, the RDC undertook an independent audit of the MCC in 2004. This audit clearly revealed the validity of accusations of mismanagement and misappropriation of CAMPFIRE funds by the élite within Mahenye.

According to the RDC Chief Executive Officer (CEO) the situation in Mahenye is thus 'a big mess' which has largely occurred because 'one individual is no longer accountable' which is bringing the RDC into disrepute:

> *Chipinge is proud of being the birth place of the CAMPFIRE concept, but now we are failing to live up to our reputation. We view it as a priority that things are put right.*

The RDC's chosen strategy has been to analyse what they see as the two elements of the problem: lack of accountability, and conflicts between the broader community and the safari operator:

And now we will approach the issues in stages. Our first priority is to sort out the problems with the safari operators. Once this is done we'll address local problems of representation. Elections with a secret ballot need to take place, and new safeguards developed to make sure authority isn't abused.

They are well aware of the demands for greater fiscal devolution regarding which the CEO says:

Personally I don't have a problem with the hunting fee going directly to the community but we have to sort out the abuses first and the decision isn't only mine to make.

The story according to the RDC is that they are aware of problems and are in the process of making a measured and responsible determination of how to proceed, which will respond to the demands and needs of their constituency. Given such a reasonable response it is fair to speculate why action has been so slow in forthcoming. The audit – which clearly illustrates fraud and corruption – was carried out in August 2004, whilst the Commission of Inquiry took place in May 2005. And yet by October 2005, despite the CEO acknowledging that it was a priority for the RDC, no action had been taken. This may simply be a result of bureaucratic ineptitude, but once again it is possible to identify alternative reasons.

Chief Mahenye's position provides him with networks linked to politically powerful national factions that may have an influence on the strategies adopted by the RDC. For example, the Deputy Minister of Local Government, Rural and Urban Development has attended meetings with the Mahenye CAMPFIRE committee at which discussions were held relating to securing greater financial devolution from the RDC. The Chief has also worked closely with the former District Administrator of Chipinge (himself now a Member of Parliament) to influence the Mahenye vote for the ZANU-PF MP candidate. These personal national networks and political affiliations provide an additional level of complexity in local power struggles which impact on the balance of power between the RDC and traditional authorities, and this may at least partially account for the reluctance of the RDC to take any decisive action.

Non-governmental organizations (NGOs)

The marginalization of civil society from policy-making and implementation in Zimbabwe's politically contested rural areas has had significant impacts on CAMPFIRE. The consequence of this marginalization is that those former CAMPFIRE Collaborative Group (CCG) members (particularly NGOs such as WWF and Zimbabwe Trust) who formerly played key roles in institutional development within Mahenye are no longer able to do so.

Some scholars have criticized NGOs for this (e.g. Balint and Mashinya, 2006), but this glosses over the reality that Zimbabwe's national political context since

2000 has served to marginalize and exclude those NGOs from the local governance arena. This has occurred by denying NGOs access to funds but also by removing their mandate. NGOs formerly active in Mahenye have been aware of the problems there but have no means or resources with which to address the problem, and also felt intimidated to try to do so. As expressed by one NGO officer formerly active in the area for a decade:

> *[Our friends] in the RDC tell us Mahenye is a mess, the Chief and Chairman have taken over. I hate to hear it after years of working with them but with no vehicles, no fuel, and no reason to go there, what can we do? Anyway, I'm known as MDC, the Chief is ZANU-PF, it wouldn't be good for my health.*

The one NGO that is still highly active in CAMPFIRE implementation is the CAMPFIRE Association (CA). They are familiar with the current situation in Mahenye and are involved with the RDC in seeking a solution to the problems based on their understanding that:

> *There are a lot of undeclared interests at play in Mahenye. There's a need to identify the root cause of the problem and sort the institutional problems. We strongly felt as a commission there was need for changes in tenure of office, to elect a new committee.*

As in the case of the RDC narrative, there is also a sense of some deadlock in taking actions or decisions in the discourse of the CA; particularly given this is precisely the institution taxed (literally, given that the CA membership fees are deducted from Mahenye revenue) with the task of linking the producer communities of CAMPFIRE with district and national agencies and with the overall coordination of the programme.

Discussion

In discussing contemporary CAMPFIRE and natural resource governance evolutions in Mahenye, a good place to begin is to recognize the complexity of the current situation both in Zimbabwe and in Mahenye, but also the extent to which there is remarkable congruence and depth in the narratives of local, district and national scales about existing challenges and the most urgent next steps to take. At the crux of these stories is a multi-tiered and interrelated set of politically and socially constructed stalemates inhibiting those steps from being taken and governance problems being addressed. As noted in the previous section by one interviewee: 'people are not happy, but they don't know where to complain'.

Local governance, CBNRM institutions and historical precedent

One of the paradoxes and strengths of the case of Mahenye is the degree of adaptation and cross-scale linkages that characterize local governance dynamics over the course of the past two decades. Mahenye had, by the mid- to late 1990s, developed a complex set of multi-tiered natural resource governance linkages involving upward delegation and downward accountability depending on political agency and ecological and social scale requirements (cf. Murphree, 2000; Rihoy and Maguranyanga, 2007). It had in that decade moved beyond the 'chicken and egg' structural dilemma of full devolution as prerequisite for CBNRM versus fragile local common property regimes as a cause of failure of CBNRM. The egg had produced the chicken and chicken produced the egg in a context, as described earlier, of happy congruence where the strengths of the local society (not one mired in feudal, hierarchical condition – as characterized, for example, by Balint and Mashinya (2006) – but mixing both modern and customary) was linked to higher scale organizations of the state, private sector and NGOs, with powerful economic incentives and political capital supporting these evolutions. The challenge was to come from 2000 with the series of connected local and national events which generated the dramatic distortions to economic incentives, political dynamics and local leadership. The informal and precedent basis of the Mahenye 'constitution' was inadequate to counterbalance these profound changes. In simple terms, the devolution-jurisdictional egg was hatching out in a much rougher neighbourhood.

But it is important to stress, as do the majority of the local narratives from Mahenye, that this does not preclude local ability to react or adapt. The fact that the precedent of tackling significant challenges from 1982 to 1991 existed, and the widely agreed strengths of the institution then until 2000 were established, provides hope that the scenarios and strategies for change envisaged by most Mahenye people can engage with contemporary crises.

National to local links, mirrors and influences

Whilst the past decade's problems in CAMPFIRE in Mahenye do indeed reflect 'local failures in governance and capacity' (see Balint and Mashinya, 2006), those changes in local governance are fundamentally shaped by developments at the national scale. The situation in Zimbabwe, where political trends since 2000 have resulted in the promotion of those institutions and individuals associated with the ruling party, whilst those affiliated in any way with opposition parties and politics have been marginalized, has been comprehensively documented by many analysts, both Zimbabwean and foreign (e.g. Raftopoulos and Savage, 2005; Bauer and Taylor 2005). The Mahenye situation in this regard mirrors that of the nation; the impact has been profound in determining the balance of power between various local actors in Mahenye, as well as determining which individuals continue to play active roles within institutions, based upon their political affiliations.

One of the most significant legislative changes promoting shifts in the institutional dynamics and balance of power within Mahenye has been the Traditional Leaders Act (TLA) of 2001, which has strengthened the power of traditional authorities nationally whilst also bringing them under the influence of the ruling party, ZANU-PF. Until the passing of this Act, policy since independence had strengthened the role of elected RDCs at the expense of traditional authorities.

The TLA is a significant shift in direction, empowering traditional leaders not least in terms of natural resource management. A widespread interpretation of the TLA is that it aims to co-opt traditional leadership to ensure political penetration of the ruling party into rural areas. This Act has not only enhanced the authority of chiefs locally but has also changed the nature of the relationship between chiefs, the RDC and the private sector.

Other changes which have influenced events in Mahenye include the creation of new and powerful institutions representing the party at local level. These include the Ward Coordinator (an employee of the Ministry of Youth, Gender and Employment Creation), while formerly relatively insignificant institutions, such as the Ward Chairman of ZANU-PF, have taken on new prominence. Compounding this is that the modern development structures and their representatives, notably the Ward Councillor, have also come increasingly under the influence of and are accountable to the ruling party and are under pressure, sometimes violent, to represent party interests in rural areas (see Hammar, 2003 for a detailed account).

But changes in the national context have not been limited to legislative or administrative changes. The year 2000 saw a dramatic and public shift in the political dynamics of Zimbabwe, culminating in an increase in politically motivated violence and in the collapse of the rule of law (Raftopoulous, 2005). This situation was underlain by a racial and populist moral discourse about the return of 'African soil' to Africans adopted by the ruling party, which served to marginalize and vilify whites and, by inference, political opponents of the ruling party. At local levels this often translated into the violent persecution and marginalization of MDC supporters and introduced greater suspicion of wildlife management as it was considered to be 'a ploy of whites to forestall land acquisition and justifying multiple and extensive land holdings' (Wolmer et al, 2003, p8). Many of those interviewed noted that the impact in Mahenye has been to marginalize key figures who were known to be opposition supporters and a further reinforcement of the powers of the Chief.

Thus the relationship between the traditional and ruling party institutions has fundamentally changed, with the result that the power and influence of traditional authorities has been enhanced but at the expense of increased dependency on the ruling party. In Mahenye this has allowed for the creation of one institution within which all power is vested: that of the Chief (as distinct from the institution of customary authority). This has occurred because of the mutually beneficial relationship and endorsement from ZANU-PF and the other newly created or co-opted institutions such as the MCC under the current Chairman. The new roles acquired by the Chief and his family translate into real power over and above that traditionally extended to them.

The national context has enabled the Chief to translate his newly enhanced legal position as regards natural resources and his new position as powerful ZANU-PF representative to divert the claims of others and validate his own claims over these resources, thus expanding his control over development in Mahenye. One of the first actions undertaken by the Chief on his ascendancy in 2001 was to ensure that CAMPFIRE and its benefits were brought under his control.

Economic returns and incentives

Contemporary realities in Mahenye illustrate that the local and national institutional distortions are equally present in the economic and revenue context. The collapse of local democratic governance is equally evident in the declines in CAMPFIRE household dividends between the late 1990s and 2004 from around US$20 to US$0.03. The real decline of the proportion of revenue allocated to household dividends fell from around 50 per cent to less than 1 per cent. Effectively the ward residents (beyond those employed in the lodge and/or hunting industry and the élite of MCC) are getting no economic returns from their wildlife management or recompense from the costs of living with wildlife. CAMPFIRE revenue mechanisms are now effectively a long pipeline of massive leakages – exposed to foreign exchange losses, inflation at the world's highest rates, ad hoc taxes, fraud and minimal transparency.

Networks, patronage and power

By effectively capturing CAMPFIRE operations in Mahenye, the traditional authorities have essentially created a powerful patronage tool for themselves through which they can construct and reproduce power relationships and perpetuate their authority. CAMPFIRE provides the means by which to develop a strong network of loyal supporters. This begins with the enrolment of other members of their extended family as MCC members, ensuring that they receive significant financial benefits in the form of sitting allowances, access to valuable transport and prestige. The Chairman and Chief have ensured that these people are beholden to them. By extending participation in certain key meetings to include all members of the traditional authorities and other party-endorsed positions, this network has been extended further to all those in positions of authority in the village. The network is extended outside family by the manipulation of scarce and valuable employment opportunities within the CAMPFIRE project itself. For example, posts for game monitors, grinding-mill operators and shop assistants are now decided upon exclusively by the MCC. The same is true of jobs with the private sector operators who, by wilfully maintaining the façade that the Chairman of the MCC represents 'the community', give him leverage over who is appointed to these positions. By consolidating their positions of power in other institutions outside the MCC, the Chairman and Chief can threaten retribution to any who question their decisions, not just in the form of losing the benefits that have been forthcoming from being part of their network but also through the potential loss of access to food aid, land or being labelled an opposition supporter. This last threat can also be extended to private sector operators and the RDC through the manipulation of national political networks.

Thus the Chief and Chairman would appear to have built themselves an unassailable position of power and authority. Yet this is clearly not the case. There is unanimous condemnation of the Chairman – although many, particularly the traditional authorities, were careful to draw a distinction between the Chief and the Chairman – and on the need to find a solution to the current problems, even though such a solution would probably lead to some people losing privileged positions as network beneficiaries. However, whilst there is unanimous discontent, the situation within Mahenye is effectively a socially and politically constructed stalemate with no local means of sufficient agency or power to break the deadlock. Therefore people have identified alternative mechanisms to assist them to solve their problems. The long and successful history of CAMPFIRE in the area has ensured that there is considerable local knowledge about the process, including a widespread understanding of the roles and responsibilities of various governance bodies. Thus whilst the RDC is widely distrusted on the grounds that it has its own agenda in relation to the safari operations and securing its own revenue, there is nevertheless clear recognition within Mahenye that it has a legal responsibility to step in to break the local stalemate and the – albeit so far latent – political agency and state–party linkages to do so.

It is generally recognized locally that improving the existing situation involves two different but interconnected activities. First, addressing issues of local governance and second, addressing fiscal accountability and use of revenue. Only once these issues have been resolved do the majority of people in Mahenye want to see greater fiscal devolution occurring. That is to say, their scenario for change is a sequence of events in rebuilding a process of devolution based on local responsibilities and authority but also with strategic linkages and practical politics to get there.

Building accountability from local to district scale

The situation in Mahenye suggests that one of the most significant impacts of CAMPFIRE over the last 20 years has been to empower local people by making them aware of the value of the natural resources in their areas and their (albeit restricted) rights to these, whilst raising awareness of mechanisms through which they can exercise those rights.

Mahenye illustrates that community members can have the knowledge, confidence and organizational awareness to counter local élites who are usurping power and undermining democratic decision-making, and to articulate demands to their political representatives at the district level to assist in resolving the problem. Thus despite the fact that local political mobilization has had to be largely covert in recent years due to fear of reprisal, it has nevertheless created space for political negotiation between the local and district level and catalysed two external and damning investigations. This could ultimately lead to greater accountability of the RDCs to their local constituents. Allied with a strategy of practical politics in a win–win approach to the revenue and economic incentives for the residents of the Ward, the RDC and the private sector, the potential for breaking the current stalemate certainly exists.

Conclusions

The foremost lesson from the experiences of Mahenye is that CBNRM is a process of applied and incremental experiments in local democracy and most valuable in this because it involves not a single idealized state of full devolution but the interaction of tiers of governance over time in adaptive processes. What could be construed as a 'failure' or 'crisis' at any one moment is in reality part of an ongoing process of development which, in this case, contains the seeds of opportunity through which rural people can develop organizational mechanisms and abilities to voice their demands. The analysis, as drawn out in the narratives presented here, demonstrates that CAMPFIRE has had a real impact in terms of empowering local residents, providing them with incentives, knowledge and organizational abilities to identify and address their own problems, recognize the constraints that they are operating within and identify where external interventions are required.

It is apparent that alliances and boundaries are formed throughout these processes, and when situations change these alliances and boundaries shift and reconfigure the landscape of governance and politics of natural resource management. The situation currently facing Mahenye is, in the stories of the residents themselves, just a snapshot of a moment in time. Their eye is on the future and how to effect an outcome that is favourable to all people in Mahenye, not just temporarily powerful local élite. Thus what an observer may view as a crisis is viewed by many local inhabitants as part of an ongoing contest for control over resources within which lie opportunities for positive change. This has been readily apparent in other CAMPFIRE locales during the past decade, notably the community of Masoka which used the crisis brought about by unprecedented RDC appropriation of revenues in 2004 to force a process of renegotiation which led to record benefits being realized by the community only two years later (Taylor and Murphree, 2007).

The situation in Mahenye illustrates the centrality of political dynamics at multiple scales to natural resource governance outcomes. A core concern of CBNRM is therefore working towards the recognition and translation of political capital into a political tool for mobilizing power and bringing local demands to bear on relevant authorities in order to support communities to capture and enlarge the political and policy spaces fundamental to local participation. While in Zimbabwe RDCs are notoriously associated with 'capturing' CAMPFIRE revenues (Bond, 2001; Katerere, 2001; Shackleton and Campbell, 2001; Child et al, 2003), in the current context of Zimbabwe RDCs could provide a system of checks and balances at the local level which can prevent capture of the process by local élites.

But our argument goes further than simply acknowledging the vital role of local government and addresses the broader issue of democratization. Local government has a vital role to play in ensuring democratic outcomes. Mamdani (1996) argues that emphasizing local participation or empowerment in an isolated or autonomous fashion, at the expense of cross-scale alliances and representative forms of democracy, can serve to reinforce authoritarian local structures. He concludes that 'to create a democratic solidarity requires joining the emphasis on autonomy with the one on alliance, that on participatory self-rule with one on representational politics'.

Put simply, a properly democratic system requires the effective linking of the local and national. CBNRM provides a means and incentives by which this can be done. Mahenye, albeit based on informally legitimized institutional foundations (the bylaws) was in the process of doing this in the late 1990s; now in more complex times it retains the potential to do so again and to provide continually evolving political and structural applications of CBNRM.

Despite the manifest problems facing CBNRM in contemporary Zimbabwe, our interpretation of local narratives at Mahenye draws optimism from the capacity for local adaptation and resilience. At the community level, there is ample evidence that many of those factors which Murphree (2001) identified as decisive to their overall success are still in evidence, notably that of intra-communal cohesion, but also resource richness, social energy, flexibility and evolution and acceptance of risk. But it also provides evidence that CAMPFIRE continues to evolve and has empowered local communities with the means and incentive to engage and negotiate with their local government representatives.

Postscript: Mahenye in 2008–2009

Since the research that this chapter is based on was carried out in 2005, a number of macro-political changes have occurred in Zimbabwe, as well as evolutions in Mahenye CAMPFIRE itself and local tiers of governance.

In March 2008 there were disputed national elections in which a majority of parliamentary seats were won by the opposition parties, while the presidential contest led to a presidential run-off in June 2008 between the ZANU-PF and the MDC candidates which was marked by violence. Conflict over both disputed presidential elections and the composition of the new government authorities, led in early 2009 to the signing of a Global Political Agreement (GPA) and the formation of a Government of National Unity (GNU) comprising power sharing between ZANU-PF and MDC with agreement to devise a new Zimbabwean Constitution prior to further elections. The GNU has enabled an improvement in the basic economic situation with the adoption of the US$ as currency and the end of the inflationary spiral that characterized the previous nine years. However, both the implementation aspects of power sharing of the GPA and GNU have encountered serious challenges with considerable powers retained by ZANU-PF in key political, ministerial and administrative structures to the extent that real authority outside the area of macro-finance remains relatively unchanged or highly disputed. This is illustrated by the 'new wave' of forced asset transfers in land and resources sectors by members of the ZANU-PF élite, the retention by this élite of control over the lucrative eastern diamond fields, the retention of Provincial Governors with considerable local powers as ZANU-PF appointees, disputes over the extent of civil society involvement in the new Constitution and a general maintenance of ZANU-PF dominance of local government irrespective of election results. In these macro-scale political struggles the control over both land and the most valuable natural resources or benefits (wildlife hunting concessions, ivory and rhino horn illegal trade, diamond trade, commercial farmland) remain particularly marked and increasingly complex.

At the level of local governance evolutions and the CAMPFIRE Programme in Mahenye, there is considerable evidence for continual mirroring of macro-politics at the local scale, as well as the considerable community agency and ingenuity to continue to address stalemates or distortions in governance.

Following local concerns of distortions of the MCC 'bylaws' and election procedures noted above, new MCC elections were held in March 2006 at the demand of local residents and with the Chipinge RDC as observers. The Mahenye community insisted on holding open elections (lining up behind the candidate of their choice in public) so as to ensure transparency and prevent disputed results. The outcome was the nearly unanimous election of a new Chair and Members of the MCC. The previous Chairman that was rejected by the community was to re-appear again in local governance in 2008 following the sudden death of his brother the Chief (a death locally ascribed to poisoning). This individual's assumption as the new 'Acting Chief' was not on the basis of customary means but was a political appointment by the District Administrator and ZANU PF candidate during campaigns in the period prior to the contentious and disputed 2008 national election process.

The elected Mahenye Ward Councillor of the MDC party also died after a short illness in early 2009 and the MDC supporters in Mahenye alleged Chipinge RDC accepted the ZANU-PF candidate (who had received less than 5 per cent of the ward vote) as the acting Ward Councillor – despite the lack of a procedural basis to do this. Both the new 'Acting Chief' and the 'Acting Ward Councillor' (who are relatives) have little legitimacy, either in formal democratic or customary terms, but are influential representatives of a political party (ZANU-PF) with minimal local support. In these roles they are able to considerably influence MCC decisions on natural resource management and benefit distribution through their claims to be themselves the prime representatives of the 'community' as well as the main representatives of the dominant political party. The paradox that the local electorate, the Mahenye CAMPFIRE constituency and the customary system have all rejected this centrally-delegated local governance cartel is a marked feature of Mahenye narratives at present. That it persists is an indication of the powerful forces that have constructed this governance stalemate both at district-ward level and in national politics, and the significance that control over natural resources such as wildlife has assumed within élite political networks at all levels.

In 2008 the 'informal contract' that existed (illegally) between the RDC and a hunting company was cancelled and new processes for granting this concession through tender took place. This process was administered by the RDC with support from the CAMPFIRE Association. However, the actual tender reviews and agreement on a new hunting company contract for 2008–2010 were noted by MCC members as having been carried out by the RDC without their detailed input and in a process that lacked transparency. Revenues have largely been from hunting (Chilo Lodge payments in 2008 were in Z$ and made effectively worthless by inflation, and 2009 payments in US$ remain to be made). Payments to the community/MCC from hunting remained from 2005 (previous research) until the end of 2008 in Z$ paid in arrears to the extent that the income was effectively zero because of hyperinflation. As of early 2009, the MCC opened its own foreign exchange account and can now receive income in US$. The main beneficiaries of the hunting revenue in 2007–2008 were the RDC, which was able to secure its payments in US$, unlike either the CAMPFIRE Association or the MCC. In 2008 for example, the RDC received US$42,000 in income (compared to effectively zero for the MCC), representing one of the largest income streams for the District and thus a key incentive to retaining controls over decisions. With all parties now able to retain income in US$, the contest over distribution of funds and allocation of them represents a new set of challenges. Contrast the present distribution system to that of the late 1990s, in which the RDC received 20 per cent of income for its support functions, CAMPFIRE Association a level of 2 per cent for its membership support and the balance of 78 per cent was managed by the MCC (with 50 per cent allocated for household cash dividends). Currently, with combined revenues of around US$100,000 likely for 2009, the distribution basis is: around 50–55 per cent for the RDC and 4 per cent to CAMPFIRE Association – both thus with increased income shares – and the remainder (~45 per cent) to the MCC. The end of 2009, when payments will be made to all parties, is likely to see further contestation of distribution and actual incomes both between the three main beneficiaries (RDC, CA and MCC) and within the local context (MCC and the Chief/Councillor).

What remains clear in a situation whose complexity has increased since research in 2005 is that the Mahenye community has explored virtually all the available avenues from national democratic politics to local elections, to changing the MCC composition, to lobbying its RDC and CAMPFIRE representative bodies to find solutions to their natural resource governance challenges. The story continues to reveal a considerable level of community agency to find the governance route that will produce the results it wishes. Current efforts aim to use the customary governance 'checks and balances' structures of the Mahenye Headmen to challenge the illegitimate assumption of power by the 'Acting Chief' and free up local democratic space.

As summed up by one Mahenye resident and long-term contributor to the MCC:

We are between a hammer and a nail. I don't have a good view of today or tomorrow. The will of the people is being ignored. Only a change of politics in Zimbabwe will bring this better. But we can try to change things also here and we are not afraid.

Notes

1   This chapter was published in an earlier form in 2007 as: E.C. Rihoy, C. Chirozva, and S.G. Anstey. (2007) *'People are not Happy' – Speaking up for Adaptive Natural Resource Governance in Mahenye*, Occasional Paper No. 31, Programme for Land and Agrarian Studies, University of Western Cape, Cape Town, South Africa. This version has been shortened and modified, with a postscript added based on the situation in the study area as of 2008–2009 in order to update the rapidly changing social and political landscape of present-day Zimbabwe.

2   Narratives and counter-narratives draw on the work of Roe (1991) and are used to explore the significance of particular sets of ideas or discourses or stories and the ways that they are contested and evolve; and provide plausible explanations and can persist in the face of even strong empirical evidence against their story lines (see Adams and Hulme (2001) for more discussion). Used here for stories from or about Mahenye (and told by policy-makers, academics, local officials and community members) these narratives are not necessarily the 'truth' but more importantly are valid as their own explanation for reality and its causal features.

3   Given the sensitivity of the information collected, the authors have withheld names of most interviewees.

4   At the time of research in 2005, out of a total of 37 staff employed, 32 are from Mahenye, including one in a management position. The construction of the lodges has also led to improved local infrastructure such as transport links, electrification, borehole construction and telephone connections.

5   This three-sentence comment is also a powerful summary of the now highly politicized Zimbabwe rural landscape and the distortions of three normally separate institutions – the Chief (traditional authority), District Administrator (civil servant) and ZANU-PF (political party) – in becoming inter-linked.

References

Adams, W. and Hulme, D. (2001) 'Changing narratives, policy and practices in African conservation', in D. Hulme and M.W. Murphree (eds) *African Wildlife and Livelihoods: The Promise and Performance of Community Conservation*, James Currey, Oxford

Balint, P. and Mashinya, J. (2006) 'The decline of a model community-based conservation project: Governance, capacity and devolution in Mahenye, Zimbabwe', *Geoforum*, vol 37, no 5, pp805–815

Bauer, G. and Taylor, S.D. (2005) *Politics in Southern Africa: State and Society in Transition*, Lynne Rienner, New York

Booth, V.R. (1991) *An Ecological Resource Survey of Mahenye Ward, Ndowoyo Communal Land, Chipinge District*, WWF Multi-species Animal Production Systems, Project Paper No. 20, WWF, Harare, Zimbabwe

Borrini-Feyerabend, G. (1997) *Beyond Fences: Seeking Social Sustainability in Conservation*, IUCN, Gland, Switzerland

Bond, I. (2001) '"CAMPFIRE" and the incentives for institutional change', in D. Hulme and M.W. Murphree (eds) *African Wildlife and Livelihoods: The Promise and Performance of Community Conservation*, James Currey, Oxford

Chabal, P. and Daloz, J.P. (1999) *Africa Works: Disorder as Political Instrument*, James Currey, Oxford

Child, B. (2004) 'The Luangwa integrated rural development project, Zambia', in C. Fabricius, E. Koch, H. Magome and S. Turner (eds) *Rights, Resources and Rural Development: Community-based Natural Resource Management in Southern Africa*, Earthscan, London

Child, B., Jones, B., Mazambani, D., Malalazi, D., and Moinuddin, H. (2003) *Final Evaluation Report – CAMPFIRE Programme*, Zimbabwe Natural Resources Management Programme, USAID/Zimbabwe Strategic Objective No. 1, Final Report submitted to USAID, Harare, Zimbabwe

Dell, C. (2005) 'Plain Talk about the Zimbabwean Economy', Speech delivered at Africa University, Mutare, 2 November 2005

Duffy, R. (2000) *Killing for Conservation: Wildlife Policy in Zimbabwe*, James Currey, Oxford

Dzingirai, V. and Breen, C. (2005) *Confronting the Crisis in Community Conservation: Case Studies from Southern Africa*, Center for Environment, Agriculture and Development, University of KwaZulu-Natal, South Africa

Hammer, J. (2006) 'The hidden links between American hunters and Zimbabwe's dictatorship', *Newsweek* 30 January 2006

Harold-Barry, D. (2004) *Zimbabwe: The Past is the Future*, Weaver Press, Harare, Zimbabwe

Hill, G. (2005) *What Happens after Mugabe: Can Zimbabwe Rise from the Ashes?*, Zebra Press, Cape Town, South Africa

Jones, B. and Murphree, M.W. (2001) 'The evolution of policy on Community Conservation in Namibia and Zimbabwe', in D. Hulme and M.W. Murphree (eds) *African Wildlife and Livelihoods: The Promise and Performance of Community Conservation*, James Currey, Oxford

Katerere, Y. (2001) 'Community public–private partnerships in CBNRM: The real challenges?', in B. Cousins and T.A. Benjaminsen (eds) *Contested Resources: Challenges to the Governance of Natural Resources in Africa*, Programme for Land and Agrarian Studies, University of Western Cape, Cape Town, South Africa

Keeley, J. and Scoones, I. (2003) *Understanding Environmental Policy Processes: Cases from Africa*, Earthscan, London

Makumbe, J. (1998) *Democracy and Development in Zimbabwe: Constraints of Decentralization*, SAPES Books, Harare, Zimbabwe

Mamdani, M. (1996) *Citizen and Subject: Contemporary Africa and the Legacy of Late Colonialism*, James Currey, London

Mapedza, E. (2007) *Keeping CAMPFIRE Going: Political Uncertainty and Natural Resource Management in Zimbabwe*, Gatekeeper Series No. 133, International Institute for Environment and Development, London

Murombedzi, J. (2003) 'Revisiting the principles of CBNRM in southern Africa', in *Proceedings of the Regional Conference on CBNRM in Southern Africa: Sharing Best Practices for the Future*, NACSO, Windhoek, Namibia

Murphree, M.W. (2005) 'Congruent objectives, competing interests, and strategic compromise: Concept and process in the evolution of Zimbabwe's CAMPFIRE, 1984–1996', in J.P. Brosius, A.L. Tsing and C. Zerner (eds) *Communities and Conservation: Histories and Politics of Community-based Natural Resource Management*, AltaMira Press, Walnut Creek, CA

Murphree, M.W. (2001) 'Community, council and client: A case study in ecotourism development from Mahenye, Zimbabwe', in D. Hulme and M.W. Murphree (eds) *African Wildlife and Livelihoods: The Promise and Performance of Community Conservation*, James Currey, Oxford

Murphree, M.W. (2000) *Boundaries and borders; the question of scale in the theory and practice of common property management*, Paper resented at the Eighth Biennial Conference of the International Association of Common Property (IASCP), Bloomington, IN

Murphree, M.W. (1995) *The Lesson From Mahenye: Rural Poverty, Democracy and Wildlife Conservation*, Wildlife and Development Series No. 1, International Institute for Environment and Development, London

Murphree, M.W. and Mazambani, D. (2002) 'Policy Implications of Common Pool Resource Knowledge: A Background Paper on Zimbabwe', Unpublished report, Department of Geography, University of Cambridge and DfID, UK

Nemarundwe, N. (2005) 'The performance of CBNRM in the face of socio-political dynamism: A case study of CAMPFIRE in Masoka, Zimbabwe', in V. Dzingirai and C. Breen (eds) *Confronting the Crisis in Community Conservation: Case Studies from Southern Africa*, Centre for Environment, Agriculture and Development, University of KwaZulu-Natal, South Africa

Ostrom, E. (1990) *Governing the Commons: The Evolution of Institutions for Collective Action*, Cambridge University Press, Cambridge, UK

Peterson, J.H. (1991) *A Proto-CAMPFIRE Initiative in Mahenye Ward, Chipinge District: Development of a Wildlife Programme in Response to Community Needs*, Centre for Applied Social Sciences, University of Zimbabwe, Harare, Zimbabwe

Raftopoulos, B. (2004) 'Current politics in Zimbabwe: Confronting the crisis', in D. Harold-Berry (ed) *Zimbabwe: The Past is the Future*, Weaver Press, Harare, Zimbabwe

Raftopoulos, B. and Savage, T. (2005) *Zimbabwe: Injustice and Political Reconciliation*, Weaver Press, Harare, Zimbabwe

Ribot, J. (2004) *Waiting for Democracy: The Politics of Choice in Natural Resources Decentralization*, World Resources Institute, Washington, DC

Rihoy, E.C. (forthcoming) 'Devolution and democratisation: Policy processes and community-based natural resource management in Southern Africa', Unpublished PhD Thesis for submission (November 2009) to Programme for Land and Agrarian Studies (PLASS), University of Western Cape, South Africa

Rihoy, E.C. and Maguranyanga, B. (2007) *Devolution and Democratisation of Natural Resource Management in Southern Africa: A Comparative Analysis of CBNRM Policy Processes in Botswana and Zimbabwe*, CASS-PLAAS CBNRM Occasional Paper No. 18, Programme for Land and Agrarian Studies, University of Western Cape, Cape Town, South Africa

Roe, E. (1991) 'Development narratives or making the best of blueprint development', *World Development*, vol 19, no 4, pp287–300

Shackleton, S. and Campbell, B. (2001) *Devolution in Natural Resource Management: Institutional Arrangements and Power Shifts – A Synthesis of Case Studies from Southern Africa*, USAID, WWF, EU, CIFOR and CSIR, Bogor, Indonesia

Taylor, R.D. and Murphree, M.W. (2007) *Case Studies on Successful Southern African NRM Initiatives and their Impacts on Poverty and Governance. Zimbabwe: Masoka and Gairezi*, International Resources Group, Washington, DC

Wolmer, W., Chaumba, J. and Scoones, I. (2003) *Wildlife Management and Land Reform in Southeastern Zimbabwe: A Compatible Pairing or a Contradiction in Terms?* Research Paper 1, Sustainable Livelihoods in Southern Africa Programme, IDS, Brighton

9

The Rise and Fall of Community-Based Natural Resource Management in Zambia's Luangwa Valley: An Illustration of Micro- and Macro-Governance Issues

Rodgers Lubilo and Brian Child

Introduction

Community-based natural resource management (CBNRM) is essentially an institutional process concerned with restructuring the governance and allocation of natural resource use. CBNRM combines the twin goals of environmental conservation and rural development because localized institutional arrangements can facilitate both aims. Economic institutions such as property rights and contract law are important for adding value to natural resources and increasing benefits from sustainable use. Of equal importance are political and organizational rules, norms and arrangements that empower rural people to control their own lives through effective and meaningful participation and governance.

Redesigning or reforming economic and political institutions is broad, complex and inherently contested process. Consequently CBNRM implementation has not always lived up to its conceptual expectations, at least in the time that it has been allowed to evolve (Roe et al, 2009; see also Nelson, this volume, Chapter 1). The practical challenge facing CBNRM thus lies in processes surrounding implementation rather than in the concept of local resource governance itself. Indeed CBNRM, combining a range of interconnected political and economic dimensions, is analogous to democratization writ large and brings into play on a smaller scale broader social struggles over political authority and control over resources.[1]

Many of the fundamental challenges to CBNRM lie in the definition of roles and responsibilities and in the configuration and competition over power and resources between and across different scales (see Figure 9.1). The importance of

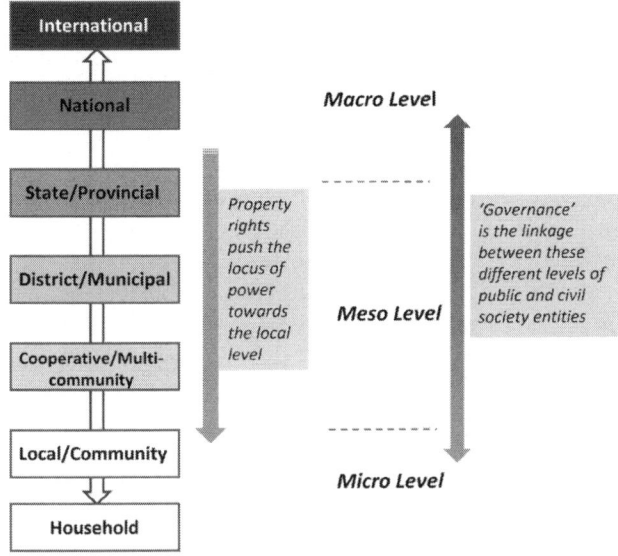

Figure 9.1 *Governance and scale*

these relationships is widely recognized, including by leading deductive (Ostrom, 1990) and inductive social scientists (Murphree, 1991; Murphree, 2000a).

In this chapter we discuss natural resource governance in Zambia at the local level as well as across scales within the broader political environment. Using the case of the Lupande Game Management Area (GMA), where 65,000 people live alongside the South Luangwa National Park, the country's leading wildlife protected area, we contend that the conditions for CBNRM to operate effectively at the local scale are available. There is no technical excuse not to be successful, although many programmes do not achieve their aims because they do not apply rigorous principles based on local democratic governance. However, an additional and perhaps paramount challenge is to facilitate conditions that enable effective local natural resource governance regimes to emerge and persist within the complex political arena within which power is negotiated and renegotiated. Moreover, to understand this, we need to understand the nature of the governing polity itself. Of particular importance is the difference between highly personalized, patrimonial states and the more impersonal and institutionalized economies associated with liberal democracy.[2]

The CBNRM programme in the Luangwa Valley is useful for investigating intra-community and cross-scale governance because it has experienced three distinct phases marked by institutional changes in decision-making in relation to wildlife management and associated revenues, which have occurred over the course of the past 30 years. CBNRM in Luangwa was conceived as a technically strong and decentralized Integrated Resources and Development Project, essentially establishing a mini-government for the Lupande GMA that was well-funded by the Norwegian government and protected politically by then-President Kenneth

Kaunda (Gibson, 1999). This stage lasted from the initiative's inception in the mid-1980s until 1995. In 1996, the programme adopted a much more democratic approach to community participation, drawing ideas as well as personnel from CBNRM initiatives in Zimbabwe (see Rihoy et al, this volume). This second phase led to the devolution of all revenues from wildlife use in Lupande GMA to the community at various levels, with 80 per cent of revenues controlled within villages and used according to processes of direct democratic, rather than representative, decision-making. Despite the relative success of this approach, wildlife revenues were subsequently recentralized in 2003, a situation which continues to the present. We describe the technical outcomes of the three phases and provide a preliminary analysis of why these changes happened. Our perspective is that of field practitioners who worked on CBNRM in Luangwa during many of the years in question, with one of us (R. Lubilo) continuing to permanently reside and work in the area. As such, we have directly observed many of the changes in resource governance during these phases and have participated directly or indirectly in many, but by no means all, of the political processes and negotiations that occurred.

The emergence of CBNRM in Zambia

Zambia's enormous potential as a wildlife-driven economy has never been fulfilled. Some 40 per cent of the country is gazetted as national park, forestry area or GMA, but in most of these areas the wildlife population is depleted (although the habitat is intact) and Zambia earns an order of magnitude less from its wildlife than its neighbours in both southern and eastern Africa because of inappropriate policy and poor governance. Zambia's wildlife management practices include both promotion of non-consumptive or photographic tourism, which occurs primarily in national parks such as South Luangwa, and trophy hunting, which operates in the GMAs. These GMAs are inhabited by rural communities, who hold customary rights to the land which is exercised by traditional chiefly authorities (Lewis and Alpert, 1997; Simasiku et al, 2008).

Politically, Zambia gained independence from Britain in 1964, and followed a pathway of personalized rule as a one-party socialist state under Kenneth Kaunda for 27 years. With neo-patrimonial imperatives being paramount over public or technocratic developmental interests, Zambia rapidly became a highly inefficient state. The country, led by President Kaunda, adopted a socialist centrally-planned economic model which was highly dependent on global copper prices, while the control of natural resources was noticeably centralized (HURID, 2002). After the collapse in copper prices in the 1970s, Zambia came to depend on the largesse of western donors, before entering a phase of multiparty democracy in the 1990s characterized by 're-cycling' the same set of politicians through different competing political parties (Simon, 2005). In the rural areas chiefs are exceptionally strong, and the economy as a whole is dominated by a relatively small number of powerful individuals (cf. Brown, 2003). The institutions of property rights, legal contracting and the judiciary are unreliable and subject to informal negotiations. Corruption is widespread (Szeftel, 2000) and Zambia was ranked 75th in

2001 and 115th in 2008 in Transparency International's Corruption Perceptions Index (Transparency International, 2009). Thus, North et al (2009) would describe Zambia as a personalized economy with high transaction costs, while Hyden (2006) would recognize the essential features of a neo-partimonial state in the personalized loyalties of the civil service and the patronage-based rather than public orientation of policy-making.

Integrating conservation and development in Zambia

In the 1970s and early 1980s, Zambia's elephant and rhino populations were ravaged by commercial poaching, with rhino becoming extinct and over 100,000 elephant being killed (Jachmann and Billiouw, 1997). In response, a national workshop was held in 1983 at Nyamaluma Training Institute in the Luangwa Valley (Dalal-Clayton and Lewis, 1984). The workshop identified poverty as the main reason for rampant poaching and recommended that local communities should participate in both management of, and sharing of benefits from, wildlife. Thus, ideas about integrating wildlife conservation with rural development began to take shape in Zambia, even as experiments with CBNRM arose in neighbouring countries such as Zimbabwe. The basic idea underpinning CBNRM, as it evolved across southern Africa, is that wildlife has to be of value to the local people who live with it if it is to survive. In the early 1980s, regional wildlife managers began to promote the idea that local communities should be allocated concessions to use wildlife (Bell, 1987). This ran counter to a generation of wildlife managers who considered wildlife to be the exclusive property of the government. However, wildlife under such institutional arrangements had no value to local communities and landholders, and during the second half of the 20th century was put under severe pressure, crowded out by alternative land uses and decimated by commercial poachers.

In Zambia, two parallel programmes, the Administrative Management and Design for Game Management Areas (ADMADE) and the Luangwa Integrated Resources and Development Project (LIRDP) emerged (Gibson, 1999). The national ADMADE programme was implemented by the National Parks and Wildlife Service across Zambia, but most prominently in the Luangwa Valley. In designing these programmes, President Kaunda collaborated with Norwegian bilateral aid agency staff to cut South Luangwa out from the purview of the notoriously ineffective National Parks and Wildlife Service (NPWS). Mistrusting NPWS, Kaunda placed the LIRDP under the Commission for Economic Planning and Development as a pilot programme for community development in the Lupande GMA, and for antipoaching in and around the South Luangwa National Park. This established a competitive relationship between the two experimental community wildlife programmes that is well documented by Gibson (1999).

Administrative Management and Design for Game Management Areas (ADMADE)

For the sake of historical completeness, we briefly describe the ADMADE programme (Lewis et al, 1990). ADMADE emerged out of the experimental Lupande Development Project (1984–87) which was originally designed to examine the damage caused to woodlands by elephants restricted to certain areas of the park by human disturbance, to involve local people directly in the protection and sustainable use of wildlife and to return a significant level of wildlife revenues to them (Lewis et al, 1990). Following the 1983 Nyamaluma Workshop (Dalal-Clayton and Lewis, 1984), ADMADE established a central Revolving Fund at NPWS headquarters and worked closely with Nyamaluma Training Institute to provide capacity-building for rural leadership to participate in wildlife conservation. The Revolving Fund collected revenues from trophy hunting in GMAs, and apportioned that revenue from national to local scale as follows:

- 35 per cent to local authorities (i.e. chiefs) for community development;
- 40 per cent for wildlife management in GMAs;
- 25 per cent for NPWS's general management operations.

What is often not mentioned in public documents is that these proportions only apply to 50 per cent of trophy hunting revenues, with the other 50 per cent being retained by the Treasury. Further, records and audits of the Revolving Fund were notoriously incomplete (Gibson, 1999), so communities were seldom aware of how much money they were getting, and the relationship between the amount of income generated in a community and the income paid back to them was never defined and was tentative at best.

Using the 40 per cent allocated for wildlife management in GMAs under ADMADE's revenue-sharing formula, ADMADE instituted a village game scout programme as a way of involving communities in the management of wildlife, albeit under the supervision of NPWS antipoaching staff. ADMADE created wildlife sub-authority committees at chiefdom level for liaison purposes and to implement projects, and placed an NPWS Wildlife Officer as Unit Leader in order to support this process. ADMADE catalysed broader thinking on how to involve communities in the integrated management of wildlife in Zambia so that promoting greater local involvement and benefits from wildlife came to be seen as a desirable conservation strategy. However, while the village scout programme and associated training was a move in a positive direction, the overall performance of ADMADE was hampered by recentralization at the local level and accompanying problems of élite capture and financial non-transparency, and because very few wildlife benefits, except employment as village scouts and a few projects, ever reached individuals (see Gibson and Marks, 1995; Marks, 2001; Bwalya, 2003). The personal alliances leading this programme were shattered in the drawn-out and politicized transformation of NPWS into the parastatal Zambia Wildlife Authority between 1998 and 2003.

Luangwa Integrated Resources and Development Project (LIRDP)

Piloted in six Kunda chiefdoms in the Luangwa Valley, LIRDP's first manifestation was as a large multi-sectoral project designed to coordinate development planning in the district and to provide basic social services, including water, forestry, agricultural research and extension, etc. The programme's mandate was the integrated management of an area of 15,000km^2, including South Luangwa National Park (9,050km^2) and Mambwe District in the Eastern Province of

Zambia. Outside the park, not less than 65,000 indigenous people depend on subsistence farming of maize, rice and sorghum, and more recently, on cotton as a cash crop. LIRDP was in essence a mini-government for the Luangwa Valley, financed largely by the Norwegians and administratively shielded from other bureaucratic interests by the dual influences of that foreign donor and President Kaunda. LIRDP initially spent heavily on coordinating meetings which, in the final analysis, was probably essential to buy political support from the various departments that benefited from participation (including through 'sitting allowances') for the then-radical idea of wildlife-based development (Dalal-Clayton and Child, 2003).

At Cabinet level, an inter-ministerial committee chaired by the President (until 1991) oversaw the project, and two weeks each year were spent in lavish meetings. At district level, numerous coordinating committees met regularly, wrote reports and absorbed sitting allowances. Unfortunately, this led to LIRDP becoming an organization oriented towards spending money on administrative functions and which was regularly criticized for inefficiency, employing between 350 and 600 people and having over 40 Toyota Land Cruisers in use. Moreover, LIRDP did not have an easy task. Administrative structures in the district were complex and confused. For instance, the formal district administrative structure, Mambwe District Council (comprising 13 political wards with elected councillors, and an area Member of Parliament) often could not pay its technical staff for months at a time, while its authority relative to other government departments, and particularly the traditional leadership, was never clear. The project area included six chiefdoms under the leadership of Senior Chief Nsefu. Each chief is advised by a team of *indunas*,[3] while groups of households are administered by a Village Headman. *Indunas* and headmen play a key role in resource utilization at community level, allocating land for farming and settlements subject to the approval of the chief.

South Luangwa National Park is Zambia's premier tourism destination (after the Victoria Falls). In the central planning mode, LIRDP[4] tried to run tourism and hunting operations itself. This was heavily subsidized by the donor, and generated income of about US$150,000 from park fees compared to expenditures for the park and GMA exceeding US$3 million annually. This partly funded LIRDP antipoaching operations, which were most effective between the mid-1980s and mid-1990s. This stopped rampant elephant poaching, allowing populations to recover from roughly 5,000 to 10,000 at the same time that elephant populations elsewhere in Zambia continued to decline (Jachmann and Billiouw, 1997; Patterson, pers. comm.[5]). However, the park only approached financial self-sufficiency in the late 1990s when it was managed as a self-financing cost centre and adopted a new commercial model based on private sector investment. There are now 50 lodges and campsites with 300 beds in total capacity in and around the park generating some US$1 million in park fees annually (SLAMU, 2008). This created the first employment-based economy in the GMA with both positive effects (e.g. economic development) and negative ones (e.g. unplanned settlement growth). The GMA is one of Zambia's prime areas for trophy hunting, and in the 2007 hunting season, for example, generated US$488,000 (SLAMU, 2007).

The rise and fall of community wildlife management in the Luangwa Valley

After the idea of community conservation emerged in the Luangwa Valley in the early 1980s (Dalal-Clayton, 1984), the subsequent evolution of LIRDP can usefully be characterized according to three district phases.

1 In the first phase of LIRDP (1986–1995) all wildlife revenues generated by the park and GMA were retained by the programme, and 40 per cent of these revenues were channelled to local communities through traditional leaders, the chiefs.

2 In the second phase (1996–2002) the community retained 100 per cent of revenues from trophy hunting in the GMA, and more than 80 per cent of this was allocated through some 45 Village Action Groups (VAGs). By this time, hunting revenues had risen to over US$225,000 annually. The communities did not receive any of the revenue generated by South Luangwa National Park, which was treated as a self-financing management unity.

3 Following the transformation of the government department, NPWS, into the self-financing parastatal, the Zambia Wildlife Authority (ZAWA), wildlife income was recentralized in Lusaka. ZAWA officially allocates 50 per cent of trophy fees and 20 per cent of concession fees from trophy hunting to GMAs, and makes sporadic payments to Community Resources Boards (CRBs) which have been established at the level of a chiefdom, far more removed from local communities than the village-level VAGs.

These phases are described in tables and figures to clarify key issues of scale and authority in the Zambian context. Figure 9.2 shows how policies associated with the three phases substantially affect the locus of financial decision-making and the configuration of power between the levels. Note how, in the recentralization phase, governance is re-personalized, with ZAWA scaling revenues back upwards to itself and empowering chiefs in relation to CRBs. Predictably, this virtually eliminated VAG-level activity by removing financing and, indeed, information. Table 9.1 summarizes performance in terms of participation, benefit flows, financial accountability and access to information at three levels in the community over the three phases of the project.

Local participation in wildlife management through top-down benefit-sharing (1985–1995)

Following an initial planning phase, LIRDP received substantial funding from the Norwegian government and two co-directors were employed to oversee the development of a viable wildlife-based development programme in the Luangwa Valley: Fidelius Lungu, a confidant of President Kaunda, and Richard Bell, a leading southern African wildlife manager and CBNRM innovator.

Several factors aligned in the emergence of this new conservation model in Zambia in the early 1980s. As mentioned, Zambia faced a serious poaching crisis.

Table 9.1 An assessment of annual performance (participation, benefits, financial accountability, information flows) at different levels of community administration in the three phases of the programme

Performance metrics	First (benefit-sharing) phase	Second (participatory democracy) phase	Third (recentralization) phase
Participation			
Level 3: GMA	80 man days (Chiefs + 2 *indunas* meet quarterly)	20 man days (seldom meet because of conflicts)	Nil
Level 2: ADC/CRB	Informal	600 man days (6 committees met monthly)	240 man days (6 committees meet quarterly)
Level 1: VAG		81,000 days	No meetings
Ordinary people		(45 VAGs, 300 people, 3 quarterly GMs, 1 3-day AGM)	
Benefits			
Household benefits	Nil	20,500 people get benefits	Nil
Projects	A few	262 projects	Nil
Wildlife management	Nil	Allocation increase to 14% of income; employed 78 Village Scouts	??
Financial Accountability			
Level 2&3: LIRDA, ADC, CRB	No accounts but many rumours	40% misallocated (mainly 2 chiefs with HIV/AIDS)	No records but unhappy rumours
Level 1: VAG	No income	>98% of $175,000+ accounted for by year 2000	No income
Information flow			
Levels 2&3: Committees/chiefs	General information on project; rough accounting of income (no records of expenditure)	As below	Not known
Level 1: Ordinary people	General idea of project	Income and Expenditure plus audit reports Quotas. Wildlife values. Their rights. Procedures. HIV/AIDS	Very little

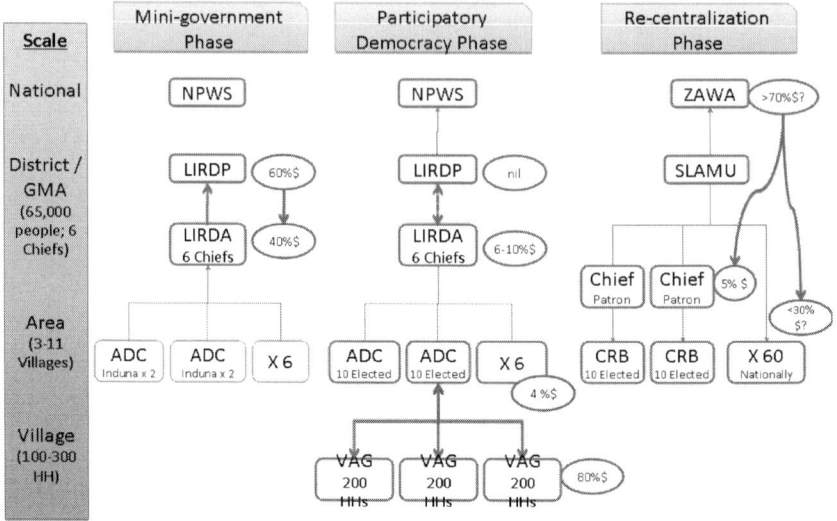

Figure 9.2 *A comparison of the organization structures and revenue flows of different organizational levels in the three project phases*

At the same time concerned individuals (e.g. Norman Carr), researchers (e.g. Dale Lewis), NGOs (e.g. WWF) and government officials (e.g. Gilson Kaweche) were engaged in a regional debate about the potential of wildlife-based development and the merits of citizen- and incentive-led conservation (Suich et al, 2008). As it happened, the Norwegians had recruited an energetic polar bear expert (Thor Larsen) to their Lusaka Embassy. The financial foundation for LIRDP was laid when Larsen tracked President Kaunda to his private lodge in South Luangwa National Park and together they developed the initial idea for LIRDP. President Kaunda had a fondness for wildlife, and both he and his wife had their political and personal roots in eastern Zambia, with his wife coming from Mambwe District.

President Kaunda removed the new initiative from the control of NPWS, the Norwegians funded LIRDP, and Bell and Lungu managed it. Bell was clearly aware of the problems of an isolated project approach, having written about similar problems arising from early Zimbabwean CBNRM efforts (Bell, 1987). Nevertheless, LIRDP adopted a stand-alone programmatic model. Perhaps it was impossible to alter Zambia's model of central planning quite so radically, while Bell and Lungu may have believed that central planning worked if the central planners were situated locally and were technically competent, as both these men were. Moreover, at the time, critical lessons about representational and participatory local governance had not yet emerged from experiential learning across the region.

The net result was a top-down system where the use of the 40 per cent of wildlife revenues allocated under LIRDP for local revenue-sharing was decided locally by the Local Leaders Sub-committee comprising 6 chiefs, 12 *indunas* (one male and one female from each chiefdom), 4 elected councillors and other invited stakeholders. This 40 per cent was shared equitably among the chiefdoms, which covered a total of 65,000 people, based on needs and was targeted towards infra-structure and service provision. No financial statements describing the use of these wildlife revenues have ever been made available. Judged by output (e.g. lack of projects), expenditure was inefficient and used personally, it is said, by local élites.[6] Funds generated by the park and hunting in the GMA were also mixed with donor funds in their operational use.

A culture of spending emerged, based partly on the availability of external donor funds, providing services that could never be sustained. The provision of social services including water, rural development, women's projects, agricultural exten-sion, forestry, roads and wildlife management, was implemented in a conventional bureaucratic style. The communities' general cynicism about projects and service provision during this period corresponds to the poor record of service delivery. Building the capacity of the local community was largely ignored, and local partic-ipation was limited to interactions with chiefs, who were the principal decision-makers at the local level. Though the intention was good, the results were poor in terms of empowering the local people and changing their attitudes towards wildlife. The project also engaged in entrepreneurial projects including Malambo Milling, Malambo Transport, Malambo Safaris and a game-cropping scheme to generate income and employment. These businesses all failed, and absorbed significant donor funding. The business model relied on almost unlimited access to donor financing and was never distanced from the personal attention and benefit of the local élites (i.e. the chiefs).

The chiefs and LIRDP staff took all key decisions, and the centralized decision-making system did not encourage local people to link wildlife conservation with benefits received. Most people assumed the services were being funded by donor aid grants. A series of studies trace a shift from negative attitudes towards wildlife in the mini-government phase of LIRDP, largely because of human–wildlife conflict and non-participation (Balakrishna and Ndlovu, 1992; Wainwright, 1996), with attitudes then improving markedly, initially because of tourism (Butler, 1996), but by 1998 direct (cash) benefits were prominent in people's responses (Phiri, 1996; Butler, 1998).

Transitioning to a bottom-up approach (1992–1996)

After 27 years as a one-party state, the 1991 elections in Zambia saw the startling defeat of President Kaunda and the end of socialism as the dominant develop-ment discourse. Frederick Chiluba, a former labour activist and opposition leader with the Movement for Multiparty Democracy (MMD), unseated Kaunda as Zambia transitioned towards a more liberalized economy under pressure from donors' structural adjustment programmes and conditional loan requirements. In 1992, NPWS wrested control of LIRDP back from the National Commission for Development Planning and replaced the two LIRDP co-directors with an NPWS employee.

With income of about US$200,000 and expenditure approaching US$3 million, a proposal was submitted for a third phase of Norwegian funding to LIRDP in 1992. This was heavily criticized by consultants reviewing the proposal for replicating a bureaucratic behemoth while claiming to be seeking financial sustainability, and for perpetuating paternalistic and weakly accountable community conservation structures with only 2 per cent of the budget devoted to community development (Scanteam, 1993). Subsequent revisions emphasized returning functions to line ministries, reorganizing the project with clear and funded core functions, and strengthening CBNRM through more devolved forms of grassroots organization.

In 1996, the project hired a technical advisor from Zimbabwe to develop a more participatory and 'bottom-up' system for community wildlife management.[7] This led to an internal planning process that re-engineered the programme from within, recognizing that only a modernized organizational culture would support decentralized CBNRM. LIRDP sought financial sustainability by eliminating many unfunded service mandates, and by devolving planning, budgets and authority to nine cost centres through a performance management system. It also recruited new Zambian staff with a more commercial and business-oriented outlook.

Simultaneously, a series of workshops with the six Area Development Committees (ADCs) indicated that few projects were being implemented, that communities were not benefiting, and that the project and wildlife were viewed negatively at the local level. In April 1996, and following a visit to Zimbabwe's CAMPFIRE programme, senior project management met and agreed to transform the approach to CBNRM. LIRDP produced a four-page policy document that clearly described new financial procedures and responsibilities for each of the administrative layers in the programme – LIRDP, the chiefs, ADCs and community members through the mechanism of participation in Village Action Groups (VAGs).

Under this new approach, all revenue from trophy hunting carried out in the GMA would be banked in a community account. As soon as conformance monitoring verified that proper procedures were followed, including elections, participatory budgeting and financial reporting (both to LIRDP and the community), 80 per cent of this money would be divided amongst the 45 VAGs. Ordinary people could choose to allocate this revenue for personal or collective benefits at the village scale, as well as for wildlife management and administrative overheads, without interference from the chiefs or the LIRDP management. The ADC received 4 per cent for general coordinative functions, the chiefs were redefined as 'patrons' and were effectively paid off with a 6 per cent share, and 10 per cent remained in the account as a contingency fund.

This proposal, representing a radical departure from the way wildlife revenues were allocated under the prior LIRDP phase, was presented to the national Policy Committee that oversaw LIRDP and was attended by Permanent Secretaries from at least five ministries. Amazingly, it was accepted almost without comment despite almost no pre-meeting lobbying by LIRDP staff. Unlike Zimbabwe and Namibia, where CBNRM arrangements were built into primary legislation, in the Luangwa Valley the enabling framework was an administrative agreement made by this committee and strengthened by the overarching Norway–Zambia bilateral cooperative agreement.

Support for the new approach was provided for the first revenue distribution in Malama chiefdom through the attendance of senior officials from both NPWS and the Norwegian Embassy, a ceremony preceded by considerable participatory planning and budgeting (Child, 2006). The community had allocated money to schools and other social projects, and were excited when the trunkful of cash for household cash dividends and projects arrived. Nonetheless, the revenue distribution was cancelled when Chief Malama conspicuously drove away in his vehicle to visit nearby relatives. Thus began a four-year battle over fiscal devolution between the chiefs in the Luangwa Valley and their subjects.

In the short term, the concept of fiscal devolution through face-to-face financial budgeting and the rights to individual and collective choice over investments was saved by Chief Msoro. He allowed local revenue distribution according to the new LIRDP formula to continue in his chiefdom. Social pressure within the community led even Chief Malama to approach LIRDP with his reconsideration. The chiefs now legally received a significant annual honorarium from wildlife, but it is likely that they benefited far more from the non-transparent and top-down system that this replaced. A battle of wills ensued, with some of the chiefs trying to force their subjects to spend money in certain ways. Ordinary community members often asked LIRDP to challenge the chiefs on their behalf. LIRDP recognized that it could only lose by getting caught in the middle of this political struggle, and simply insisted on financial transparency, enabling and insisting that communities produced accurate accounts and made these widely available within the community at least four times per year. The conflict over money raged for at least four years, and LIRDP staff were harangued for many hours at formal meetings with chiefs, and sometimes by politicians and bureaucrats. After four years these conflicts somehow faded in the course of interactions between the communities and their chiefs.

The new LIRDP approach did not arise organically from within communities, but was designed by external programme staff, and then explained village-by-village through a process of participatory constitution development followed closely by experiential learning when each VAG was facilitated through a three-day process of budgeting their money, running elections and paying out cash dividends. Although this neo-liberal democratic approach was imposed on local communities, who had little capacity to aspire to an approach they had never seen before, it was absorbed almost seamlessly. Indeed, the chiefs took their dissatisfaction with this democratic approach to the national Policy Committee, who ruled that people should be allowed to vote on which approach they preferred. A poll was organized in one village in Chief Mnkhanya's area. In an energetic process over 130 people supported the new system with only seven votes against it. The chiefs subsequently objected to such polls as being non-traditional, but the point had been made.

CBNRM as fiscal devolution and participatory democracy (1996–2002)

The crucial mechanism for creating participation and financial accountability was to devolve the allocation and control of 80 per cent of wildlife revenues to Village Action Groups (see Figure 9.2), and to insist on conformance to face-to-face procedures for democratic accountability. This also prised financial control away from the chiefs. When face-to-face meetings became to big too handle, communities sub-divided themselves, and through this organic process each chiefdom was divided into between 3 and 11 VAGs. The Project redefined its role as facilitating participatory democracy by emphasizing the flow of information (e.g. finances, wildlife off-take and prices), insisting on conformance to key democratic principles, and providing supporting training and facilitation (e.g. constitution formation and reinforcement). The Project ensured compliance with the new democratic procedures, but did not interfere in the VAGs' choices about spending, except that fiscal management was participatory and money was accounted for. Some programme staff and government officials struggled to accept this hands-off role. Individual members of the community were placed at the centre of all decisions, while ensuring (through 45 quarterly community assemblies and the 6 ADCs) that their decisions were informed by quality information and regular discussions and presentations on constitutions, roles and responsibilities, and members' rights, financial expenditure and wildlife utilization.

The overall management system was loosened by devolving decisions to ordinary people and allowing them the full choice of how to use their money, including household cash.[8] However, procedurally, the system was tightened; revenue was only made available to communities once they had conformed to requirements for face-to-face budgeting, face-to-face control of previous finances, the transparent financial records necessary for this and annual elections. Accountability was further strengthened as committees were downwardly accountable to the membership and upwardly accountable to LIRDP, and to the ADC and the district-level Luangwa Integrated Rural Development Authority (see below). Key mechanisms were, respectively:

1   well-organized quarterly village assemblies;
2   conformance monitoring implemented by the programme that summarized oversight of each community using a simple one-page checklist.

At the VAG Annual General Meeting, at least 60 per cent of the community met face-to-face to decide how to spend their money. They compiled a simple budget and work plan, elected new leaders, signed off on financial and progress reports, and updated and revised the membership register. At quarterly general meetings, actual expenditure was compared to agreed budgets and work plans with support from LIRDP staff in the form of financial and technical audits. Thus, ordinary people made decisions and checked that they were implemented. These arrangements enabled the communities to give instructions to their village-level committees, instructions which could not be changed without their authority as reinforced through these assemblies. This helped prevent committees from changing budgets, prolonging the terms of office bearers, terminating membership and hiding information.

The result was energetic acceptance of the programme, a burst of community projects and voluntarism, and a drastic reduction in poaching in Luangwa. An important lesson imported from CAMPFIRE in Zimbabwe (Child et al, 1997; Rihoy et al, this volume) and confirmed in LIRDP was the power of household-level cash dividends, with some 20,500 people benefiting directly each year. Although this was often criticized by bureaucrats as amounting to only US$10 or so annually, it was critically important, not only to cash-starved households, but also in symbolizing community ownership and authority, in bringing communities together to resolve their own problems, and in linking benefits directly to wildlife. This linkage was emphasized with a careful and full accounting of all wildlife off-take and income in every community using flipcharts, in marked contrast to the unexplained sources of local benefits as occurred during the previous programme phase.

While a four-level hierarchical structure that looked good on paper was officially accepted, the primary levels of actual decision-making were the VAGs and the LIRDP itself, with the ADC performing light functions and the LIRDA becoming almost irrelevant. We describe the roles of the different layers of local governance during this phase of LIRDP in greater detail below.

Institutions at district level

The Lupande Integrated Rural Development Authority (LIRDA) was a district-level assembly chaired by the chiefs with representation from *indunas*, councillors and LIRDP project staff. It was supposed to be a policy body debating principles and key decisions, but conflicts between LIRDP and chiefs over fiscal devolution, and between chiefs over the share of revenues, rendered this entity virtually non-functional. As noted, the chiefs had rejected the principle that wildlife revenues should accrue proportionally to the local communities that lived alongside wild-life, and which produced the wildlife used for trophy hunting, and wanted funds shared equally across the six chiefdoms of the 'Kunda nation'. However, the chiefs adjacent to the park, where agriculture was less successful and human–wildlife conflict more serious, soon began to lobby for a greater share of benefits, and this and other conflicts made it difficult to bring the chiefs together.[9]

The six chiefdoms

At chiefdom level, the role of the Area Development Committee (ADC) was restricted by cutting their share of the budget to 4 per cent to cover administrative costs, meetings, travel expenses and allowances. The role of ADCs was redefined as the coordination of VAGs and ensuring compliance to the agreed programmatic principles of democracy, transparency and accountability. The ADCs were encouraged to use village general meetings to raise awareness of problems and ask the people to take appropriate action but had no power to alter the budget of any village.

Village Action Groups (VAGs)

The foundation of the programme during this phase was the 45 VAGs, where individuals assembled face-to-face to make decisions about wildlife management, revenue distribution and project development. With control over 80 per cent of the wildlife income generated in Lupande GMA, VAGs became vibrant organizations. On average, the VAGs apportioned their income, very roughly, as follows:

- 10 per cent for administration;
- roughly 10 per cent (but up to 14 per cent by 2000) for wildlife management including the employment of some 78 village scouts, patrolling and the construction of wildlife dams;

- roughly 40 per cent for household cash dividends;
- roughly 40 per cent for social projects including the construction or renovation of schools, wells, clinics, teachers' houses, and shelters and investments in sewing machines, food and even football clubs.

In six years, some 232 projects were built compared to, perhaps, ten (there were few records) grain-storage sheds, classrooms and clinics during the previous programme phase, which had been built on behalf of the communities and often associated with conflict and incompletion. Notwithstanding the allocation of 60 per cent of the communities' income as cash benefits, wildlife management and administration, the number of projects increased by a factor of well over 20, presumably because of increased accountability, voluntarism (e.g. brick-making, digging, carrying water), and using scarce cash only for items such as metal roofing and door frames (Dalal-Clayton and Child, 2003). In addition, communities began to set aside land for wildlife conservation and attitudes towards wildlife improved measurably (Lubilo, 2007). Nevertheless, some officials and traditional leaders regularly complained that development was being squandered because people took a proportion of their revenues as cash and, sin-of-sins, sometimes bought beer with those dividends.

Constitutions were crafted carefully so that power lay with individuals, who were empowered to change their leaders, approve all financial decisions, request and require financial and technical reports and other information. People met quarterly to review performance through reports from the chair, treasurer and secretary. The process of participatory revenue allocation and tracking provided a strong foundation for improved natural resource governance. People met under the tree at the centre of villages to decide how much money to take as cash or to invest in projects or administration (e.g. meetings, allowances, transport and communication). The cash distribution signalled a positive and independent choice for the local community and enhanced power to manage their own affairs. Consequently, people learned how to account for cash, develop infrastructure and service provision projects and to manage wildlife. This built strong proprietary interest in the programme and created confidence amongst local people.

The collapse of participatory democracy (2002–present)

Restructuring NPWS from a government department into the self-funding parastatal Zambia Wildlife Authority (ZAWA) seriously damaged CBNRM in Zambia. A poorly conceived transition meant that ZAWA often could not pay its own staff's salaries, and institutionalized a bureaucratic dependence on revenues from GMAs, effectively extracting resources from Zambia's rural poor. ZAWA officials used the organization's financial crisis, which saw staff go for several months without salaries, to undermine the extant LIRDP approach to wildlife management, and to argue against communities receiving cash dividends. This was exacerbated by a trophy hunting ban put in place nationally between 2001 and 2003, which not only affected ZAWA's finances, but meant that communities went without income for two years, so that ZAWA's new policy of not giving communities revenue from wildlife was less obvious.

The transformation process which replaced NPWS with ZAWA was rancorous, lengthy and associated with political intrigue, as different factions struggled for control of Zambia's wildlife. Legally, ZAWA was established through the Zambia Wildlife Act No. 12 of 1998, followed by a commencement order issued in 2000. This legislation provided a firmer legal basis for CBNRM through newly legislated Community Resources Boards (CRBs). Unfortunately, the framework for CBNRM in the Act provided a lot of administrative detail about how CRBs were to function (with little room for flexibility), but missed the lesson that accountability arises through well-organized bottom-up processes. ZAWA established representational CRBs at the scale of approximately 10,000 people, defining accountability from the top-down but without any logistical capacity to implement requirements such as regular audits. The Act could nevertheless be interpreted to entrench further devolution using subsidiary legislation and guidelines, but in practice was used to recentralize CBNRM both nationally and locally, as well as to extract income from wildlife living in rural areas. To understand why it played out in this way, we describe the transformation process in more detail.

The rapidly improving financial and technical performance of LIRDP in the late 1990s, and of tourism in Zambia more generally, excited considerable donor interest in protected areas as an option for economic development. Delighted by their success in Luangwa, the Norwegians sought to scale this up by supporting the transformation of NPWS into the parastatal ZAWA in the hope of extending progress countrywide,[10] and especially to Kafue National Park, one of the country's other major wildlife areas. The challenge was to create new rational-legal institutions to replace the personalized rule within a state with a heavy interest in the wildlife sector and its patronage possibilities. The potential gains in economic growth, poverty reduction and wildlife conservation were considerable.

Inexplicably, the Norwegians, who led this multi-donor push for reform,[11] changed their management model in the midst of this complicated transition from NPWS to ZAWA. They phased out external technical assistance, and stopped ring-fencing and protecting South Luangwa to demonstrate their solidarity with ZAWA. But most importantly, they reinterpreted their definition of 'recipient responsibility'. The strategy of facilitating LIRDP to develop objective-orientated, measurable annual and four-year plans, holding LIRDP accountable to the performance metrics in these plans, and insisting that the purpose of the project was to 'benefit Zambians at a household level'[12] was a major factor in the turnaround of LIRDP. Norway's programmes in Luangwa (and also through direct payment to scouts for antipoaching efforts in Kafue) clearly demonstrated the effectiveness of linking funding to measurable performance. Possibly influenced by a general return of donors to basket funding rather than project support in the early 2000s, Norway (and others) began to fund ZAWA centrally yet with far less emphasis on linking payments to performance than before. Providing money to headquarters, with weaker links to metrics of performance, enabled ZAWA's managerial culture to orient less towards technical delivery (and decentralization) and more towards political and patronage ends and centralization.

During the negotiations over aid support to ZAWA, a small group of advocates attempted to persuade the donors to use their financial muscle to support ZAWA, but on condition that ZAWA protected the rights of communities to benefit from wildlife on their lands (DSI, 2002). In the event, ZAWA hauled in money from both the donors and the communities, with the associated collapse of considerable investment in CBNRM by both ADMADE and LIRDP.

ZAWA recruited key staff from LIRDP, especially those with competencies developed outside the government system, but their technical skills were not up to the political intrigue of the ZAWA transformation and they were eventually lost from the system. At the same time, Norway phased out its last two technical assistants. This broke up LIRDP's management team, and little capacity remained to support local rights and interests. At the same time, the ZAWA transformation lacked technical capacity, especially but not only related to CBNRM. Institutional memory was eroded even further by simultaneous staff changes in the Norwegian Embassy which, as mentioned above, may have largely accounted for the emphasis on local benefits and accountable performance being dropped in favour of granting large-scale financial support to ZAWA. Norwegian priorities and rhetoric also changed radically.

In the early 2000s, LIRDP was lauded as a flagship programme to the extent that Norway's Environmental Action Plan highlighted the 'conservation and sustainable use of ecosystems' and 'giving local communities, including indigenous people, access to natural resources and the fair and equitable sharing of the benefits arising out of the utilization of genetic resources'. Norwegian officials suggested that Norway wanted to become the premier supporter of community conservation. However, this was rapidly dropped in favour of a focus on climate change, while in Zambia, commitment to CBNRM was replaced with new rhetoric that cast doubt on the effectiveness of CBNRM.[13] Consequently, as Zambia's wildlife sector was transformed with considerable donor investment, the Luangwa communities and CBNRM more broadly had fewer technical and political supporters.

From Village Action Groups to Community Resource Boards

Despite the experiences over the previous six years in Luangwa that clearly demonstrated the advantages of participatory democracy over more remote and large-scale representational governance structures, ZAWA has shown a preference for the latter. ZAWA institutionalized a system of Community Resource Boards across the country, effectively re-establishing the ineffective top-down approach associated with the first phase of LIRDP. The main nominal change in the CRBs, in comparison to the first phase of LIRDP, is that chiefs are supposedly distanced from the operations of the CRB which, however, coincide administratively with chiefdoms.

Participatory democracy in the Lupande GMA, based on VAGs, was replaced by a representational organization comprised of officials elected from the community over a vastly larger area. Community assemblies all but ceased, and information is no longer flowing at the village or household scale (Lubilo, 2007). The underlying cause is the re-introduction of a representational form of governance and the recentralization of wildlife finances and associated loss of transparency and accountability. In June 2002, ZAWA called together the chairs of Zambia's 60 CRBs to discuss revenue-sharing. The workshop report (Mwape, 2002) states that the meeting agreed to share revenues as follows:

- CRBs 45 per cent;
- patrons (chiefs) 5 per cent;
- ZAWA 40 per cent;
- Government/Zambia Revenue Authority 10 per cent.

This report notes that based on this revenue-sharing formula, local communities will effectively receive considerably more money than they used to receive before (Ibid.)

However, participants who were subsequently interviewed noted that the workshop was confused and did not reach a consensus for ZAWA to retain 40–50 per cent of wildlife revenues. The distortion went further, with ZAWA failing to mention that this proportion applied only to trophy fees and that it intended to retain 80 per cent of concession fees, or some 70 per cent of GMA gross wildlife income.

The flow of revenues was also centralized. Instead of being paid directly into the community bank account in Lupande, hunting fees are now collected at ZAWA headquarters in Lusaka. With ZAWA sometimes unable to meet its own salary bills, it is hardly surprising that communities are paid out somewhat sporadically. Moreover, payments are not associated with a full accounting of wildlife off-take, further breaking the links between wildlife use, benefits received and accountability in decision-making.

In 2007, we interviewed some 463 individuals in the Lupande GMA, as well as key informants amongst traditional leaders, government officials and the tourism sector (Lubilo, 2007). The VAGs had collapsed, with few meetings, loss of income to communities and individuals, lack of projects, and weakened systems of checks and balances. Local communities were no longer in charge, and the sense of proprietorship and procedural accountability had been lost. The absence of constitutions made it difficult to organize CRBs and local people are of the opinion that there is too much scope for corruption in a system that has been recentralized under the control of a small élite. Indeed, almost nothing has been done to build the capacity of CRBs or to address their accountability to the village scale. LIRDP has lost its technical expertise in CBNRM, including a cadre of trained Zambians. At the national level, ZAWA did away with the directorate dealing with communities in GMAs. Finally, the donors driving the transformation of the wildlife sector no longer appear strongly committed to CBNRM.

The failure of CRBs has seriously eroded the confidence of the communities in the new system. The system of regular financial auditing of community accounts had collapsed, and performance is unlikely to differ from similar CRB systems around Kafue National Park, where no money benefits local people and over 80 per cent of income is not accounted for (Malenga, 2004, p363). The 2007 survey showed that CRBs have failed to provide information on wildlife income or expenditure to people, public meetings had all but ceased, and CBNRM activities were limited to routine committee meetings. Indeed, the transition from participatory to representational governance reduced the number of people with some knowledge of wildlife income and expenditure from an average of 72 per cent to 20 per cent (Table 9.2). It is interesting to note that in Malama CRB the proportion of people with an understanding of finances was large unchanged or even slightly increased (from 50 per cent to 56 per cent of the sample). Malama CRB, with less than 100 households, retains the scale necessary for participatory governance and decision-making.

Table 9.2 *A comparison of information on finances in communities between the 'participatory' (1997–1999) and 'recentralization' (2007) phases*

Name of CRB	1997–99 (40%+)	2007 (All + Some)
Jumbe	80%	16%
Kakumbi	93%	12%
Malama	50%	56%
Mnkhanya	53%	14%
Msoro	66%	
Nsefu	78%	11%
Overall %	72%	20%
n	851	451

Note on methodology: In 1997–99 community members were interviewed to assess if they understood roughly 0 per cent, 20 per cent, 40 per cent, 60 per cent, 80 per cent, 100 per cent of community wildlife finances. In 2007, community members were asked if they got 'all', 'some', 'none', 'didn't know' information about community finances.

Recentralization has reduced local people's participation, largely destroying the spirit of voluntarism that had been developed. Interviews suggested that although people supported CBNRM they thought that the Luangwa programme was on the verge of collapse because the CRB and ZAWA made all decisions on the use of funds. This undermined a strong sense of community ownership; instead of some 75,000–100,000 meeting days discussing wildlife (see Table 9.1), people now shun conservation meetings because they do not see meaningful direct benefits which would warrant their commitment – only 4 per cent of people said they got cash benefits in 2007 compared to nearly all adults seven years previously. This malaise is not limited to Lupande GMA. Across the country we generally observe little participation or agitation even when ZAWA delays the release of funds to CRBs. Within-community accountability has broken down, but so has the accountability of ZAWA to the communities where wildlife income is generated.

Chiefs are held in high esteem in Zambia, where their role is enshrined in local government legislation, as well as the Zambia Wildlife Act of 1998, which recognizes chiefs as patrons to the CRBs. The hope was to satisfy chiefs with non-administrative powers and a 5 per cent honorarium, but in practice they again influence the use of funds, and are said to be a major factor in the misappropriation of funds by CRBs, just as they were during the top-down phase of LIRDP. Despite legal niceties and their honoraria, chiefs are said to 'collect huge sums' from the CRBs (see Lubilo, 2007). ZAWA has also given chiefs the mandate to vet people who stand in elections whether at VAG or CRB level.

Local people nevertheless agree that chiefs have an important role to play in CBNRM by encouraging community mobilization, voluntarism and participation, and having the power to allocate land for settlements, farming and other uses. However, many lament the loss of the system whereby, if chiefs wanted extra money from the community for such activities as vehicle maintenance, they were allowed to present their budget proposal to each village Annual General Meeting, with some villages agreeing to the requests and others refusing. Indeed, people agree that the chiefs had adjusted somewhat to the principles of participatory democracy, and even played a part in contributing to strengthening local participation. While the chiefs have taken advantage of the loss of accountability to reassert patrimonial governance practices, they are also complaining about the loss of local control of funds and ZAWA's unreliability in disbursing these.

The reaction to changes in CBNRM in Lupande GMA amongst government officials is mixed. Those responsible for working in the communities on a daily basis express concern that ZAWA has effectively undermined a decentralized system which was delivering some positive outcomes for local people and for wildlife management. However, more senior officials are impressed with the current status quo and overall ZAWA favours representative rather than participatory democracy where CRBs have a committee that is elected every three years.

In summary, the replacement of village-level VAGs with CRBs eroded accountable and participatory local governance with less accountable, higher-scale institutional arrangements. It recentralized financial management in a way that facilitates greater élite capture and precludes prior forms of individual benefits through cash dividends. The local communities in Lupande GMA lost over 70 per cent of their income, all VAG accounts were closed, the weakening of local institutions led to renewed alienation from wildlife resources and heightened tensions between local communities and governmental wildlife officials.

Political dimensions of CBNRM in Zambia

The recent history of CBNRM programmes in Luangwa represents a microcosm of the struggle over 'good governance' in African development, and in particular efforts to replace personalized neo-patrimonial systems with governance based on property rights, markets and the rule of law (Hyden, 2006). The differences between impersonal and institutionally-based governance on the one hand, and personalized or neo-patrimonial rule on the other (North et al, 2009), greatly affect whether the macro political-economic environment enables or disables the emergence of effective local governance.

Our political interpretation of the collapse of participatory wildlife governance in Lupande GMA is based on personal experience in a time of considerable inter-factional intrigue. Our preliminary observations suggest that more political-economic research is needed to pull back the curtain on how natural resource policy and governance decisions are actually made. Nevertheless, the logic of our argument is consistent with the neo-patrimonial and personalized nature of the Zambian state. Formal community institutions that had begun to work shifted power towards ordinary people, but were dismantled, either purposefully or through ignorance. This undermined emerging processes of participation, accountability and fiscal devolution, but opened the door for neo-patrimonial capture of valuable resources. The Zambian state is not monolithic, with some professionals favouring technically viable policies that promote the public good (Simasiku et al, 2008), but in the end emerging impersonal institutions of transparency, accountability and democracy (as developed in Lupande GMA) threatened patronage systems and did not survive. Taking advantage of the confused transition of NPWS to ZAWA, influential individuals at local and national levels were able to weaken effective local controls over wildlife. ZAWA took advantage of declining protection of grass-roots institutions by foreign donor supporters to absorb some 70 per cent of hunting income that, it could be argued, rightfully belonged to communities living with wildlife. Moreover, an emerging process of institutionalized neo-liberal economic and political participation has been superseded by new configurations of power that marginalize community members and privilege personal relationships between leaders in the wildlife sector, political patrons and clients at the local level (including chiefs). Personalized power relations regained the upper hand over formal institutional rules.

Conclusion

This case illustrates the quantum performance advantages associated with face-to-face scale and participatory democracy at the village level compared to larger-scale representational systems of local governance. However, it also shows how susceptible emerging local regimes are to changes in the macro-political environment. Thus, Zambia's shift from a one-party state to multiparty democracy in the early 1990s opened the door for the brief emergence of participatory democracy in Lupande, fortunately for long enough to be able to measure the superior performance of this system in terms of generating local benefits from wildlife. During this period, the personal relationships between politicians and businessmen in the allocation of state-owned resources such as wildlife were briefly in disarray, while Norway's influence as a major donor in a donor-dependent economy enabled it to ring-fence LIRDP as a neo-liberal community conservation programme from dealings in Lusaka. However, the patrimonial logic of the gatekeeper state soon re-exerted itself. By the late 1990s, politician–business relations and patronage networks were re-solidifying, even as the era of multiparty democracy brought notably little reformation of political rights and governance patterns in the Zambian state (Simon, 2005). Simultaneously, and ultimately unfortunately, foreign donors re-initiated centralized basket financing mechanisms which inverted the direction of accountability and re-empowered the centre at the expense of ordinary people at the margins. For instance, instead of South Luangwa's budget being dependent on its own performance, and ZAWA headquarters needing to facilitate a surplus, the donors began to fund ZAWA headquarters, which naturally began to expand in line with the resources provided, and to arrogate decision-making power to itself. Unfortunately the surge in funding aimed at transforming the wildlife sector into an engine for economic growth focused on building the state wildlife agency, and actually disenfranchised communities in GMAs. Systems of local accountability that were working well in Luangwa were rapidly dismantled. Face-to-face institutions like VAGs were replaced by representational CRBs, despite data that showed this was clearly a retrogressive move, at least from the perspective of wildlife and communities. Money that was accruing to people who were poorer by a third than others in Zambia (Simasiku et al, 2008) was redirected to keep a bureaucratic institution alive.

Murphree (2000b) concluded a decade ago that successful community-based conservation remains elusive because it 'has not to date been tried and found wanting; it has been found difficult and rarely tried'. Similarly, the experience from South Luangwa demonstrates that we know how to design institutions that simultaneously promote measurable improvements in wildlife conservation, livelihoods and democratization. However, efforts to operationalize such approaches often fail because they are incompatible with the political-economic status quo. An old system of doing things characterized by political logic and informal and personalized rule trumps the evidence that carefully institutionalized devolution and participatory governance can generate both conservation and development. Is this not also the general challenge of the development state in Africa?

Notes

1 Although the emergence and maintenance of democratic governance is invariably subject to violent conflict and negotiation, on economic grounds it is hard to argue that democracy is not worthwhile given that all of the world's 30 countries with a per capita income exceeding US$20,000 are democracies, except for four small oil-producing states (North et al, 2009).

2 These concepts are developed in some detail by North et al (2009) and in the African context by Hyden (2006).

3 '*Induna*' denotes a senior official and advisor appointed by the traditional leader or chief, and is a position of some power in rural communities in Zambia.

4 When LIRDP was absorbed by ZAWA in about 1998, it was renamed South Luangwa Area Management Unit (SLAMU). For purposes of simplicity and clarity, we use the acronym LIRDP uniformly throughout the chapter to refer to the programme both before and after this change.

5 Patterson's aerial survey data in the mid–late 1990s suggested that elephant populations in Kafue National Park had recently declined from 8,000–10,000 to about 4,000–5,000. These results were never made public.

6 This conclusion emerged from a series of participatory rural appraisal exercises carried out in the Lupande communities in 1996. Further, LIRDP was unable to compile a list of these projects nor an accounting of them. For example, one chief sold a lot of meat from the culling programme and money was never accounted for. Similarly, when the chiefs sold the bus from Malambo Transport the money was not accounted for.

7 This advisor was one of the chapter authors, B. Child.

8 See Peters and Waterman (1982) for a useful conceptual framework of 'loose' versus 'tight' management systems.

9 Interestingly, and perhaps sensing the inevitability of this principle, Chief Msoro, who resides well way from the park, set aside a large area of wild land, invested in water and antipoaching to develop his wildlife resource, and began to seek private partners.

10 In September 2000 the Government of the Republic of Zambia and the Government of the Kingdom of Norway signed a Memorandum of Understanding concerning Development Cooperation that prioritized (1) good governance (2) basic education (3) the road sector and (4) environmental management with the main focus on wildlife management. Norway commissioned a confidential review of the wildlife sector because of its concerns about political manoeuvring and went ahead following a recommendation that the worst option was not to try to address the sector.

11 Donors investing in the wildlife sector included Norway, Denmark, US, the World Bank and UNDP/GEF.

12 Opening statement by Norwegian representative, Mr Magne Grova, at LIRDP Annual Meeting, 2001.

13 Personal observation by the authors.

References

Balakrishna, M. and Ndlovu, D. (1992) 'Wildlife utilization and local people: A case study in Upper Lupande Game Management Area, Zambia', *Environmental Conservation*, vol 19, no 2, pp135–144

Barnes, G. (2009) 'Carbon as a community based natural resource?', Keynote Address, Conference 'Transforming CBNRM Education in Southern Africa', Pretoria 20–24 July 2009

Bell, R. (1987) 'Conservation with a human face: Conflict and reconciliation in African land use planning', in D. Anderson and R. Grove (eds) *Conservation in Africa: People, Policies and Practice*, Cambridge University Press, Cambridge

Brown, T. (2003) 'Contestation, confusion and corruption: Market-based land reform in Zambia', in S. Evers, M. Spierenburg and H. Wels (eds) *Competing Jurisdictions: Settling Land Claims in Africa*, Bril Academic Publishers, The Netherlands

Butler, C. (1996) 'The development of ecotourism in South Luangwa National Park, Zambia', Master's Thesis, Durrell Institute of Conservation and Ecology, University of Kent

Butler, C. (1998) 'Case Studies in Tourism and its Relation to Communities. Kakumbi and Nsefu Chiefdom, Lupande GMA, Zambia', Unpublished manuscript

Bwalya, S.M. (2003) 'Understanding community-based wildlife governance in Southern Africa: A case study from Zambia', *African Journal of the Environment and Management*, vol 7, pp41–60

Child, B., Ward, S. and Tavengwa, T. (1997) *Zimbabwe's CAMPFIRE Programme: Natural Resource Management by the People*, Canon Pres, Harare, Zimbabwe

Child, B. (2006) 'Revenue distribution for empowerment and democratization', *Participatory Learning and Action*, vol 55, pp20–29

Dalal-Clayton, B. and Lewis, D. (1984) 'An integrated approach to land use management in the Luangwa Valley', in *Proceedings of the Lupande Development Workshop, Nyamaluma Wildlife Camp, Lupande Game Management Area*, Government Printer, Lusaka, Zambia

Dalal-Clayton, B. and Child, B. (2003) *Lessons from Luangwa: The Story of the Luangwa Integrated Resource Development Project, Zambia*, International Institute for Environment and Development, London

DSI (Development Services International) (2002) 'Strategic Framework for Emergency Support to ZAWA', Presentation to ZAWA Board and Wildlife Sector Donors, April 2002, Lusaka, Zambia

Gibson, C.C. and Marks, S.A. (1995) 'Transforming rural hunters into conservationists: An assessment of community-based wildlife management programs in Africa', *World Development*, vol 23, no 6, pp941–957

Gibson, C.C. (1999) *Politicians and Poachers: The Political Economy of Wildlife Policy in Africa*, Cambridge University Press, Cambridge

HURID (Institute for Human Rights, Intellectual Property and Development Trust) (2002) *Policy and Legislation Review of the Fisheries, Forestry, Wildlife and Water Sectors vis-à-vis Community Based Natural Resource Management*, Prepared for Community Based Natural Resource Management and Sustainable Agriculture Project, USAID, Lusaka, Zambia

Hyden, G. (2006) *African Politics in Comparative Perspective*, Cambridge University Press, Cambridge

Jachmann, H. and Billiouw, M. (1997) 'Elephant poaching and law enforcement in the central Luangwa Valley, Zambia', *Journal of Applied Ecology*, vol 34, no 1, pp. 233–244

Lewis, D., Kaweche, G.B., and Mwenya, A. (1990) 'Wildlife conservation outside protected areas: Lessons from an experiment in Zambia', *Conservation Biology*, vol 4, no 2, 171–180

Lewis, D.M. and Alpert, P. (1997) 'Trophy hunting and wildlife conservation in Zambia', *Conservation Biology*, vol 11, no 1, pp59–68

Lubilo, R. (2007) 'A Comprehensive Report on the Status of Governance and Participation in Lupande Game Management Area of South Luangwa Area Management Unit in Zambia', Unpublished report

Marks, S.A. (2001) 'Back to the future: Some unintended consequences of Zambia's community-based wildlife program', *Africa Today*, vol 48, no 1, pp121–141

Murphree, M.W. (2000a) *Boundaries and borders; the question of scale in the theory and practice of common property management*, Paper presented at the Eighth Biennial Conference of the International Association of Common Property (IASCP), Bloomington, IN

Murphree, M.W. (2000b) *Community-based conservation: Old ways, new myths and enduring challenges*, Paper presented at a conference on African Wildlife Management in the New Millennium, College of African Wildlife Management, Mweka, Tanzania

Murphree, M. (1991) *Communities as Institutions for Resource Management*, Centre for Applied Social Sciences, University of Zimbabwe, Harare, Zimbabwe

Mwape, Ernest (2002) 'Report on the ZAWA-CRB workshop', Garden House Motel, Lusaka, 3 and 6 June 2002, Workshop report prepared by CONASA Policy Component Manager

North, D.C., Wallis, J.J. and Weingast, B.R. (2009) *Violence and Social Orders: A Conceptual Framework for Interpreting Recorded Human History*, Cambridge University Press, Cambridge

Ostrom, E. (1990) *Governing the Commons: The Evolution of Institutions for Collective Action*, Cambridge University Press, Cambridge

Peters, T. and Waterman, R.H. (1982) *In Search of Excellence: Lessons from America's Best-run Companies*, Harper-Collins-Business, London

Phiri, E. (1996) 'Community-based management programme: A case study of Luangwa Integrated Resources Development Project, Zambia', Master's Thesis, University of Dresden, Germany

Roe, D., Nelson, F. and Sandbrook, C. (2009) *Community Management of Natural Resources in Africa: Impacts, Experiences and Future Directions*, IIED Natural Resource Issues No. 18, International Institute for Environment and Development, London

Scanteam (1993) *Luangwa Integrated Rural Development Project: Project Appraisal*, NORAD, Lusaka, Zambia

Simasiku, P., Simwanza, H.I., Tembo, G., Bandyopadhyay, S. and Pavy, J.-M. (2008) 'The impact of wildlife management policies on communities and conservation in Game Management Areas in Zambia', in Message to Policy Makers', Natural Resources Consultative Forum, Lusaka, Zambia

Simon, D. (2005) 'Democracy unrealized: Zambia's Third Republic under Frederick Chiluba', in L.A. Villalón and P. VonDoepp (eds) *The Fate of Africa's Democratic Experiments: Elites and Institutions*, Indiana University Press, Bloomington, IN

SLAMU (South Luangwa Area Management Unit) (2007) *Annual Report, 2007*

SLAMU (South Luangwa Area Management Unit) (2008) *Tourism Alternatives Study Report, 2008*

Suich, H., Child, B. and Spenceley, A. (2008) *Evolution and Innovation in Wildlife Conservation: Parks and Game Ranches to Transfrontier Conservation Areas*, Earthscan, London

Szeftel, M. (2000) '"Eat With Us": Managing corruption and patronage under Zambia's three Republics', *Journal of Contemporary African Studies*, vol 18, no 2, pp207–224

Transparency International (2009) 'Corruption perceptions index', www.transparency.org/ policy_research/surveys_indices/cpi/2008 and www.transparency.org/policy_research/ surveys_indices/cpi/2001 Accessed 30 September 2009

Wainright, C. (1996) 'Evaluating community based natural resource management: A case study of the Luangwa Integrated Resource Development Project (LIRDP), Zambia', Master's Thesis, Durrell Institute of Conservation and Ecology, University of Kent

10

External Agency and Local Authority: Facilitating CBNRM in Mahel, Mozambique

Marta Monjane

This chapter presents a case study of community-based natural resource management (CBNRM) in Mozambique, using the locale of Mahel in southern Mozambique. The chapter first provides a brief overview of the conceptual evolution of CBNRM in Mozambique in the post-civil war (1992–present) period and subsequently explores the linkages and implications of institutional and governance assumptions for CBNRM implementation and effective communal management of natural resources.

The evolution of CBNRM in post-civil war Mozambique

Community-based natural resource management encompasses a range of concepts and terms such as 'community conservation', 'community-based conservation' and 'park outreach', all of which aim generally to promote greater local involvement in natural resource management (Hulme and Murphree, 2001; Fisher et al, 2005). The overall thrust is to 'give those who live in rural environments greater involvement in managing the natural resources (soil, water, species, habitats, landscapes or biodiversity) that exist in the areas in which they reside (be that permanently or temporarily) and/or greater access to benefits derived from those resources' (Hulme and Murphree, 2001, p4).

Perceptions of the positive impacts of CBNRM initiatives elsewhere in southern Africa, particularly neighbouring Zimbabwe's CAMPFIRE programme, were critical to the emergence of CBNRM in Mozambique. CBNRM was perceived as a pragmatic approach for providing local people with environmentally sound and economically sustainable alternatives to destructive land use; a strategy to promote forest and wildlife conservation; and a form of local democratic governance (Salomão, 2002; Nhantumbo et al, 2003; Salomão and Matose, 2007).

In the 1990s, CBNRM took shape as a stimulating and challenging development and research concept. Many discussions were held among Mozambican officials and academics on two key themes: first, how to involve local people in natural resource management; and second, what appropriate practices should be disseminated by the extension services in order for local people to obtain economic benefits from the country's vast natural resources in a sustainable fashion (Ribeiro, 2001). Welcomed by funding agencies, these new ideas were soon converted into practice, being incorporated into both development and research projects, and CBNRM began to influence the reformulation of national policies in the post-war period (Anstey, 2005).

From 1992, and over the next decade, the former rhetoric of paramilitary-style state management of protected areas was transformed into one of local community participation in wildlife and forest management (Anstey, 2001). Community participation was seen as being essential for the success of projects. Community-based initiatives started to proliferate with support from both government and donor agencies. The first experiences came from the Tchuma Chato project in west-central Mozambique and the Chipanje Chetu project in Niassa Province in the far northern part of the country (Johnson, 2004; Anstey, 2005) and by 2004 over 60 CBNRM initiatives had been already established in Mozambique (Couto, 2004). CBNRM was formally recognized by the government through provisions of protection of community rights to land and natural resources, in the Land Law (1997) and in the Forestry and Wildlife Law (1999).

From its inception in the early 1990s until the present, the Mozambican approach to CBNRM has evolved, largely based on in-country contextualization and analysis, recognizing that its adoption was based in wildlife-based initiatives and experiences from other countries in the region (e.g. Namibia, Botswana, Zambia and Zimbabwe). In these countries' programmes, financially-based economic incentives were central to promoting local incentives for conservation, whereas in Mozambique the abundance and richness of wildlife resources remains relatively limited. Initially viewed as a sectoral strategy (forestry or wildlife) CBNRM came to target interventions around community organization, capacity building and empowerment for natural resources planning and use. Two key questions confronted CBNRM initiatives at the time:

1   the extent to which the government was prepared to devolve the rights of the management of natural resources to local communities;
2   the extent to which communities were prepared to take the responsibility for sustainable management of natural resources.

The existing legal framework presented gaps in the operational mechanisms available to respond clearly to these questions. Unlike the land rights campaign before and after the 1997 land law reform, which focused on wide dissemination of information about people's rights and obligations in relation to land access and tenure, the awareness of access and tenure rights in relation to forests and wildlife was limited in part due to the fluid and rapid policy change related to forest and wildlife resources, and partly because of limited capacity for its implementation. By 2000, Mozambique's CBNRM approach progressively evolved from a strong sectoral and conservationist emphasis, to a broader rural development strategy, and as such was perceived to require a more integrated development approach (Mansur and Cuco, 2002). The CBNRM model (Figure 10.1) developed in Mozambique attempts to recognize the importance of existing local institutions; highlights the need for partnerships between conservationist and development interests and agencies; takes account of the legitimate needs of communities for deriving tangible benefits from natural resources use; and promotes effective devolution of decision-making rights to appropriate local-level bodies.

CBNRM in the Mahel community

Socio-economic and ecological context

Mahel is an administrative unity within Magude District, located to the northwest of Maputo Province in the southern part of Mozambique. Mahel covers an area of approximately 33,000 hectares and is registered under the 1997 Land Law as belonging to the people of Mahel (Mahel centre and ten sub-villages), through the recognition of customary rights (see Tanner et al, 2006 for background on the land tenure context). The population of Mahel is estimated at 1,560 inhabitants grouped in 560 households.

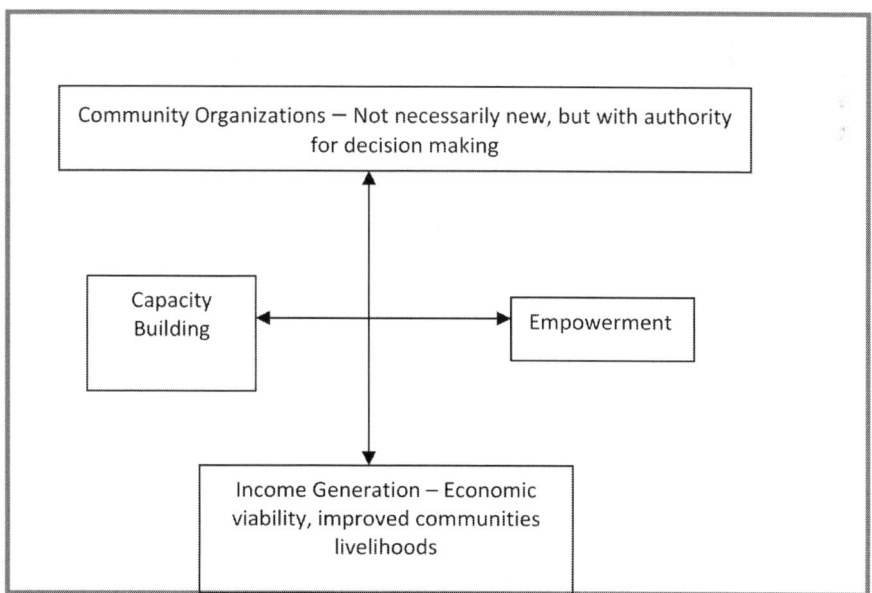

Source: Mansur and Cuco, 2002

Figure 10.1 *General elements of the CBNRM model in Mozambique*

The Mahel community relies considerably on natural resources for its livelihoods. Charcoal production is the main community-managed income-generating activity in the area, while animal husbandry plays an important role in providing household income, with varying levels of importance depending on household wealth. The average income per capita in the community is estimated at US$0.37 per day (Shepherd, 2008). Other livelihood activities and sources of income include small-scale agriculture and local commerce. Mahel faces severe periodic droughts, and a general lack of an appropriate commercial network and employment opportunities are characteristics of the area.

The vegetation of Mahel is characterisitic of the southern African Mopane ecosystem, characterized by the predominance of the Mopane tree (*Colophospermum mopane*). The Mopane flora is not particularly diverse in terms of tree species, but it is estimated that the ecosystem holds nearly 2,000 vascular plants. Wildlife found in the area include large mammals such as elephant and lion, in reduced numbers, and a relatively great richness in avifauna.

Mahel has been targeted for many years for illegal logging and heavy poaching. Human–animal conflicts constitute a problem in the area and water shortage is severe and a key livelihood concern.

Initiation of CBNRM in Mahel

Following the national land and natural resource policy reforms in the late 1990s, which generally promoted devolution of rights and participatory management of natural resources, the richness of wildlife was seen to offer promising opportunities for community-based ecotourism and associated services in Mahel. The engagement of local communities in wildlife management, conservation and benefit sharing, looked highly promising as a way to reduce illegal logging, human–wildlife conflicts and conserve biodiversity while improving the livelihoods of local people.

It was against this background that a project led by the Ministry of Agriculture, with financial support from the Government of The Netherlands and the technical assistance of the United Nations Food and Agriculture Organisation (FAO), was initiated in Mahel starting in late 1999. The project aimed to support community organization for the management of natural resources in the area. Two central specific objectives were to establish a community-managed game farm, initially planned to cover 14,000 hectares, and to promote sustainable local charcoal production.

With support from the FAO project, the Mahel community was officially registered as an association, giving it legal form, in 2004. The project supported activities ranging from local organizational development through establishment and training of resource user groups, including community scouts, charcoal, beekeeping, sawing, agriculture and livestock groups. The FAO project initiated the definition and demarcation of the community's land area and the process for acquiring the land certificate for that area. Later in 2005, the Department of Land and Forestry partnered with the Mahel community to develop and implement a two-year follow-up phase of the FAO project with financial support from the United Nations Development Programme (UNDP) Small Grants Programme.

In late 2007, IUCN launched the Livelihoods and Landscape Program (LLS) in Mahel with the intent to build on the initial efforts of the FAO project. The main goal of the LLS programme in Mahel was to contribute to the integrated management of the community land and associated forest and wildlife resources, with the view of attaining improved livelihoods and conserving natural resources. Specifically, LLS intended to focus on facilitating local organizational development processes for managing the community game farm and to support the establishment of the game farm infrastructure.

At the inception of the LLS programme, the active local organizations were the registered Community Association, which operated through a management committee, and the charcoal production groups (charcoal producers and community patrols) who worked under direct supervision of the committee leaders. Other resource user groups established during the FAO project were dissolved, allegedly due to organizational and institutional issues and/or the lack of markets.

A participatory planning process was carried out, through which interventions were identified and implementation initiated. The community committee and government officers jointly welcomed the initiative. The participation and commitment of committee members (with the exception of the Committee President) and the government representative indicated a good collaboration and relationship between the local association and the district government. The district government representative took a leading role in the programme implementation and liaison with facilitator agencies.

The first challenges arose at the stage of strengthening community organizational structures established during the inception of CBNRM in Mahel, and the facilitation of private sector partnerships with the communities. Requests to review relevant documentation on association and committee statutes as well as the draft agreement with the private sector were not successful, suggesting lack of trust towards the facilitators. Further challenges were faced in the design and establishment of the game farm infrastructure, following the hiring of a private ecolodge owner to provide strategic guidance and technical expertise. This was perceived as a threat by the community committee to the existing agreement between the communities and a private investor.

The process and outcomes of carrying out a combined wealth-ranking exercise; training on participatory planning, monitoring and evaluation; and action learning sessions indicated the presence of governance and institutional issues in Mahel that posed fundamental challenges to CBNRM implementation and had serious implications for effective communal management of natural resources. It became evident that there were problems with a number of assumptions made at the outset of establishing CBNRM in Mahel as well as with the process of implementing the various project components.

Revisiting assumptions about CBNRM

The establishment and implementation of CBNRM in Mahel followed the approaches and assumptions which were widespread at the time, particularly with reference to CBNRM as implemented elsewhere in southern Africa. Several assumptions are highlighted here:

- the need to create new local organizational structures to manage natural resources;
- external agencies as a neutral facilitator and with the know-how and responsibility to build operational capacity at the local level;
- the relevance of collective natural resource management as a livelihood strategy for targeted communities;
- the community as a homogeneous group with common shared interests in natural resources management;
- the existence of an enabling legal framework and political context for natural resources conservation and devolution of rights to local-level institutions.

Need and ability to facilitate the establishment of local organizational structures to manage natural resources

Central to the initial establishment of the CBNRM initiative in Mahel was the need to create a local organization responsible for overseeing the management of the collective use of natural resources in the area. The formation of such an organization was guided by, amongst others, principles of democracy, inclusiveness and representation. The approach has been to sponsor new organizational structures and place emphasis on forming committees and resource user groups rather than exploring and developing the existing local institutional base of shared norms and behaviours.

The external agent as neutral facilitator

The facilitating agencies, all of which were large-scale, transnational organizations operating through national programme offices, framed within their own organizational and institutional arrangements and knowledge, often portrayed themselves as neutral agents in the process of forming local organizations. The facilitation process, however, by means of providing guidance, drafting organization statutes, training and other inputs, is shaped by these organizations' own beliefs, political concerns, knowledge and organizational and institutional arrangements. These sources of bias may have a positive or negative effect in different contexts. In addition, communities often do not perceive the facilitators as neutral. This is certainly the case in Mahel, where the community has clearly expressed the view that the facilitating agencies have their own agendas. These include using communities to justify expenditure of funds and using the social surveys to gather information for the sole purpose of writing articles and publishing the findings elsewhere.

The local community as a homogeneous group with common interests in managing and conserving natural resources

Both the Land Law of 1997 and the Forestry and Wildlife Law of 1999 define 'local community' as a group of families and individuals living in a limited territorial space, with the size of a locality or smaller, and who wish to safeguard common interests through the protection of their areas of residence, agricultural land, forests, sites of cultural significance, grazing fields, water sources, hunting and expansion areas. Stemming from the above and in spite of the subjectivity of its interpretation, two key factors led to the assumption that there would be a common interest on the part of the Mahel 'community' in managing natural resources and ensuring more sustainable use. Firstly, Mahel traditional jurisdictional boundaries coincide with the limits of the Mahel administrative entity. Secondly, the ongoing hunting, charcoal, human–wildlife conflict presumably affects the entire community, and as such provides an incentive to revert the accrued benefits from capture by outsiders to the local community.

National decentralization and devolution processes provide an adequate framework to enable CBNRM

A significant number of strategic policy documents developed during the 1990s created a general perception of there being an emergent enabling institutional environment for CBNRM in Mozambique. This policy narrative highlighted the value of rural poor and local communities in the sustainable management of natural resources (Anstey, 2001).

At macro-level, the Constitution of the Republic of Mozambique expresses that the state aims to promote the rational use and valuation of natural resources, sustaining resources for future generations, and determining conditions of their use while safeguarding national interests. The National Sustainable Development Strategy (EADS) promotes the equitable access, management and exploration of the land and other natural resources in such a way that they maintain their functional and productive capacity for future generations. The Action Plan for Absolute Poverty Reduction (PARPA) also highlights the importance of environmental conservation and the sustainable use of natural resources in relation to poverty reduction and calls for sustainable management and balancing the interests of communities, the private sector and the state on the use of natural resources and the environment.

At the sectoral level, the legal reforms affecting environment, forestry, wildlife, land and local government have all been key in enabling CBNRM development. The Environmental Law (1997) provides the legal framework for the use and management of environmental resources for sustainable development. The Land Law (1997) safeguards the rights of communities to settlement, agricultural, forestry, pasture lands and water sources to support their livelihoods. The Forestry and Wildlife Law (1999) makes provision for rights and benefits of the forest-dependent communities including subsistence use, participation in co-management, consultation when transferring rights to third parties, and returning to communities of 20 per cent of forestry logging fee/tax revenue and a percentage of fines received from law enforcement. Under the 2005 local government legislation, the local leadership or community authorities are recognized by the appropriate government representative, and are legitimated by the local communities usually based on historical lineage.

What actually happened, and why?
Theory and practice in local resource governance

Sponsoring community organization: Understanding local power structures

Social and economic life in Mahel is governed by the local authority comprising the traditional leader (*régulo*) and an advisory group of elders (*madodas*). Formal local governance bodies comprise the formal Community Association represented by the Community Committee for Natural Resources Management (led by the traditional leader, in spite of the law on local governing organs clearly stating that the local leaders cannot hold dual positions) and the local government representative (Chief of the administrative post of Mahel). While a socio-economic study had been undertaken at the outset of the CBNRM initiatives, this study did not identify nor assess the local institutions and actors involved, which, as was later realized, are key to natural resource governance in the area. It became evident that there were insufficient insights into and understanding of the history and context, particularly with regards to 'people processes' in Mahel.

From the roles, responsibilities and duties established under Mozambican local government legislation it is clear that the legal authority to govern the development of the administrative post rests with the head of the administrative post nominated by the government, while the traditional authorities have more of a supporting role and act as the intermediary body between the government and the communities. The law does not clearly vest authority and decision-making power with the local traditional leader (*régulo*) and the traditional authorities (*madodas*) or with the community organizations and/or association. The lack of a clear legally bound distinction with regards to the mandates of these different local actors results in conflicting interpretations of the duties and responsibilities between the different actors and the apparent overlap of these rights and responsibilities. This lack of clarity around roles and boundaries of authority inevitably led to serious tensions and power struggles at the local level.

In Mahel, tensions revolved around the committee's activities, including tension between committee members, between the community and the local government, and between committee members and the external facilitation team and partners. The tensions evolved around determining the appropriate authority to host the programme, the appropriate decision-making body on matters related to the Mahel program, and the leading role of the local government representative in affairs pertaining to the community committee and the local association. These conflicts also related to the lack of clarity around the custody and ownership of the material and equipment delivered to support the game farm infrastructure establishment.

The relationship between the local government representative (Chief of Post at Mahel) and the traditional leadership (*régulo* and *madodas*) has been and continues to be difficult, appearing to be a struggle for power, status and control over resources within the community. Committee members explicitly demonstrated their lack of trust towards the local government representative and engaged in a serious argument that led to breaking off communication between the two parties. This led to the local government representative deciding to move away from the site and not participate in the training and the activities that were being carried out under the programme.

Relationships within the committee are opaque and difficult to fully understand from the outside. The committee president dominates proceeding and does not allow for free expression of views by the other members. While there were some incidents where his authority was challenged, these were rare and often fleeting. Some individuals apprehensively raised the issue of the (nominally illegal) dual role currently being played by him as committee president and traditional leader (*régulo*) but this challenge quickly faded during subsequent conversations (Pabari and Monjane, 2009).

In addition, there was a distinct reluctance by the committee (particularly the committee President) to convene discussions with the wider community about the game farm. The wealth-ranking process also revealed that three sub-villages which were significantly affected and had a stake in the game farm were being left out of the developments and the decision-making processes of the Community Association, which itself was centred on an élite group of individuals from central Mahel village comprising the traditional leader and other committee members (Ibid.).

Challenging external facilitators

One of the reasons Mahel was selected as a site for CBNRM was that there had been previous initiatives in the area that LLS could build upon, which included the FAO project and UNDP Small Grants projects. It was later discovered that the way in which these projects had been implemented had important implications for the LLS activities, many of which were negative in the sense that the committee had perceived that the funds were being used mainly for individual gain through daily meeting allowances and expectations that LLS funds would be channelled directly to the committee to manage and utilize as was done before.

Limited insights on documenting and understanding the processes and outcomes of past projects, and the perceptions of local communities, led to tensions between the committee, IUCN project facilitators and the local administration. It was evident that there was insufficient trust by the committee, particularly the committee President, of the facilitators, whose role and legitimacy were was challenged in a variety of ways.

Such challenges were manifested through various insinuations around IUCN's interest in the game farm, relations with private investors and the ownership of information used for research papers. It emerged that some of the reasons behind the local lack of trust included the hiring by IUCN of a private game farm owner to provide technical advice and assist with some of the initial activities. Prior to this, the committee had signed a Memorandum of Understanding with another private investor and seemed to feel that the technical advisor brought in by IUCN threatened their arrangement with the latter.

Different perceptions and interests in natural resources

Stemming from the local governance issues outlined above, it became clear that in Mahel there are different perceptions within and between communities on the importance of the area intended to be used for the game farm. There is a general lack of trust that the game farm will actually bring benefits to the wider community, partly as a result of the shortcomings of various other local projects and programmes that have not yet provided tangible benefits in this regard, as well as lack of clarity at the local level on the market feasibility of the game farm, and finally due to existing institutional issues in the area.

The members of sub-villages adjacent to the game farm area have also expressed concerns in relation to the game farm boundaries and land use implications. The initial 14,000ha have been reduced by 2,000ha, apparently by a decision taken by the *régulo*/committee President to provide land for charcoal production and grazing. However, this area favoured mainly the central sub-village residents of Mahel. The three sub-villages on the northern boundary of the game farm area have been requesting an additional area for grazing by further reducing the size of the game farm, but the community committee or the *régulo* has not yet decided on the matter.

Further concerns relate to lack of transparency on the use of existing local revenues derived from the 20 per cent of forest tax revenue and charcoal production received by the community from the central government, and a widespread scepticism if the game farm goes ahead about whether it would actually benefit the wider community and not simply select local élites.

Rethinking assumptions

Institutions and organizations

The approach in Mahel, as in many other CBNRM initiatives, has been to sponsor new organizational structures and emphasize the establishment of formal local committees and resource user groups, regardless of their sustainability in the absence of project support (Gilmour, 2000). The process in Mahel, by eventually deriving a better understanding of the committee composition through discussions held with the wider community, revealed that there was not a wide level of acceptance or trust in the committee. This drove home the realization on the part of the facilitators that the Association was not representative of the community as a whole and was not inclusive in its decision-making processes.

The individual actors within the committee were recognized by the wider community because they were also the traditional leaders. However, the organizational structure, rules and regulations of the committee and the Association were not, and did not fit with the traditional norms and customs. Mahel's experience suggests that the traditional local governance institution, with its own set of rules, authority and power was more accepted by the wider community. This clearly points out the relative importance and relevance of local (indigenous) institutional arrangements, whether formal or informal, and their functions (the institutional base of shared norms and behaviours) on natural resources management compared to the creation of new formal organizations.

Limitations of the legal framework

Mozambican legislative reforms provide for the protection of community access rights to natural resources, including land, forestry, wildlife and fisheries. However, the various laws governing these resources regulate the extent and nature of community access in significantly different ways.

While the Land Law enables the transfer of real rights to land (which can be subject to transaction), the Forest Law erodes those by restricting resource use to non-commercial subsistence levels. The potential for commercial gains from forest resources remains dependent on the successful application for a concession or a simple licence, thus effectively putting communities on the same playing field as the private sector (Johnstone et al, 2004).

In addition, local government legislation attempts to decentralize power but separates the role of local natural resource management organizations from the role of the local authorities, granting the former advisory functions only in relation to natural resource management. This somewhat excludes the local organizations, established in order to manage communal natural resources, from actually exercising effective decision-making power in relation to communal forest and wildlife resources.

'Neutrality' and external facilitation

External facilitating agencies are not neutral and more often than not, come with their own biases and interests which influence, in one way or another, the shape that externally-introduced resource management initiatives take at the local level. From the principles governing the formation of local organizations (democracy, transparency, representation and inclusiveness) to the institutional arrangements (often based on legal statutes) used, a range of external preferences are inevitably imposed by the external agent. In the process, the external agent often is not cognizant of imposing norms and behaviours whose local recognition, adoption and enforcement are not only overlooked, but framed to the specific organizational, institutional and operational arrangements and knowledge of the external agent itself. These impositions can positively or negatively influence the existing local context and the outcomes of the interventions, but inevitably reshape local power relations in important ways.

Implications for CBNRM

In southern Africa, community-based natural resources management projects have often been externally driven, with the ideas of community conservation imposed on local communities and societies. For instance, Barrow and Murphree (2001) note that, with some important exceptions, the prevalence of community conservation programmes in Africa is mostly a product of initiatives by international conservation agencies and conservation professionals, state governments and international donors.

What emerges from the experiences in Mahel are lessons relating to the agency and influence of externally-driven programmes and patterns of project management, planning, mobilization and implementation on the part of supporting NGOs and donor agencies. Additionally, the Mahel experience also demonstrates the importance of having the skills and knowledge to engage effectively with local political processes including personal and informal relationships, power and group dynamics and conflict management, as well as the more technical processes related to natural resource management. This suggests the need for continued stronger linkages between conservationists and social sciences; had such linkages been established at an ealier stage in Mahel, many subsequent problems and challenges might have been avoided. This also calls for greater internal reflection within external agencies in terms of their structure and mode of operations in planning, implementing and delivering on intended outcomes. It became clear that there was a mismatch between the intended outcomes and the actual capacity to deliver in Mahel.

The existing local power relations and internal dynamics in Mahel, within the committee, between the committee and wider community, as well as between the committee and government representatives inhibit open dialogue and collective decision-making processes. There are numerous case studies and examples of challenges that often emerge in similar situations, such as tensions and open conflict arising from real or perceived inequitable decision-making power and/or distribution of benefits and costs arising from natural resource uses.

The lack of trust between the different actors at the local scale is problematic and extends to the external facilitating agencies. 'Trust' between individuals and groups is a key element of local social capital that can help enable collective decision-making proceses and thus CBNRM. The absence of an environment where community members can voice opinions inhibits sharing information, holding local governance organs and leaders accountable, and resolving local conflicts.

There is a need to improve the capacity of external agents to act as 'honest brokers'. This is particularly important where the role of a mediator is potentially instrumental for resolving challenges emerging from existing local power relations. This requires rethinking our 'theories of change'; taking into account our own institutional frameworks and their potential to influence positively or negatively the existing context and how they could best fit with communities and particularly assumptions that particular formal institutional arrangements are necessary or applicable. External agents need to be able to present clearly the programme and ensure the message is understood and widely communicated to the relevant stakeholders; to understand and negotiate relationships between different forms of power as part of the process; to understand diverse forms of knowledge; to clearly identify locally-agreed norms and processes and where appropriate work to strengthen existing institutions as opposed to focusing on 'sponsored' organizations; to better understand the various groups and actors within the area and pursue explicit commitments by communities through participation with tangible inputs to the programme; and to develop the capacity to inform policy and to bridge the gaps between formal and informal institutions.

References

Anstey, S. (2005) 'Governance, natural resources and complex adaptive systems: A CBNRM study of communities and resources in northern Mozambique', in V. Dzingirai and C. Breen (eds) *Confronting the Crisis in Community Conservation: Case Studies from Southern Africa*, University of KwaZulu-Natal, Pietermaritzburg, South Africa

Anstey, S. (2001) 'Necessarily vague: The political economy of community conservation in Mozambique', in D. Hulme and M. Murphree (eds) *African Wildlife and Livelihoods: The Promise and Performance of Community Conservation*, James Currey, Oxford

Barrow, E. and Murphree, M. (2001) 'Community conservation: From concept to practice', in D. Hulme and M. Murphree (eds) *African Wildlife and Livelihoods: The Promise and Performance of Community Conservation*, James Currey, Oxford

Couto, P. (2004) 'Community-based natural resource management: Some challenges, in the pursuit of the objective of poverty reduction through the promotion of social and economic development', in I. Nhantumbo, M. Foloma and N. Puná (eds) *Memórias da III Conferência Nactional sobre o maneio Comunitário dos Recursos Naturais*, 21–23 June 2004, Maputo, Mozambique

Fisher, R., Maginnis, S., Jackson, W.J., Barrow, E. and Jeanrenaud, S. (2005) *Poverty and Conservation: Landscapes, People and Power*, Landscapes and Livelihoods Series No. 2, IUCN Forest Conservation Programme, IUCN, Gland, Switzerland and Cambridge, UK

Gilmour, D. (2000) Strategies, methodologies and gender approaches for CBNRM development in Mozambique, FAO Project GCP/MOZ/056/NET Maputo, Mozambique

Hulme, D. and Murphree, M. (2001) 'Community conservation in Africa: An introduction', in D. Hulme and M.W. Murphree (eds) *African Wildlife and Livelihoods: The Promise and Performance of Community Conservation*, James Currey, Oxford

Johnson, S. (2004) 'The Thumo Tchato project in Mozambique: Community-based natural resource management in transition', in C. Fabricius, E. Koch, H. Magome and S. Turner (eds) *Rights, Resources and Rural Development: Community-based Natural Resource Management in Southern Africa*, Earthscan, London

Johnstone, R., Cau, B. and Norfolk, S. (2004) *Forestry Legislation in Mozambique: Compliance and the Impact on Forest Communities*, Tera Firma Lda in association with the IIED Forest Governance Learning Group, Maputo, Mozambique www.policy-powertools.org/Tools/Engaging/docs/Mozambique_study_Johnstone_et_al.pdf Accessed 1 October 2009

Mansur, E. and Cuco, A. (2002) 'Building a community forestry framework in Mozambique: Local communities in sustainable forest management', in A. Sherwood (ed) *Second International Workshop on Participatory Forestry in Africa. Defining the Way Forward: Sustainable Livelihoods and Sustainable Forest Management through Participatory Forestry*, 18–22 February 2002, Arusha, Tanzania, FAO, Rome

Nhantumbo, I., Norfolk, S. and Pereira, J. (2003) *Community Based Natural Resources Management in Mozambique: A Theoretical or Practical Strategy for Local Sustainable Development? The Case Study of Derre Forest Reserve*, Sustainable Livelihoods in Southern Africa Research Paper No. 10, Institute of Development Studies, Brighton

Pabari, M. and Monjane, M. (2009) 'PM&E community training report in Mahel, June 2009,' IUCN Livelihoods and Landscapes Programme, IUCN, Maputo, Mozambique

Ribeiro, A. (2001) *Natural Resource Management Policy in Mozambique: An Overview*, Marena Research Project, Working Paper No. 7, University of Sussex www.geog.susx.ac.uk/research/development/marena/pdf/wp7.pdf Accessed 2 October 2009

Salomão, A.I.A. (2002) *Participatory Natural Resource Management in Mozambique: An Assessment of Legal and Institutional Arrangements for Community-based Natural Resource Management*, Draft Working Paper, Institutions and Governance Program, World Resources Institute, Washington, DC

Salomão, A. and Matose, F. (2007) *Towards Community-based Forest Management of Miombo Woodlands in Mozambique*, Centre for International Forestry Research, Bogor, Indonesia www.cifor.cgiar.org/miombo/docs/CBNRMMozambique1207.pdf Accessed 2 October 2009

Shepherd, G. (2008) *The Ecosystem Approach: Learning from Experience*, IUCN Commission on Ecosystem Management, IUCN, Gland, Switzerland

Tanner, C., Baleira, S., Norfolk, S., Cau, B. and Assulai, J. (2006) *Making Rights a Reality: Participation in Practice and Lessons Learned in Mozambique*, LSP Working Paper 207, FAO, Rome

11

Adaptive or Anachronistic? Maintaining Indigenous Natural Resource Governance Systems in Northern Botswana

Masego Madzwamuse

Introduction

This chapter reviews the interactions between indigenous natural resource governance systems of the Basarwa/San[1] communities of northern Botswana's Okavango Delta, and external resource governance interests and discourses, including formal community-based natural resource management (CBNRM) initiatives. The chapter highlights the challenges facing local politically marginalized communities in maintaining their resource governance systems in the face of power imbalances and national-level debates over resource use.

Although local and indigenous communities such as the Basarwa are said to have knowledge that could contribute to sustainable natural resource governance (Berkes, 1999; Berkes and Folke, 2002), these communities continue to be alienated from the use and management of natural resources in their areas. As this chapter demonstrates, traditional communities have always practised adaptive resource management which is essential for building the resilience of social and ecological systems. Even with good examples of local knowledge and institutions capable of sustainably managing natural resources (Gunderson, 1995; Berkes and Folke, 1998a, 1998b; Gunderson, 1999; Ostrom, 1999), such evidence is not enough to guarantee increased participation and involvement of local communities in natural resource governance. Communities are often far removed from the decision-making structures responsible for natural resource management at national level, despite the dependence of local livelihoods upon such resources. Recent insights on attributes of governance systems and capacities to manage resilience in social and ecological systems acknowledge the fact that decisions about how to manage resources are political and are often influenced by agendas that shape the contexts within which actors contest decisions that determine access to resources (Ostrom, 2003; Lebel et al, 2006). However, the political aspects of natural resource governance have not been adequately explored, particularly in the realm of community-based natural resource management.

The material presented in this chapter is based on a study involving two months of qualitative data collection carried out in Khwai and Xaxaba in May 2000 and March 2001 (Madzwamuse, 2009). Secondary household survey data was collected from the Every River Project in 2001, focus group discussions and key interviews were held with members of the communities of Khwai and Xaxaba, two Basarwa communities comprising about 419 and 78 people, respectively, located in the Okavango Delta. Key informant interviews were held with experts on Basarwa research, NGOs and government officials. The key informants were drawn from the Department of Wildlife and National Parks (DWNP) Community Service Division, DWNP staff based in Maun and Khwai, NGOs active in the Delta (Conservation International, Kuru and Kalahari Conservation Society), private sector and fellow researchers. A total of 17 people were interviewed using this method. The study is also based on an extensive review of anthropological research on the Basarwa and a review of literature on CBNRM in Botswana and other parts of the region. Some of the analysis is based on the observations of the author as a participant in the National CBNRM Forum from 2001 to 2006.

Background on the Basarwa

The ethnic Basarwa have been historically associated with a hunting and gathering lifestyle which is significantly different from Botswana's dominant Tswana ethnic group and the less dominant Kalanga, both of whom have historically been associated with an agro-pastoral way of life. While hunting and gathering is noted as a central marker of the Basarwa's cultural identity, it is also noted that they have for centuries engaged in mixed economies involving agriculture, herding and small-scale rural industries in the form of craft production (Motzafi-Haller, 1994; Taylor, 2000; Twyman, 2000). The language the Basarwa speak is simplistically referred to as SeSesarwa, although there are in fact several different languages indigenous to the Basarwa. Much of the interest in the Basarwa has arisen from their remarkable adaptation to one of the harshest environments in the world, the Kalahari Desert (Saugestad, 1998). Their ability to survive in an environment that for large parts of the year provides no surface water has depended on a locally appropriate combination of hunting and gathering techniques and a form of social organization facilitating the flexible use of large territories based on patterns of seasonal changes (Lee, 1972; Cashdan, 1993; Madzwamuse, 1998; Saugestad, 1998). A much less-known group of the Basarwa is the so-called River Bushmen who live in and around the Okavango Delta (Heinz, 2001; Bolaane, 2004a). The River Bushmen include groups such as the Bateti, named after the Boteti River; the BaXhanikwe, found north of the Delta (e.g. Xaxaba), the BaBugakhwe to the south and middle of the Delta (e.g. Khwai), and several smaller groups like the Bagumaii who live scattered throughout the Delta area (Tlou, 1976). The groups found in the Okavango Delta make up roughly 20 per cent of Botswana's Basarwa population of 55,000, while the rest of the Basarwa population is found in the more arid Gantsi and Kgalagadi Districts.[2]

Interaction with other ethnic groups has often been and continues to be to the disadvantage of Basarwa communities, and in turn translates into both political and economic marginalization. A central problem has been the failure by other groups to recognize hunting and gathering as a legitimate land use, which has ultimately had far-reaching consequences for the Basarwa, such as loss of land and land rights. The cultural differences between the Basarwa and the dominant Tswana agro-pastoral society have been important in defining the relations between those two groups, and the way each relates to and uses land. The agro-pastoral Batswana, for instance, came to dominate the hunter-gatherer Basarwa, imposing a system of land tenure that gave precedence to the agro-pastoral use of land. This has been reflected in the definition of land rights in Botswana's Constitution and in the Tribal Land Act of 1968 and its 1993 Amendment. The cultural dominance of the Tswana has further influenced the economic policy directions in the country wherein national policies are influenced by political élites' bias towards the live-stock sector (Taylor, 2007; Rihoy and Maguranyanga, this volume). Culture has an influence on policy formulation, interpretation and implementation, particularly the cultures of the dominant social and political groups (Peters, 1994). This has been evident throughout the history of natural resource governance in Botswana. As a result the livestock producers' interests intersect with development policy, resource use policy and national politics (Ibid.). I later argue that this is one of the reasons why communities targeted by CBNRM programmes do not have a significant political influence on the shape of national CBNRM policy decisions.

Drawing on the developments around land policy in Botswana, most government officials and policy-makers have assumed that the Basarwa did not have a clearly defined traditional land use system (Ng'ong'ola and Moeletsi, 1995; Ng'ong'ola, 1997). Because of the problem of defining land rights, tracts of land 'belonging' to the Basarwa were incorporated into state lands, national parks and game reserves, wildlife management areas, and even 'private' lands such as the Tribal Grazing Land Policy (TGLP) ranches (Alden Wily, 1994; Saugestad, 1998; Bolaane, 2001; Ellis, 2001; Madzwamuse, 2007; 2009). The lands belonging to the Basarwa were regarded as 'vacant lands' and parcelled out as TGLP farms. This has resulted in Basarwa being landless and consequently increasing their poverty given that land is the basic means of production for rural households that depend on agri-cultural production or the gathering of wild foods in order to survive (Ratcliffe, 1976; Arntzen et al, 1982; Alden Wily, 1994; Mogwe, 1994; Selolwane, 1995). Alden Wily (2006) argues that such developments do not necessarily arise out of ignorance about tenure on the part of policy-makers, but that in fact these are convenient moves enabling state-building administrations of the colonial and post-colonial eras to secure vast areas of common property for themselves, particularly where high value resources are present.

Government policy can be seen as a formalization of British colonial actions when Botswana was a protectorate under British rule. Cecil Rhodes settled Boer and English pioneers on the Gantsi ridge in the western part of the country, who were intended to act as a buffer against German expansion from South West Africa (contemporary Namibia) (Ng'ong'ola and Moeletsi, 1995). During colonial rule, native reserves were mainly delineated for the Tswana-speaking tribes or communities. Crown land (land retained under the Bechuanaland Protectorate administration) essentially consisted of those areas belonging to Basarwa, Bakgalagadi and other voiceless minority ethnic groups not incorporated into the recognized Tswana tribes and territories. Furthermore, by virtue of living on what was referred to as Crown land, the Basarwa were those most directly affected by the evolution and implementation of conservation laws. The Wildlife Conservation and National Parks Act of 1992 reduced Basarwa peoples' access to their traditional territories and, together with land policies discussed above, trapped the Basarwa into smaller areas that could not accommodate their traditional livelihood strategies (Madzwamuse, 2009). By criminalizing one of the central markers of Basarwa identity, hunting regulations such as the Fauna Conservation Act and the Unified Hunting Regulations of 1977 symbolically marginalized Basarwa from mainstream society (Taylor, 2000). The numerous and complicated rules and regulations of those laws were formulated and implemented without consultation with the Basarwa, nor with sufficient regard of the importance of hunting and gathering to the affected communities (Ng'ong'ola and Moeletsi, 1995). Even though the Basarwa occupy most of the Wildlife Management Areas where the bulk of CBNRM activities are taking place (Rozemeijer and van der Jagt, 2000), the CBNRM policy has done very little to adequately address the needs of the Basarwa and the security of resource tenure issues in general (Madzwamuse, 2007).

Indigenous natural resource governance systems

Discussion of indigenous natural resource governance systems often generates discomfort amongst CBNRM practitioners in southern Africa who are concerned with the danger of local chiefs usurping all rights and benefits at the expense of the ordinary members of the local communities. These reservations stem from the conflation of traditional management systems with the role of chiefs and/or traditional authorities and the somewhat tainted history of chieftaincy and its colonial ties in southern Africa (Murombedzi, this volume). I look beyond the traditional leadership structures, using the case of the Basarwa to highlight the broader relevance of indigenous knowledge systems (IKS), norms, values and practices that are tied to conservation. While chiefs have played a central role in governing the use of natural resources in Botswana, this aspect will not be examined here as this was not part of the indigenous governance structures of the Basarwa.

As with many other indigenous societies, the Basarwa's adaptive strategies for using natural resources were based on traditional ethics, norms and rules – both formal and informal – that governed the use of land and natural resources (Spinage, 1992). These systems reflect what Berkes (1999) terms a knowledge-practice belief complex which involves local knowledge of land, plants and animals; embodies land and resource management systems; defines social institutions and reflects a certain worldview capturing the religious beliefs about the use of the resources and ritual practices associated with them. Thus the Basarwa's traditional governance systems embody a holistic view and approach to natural resource management, which is central to the realm of communal governance of natural resources and community conservation.

The Basarwa's traditional management strategies were designed to be responsive to a highly variable climatic environment involving fluctuations in resource availability, with water being the most important resource determining settlement patterns and the size of communities. Tenurial rights and access to land and natural resources were restricted to members of a group with a given territory. This membership and accompanying tenurial rights were obtained through birth, marriage and residence (Madzwamuse, 1998).

The Basarwa's traditional strategies for managing natural resources included seasonal mobility, detailed ecological knowledge and appropriate skills to capitalize on this knowledge. Flexibility was a key strategy that the Basarwa used in relation to group size and social organization, leadership structures and resource use in order to respond to changes in their local environment (Madzwamuse and Fabricius, 2004; Madzwamuse, 2009). Anthropological studies on the Basarwa living in the Kalahari by Cashdan (1983) and Barnard (1992) on the G/wi, !Xo, !Kung and Naro reveal differences in the strategies pursued by various San groups. The !Kung who lived in areas with permanent water sources exploited natural resources in more fluidly composed groups, involving two or more clans that came together in the dry season to exploit permanent wells. In the wet season, when water and food were abundant, the !Kung dispersed into smaller (family) groups. The territories of the !Kung overlapped with each other, with areas rich in natural resources being used by more than one clan. The clans would disperse deep within their territories in the summer when resources were more abundant. The G/wi, who occupied areas with less rainfall and resource abundance, did the opposite in managing access and using natural resources. They congregated in the wet season and dispersed in the dry season, as they did not have any permanent water sources to exploit in the dry season. Flexibility in group size was employed as a strategy to adjust to seasonal changes and the consequent availability of food and water (Madzwamuse and Fabricius, 2004; Madzwamuse, 2009).

The !Xo lived in areas where natural resources were most sparsely and least predictably distributed, and therefore tended to be more territorial than the other groups. For this group, territoriality not only operated at the clan level but also extended to groups that were related to each other through kinship, friendship or ritual bonds (Barnard, 1992). The !Xo dispersed in both wet and dry season and scarcity of resources necessitated smaller community sizes (Ibid.). The Naro, on the other hand, lived in areas well-favoured with water and natural resources, making them less territorial, compared to the !Kung, G/wi and !Xo. Because of abundance in food resources and water, the Naro did not need to disperse at any time. The group congregated in both dry and wet seasons (Cashdan, 1993).

Another element important to the traditional adaptive strategies of the Basarwa was the size of territories within which natural resources were accessed and seasonal mobility was employed. The Basarwa who lived in resource-abundant areas moved within relatively smaller territories compared to those who lived in resource-poor areas. In other words, seasonal mobility was more extensive for the !Xo compared to the three other groups.

Clearly defined rules and territories governed access to natural resources amongst all Basarwa communities, with tenurial rights obtained through birth, marriage and residence. Cashdan (1983), for instance, notes that among the BaXhanikhwe, kinship controlled access to land, whether for resource exploitation or residence. Cashdan found that people sought permission to use land where they had close relatives, and consequently permission was rarely if ever denied. Furthermore, sanctions for trespassing existed and were used when needed. The rules operating in these institutions differed from clan to clan, in response to micro-environmental factors that influenced the way in which people used natural resources. There was considerable movement across territory boundaries and between social groups, such that groups would typically have overlapping rights and access rights to more than one territory.

Although research on the settlement patterns of the Basarwa in the Okavango Delta is scant, one can safely assume that seasonal mobility was not as extensive as it was for the !Xo and other desert Basarwa because of the abundance of resources and availability of permanent water sources. In fact Bolaane (2004b) states that the BaXhanikhwe and Babugakhwe did not follow defined annual cycles similar to those of Basarwa living in the Kalalahari. Those more sedentary Basarwa communities rather followed movements according to trade-offs between being close to stretches of permanent water and the desire to avoid areas infested by tsetse fly. The movements of the BaXhanikwe and Babugakhwe were nevertheless still within their territories.

An interview with village elders in the Xaxaba community revealed examples of rules and practices that governed access to natural resources amongst some of the Basarwa groups in the Okavango Delta. Describing local rules governing hunting rights, the elders in Xaxaba noted that outsiders would have to seek permission from a group in order to gain access to wildlife within the Xhanikhwe territory. Permission was not sought from the group leader alone but also from the ancestors. One of the elders in the Xaxaba community described the process as follows:

> *Bayei[3] would bring with them maize, sorghum and other gifts to the locals when seeking permission to hunt or collect medicinal plants in a territory which belonged to the BaXhanikwe. The first person to receive these visitors will then give the Bayei a place to rest for the night. The following day in the morning they would be taken to the clan leader where their request is made official. They would state, 'we have come to seek permission to hunt and we bring with us gifts in the form of food'. The food would be prepared and shared with the rest of the clan. The next day, strong Xhanikhwe [another term for BaXhanikhwe] men are selected to accompany the visitors on their hunting expedition. It was necessary for the visitors to be escorted because they did not know their way around the said territory, i.e. where to find different types of animals.[4]*

By accompanying the visiting hunters, the Xhanikhwe made sure that their rules were not broken. They ensured that there was no hunting of expectant female wildlife or of productive male animals and that the visiting hunters did not go beyond the boundaries of the Xhanikhwe territory. This way they retained the power to decide where and how much hunting was to take place, again as recounted by a Xaxaba elder:

> *The visitors and the Xhanikhwe men appointed to accompany them would take guns and go to a sacred tree known as Kgaka where a fire is made and the ancestral spirits are contacted to safeguard the men on the hunt. After this the Basarwa would take the Bayei to an island where the hunting is going to be; they did not hunt female animals, only old male animals were hunted. The animals would then be skinned and meat dried at the hunting site; the kill would all be given to the visitors. The land was protected [said with emphasis]; people who hunted without being given permission were, if found, required to give an explanation and state who had given them permission to hunt.*

The above not only highlights territoriality but also a point noted by Berkes (1999), which is that often where traditional ecological knowledge and management systems are concerned, the ecological aspects cannot be divorced from social and spiritual realms. Elders in Xaxaba emphasize that natural resource governance was beyond the powers of ordinary individuals in the community, and was vested in those with supernatural powers, such as rainmakers, trance dancers with healing powers, and so forth. Elders also gave examples of taboos, which were embedded in natural resource management systems and livelihood strategies in general. They spoke of what they term *Setema*, referring to people who had the powers of lions. They said if someone spilled water as they were returning from the river where they collected it, lions would surround the village that very evening. Those with the powers of the lions would then have to apologize on behalf of the wasteful person(s), and only then would these lions go back to where they had come from. The fear of attracting lions to the village deterred clan members from wasting water. The lions could also be attracted to the village by someone returning to the village with thatch grass after sunset. To avoid this, the grass collectors were required to leave the grass outside the village and bring it in the morning or any other time during the course of the day. Such beliefs deterred people from being wasteful and encouraged sustainable natural resource management practices. For example, among the G/wi, animals are *kx'oxudzi* (things to be eaten), but they are N!adima's creatures (that is, God's creatures), and 'As his property they must be respected, not abused' (Silberbauer, 1981, cited in Spinage, 1992, p31). They may be killed in self-defence or for food or to avoid an attack that is believed to be imminent. The G/wi disapprove of what is seen as greedy hunting, fearing that it will displease N!adima and they will suffer unpleasant consequences in some way (Ibid.).

Other rules governing the use of natural resources involved observing ceremonies marking the arrivals of the first wild fruits. The elderly women in Xaxaba[5] stated that the very first fruits, berries and honey of the season (usually in late October and early November for most fruit species) were collected and burnt so that the smoke could go up to the ancestors, as a tribute to them (Madzwamuse, 2009). Thereafter, the remainder of the collected fruits would be given to old women and to successively younger age groups. By the time the youngest group has had its share there would be an abundance of fruits in the wild, and the members of the community would then be free to go out and collect the fruits at will. This, they said, ensured that fruits were collected on a large scale only when there was enough supply to avoid over-harvesting (Ibid.).

Often, when highlighting the importance of traditional institutions in governing resource use, we are confronted with the question of the relevance of these systems to contemporary resource management scenarios. Lewis (1993) points out the limitations of using the term 'traditional', as it may be dismissed or denigrated by those in positions of power and authority as the custodians are considered as no longer 'traditional'. Such views assume that traditional systems are static and fail to change with the times. 'Traditional' does not imply an inflexible adherence to the past, it simply means time-tested and locally adaptive systems (Berkes, 1999). This type of knowledge is cumulative and dynamic, building on experience and adapting to changes (Ibid.). In the case of the Basarwa, while seasonal mobility may no longer be a feasible strategy because of the prevailing land tenure system in the country and patterns of economic development and population growth, seasonality and fluctuating resource availability remain realities which face the Basarwa and other local communities. Therefore, in contemporary times, in order to respond to these fluctuations and take into account traditional adaptation strategies, a fair amount of flexibility is needed on the part of government policies. Government could for instance secure access to dryland resources found in protected areas for certain parts of the year.

While one is careful not to make exaggerated claims on the relevance of indigenous knowledge systems a more relevant question to ask is: do modern forms of knowledge such as science and modes of governance provide space for locally adapted practices and institutions? In modern Botswana, indigenous management strategies, rules and regulations have been rendered largely irrelevant. Privatization of land, agricultural and livestock policies and modern conservation laws have alienated local communities from the direct management of land and natural resources and undermined traditional management systems.

Indigenous knowledge systems and external resource governance interests

CBNRM and interactions with indigenous knowledge systems

The previous section highlights how indigenous management systems have contributed to resource conservation, demonstrating that the Basarwa and other local communities have always practised community-based natural resource management in a substantive sense. These practices were undermined by broader external measures governing the use of land and natural resources, such as various agricultural and conservation polices imposed on the Basarwa by the colonial and post-colonial nation-state. In most cases this process led to a breakdown of local governance institutions, thereby resulting in open access to resources in communal areas. Local management systems continue to be overlooked in the current implementation of CBNRM in Botswana.

In the early 1990s CBNRM was introduced in Botswana as a rural development and conservation strategy, based on experiences from neighbouring countries such as Zimbabwe and Namibia and strong external donor support (Rihoy and Maguranyanga, this volume). The aim of the CBNRM programme, as captured in the CBNRM Draft Policy of 2001, was to improve the living conditions of people residing with natural resources so as to improve their attitudes towards wildlife and demonstrate the value of conserving those resources for future generations. Local communities were supported to set up legal entities in the form of community-based organizations (CBOs) or Village Trust Committees (VTCs). The VTCs were tasked with managing natural resources within a designated Wildlife Management Area and Controlled Hunting Areas as well as to oversee CBNRM activities on behalf of the community.

The VTCs are required to manage CBNRM programmes using participatory processes sanctioned by district government authorities (Madzwamuse, 2009). In this instance acceptable participatory processes refer to the *kgotla* which in itself is not a Sarwa construct but rather a Tswana institution. Not only do the cultural practices of the Tswana influence policy as indicated by the Land Act and the TGLP, but this also extends to what is regarded as acceptable definitions of traditional democratic spaces and practices within CBNRM. The challenges and experience in this regard are more pronounced in the case of the Basarwa who are politically marginalized in the context of the Botswana state. Peters (1994) notes that the *kgotla* does not necessarily grant a culture or class free space to engage with and influence decision-making, and that participation in these fora is highly stratified, with the result that the voices of the marginalized are not heard in this space.

The case of Khwai

Khwai is situated on the northern border of the Moremi Game Reserve within a Wildlife Management Area and 140km from Maun (see Figure 11.1). The settlement is almost exclusively Basarwa (Babugakhwe) with a history of hunting and gatherering. The village arose from the settlement of various small family groups resettled following the establishment of the Moremi Game Reserve in the 1960s (Alexandra, 1993; Madzwamuse, 2009). In the mid-1990s the group was forced to relocate once again when the boundaries of the Moremi Game Reserve were extended (Alexandra, 1993).

The settlement has a population of 419 with an average household cash income of P2,100 (~US$350) per month, the bulk of which is earned during the tourism peak season (Madzwamuse, 2009). In 1996, the Khwai community formed a CBO and was allocated a concession area covering 1,815km². However, as described by Rihoy and Maguranyanga (this volume), the CBNRM activities in Khwai were delayed and did not begin formally until 2000. The community lease was withheld by local authorities on the grounds that the constitution drawn up by the community was discriminatory. The constitution required non-Basarwa persons to apply for the Trust membership whereas the Basarwa themselves were not required to apply. The members of the Khwai community had taken it upon themselves to define and restrict community membership as a strategy to possibly protect themselves from domination by other ethnic groups (Madzwamuse, 2009). This

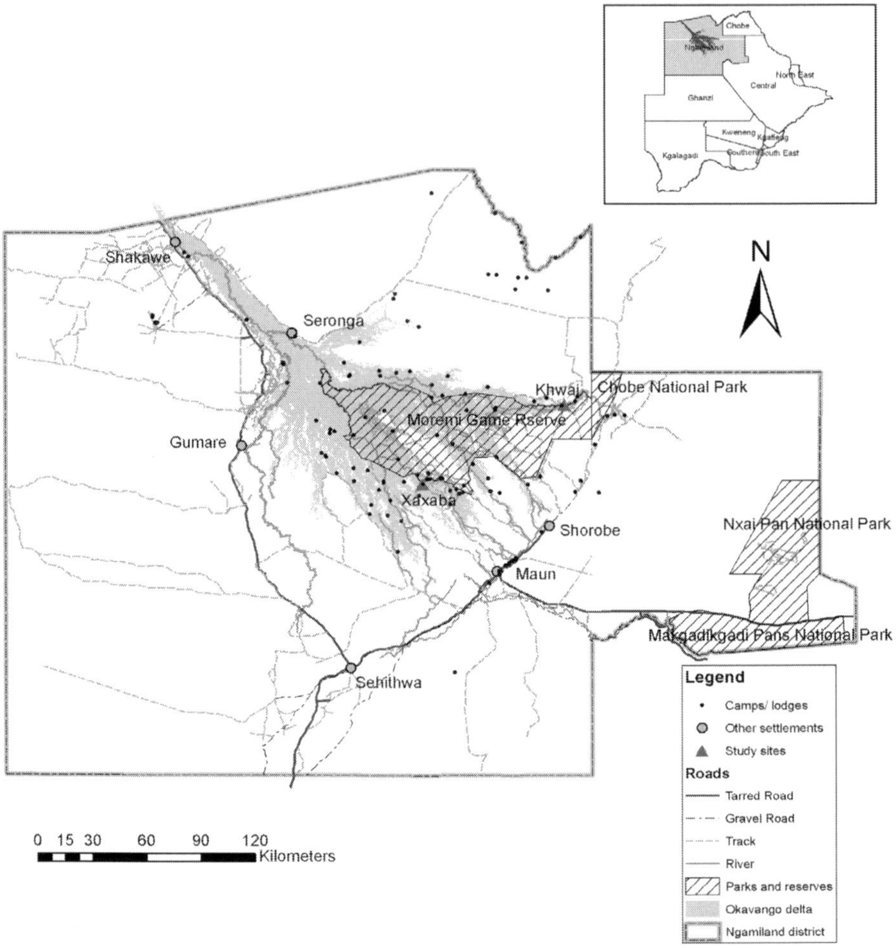

Figure caption and map:

Figure 11.1 *Map indicating the location of Khwai and Xaxaba*

Source: Madzwamuse, 2009

provision was not allowed by the district authorities responsible for sanctioning participatory processes at the community level and issuing land leases to the CBOs. The district authorities were reluctant to support a CBNRM initiative built exclusively around cultural identity (Bolaane, 2001). The Khwai community was left with no choice but to amend their constitution and they were consequently allocated a hunting quota for their concession in 2000.

Having overcome the first obstacle concerning their constitution, Khwai embarked on a number of CBNRM activities which included marketing part of their hunting quota to commercial outfitters, subsistence hunting for part of their quota and trading in crafts and thatching grass (see Table 11.1). Internally, the community continued to tap into aspects of their traditional management practices, particularly with regards to the harvesting and trading of thatch. The residents of Khwai formed a committee that controls the collection of thatching grass to ensure that harvesting does not take place outside the June to September period (Madzwamuse and Fabricius, 2004; Madzwamuse, 2009). However, with limited legal and policy backing for the use of veld products, the residents of Khwai could not control access by members from outside their community. The community generally had difficulties reaching consensus on matters relating to the use of natural resources, with widespread conflicts on decisions. In a focus group discussion with Department of Wildlife and National Parks (DWNP) officials in Khwai, the officials argued that it would be difficult for the Khwai community to successfully run their own CBNRM projects because there is a lot of conflict at community level, mostly in connection with the question of who has the right to be a member of the community.[6] A community mapping exercise carried out with the residents of Khwai also revealed the source of these tensions as revolving around group membership legitimacy. Respondents repeatedly made reference to 'old' Khwai and 'new' Khwai within the village. 'New' referred to areas where recent settlers lived, and even after 20 years of being part of this community their rights to access resources in Khwai were being questioned by members of the community (Bolaane, 2001; Madzwamuse, 2009).

Table 11.1 *Annual benefits derived from CBNRM activities in Khwai and Xaxaba*

	1999	2000	2001	2002	2003	2004	2005
	Annual Benefits in Pula (1P=~US$0.15)						
Khwai Development Trust	–	1,200,000	600,000	1,211,533	389,000	1,272,900	1,318,560
Okavango Kopano Mokoro Trust	750,000	1,100,000	1,200,000	1,300,000	2,213,545	1,767,155	1,855,655

Source of Data: CBNRM Status Reports 2003–2006

At an operational level the Khwai community continued to face other challenges in implementing CBNRM activities and working with external agencies in the form of local government, NGOs and private companies. The community gained a reputation for being a 'difficult' community and often dominated the agendas of the National CBNRM Forum and the Ngamiland District Forum. In 2003 a case study that was commissioned by the CBNRM National Forum revealed the tendency by local élites in Khwai to use community benefits for individual benefits (Potts, 2003). This overshadowed what started off as a struggle for self-determination and control of the operations of the affairs of its governing trust with minimal interference from what they regarded as external agencies. The case of financial mismanagement in Khwai would have far-reaching policy and political implications, contributing to the recentralization of national CBNRM policy in Botswana in subsequent years (Rihoy and Maguranyanga, this volume).

The case of Xaxaba

Xaxaba settlement is on an island referred to as Sedibane or Ncoega by the locals (see Figure 11.1). It has a small population of 78 people consisting of Basarwa (from the Xhanikhwe group), Bayei and a few Batawana. The average household income is P1,600 (US$267) per month and like Khwai fluctuates depending on the performance of the tourism industry. The tourism industry also has an impact on the population size of this settlement. Xaxaba has been described as a transient community hosting mobile people seeking employment in surrounding camps who leave as soon as their contracts end. A national census carried out in 1991 counted 212 people and subsequent surveys in 1999 estimated the population at 400 (Cassidy, 1999). The more permanent residents of this settlement claim to have originated from Tsobaoro, which is modern-day Chief's Island, one of the islands in the Okavango Delta (Madzwamuse, 2009). The villagers were attracted to the current location by the construction of the first safari camps in the Okavango in the 1960s. The elders in the village confirm that the settlement was part of their traditional territories.

Xaxaba was originally omitted when the CBNRM programmes started in Botswana in 1993. To rectify this situation the Xabaxa community was included in the trust charged with managing the Ngamiland 32 wildlife use concession, in concert with five other settlements (Ditshiping, Quxau, Daonara, Xharaxao and Boro). The trust in question is the Okavango Kopano Mokoro Trust (OKMT) which has been allocated an area of 1,223km^2 and has a total membership of 2,400 people. This trust has been operational since 1997 and is involved in a number of commercial activities ranging from selling a trophy hunting concession to safari operators, managing a campsite, and selling grass, reeds and palms. As a result of being included in the OKMT, the government also withdrew Special Game Licences in Xaxaba which had a profound effect on the food security of several households (Cassidy, et al, 2001).[7] In 2000, Xaxaba received P15,000 (US$2,500) from the proceeds of OKMCT which was used to open a community shop. Subsequent benefits were used to purchase a vehicle and boat for the community (see Table 11.1 for revenue generated).

Apart from VTC members, most of the residents of Xaxaba who were interviewed about CBNRM did not seem to fully understand what it was about, or even how they should be involved in decisions on the use of funds derived from CBNRM projects.[8] One of the old women interviewed stated, 'It is not our money, it is for developments [referring to infrastructural development] in the village.'[9]

What I observed during my last stay in Xaxaba in March 2001 was that the elderly members of the community did not attend VTC public meetings, and thus gained only second-hand information on what the affairs of the VTC were. By the time this information reached them it was either incomplete or distorted. The VTC board members are not well-known to the general membership of the CBO. This has led to mistrust, accusations of misappropriation of funds and to tensions between the residents of Xaxaba and other members of OKMT (Madzwamuse and Fabricius, 2004). DWNP and PACT (2001) in their CBO assessments concluded that it is difficult for a multi-village CBO to achieve acceptable levels of participation and benefit-sharing, yet up to this day the membership and structure of OKMCT remains unaltered. The grouping of these villages was not informed by prior understanding of how these communities relate to each other in terms of resource use, access and rights. The decision was based on proximity to a Controlled Hunting Area demarcated by government agencies.

Regardless of CBNRM activities being in place, the residents of Xaxaba, similarly to Khwai, still complain about the difficulty in controlling access to natural resources in their locality by outsiders. Some of the resources and territories that were previously accessible only to clan members are now open access resources. For example, in both villages leaves of palm (*Hyphaene petersiana*) used for crafts, reeds, water lily (*Nymphaea nouchali*, referred to as *Tswii* by residents) and thatch grass in their area are also collected by people who come from as far as Maun for commercial purposes. The residents of Khwai argue that in the past, when their clan was comprised of BaBugakhwe alone, cooperation at community level was very high, resulting in easier management and control of resource use. They also argued that within their community they are in a position to regulate the collection of thatch grass, but they are not in any position to control outsiders who are accessing the natural resources in their area. The reason is that their local rules are not supported by the present legal system. The 1993 amendment of the Tribal Land Act of 1968 gave all citizens of Botswana the right to acquire land and settle in any part of the country, regardless of their tribal affiliation. This change, according to the communities of Xaxaba and Khwai, has complicated matters in terms of natural resource governance. An elderly resident of Khwai in her sixties described these changes as follows:

> ...*we were just on our own; the BaBugakhwe and our clan were composed of family units; that way the use of natural resources was easily managed. In the past, cooperation at community level was high, but now it is felt that things are different. For instance, having collected thatching grass and agreeing to sell it at a certain price, some people may change the price without consulting the rest of the community. Decisions are no longer made collectively at community level but rather increasingly at an individual level.*[10]

CBNRM implies active participation by local communities whereas the reality on the ground does not reflect that scenario. Sullivan (2002) argues that, in practice, CBNRM is a mere continuation of past conservation policies because the policies and projects are largely driven by external agents who tend to overlook local aspirations and regard communities as homogeneous entities.

While at the national level issues of local financial accountability and good record-keeping have dominated policy debates, at the local level communities are more concerned about issues pertaining to self-determination, identity and group definition. These concerns, as demonstrated by the case of Khwai and Xaxaba, include controlling their own group and/or community definition and controlling access and resource use in their 'territories'.

Challenges facing Basarwa in maintaining adaptive resource governance systems

Displacement of traditional management systems

Traditional institutions have been replaced by modern rules and regulations and in contrast to the traditional local institutions, which were governed by the respective Basarwa communities, new institutions in the form of VTCs are externally driven and defined. There are also differences in worldviews between outsiders and local people. The procedures for setting up VTCs are stipulated by the government, donors and other support organizations. Requirements include developing a written constitution and making use of the *kgotla* system as a forum for public consultation and participation, both of which are foreign concepts imposed on the Basarwa communities. These draw very little from local norms and practices, particularly with regards to tenure arrangements and rules governing access to land and natural resources. One of the factors determining effective resource governance is the power and control people have over their relationship to these resources (Twyman, 2000). As the preceding sections have shown, power and control over natural resources have been removed from the Basarwa. They are continually dispossessed of their lands and access to resources by conservation laws and regulations in the Okavango Delta region, and a combination of conservation and livestock policies in other parts of the country. Even with the introduction of CBNRM, communities remain passive recipients of benefits and they are not involved in active management or decision-making. The communities are allowed to enjoy increased utilization of natural resources but government retains the ultimate authority to protect species and ecological systems and continues to regulate their use (CBNRM Draft Policy, 2001).

Alden Wily (2008) notes that customary interests cannot be recognized in their own right without at the same time recognizing the existence of the (customary) regimes which sustain them. It is not adequate to establish local trusts or CBOs without taking into account and building on traditional resource governance systems. This includes accepting the heterogeneity of such local systems. A fundamental issue here is that devolving user rights to wildlife will have limited impact while communities' land tenure remains insecure. A policy direction that alienates communities from managing their land – for example through privatization, TGLP farms, and protected areas – is not compatible with efforts to enhance community participation through CBNRM. In other words, CBNRM needs to be reconciled with land tenure reform by creating space for community rights to land and natural resources (Madzwamuse, 2007; see also Murombedzi, this volume).

The power to make decisions and manage natural resources is still vested in the state. There have been problems with regards to devolution of authority in many parts of southern Africa (Hulme and Murphree, 2001; Jones, 2003; Fabricius et al, 2004). In Botswana, the government sets quotas and issues permits and commissions, and approves management plans for most uses of wildlife. Jones (2003) argues that in Botswana and Zambia, communities tend to be passive recipients of the quota as well as the associated income, without engaging in active management as the state retains considerable management authority. Murphree (2003) argues that devolution which separates responsibility from authority is fatal to institutions. As Rihoy and Maguranyanga (this volume) detail, there have been a wide set of barriers to devolution of authority over wildlife and other natural resources in Botswana, which continue to limit local rights to make decisions about rules governing use and the distribution of benefits.

Limited space for and acceptance of indigenous knowledge in CBNRM

There is a general reluctance to embrace indigenous knowledge in CBNRM as practised in Botswana by both government officials and many mainstream conservationists. Berkes (1999) argues that the use of indigenous knowledge is often inherently political because it threatens to change power relations between indigenous groups and the broader society. Indigenous knowledge provides a compelling argument for conceptual pluralism and more participatory community-based alternatives to top-down resource management (Ibid.). Acknowledging indigenous knowledge has political implications for the Government of Botswana and other governments in the region. Limited institutional capacity of local communities is often cited as a reason for not devolving rights and authority to local communities. Instead of focusing and building on the local communities' strengths and existing forms of knowledge, their capacity constraints have taken the centre stage in determining policy outcomes. The recentralization of natural resource management structures in Botswana, as highlighted by Rihoy and Maguranyanga (this volume), is justified by the shortcomings of local communities in managing the affairs of CBOs. Policy-makers and the national CBNRM discourse seldom pay attention to the positive attributes that these communities bring to the table. Botswana's CBNRM programme effectively seeks to fit community management practices into a set of pre-conceived bureaucratic norms and structures, rather than adaptively crafting governance arrangements to local institutions, customs and knowledge.

A deeper awareness in policy and planning of local knowledge and practice may foster culturally resonant, ecologically appropriate and socially inclusive dialogue regarding resource governance and development in general (Sullivan, 1999). Developing national conservation objectives appropriate for the local context implies a shift in approach that acknowledges the existence and value of cultural knowledge relating to a range of natural resources other than large mammals (Ibid.). Shackleton and Shackleton (2004) echo the same sentiment, noting that resource management interventions need to focus on the role of all natural resources in local livelihoods, suggesting that such an approach will ensure that the CBNRM agenda is guided by local priorities and needs rather than conservationist paradigms and interests. Sullivan (1999) argues that a lack of focus on details of how people currently use and manage natural resources results in an untapped potential of the value for biodiversity conservation of associated knowledge related to these resources. Communities bring significant knowledge to the table, but these local assets have been consistently undervalued in the past (Taylor, 2000). In general, indigenous knowledge holds much promise for insights and applications provided it is not used out of context (Berkes, 1999).

As noted earlier, the attitudes of most biological scientists and natural resource managers to traditional knowledge are often dismissive (Johannes, 1989, quoted by Berkes, 1999). Thus marginalized peoples not only have to struggle against the most powerful in both economic and political terms but they must also face the dominant role of externally-rooted forms of science in debates over resource use (Keeley and Scoones, 2003). The drive for a space for indigenous people and indigenous knowledge is taking place at a time when many indigenous groups, Basarwa included, are increasingly linked to new forms of market-based commerce and may be compelled to engage in activities that differ in type and intensity from traditional patterns (Berkes, 1999). While communities are required to be static in their development in order to be considered 'traditional', many indigenous communities including the Basarwa have been engaging in mixed economies for decades. What is required is trade-offs that balance conservation and development objectives of local communities.

Restricted access to natural resources

Surrounded by tourism lodges and the Moremi Game Reserve, the residents of both Xaxaba and Khwai are no longer able to engage in their traditional seasonal movements as a means to cope with resource scarcity. They feel that they are 'fenced in' and helpless to adapt to these imposed boundaries. The older residents note that during the colonial era hunting was allowed throughout the year as long as permission was sought from the colonial government. In the opinion of several people interviewed, life was a lot better then.[11] Today they have to rely on hunting safaris for meat from animals shot for trophies, on DWNP for meat from problem animals, and illegal hunting for subsistence. With the expansion of the Moremi Game Reserve to include the Boro River, the community of Xaxaba argue that the areas they can use for gathering grass, reeds and firewood, and for fishing, have been reduced significantly. The statement below captures their frustration with these restrictions.

> *It seems animals are more important than the human beings; you can judge from the sort of sentences people get for poaching.*[11]

The current CBNRM activities are not considered adequate compensation because of the distance between the village and the area allocated to OKMT, the CBO to which they belong. Furthermore, even under CBNRM, community participation is confined to the periphery; the resource-rich areas are protected and there is no space for active co-management with the communities. The Central Kalahari Game Reserve presents a good example where proposals for community use zones within the park were rejected by the Botswana government.

This restricted access does not only manifest itself in access to resources for subsistence livelihoods but it also translates to lost opportunities for communities to meaningfully benefit from lucrative income-generating activities such as ecotourism. The Basarwa are on the losing end precisely because their rights are not recognized and the leasing arrangement under CBNRM, wherein only usufruct rights are accorded and the security of these rights is at the mercy of the state, does not adequately address this. As argued by Alden Wily (2008), if these areas remain government lands, the majority of the rural poor are deprived not just of their land rights but also of a critical capital base which could help them step out of poverty.

Competition for resources with more powerful groups

Some studies have shown that the existence of Basarwa settlements in the Okavango Delta and particularly in tourism areas puts them in a position of direct competition and conflict with a more powerful tourism industry. The tourist lodges market the area as a pristine wilderness, rarely making reference to the traditional and historic occupants of the Okavango Delta. A survey of safari lodges in the Delta revealed that, out of 15 lodges or camps, the brochures of 14 make no mention whatsoever of local peoples or culture. Instead the majority illustrate the luxurious interiors of the chalets, and the type of wildlife-related activities tourists can engage in (Damm et al, 1997). In such competition the Basarwa are often on the losing end, as they have less political power compared to the tourism industry (Taylor, 2002; Mbaiwa, 2004). Despite the wealth being generated in their area, the daily tasks associated with searching for a livelihood often remain as difficult as ever for many of its inhabitants (Taylor, 2002). To the elderly members of the Xaxaba community, CBNRM has replaced subsistence hunting, which not only fitted their lifestyle but was the central marker of their identity, with a dependence on government welfare (Madzwamuse and Fabricius, 2004; Madzwamuse, 2009). During my field-work many echoed the phrase '*re a Sheta*' (direct translation: 'we are struggling') when making reference to their livelihoods.

Although CBNRM has brought substantial financial resources to marginalized communities, and opportunities exist for them to profit from the sustainable use of natural resources or tourism, Taylor (2002) highlights the fact that the inhabitants of these areas have generally found it difficult to engage effectively with an industry that is controlled far from their locality. Taylor attributes this to the reality that despite some of Botswana's most remote areas also becoming lucrative sites of capitalist production through the growth of the tourism industry, the very same rural regions have remained areas of economic deprivation, especially if one examines the benefits that accrue to the local inhabitants. Mbaiwa (2004) has narrowed this situation down to what he terms 'enclave tourism', which in the Okavango Delta is characterized by foreign ownership of tourism facilities, repatriation of funds and a failure to effectively contribute to poverty alleviation at the local or district level. Of the tourism facilities in the Okavango Delta, 53.8 per cent are foreign-owned, 27.7 per cent are jointly owned and 18.5 per cent are owned by citizens (Mbaiwa, 2002).

The share of tourism revenue that local communities such as the Basarwa capture is minimal. Due to low literacy levels the Basarwa's ability to access employment in the tourism sector is limited. Thus safari operators tend to employ non-community members as noted by the residents of Khwai. The facts appear to support this; a study carried out over a decade ago revealed that Khwai residents held only 9 of the 74 non-management posts in the three tourism lodges in the vicinity (Taylor, 2002). Competition from non-locals also extends to trade in crafts. Lodge employees sell their baskets through the curio shops at the lodges to the tourists, negatively impacting craft sales in Khwai.

Struggling for local representation in the policy arena

The Basarwa are peripheral to the political arena in Botswana, and thus do not have a strong influence on decision-making processes and policy formulation. It has only been within the past few decades that the Basarwa have been able to self-organize in a formal political sense. The earliest San community-based organization to be established was the Kuru Development Trust in 1993, which aimed to support residents of the D'Kar settlement in the Gantsi District. In 1996 the organization expanded its operations to provide support and to facilitate the establishment of CBOs in other San settlements. This led to the birth of the Kuru Family of Organisations which includes the Trust for Okavango Cultural and Development Initiatives (TOCADI) and Letloa, both operating in Ngamiland District. The aim of their Land, Livelihoods and Heritage Programme as captured on their website is to support San communities in northwest and western Botswana with sustainable development through CBNRM, land and cultural resource mapping. Other significant organizations include the First People of the Kalahari (FPK) established in 1993 as the first totally San interest group, and the Working Group for Indigenous Peoples of Southern Africa (WIMSA) Botswana set up in 1996. WIMSA, Kuru Family of Organisations, FPK and other development and human rights organizations, such as Ditshwanelo, pursued a progressive agenda to secure the land rights and development of the Basarwa. The University of Botswana and Tromso University set up a Basarwa Research Programme which has supported multidisciplinary research on various aspects of San issues in the country. However, the outcomes of these processes were not adequately used to inform the CBNRM policy debates, for instance the outcome of the Central Kalahari Game Reserve case (CKGR) which highlighted the struggles of the Basarwa to retain control of their ancestral lands as described below.

FPK and WIMSA spearheaded and won a court case between the Government of Botswana and the residents of the Central Kalahari Game Reserve in which the San opposed government-driven removals and fought to retain their rights to live within the reserve. Initially San-based organizations and human rights NGOs had responded to the relocation of the Basarwa from the CKGR by forming a negotiation team which met with government for the first time in mid-1997 and continued for many years with little success (Taylor, 2007). Although the Central Kalahari Game Reserve had been created in 1961 as a nature reserve and to protect the rights of 5,000 San and other groups living within its borders, the Government of Botswana had since the late 1990s embarked on a move to relocate the residents of the park. This move was influenced by conservationists concerned with over-hunting and veterinary control in the reserve, and the government also claimed that it was becoming increasingly expensive to provide services and development for the residents within the park. As a result, government removals began in 1997 and intensified in 2002 when services such as water, medicine, food deliveries and social welfare to the park residents were cut off.

FPK, with the controversial support of Survival International, took the government to court in 2002 in what has been noted as possibly the longest and most expensive court case in the history of Botswana (Taylor, 2007). Survival International had throughout the court case embarked on an antagonistic campaign wherein they linked the relocation of the Basarwa to diamond interests in the country and labelled the move by the government as genocide. The campaign by Survival International not only stirred animosity on the part of government but it also caused divisions among the country's citizens, and most importantly within San organizations and other partners (such as Ditshwanelo, a local human rights organization) in their campaign to have their rights recognized (Mphinyane, 2002; Saugestad, 2006a, 2006b; Taylor, 2007). The campaign by Survival International diverted attention from the real issues at hand. The key problem the case exposed is that of an authoritarian and patronizing model of socio-economic development, based on the value systems of the dominant group which had been applied for years not only on the CKGR residents but also to San and other minorities all over Botswana (Saugestad, 2005; Solway, 2007; Taylor, 2007). The court case was concluded in 2006 with a ruling allowing the return of the San to their ancestral lands. Several observers have noted this as a qualified victory which does not necessarily extend to the broader struggle of the San for their land rights. This observation is based on the government's narrow interpretation of the court ruling wherein only the 189 individuals listed in the court applications were allowed to return to the park without permits (Saugestad, 2006b; Taylor, 2007).

Although the evolution of the San organizations referred to above coincided with the development of CBNRM in Botswana, they did not actively engage with broader CBNRM processes through the National CBNRM Forum, with the exception of TOCADI and Letloa, two NGOs belonging to the Kuru Family of Organisations. As a result, the issues pertaining to the struggle for the Basarwa's land rights and the challenges that they face in implementing CBNRM did not enter the mainstream debates on CBNRM policy. Drawing from the case of Khwai and Xaxaba, the Basarwa still felt marginalized from the management of natural resources despite CBNRM programmes being in place. At the local level the communities were struggling for self-determination, identity and recognition of their local institutions and management practices, but issues of this nature were not adequately captured and highlighted in the national policy arena through the existing networks.

Apart from San-based organizations not actively engaging in the CBNRM Forum, the Forum itself shied away from highlighting the issues of the San/Basarwa, particularly during the contentious CKGR court case, because of the high political sensitivities surrounding that challenge to the Botswana state's authority. The court case began in 2002 and ended in 2006, also a critical period for the CBNRM policy wherein the 2001 draft was being considered by Government. The composition of the National CBNRM Forum was in some instances problematic, particularly when the body was faced with sensitive issues, as the group included representatives from key government departments who did not want to be seen to be advocating positions which were not in line with government thinking.

While it is accepted that the challenges the Basarwa face are shared by other communities participating in CBNRM, these challenges are more pronounced with respect to the Basarwa. The Basarwa not only rely on a diversity of livelihood strategies that directly depend on the use of natural resources, but they are also faced with an array of difficulties that most of their neighbours and fellow citizens do not encounter to the same degree (Saugestad, 1998; Suzman, 2001a, 2001b; Taylor, 2002). They are subjected to higher levels of poverty and dependency on welfare in the form of food aid or pensions; have low levels of basic literacy; weak representation in political and administrative structures, and limited capacity to advocate their own interest at a national, regional or local level; and a sense of social and political alienation from the mainstream, compounded in some instances by social discrimination and prejudice (Taylor, 2000; Suzman, 2001a, 2001b).

Struggle for identity and cultural recognition

The Basarwa in Botswana suffer marginalization through cultural exclusion. Policies are largely driven by agro-pastoral production systems of the dominant social groups while ignoring the resource-based livelihoods of ethnic minorities and most of the rural poor. Furthermore, the government refuses to recognize the Basarwa as indigenous peoples, or accept their cultural and socio-economic circumstances as markedly different from those of the rest of the population even in cases of development initiatives that are specifically targeting the Basarwa. Tracing the history of San development through the Remote Area Dwellers Programme, Saugestad (2006a, p173) sums up the issue as follows:

> ...by disregarding cultural characteristics of the San, cultural knowledge became by definition irrelevant. As underdevelopment and poverty were seen as contemporary manifestations of their 'nomadic disposition' indigenous knowledge was not only ignored it was devalued. It was not so much that the San were ignorant they had the wrong sort of knowledge.

In Botswana as well as Namibia, there is a clear need for a substantial adjustment in policy in order to meaningfully improve the status of the Basarwa relative to others. Moreover these adjustments will require the recognition of an ethnic and cultural component to the Basarwa's social, economic and political marginalization (Gordon, 1992; Saugestad, 1998; Suzman, 2001a). In support of the above view, Riddell (2002) states that, as a result of the failure to define and agree on the definition of both indigenous peoples and minority peoples, a number of states do not recognize minorities as distinct and separate. Therefore, the minorities are not recognized in law; and if they are not recognized in law, it is difficult to promote and advance their rights. It is therefore imperative that the governments of Botswana and Namibia acknowledge these differences and deal with the issues of the Basarwa accordingly. The failure to do so, to date, has as indicated resulted in further political and socio-economic marginalization of the San peoples.

Suzman (2001b), however, argues that greater scope exists in the pursuit of San rights issues within a framework of human rights, as opposed to making reference to international agreements pertaining to the rights of indigenous peoples, as the term 'indigenous' is problematic in the context of southern Africa. With regards to the rights of minorities, there needs to be a focus not merely on equality before the law but on the need for some sort of preferential treatment for minorities in order for them to be treated such that equality of opportunity can become a reality (Riddell, 2002). In relation to CBNRM, this calls for open-mindedness on the part of governments to different models of CBNRM, for example the model proposed by the Khwai community, which has so far received very little support (Bolaane, 2004b). Although the Government of Botswana has been reluctant to pursue this approach (Saugestad, 1998; Suzman 2001b), it is viewed that:

> ...*special rights do not constitute privilege as they are rooted in the rule of equal enjoyment just as is non discrimination....If group rights are rejected and preferential treatment denied, the equal enjoyment of human rights of minorities will not be realised.*
>
> (Alfredsson, 1998, quoted in Riddell, 2002, p9)

The problem, however, is that Botswana does not pursue a rights-based approach to development which requires a move from civil and political rights to embrace social and cultural rights. Botswana instead pursues a growth-led approach to development which as noted by Taillant (2002) unfortunately leaves many behind. Nthomang (2001, p133) citing Gill (1998) sums up this situation by noting that:

> ...*social policies of African governments (Botswana included) are based on traditional liberal capitalist values and philosophies that underpin economic policy as well as personal factors, stereotypes and attitudes that promote hegemony of the dominant groups in society...*

Nthomang (2001) further notes that social policies and plans are social constructs; they reflect the deeply rooted values and sectional interests of those powerful in societies (government élites, private companies) who influence policy formulation and implementation. CBNRM is not immune to these processes, and its conservation and development goals often cause it to clash directly with these interests. Ultimately it is not the voice of the politically marginalized peoples like the Basarwa which prevails in policy outcomes but that of government élites and those who have direct access to decision-making structures.

Conclusion

CBNRM in Botswana strives to achieve both conservation and development objectives. The majority of the CBOs targeted by the programme are Basarwa communities and yet their needs and issues remain peripheral to policy processes and outcomes in this area. Suzman (2001a) argues that, in the context of development, flexibility and participation are closely related concepts. For a programme to be meaningfully participatory, it must be flexible enough to accommodate what may be unpredictable local responses and desires. It should also be flexible enough to allow for the beneficiaries of any programme to respond creatively to any new challenges or problems that may arise. This is particularly important for Basarwa communities, in which the cultural gap between development agents and target communities is often the cause of conflict and confusion (Ibid.). However, the political and economic dynamics at play within CBNRM may not provide the space required for the Basarwa to have a voice. The interest and influence of the private sector and the political élite are far too powerful to overcome without a dual approach that links efforts and processes that are geared at empowering the Basarwa and building their capacity. CBNRM practitioners and the National CBNRM Forum need to engage more closely with the various NGOs and bodies that are pursuing the interests of the Basarwa. A human rights and social policy perspective needs to be strengthened within CBNRM. It was on the basis of the human rights perspective that the Basarwa won the CKGR case against the Government of Botswana. However, this case and similar situations around the world indicate that it takes more than just a human rights and social policy agenda to win such battles.

Stevens (1997) notes that in many parts of the world the lands belonging to the indigenous peoples are often the last remaining places of rich biological diversity. As a result these lands are often sought after as sites for national parks, World Heritage Sites, international biosphere reserves and other types of protected areas (Ibid.). Where co-management arrangements exist between the state and indigenous people these are often born out of conflict involving the struggle of indigenous peoples to resist state and private resource appropriation, to defend locally-based livelihoods and maintain their cultural identities (Castro and Nielsen, 2001). In most cases it takes heightened levels of conflict for co-management arrangements between the state and the local communities to be established (Ibid.). Nettheim et al (2002) observe that in the case of the Maori in New Zealand a history of conflict with European settlers saw a progression from rough equality, to denial and assimilation, to a special place of Maori in New Zealand, and ultimately to limited rights of self-determination and management of natural resources. Negotiated claims led by the Maori themselves have returned some lands to the Maori as well as provided economic compensation for historical loss of those lands.

However, as Castro and Nielsen (2001) argue, politically and economically disadvantaged rural groups, including indigenous peoples, often face great difficulties in negotiating agreements with the state and other powerful stakeholders. In such cases the indigenous people would benefit from partnerships and assistance from organizations with the capacity to negotiate on their behalf. Dangwal (1999) argues that the Van Gujjars community in India managed to secure their rights over the Rajaji National Park as a result of receiving assistance from a local NGO called Rural Litigation and Entitlements Kendra, coupled with the local people initiating change themselves. In the case of Botswana, where civil society is generally weak, the CKGR advocacy case relied on an international NGO (Survival International) but the partnership complicated matters. The international NGOs were accused of meddling, fuelling conflict and threatening the economic development of the country by both the state and citizens (Mphinyane, 2001; Saugestad, 2006a; Taylor, 2007). The involvement of Survival had a muting effect on the voice of the Basarwa (Mphinyane, 2002) as well as leading to divisions within the San-based organizations and other partners (Saugestad, 2006a, 2006b; Taylor, 2007). While international solidarity can yield positive results, experiences from elsewhere indicate that the struggles of indigenous peoples have yielded sustainable success in cases where the indigenous peoples themselves are at the forefront of these struggles.

While the natural resource management field has made advances in embracing the role of local communities in conservation through the latest developments in common property theory and resilience thinking, among other realms, these developments have not adequately incorporated the importance of political processes such as those that shape resource governance in Botswana. A critical factor is that local sustainable use and governance systems are often incompatible with higher-order political and social interests that shape resource governance in contemporary society. If indigenous resource governance systems are to be sustained, there is a need to address such political issues on both theoretical and practical grounds.

Notes

1   Basarwa is a collective term that is used in Botswana to refer to the San, the Khwe (Khoe), Bushmen or people of hunting origin (Hitchcock and Biesele, n.d.; Saugestad, 1998). While these terms are all contested due to their historical origins, I use the terms Basarwa/San interchangeably depending on context. For instance, the term Basarwa has been used by other scholars when discussing contemporary policy issues in Botswana as this is the recognized official term, and San when discussing historical material and issues that are shared by other San communities in neighbouring countries such as Namibia and South Africa (Saugestad, 1998). I have adopted this approach even though the term Basarwa itself carries a negative implication of 'those who do not have cattle' (Mogwe, 1992). This term perhaps will help to drive home the point to marginalization by cultural exclusion. The term San has academic origins having been used by the Havard Kalahari Research Group as a replacement for 'Bushmen' which was regarded as sexist and having negative social connotations (Saugestad, 1998). I stay clear of the term Bushmen which is regarded as derogatory in Botswana. The Basarwa themselves have suggested various collective names, for instance First People of the Kalahari have suggested N/oakwe a Naro term meaning red people in contrast to the black Bantu-speaking people, while some have suggested 'First People' (Hitchcock and Biesele, n.d.; Saugestad, 1998). The Basarwa also refer to themselves by the names of their individual groups such as the !Xoo, Khwe, Xhanikwe, Naro, etc. The debate on which collective term is acceptable is ongoing. The problem with terminology also reflects that there are many groups with individual names, and some 10 mutually unintelligible languages (Saugestad, 1998).
2   There are some 100,000 San peoples found in 6 different countries in southern Africa (Angola, Botswana, Namibia, South Africa, Zambia and Zimbabwe) the majority of whom reside in Botswana and Namibia (Hitchcock et al, 2009).
3   The Bayei are said to be the first Bantu-speakers to migrate to the Okavango (around 1750) from their home of Diyei, an area just west of the confluence of the Chobe and the Zambezi rivers, now within Namibia's Caprivi Strip (Tlou, 1976). They, together with the Hambukushu, introduced new technologies in the Delta in the form of fishing gear and dugout canoes (Mekoro) which enabled further penetration into the swamps. The Basarwa and the Bayei have a long history of inter-dependence (Madzwamuse, 2009). Other Bantu-speaking groups found in the Delta include the BaTawana (a Tswana group) and the Dxeriku (Bolaane, 2004a).
4   Interview with Rra Kgalelo ('village elder'), Xaxaba, May 2000.

5 Focus group discussion with elderly women in Xaxaba, March 2001.
6 Focus group discussion with game wardens at the Moremi Game Reserve northern gate, May 2000.
7 Special Game Licences were intended to legitimize subsistence hunting by the poorest members of population, most of whom were Basarwa, making it possible for them to hunt legally. With the introduction of CBNRM the Special Game Licences were scrapped, and replaced with an annual quota given to the village collectively (Hitchcock and Masilo, 1995; Taylor, 2002). The licences enabled access to the main source of protein for most of the San households throughout the year. The implications are that these households now only have access to meat during the hunting season thus negatively affecting food security during the off-season.
8 In March 2001 several focus group discussions were held with the youth, elderly, tour guides and key informant interviews with the village leadership in Xaxaba.
9 Interview with Mma Monjwa an elderly woman in Xaxaba, March 2001.
10 Interview with an elderly woman in Khwai, May 2000.
11 Focus group discussion with elders in Xaxaba, March 2001.

References

Alden Wily, L. (2008) 'Custom and commonage in Africa: Rethinking the orthodoxies', *Land Use Policy*, vol 25, pp43–52

Alden Wily, L. (2006) *Land Rights Reform and Governance in Africa: How to Make it Work in the 21st Century?* Discussion Paper, Drylands Development Center and Oslo Governance Centre, Nairobi and Oslo, Kenya and Norway

Alden Wily, L. (1994) 'Hunter-gatherers in Botswana and the land issue', *Indigenous Affairs* No. 2, April/May/June 1994

Alexandra, C. (1993) *Dialogue between Government and Basarwa: Land Use Conflict in Khwai – Living Side by Side*, CSA Botswana

Arntzen, J.W., Ngcongco, L.D. and Turner, S.D. (1982) *Policy and Agriculture in Eastern and Southern Africa*, The UN University, Tokyo, Japan

Berkes, F. (1999) *Sacred Ecology: Traditional Ecological Knowledge and Resource Management*, Taylor and Francis, Philadelphia, PA

Berkes, F. and Folke, C. (1998a) *Linking Social and Ecological Systems: Management Practices and Social Mechanisms for Building Resilience*, Cambridge University Press, Cambridge

Berkes, F. and Folke, C. (1998b) *Understanding Dynamics of Ecosystems: Institution Linkages for Building Resilience*, Beijer Discussion Paper Series No. 112, Beijer International Institute of Ecological Economics, Stockholm, Sweden

Berkes, F. and Folke, C. (2002) 'Back to the future: Ecosystem dynamics and local knowledge', in L.H. Gunderson and C.S. Holling (eds) *Panarchy: Understanding Transformations in Human and Natural Systems*, Island Press, Washington, DC

Bolaane, M. (2001) 'Fear of the marginalized minorities: The Khwai community determining their boundary in the Okavango, Botswana, through the deed of trust', in A. Barnard and J. Kenrick (eds) *Africa's Indigenous Peoples: First Peoples or Marginalized Minorities?*, Centre of African Studies, University of Edinburgh, Edinburgh, UK

Bolaane, M. (2004a) 'The impact of game reserve policy on the river Basarwa/Bushmen of Botswana', *Social Policy and Administration*, vol 38, no 4, pp399–417

Bolaane, M. (2004b) 'Wildlife conservation and local management: The establishment of the Moremi Park, Okavango, Botswana in the 1950s–1960s', Phd Thesis, University of Oxford

Cashdan, E.A. (1983) 'Territoriality among human foragers: Ecological models and an application to four bushman groups', *Current Anthropology*, vol 24, no 1, pp47–66

Cassidy, L. (1999) 'EU regional assessment of the situation of san in southern Africa – Botswana component: a general review and socio-economic baseline data', Unpublished report

Cassidy, L., Good, K., Mazonde, I. and Rivers, R. (2001) *An Assessment of the Status of the San/Basarwa in Botswana. Regional Assessment of the Status of the San in Southern Africa*, Report Series No. 3 of 5, Legal Assistance Centre, Windhoek, Namibia

Castro, A.P. and Nielsen, E. (2001) 'Indigenous people and co-management: Implications for co-management', *Environmental Science and Policy*, vol 4, no 4, pp229–239

Damm, C., Lane, P. and Bolaane, M. (1998) 'Bridging the river Khwai: Archaeology, tourism and cultural identity in eastern Ngamiland, Botswana', in A. Bank (ed) *The Proceedings of Khoisan Identities and Cultural Heritage Conference*, Institute for Historical Research University of the Western Cape, Cape Town, South Africa

Dangwal, P. (1999) 'Whose forests are they anyway? A case study of the proposed Rajaji National Park in Northwest India', in M. Colchester and C. Erni (eds) *From Principle to Practice: Indigenous Peoples and Protected Areas in Southeast Asia*, IWGIA, Copenhagen, Denmark

DWNP and PACT (2000) *Enabling Recommendations by the NG32 Strategic Planning Coordinating Team, Government of Botswana*, Gaborone, Botswana

Ellis, W. (2001) 'Bushman identity land claims and the three agendas', in A. Barnard and J. Kenrick (eds) *Africa's Indigenous Peoples: First Peoples or Marginalized Minorities?*, Centre of African Studies, University of Edinburgh, UK

Fabricius, C., Koch, E., Magome, H. and Turner, S. (2004) *Rights, Resources and Rural Development: Community Based Natural Resource Management in Southern Africa*, Earthscan, London

Gordon, R. (1992) *The Bushmen Myth: The Making of a Namibian Underclass*, Westview Press, Boulder, CO

Gunderson, L. (1999) 'Resilience, flexibility and adaptive management– antidotes for spurious certitude?', *Conservation Ecology*, vol 3, no 1, p7 www.ecologyandsociety.org/vol3/iss1/art7/ Accessed 20 August 2009

Gunderson, L.H, Holling, C.S and Light, S. (1995) *Barriers and Bridges to Renewal of Ecosystems and Institutions*, Columbia University Press, New York

Heinz, H.J. (2001) 'Territoriality and Basarwa', in P. Lane, J. Hermans and C. Molebatsi (eds) *Proceedings from the Basarwa Research Workshop*, Gaborone, Botswana

Hitchcock, R.K. and Masilo, R.B. (1995) 'Subsistence and hunting and resource rights in Botswana: An assessment of special game licences and their impacts on remote area dwellers and wildlife populations', *Natural Resources Management Programme.* Department of Wildlife and National Parks, Gaborone, Botswana

Hitchcock, R. and Biesele, M. (n.d). 'San, Khwe, Basarwa or Bushmen? Terminology, identity and empowerment in Southern Africa', www.khoisanpeoples.org/indepth/ind-identity.htm Accessed 10 September 2009

Hitchcock, R.K, Biesele, M. and Babchuck, W. (2009) 'Environmental anthropology in the Kalahari: Development, resettlement, ecological change among the San of Southern Africa', *Explorations in Anthropology*, vol 9, no 2, pp170–188

Hulme, D. and Murphree, M. (2001) 'Community conservation as policy: Promise and performance' in D. Hulme and M.W. Murphree (eds) *African Wildlife and Livelihoods: The Promise and Performance of Community Conservation*, James Currey, Oxford

Jones, B. (2003) 'Lessons learned from the philosophy and practice of CBNRM in southern Africa' in W. Whande, K. Thembela and M. Marshall (eds) *Local Communities, Equity and Conservation in Southern Africa*, Programme for Land and Agrarian Studies (PLAAS), University of Western Cape, Cape Town, South Africa

Keeley, J. and Scoones, I. (2003) *Understanding Environmental Policy Processes: Cases from Africa*, Earthscan, London

Lebel, L., Anderies, J.M., Campbell, B., Folke, C., Hatfield-Dodds, S., Hughes, T.P. and Wilson, J. (2006) 'Governance and the capacity to manage resilience in regional social-ecological systems', *Ecology and Society*, vol 11, no 1, p19, http:www.ecology and society. org/vol11/iss1/art19 Accessed 20 June 2009

Lee, R. (1972) '!Kung spatial organisation: An ecological and historical perspective', *Human Ecology*, vol 1, no 2, pp125–147

Lewis, H.T. (1993) 'Traditional ecological knowledge: Some definitions', in N.M. Williams and G. Baines (eds) *Traditional Ecological Knowledge:Wisdom for Sustainable Development*, Centre for Resource and Environmental Studies, Australian National University, Canberra, Australia

Madzwamuse, M. (2009) *Adaptive Livelihood Strategies of Basarwa Communities: A Case of Khwai and Xaxaba, Ngamiland District, Botswana*, Lambert Academic Publishers, Germany

Madzwamuse, M. (2007) 'Resource management, land tenure and land rights: The case of Basarwa communities', in B. Schuster and O.T. Thakadu (eds) *Natural Resource Management and People in Botswana*, IUCN, Gaborone, Botswana

Madzwamuse, M. (1998) 'Basarwa and the land issue: Perception of landrights held by Basarwa', BA Dissertation, University of Botswana, Gaborone, Botswana

Madzwamuse, M. and Fabricius, C. (2004) 'Local ecological knowledge and the Basarwa in the Okavango Delta:The Case of Xaxaba, Ngamiland District', in C. Fabricius, E. Koch, H. Magome and S. Turner (eds) *Rights, Resources and Rural Development: Community Based Natural Resource Management in Southern Africa*, Earthscan, London

Mbaiwa, J.E. (2004) 'The success and sustainability of community based natural resource in the Okavango Delta, Botswana', *South African Geographical Journal*, vol 86, no 1, pp44–53

Mogwe, A. (1992) *Who was There First? An Assessment of the Human Rights Situation of Basarwa in Selected Communities in the Gantsi District, Botswana*, Occasional Paper No. 10, Botswana Christian Council, Gaborone, Botswana

Motzafi-Haller, P. (1994) 'When Bushmen are known as Basarwa: Gender ethnicity and differentiation in rural Botswana', *American Ethnologist*, vol 21, no 23, pp539–563

Mphinyane, S.T. (2002) 'Power and powerlessness:When support becomes overbearing', *Botswana Journal of African Studies*, vol 16, no 2, pp76–85

Mphinyane, S.T. (2001) 'The "dirty" social scientist: Whose advocate, the devil's or the people's?' in A. Barnard and J. Kenrick (ed) *Africa's Indigenous Peoples: First Peoples or Marginalized Minorities?*, Centre of African Studies, University of Edinburgh

Nettheim, G., Meyers, D.G. and Graig, D. (2002) *Indigenous Peoples and Governance Structures: A Comparative Analysis of Land and Resource Management Rights*, Aboriginal Studies Press, Australia

Ng'ong'ola, C. (1997) 'Land rights for the marginalised ethnic groups in Botswana, with special reference to Basarwa', *Journal of African Law*, vol 41, pp1–26

Ng'ong'ola, C and Moeletsi, B. (1995) 'The legal framework for the assessment of land rights for the Basarwa and other marginalised ethnic groups in Botswana', in Chr. Michelsen Institute (ed) *Norad's Support of the Remote Area Development Programme (RADP) in Botswana*,The Royal Ministry of Foreign Affairs, Norway

Niamir-Fuller, M. (2004) 'Developing sustainable approaches for rangeland management: progress in understanding the dynamics of arid and semi-arid rangeland systems', Indigenous Vegetation Project Seminar, Gaborone, Botswana

Nthomang, K. (2001) 'Exploring the indigenous/autochthonous minefield: social policy and marginalization of indigenous peoples in Africa'. in A. Barnard and J. Kenrick (ed)

Africa's Indigenous Peoples: First Peoples or Marginalized Minorities?, Centre of African Studies, University of Edinburgh

Ostrom, E. (2003) 'How types of goods and property rights affect collective action', *Journal of Theoretical Politics*, vol 15, no 3, pp239–270

Ostrom. E. (1999) 'Coping with the tragedy of the commons', *Annual Review of Political Science*, vol 2, pp493–535

Peters, P.E. (1994) *Dividing the Commons: Politics, Policy and Culture in Botswana*, University Press of Virginia, London

Potts, F. (2003) *Khwai Development Trust: A Short Case Study*, National CBNRM Forum, Gaborone, Botswana

Ratcliffe, J. (1976) *Land Policy*, Hutchins, London

Riddell, R. (2002) *Minorities, Minority Rights and Development*, Minority Rights Group International, London

Saugestad, S. (2006a) 'San development and challenges in development cooperation', in R. Hitchcock, K. Ikeya, M. Biesele and R.B. Lee (eds) *Updating the San: Image and Reality of an African People in the 21st Century*, Senri Ethnological Studies vol 70, pp171–180

Saugestad, S. (2006b) 'Notes on the outcome of the ruling in the central Kalahari Game Reserve Case, Botswana', in *Before Farming*, www.waspress.co.uk/journals/before-farming/journal_20064/news/2006_4_10.pdf Accessed 15 September 2009

Saugestad, S. (2005) '"Improving their lives": State policies and San resistance in Botswana', *Before Farming*, vol 4, pp1–11

Saugestad, S. (1998) *The Inconvenient Indigenous: Remote Area Development in Botswana, Donor Assistance and the First People of the Kalahari*, University of Tromso, Norway

Selolwane, D.O. (1995) 'Ethnicity, development and the problems of social integration in Botswana: The Case of Basarwa', Study prepared for UNESCO

Shackleton, S. and Shackleton, C. (2004) 'Everyday resources are valuable enough for community-based natural resource management programme support: Evidence from South Africa', in C. Fabricius, E. Koch, H. Magome and S. Turner (eds) *Rights, Resources, and Rural Development: Community-based Natural Resource Management in Southern Africa*, Earthscan, London

Solway, J. (2007) 'Human rights and NGO "wrongs": Conflict diamonds, culture wars and the "Bushman question"', Unpublished manuscript, Survival International

Spinage, C. (1992) *History and Evolution of the Fauna Conservation Laws in Botswana*, The Botswana Society, Gaborone, Botswana

Stevens, S. (1997) *Conservation through Cultural Survival: Indigenous Peoples and Protected Areas*, Island Press, Washington, DC

Sullivan, S. (2002) 'How sustainable is the communalizing discourse of new conservation? The making of difference, inequality and aspiration in the fledgling "conservancies of Namibia', in D. Chatty and M. Colchester (eds) *Conservation and Mobile Indigenous Peoples: Displacement Forced Settlement and Sustainable Development*, Berghahn Books, New York

Sullivan, S. (1999) 'Folk and formal, local and national – Damara knowledge and community conservation in southern Kunene, Namibia', *Cimbebasia: Journal of the State Museum*, vol 15, pp1–28

Suzman, J. (2000) *An Assessment of the Status of San in Namibia*, Legal Assistance Centre/EU, Windhoek, Namibia

Suzman, J. (2001a) *An Introduction to the Regional Assessment of the Status of the San in Southern Africa*, Legal Assistance Centre/EU, Windhoek, Namibia

Suzman, J. (2001b) 'Indigenous wrongs and human rights: national policy international resolutions and the status of the san in southern Africa', in A. Barnard and J. Kenrick (ed) *Africa's Indigenous Peoples: First Peoples or Marginalized Minorities?*, Centre of African Studies, University of Edinburgh

Taillant, J.D. (2002) 'A rights based approach to development', Presentation to the World Social Forum on Globalisation and Human Dignity III, 2 March, Porto Alegre, Brazil

Taylor, J. (2007) 'Celebrating San victory too soon? Reflections on the outcome of the Central Kalahari Game Reserve case', *Anthropology Today*, vol 23, no 5, pp3–5

Taylor, M. (2002) 'The shaping of San livelihood strategies: Government policy and popular values', *Development and Change*, vol 33, no 3, pp467–488

Taylor, M. (2000) 'Communities in the lead: Power, organisational capacity and social capital', *Urban Studies*, vol 37, no 5–6, pp1019–1035

Tlou, T. (1976) 'The peopling of the Okavango Delta 1750–1906', Symposium on the Okavango Delta, Botswana Society, Gaborone, Botswana

Twyman, C. (2000) 'Livelihood opportunity and diversity in Kalahari Wildlife Management Areas, Botswana: Rethinking community resource management', *Journal of Southern African Studies*, vol 26, no 4, pp783–806

12

Pastoral Activists: Negotiating Power Imbalances in the Tanzanian Serengeti

Maanda Ngoitiko, Makko Sinandei, Partalala Meitaya and Fred Nelson

Introduction

Northern Tanzania's savannahs have long been a hotly contested landscape. During the colonial era large tracts of fertile land, particularly highland ranges around mountains such as Kilimanjaro and Meru, were appropriated for agriculture or ranching by European settlers. East Africa's first state-protected areas for wildlife, most notably the iconic Serengeti National Park, were created out of savannah landscapes that had been managed by pastoralists for hundreds or thousands of years. During the past 30 years, state and private interests in wildlife, tourism and commercial agriculture have continued to increase the pressure on these landscapes and the land and resource rights of resident communities. As a result, people with pastoralist livelihoods have faced escalating pressures and continuous challenges to their ability to use and access their lands and resources. A vast scholarship from the region documents how external commercial interests in wildlife and land in northern Tanzania have weakened local communities' land tenure security, undermining both livelihoods and traditional natural resource governance regimes (e.g. Lane, 1996; Neumann, 1997; Igoe and Brockington, 1999; Homewood et al, 2009). As a result, northern Tanzania has become a general reference point for the global discourse on interactions between local people and conservation goals, with case studies often highlighting the negative impacts that external global and national conservation interests have on local communities' rights and livelihoods (e.g. Dowie, 2009). Various studies highlight the role played by western conceptualizations about nature conservation (Neumann, 1998; Brockington, 2002; Goldman, 2003; Igoe, 2004); the importance of wildlife's growing economic value through tourism in terms of increasing external interest in pastoralist lands (Nelson et al, 2007; Sachedina, 2008); and the influence of globalization in terms of both private sector investors' and NGO networks' abilities to influence natural resource policies in African countries (Igoe and Croucher, 2007).

In this discourse, local communities themselves are usually portrayed as victims, with limited ability to influence decisions made elsewhere by a powerful array of external state, corporate and international interests. Although some works highlight the ways that pastoralist communities in northern Tanzania have been able to mobilize to confront external interests in order to secure their resources through emergent advocacy strategies (e.g. Neumann, 1995; Igoe, 2003), there has on balance been much more attention paid to the ways that communities are marginalized by external ideas and interests, than to the ways that local people actively negotiate these challenges.

Ngorongoro District has long been a flashpoint of tensions between community livelihoods and wildlife conservation interests. The Ngorongoro Conservation Area (NCA), which is the single most important attraction in Tanzania's rapidly growing tourism industry (Mitchell et al, 2008), has been the site of long-running tensions between livelihoods, land rights, tourism development, and wildlife conservation since the area was created a half-century ago (Homewood and Rodgers, 1991; Shivji and Kapinga, 1998; Honey, 2008).

To the north of the NCA's borders, the villages of Loliondo Division extend northwards to the Kenyan border (Figure 12.1). Loliondo borders the eastern side of Serengeti National Park, and hundreds of thousands of wildebeest and other animals pass through this area during their annual migration between Kenya's Maasai Mara National Reserve and the Serengeti plains. These villages' lands thus contain some of the world's finest terrestrial wildlife habitat. This has given some villages lucrative new opportunities to earn income from tourism concessions granted to private investors, but has also resulted in long-running pressures from

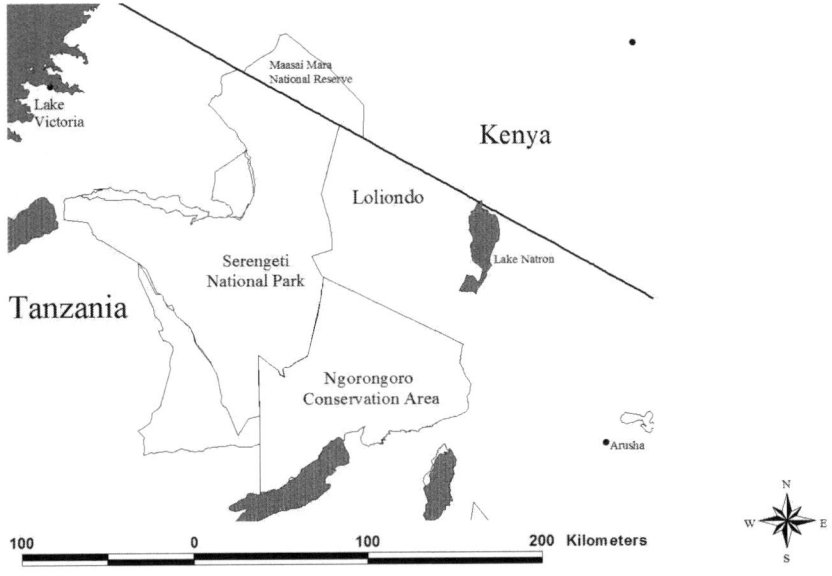

Figure 12.1 *Map of Loliondo*

central government and some private investors for land access and appropriation. The communities' natural wealth is their greatest asset and greatest source of
insecurity; few villages in Tanzania face the kind of sustained pressure that those in
Loliondo must regularly deal with in order to maintain rights over their customary
lands and resources.

In addressing these challenges, these pastoralist communities actively defend
their claims through a wide range of sophisticated political strategies. Villagers
engage directly in national policy and legislative debates, have a well-developed
understanding of their legal rights and vulnerabilities, and cultivate long-term links
to civil society organizations, private tourism investors and sympathetic government agencies or bureaucrats. In the context of Tanzania's essentially single-party
state (see Nelson and Blomley, this volume), the communities are also sometimes
able to use local and regional party institutions and electoral processes as venues
for advancing or defending their interests.

This chapter examines these local organizational strategies and negotiative
processes, based on the grassroots perspective and experiences during the past
decade of the Ujamaa Community Resource Trust, a local organization whose
work centres on facilitating community-based natural resource management and
policy advocacy at local and national levels. We review the background context of
historic conflicts revolving around natural resource management and land tenure
in Loliondo, before describing a series of specific conflicts that have emerged in
the area more recently. We focus on describing the different interests that underlie
these conflicts and examine how local communities collectively confront and
negotiate with these external interests.

Loliondo: Herds and herders of the Serengeti

The greater Serengeti ecosystem, extending for approximately 30,000km²
across the borders of Kenya and Tanzania, contains the greatest assemblage of
wild large mammals on the earth (Sinclair and Arcese, 1995). Each year over
2 million animals – including over a million wildebeest – move between the wet
season grazing and calving ground of the Serengeti plains and dry season refuges,
particularly Kenya's Maasai Mara National Reserve. This annual movement of
animals, which also attracts high densities of large predators such as lions and
spotted hyenas, passes across the land of six different state protected areas (five
in Tanzania and one in Kenya) as well as spilling out onto community lands to
the east and west of Serengeti National Park and to the north and east of the
Maasai Mara. Norton-Griffiths (1995) estimates that if the migratory animals
were not able to spill beyond the borders of state protected areas, the herds might
be reduced by about one-third.

The wildlife of the Serengeti ecosystem is not only a natural spectacle, but
an extremely valuable economic asset to Kenya and Tanzania. In Tanzania, the
Serengeti National Park (SNP) and NCA are the cornerstones of a tourism
industry worth an estimated US$1.6 billion in 2008, which has grown dramati-
cally from only US$60 million in total earnings in 1990 (Honey, 2008; Mitchell
et al, 2008). It is no exaggeration to say that the wildlife of the Serengeti

ecosystem is one of Tanzania's most important national economic resources, with wildlife-based tourism one of the fastest-growing national industries during the past 20 years.

The Serengeti is home to people as well as wildlife. The lands around the Maasai Mara in Kenya, to the east of SNP in Loliondo, and the entire Ngorongoro Conservation Area (NCA)[1] are home to Maasai pastoralists (Homewood and Rodgers, 1991). The Maasai manage their lands according to a system of tran-shumant pastoralism, based on the communal designation of different areas as dry and wet season pastures which are made available to use according to vari-able annual patterns of rainfall. This system of movement between pastures and seasonally available grazing areas and water sources mirrors the movements of wild animals in eastern African savannahs, and has facilitated the co-habita-tion of these landscapes by people and wildlife for centuries (Homewood and Rodgers, 1991). While the Maasai regularly kill predators that prey upon their stock, and kill lions ritualistically as well, they generally do not eat wild animals for food except in dire circumstances. These traditional taboos against eating wild animals, and the maintenance of grazing lands through the use of fire and exclusion of agricultural cultivation, have contributed significantly to East Africa's diversity and richness of wildlife (Western, 1989).

This historic co-existence of people and wildlife in East African savannahs has become more strained as a result of human population growth, changing life-styles and economic preferences, and the spread of conservation policies based on the segregation of people and wildlife through the establishment of national parks and other protected areas (Homewood et al, 2009). The establishment of the Serengeti during the colonial era was a formative episode in the evolution of wildlife management policies in East Africa (Neumann, 1998). The Serengeti was first established as a game reserve in the 1920s, and designated a national park in 1940, but resident communities maintained their land occupancy rights throughout those initial periods. By the late 1950s, pressure was increasing from European conservation lobbies to establish the Serengeti as a national park on the model of America's Yellowstone, where people would not be allowed to live (Neumann, 1998). Emblematic of this movement were the advocacy efforts of the founder of the Frankfurt Zoological Society (FZS), Bernhard Grzimek, who argued that the Serengeti was a priceless heritage of humankind and preserving its natural 'wilderness' was incompatible with continued human residence within its boundaries (Grzimek and Grzimek, 1960). In 1959, SNP was re-gazetted, with adjusted boundaries, and the local communities living there, including about 1,000 Maasai, were relocated to adjacent areas including the NCA and Loliondo (Neumann, 1998).

Although these events, which set the pattern for subsequent conservation efforts in Tanzania based on exclusive protected areas free of human settlement, often come across on the written page as ancient history, consigned to the dusty archives of colonial administrative records, amongst the people of the Serengeti this is living history. Amongst the residents of Loliondo's villages, the events of the past strongly colour the perceptions of the present where the interactions between local livelihoods and wildlife conservation are concerned.

Land, wildlife, and livelihoods: Challenges and opportunities in the 1980s and 1990s

Structural adjustment and 'land-grabbing'

Another formative period in the lives of Loliondo's pastoralist communties occurred during the late 1980s. During the 1980s, following Tanzania's intensifying economic crisis and the fiscal insolvency of the state from the late 1970s onwards (Nelson and Blomley, this volume), the country began a transition from socialism to more open and market-oriented economic policies. This transition was brought on largely as a result of pressure from foreign donors, particularly the International Monetary Fund and the World Bank, who made the loans Tanzania required conditional on adoption of a structural adjustment reform package (Campbell and Stein, 1991). In pastoralist areas, the late 1980s gave rise to an unprecedented period of 'land-grabbling' by various élites from both rural and urban areas (Shivji, 1998). Locally elected Village Councils were granted title deeds to customary village land areas, which was partly intended to safeguard local tenure but also effectively enabled Village Councils to sell off community lands without any formal oversight mechanisms on the part of the Village Assembly (Igoe and Brockington, 1999).

In Loliondo, as with other pastoralist areas in northern Tanzania, a series of land tenure conflicts and challenges emerged during this period. A number of land areas, some only a few hectares and some amounting to thousands of hectares, were granted under dubious circumstances by Village Councils to outside investors. Other lands were acquired without following proper procedures for allocation, or even obtaining any local authorization at all under conditions that would later lead to allegations of fraud. Many of these land allocations resulted in long-running conflicts between local communities and higher-level government authorities and private investors. In addition, government proposals emerged in the late 1980s to convert much of the Loliondo area, lying as it does in highlands which receive more rainfall than much of semi-arid northern Tanzania, to large-scale commercial agriculture. As a result of these developments, by 1989 there were 264 land claims or requests pending in Loliondo Division, covering an area equivalent to 140 per cent of the area's total land area (Ojalammi, 2006, p91).

Wildlife use: Hunting and tourism

Land tenure security in Loliondo also faced continued challenges during this time from wildlife conservation interests. National park authorities attempted to enforce an administrative 'buffer zone' in the 1980s which would prevent local economic activity in the community lands bordering SNP. Government efforts to establish this buffer zone were a main reason that communities organized to obtain title deeds to their lands by the early 1990s. In Ololosokwan village, the SNP attempted to build a ranger post at Klein's Gate, ostensibly on the boundary between the park and the community, but in fact well beyond the park's gazetted boundaries on the village's lands. In 1991–1992, the entire Loliondo area was allocated by the central government as a hunting concession for a senior official and member of the royal family of the United Arab Emirates, which sparked a national controversy and garnered international media attention because the decision was made without prior consultation and agreement of the affected villages (Alexander, 1993; Honey, 2008).

One outcome of these escalating pressures on local lands and resources in Loliondo was the formation in 1990 of one of the first Maasai community-based advocacy organizations in the area. The Koronkoro Indigenous Peoples Oriented to Conservation (KIPOC) was formed by the local parliamentary representative, Lazarus Parkipuny (Honey, 2008). The formation of this organization was also linked to broader changes in Tanzania; in 1992 the one-party state was formally abandoned through a constitutional ammendment providing for multiparty politics. Non-governmental associations, societies and organizations flourished following these and related reforms. This return to political pluralism, coupled with the growing donor influence and investment in Tanzania, much of it targeted at non-governmental organizations, helped fuel the the rise of advocacy organizations such as KIPOC in pastoralist areas (Igoe, 2003).

The early 1990s also saw the emergence of another important new development in Loliondo in the form of the first formal agreements between tourism companies and villages providing for tourism activities to be carried out on community lands. These first ventures, initiated in Loliondo in 1991, were driven both by private sector interest in tourism in these areas, but also by the perceived need on the part of tourism companies to create direct economic benefits for communities that would build incentives for conserving wildlife habitat on village lands adjacent to SNP in the face of competition from agriculture, charcoal burning and other activities (Dorobo Tours and Safaris and Oliver's Camp Ltd, 1996). With Tanzania's tourism industry expanding at roughly 10 per cent per annum throughout the 1990s, community-based tourism ventures based on contracts between villages and private operators became well-established over the course of that decade.

These tourism ventures provided communities with a direct source of income from wildlife for the first time, through private investments that were managed according to village-level contractual agreements. These ventures were important for the direct village-level income they provided, which increased from a few thousand dollars in the early 1990s to over US$300,000 across seven Loliondo villages by 2007 (TNRF, 2008). The leading income-earner was Ololosokwan village, which was home to Conservation Corporation Africa's (CCA) Klein's Camp[2] ecolodge as well as several mobile camping operations. Notably, the Klein's Camp venture arose from an earlier land dispute which the village was able to contest legally and through various political channels, forcing CCA eventually to negotiate an agreement with the village, paying it an annual rent for access to 10,000ha as well as additional fees (Nelson and Ole Makko, 2005). Perhaps just as important as the income was the fact that these tourism ventures were compatible with continued use of most concession areas as dry season grazing reserves for villagers' livestock, with the tourism ventures helping the communities to physically document their use of lands which government policy-makers often alleged were empty and unused, and therefore should be allocated to more efficient uses.

Contesting 'community-based conservation' in Loliondo

By the late 1990s the communities in Loliondo had developed their own systems for benefiting from wildlife through village-based tourism concession agreements, although these were in periodic conflict with the hunting concession granted by government for the entire Loliondo area (Honey, 2008). Villages also developed land use plans, backed up by formal village by-laws passed by both Village Councils and the District Council, which formalized the integration of tourism and pastoralism in defined areas of village land. These local land and resource management systems faced another challenge from external government and NGO interests from about 1999 to 2003, when Ministerial authorities and the Frankfurt Zoological Society (FZS) attempted to persuade the communities to form a Wildlife Management Area (WMA) according to Tanzania's 1998 Wildlife Policy (see Nelson and Blomley, this volume). The key tension resulted from several factors. First, at this time (until December 2002), the parameters of WMAs had not been legally defined and communities were thus faced with substantial uncertainty. The history of mistrust between local communities and government conservation agencies and global conservation NGOs in the Serengeti area did not ease these uncertainties. Many community members and local NGOs believed that the WMA might simply be an expedient way to place large areas of community land under central protection for wildlife, and that any tourism investments therein would primarily benefit external parties (Nelson and Ole Makko, 2005). Ultimately the WMA proposal was rejected following a long series of debates and meetings, including extensive pressure from outside for the communities to formally agree to WMA formation. It is highly notable that while debate over the advantages and disadvantages of WMAs in terms of local interests and benefits continues throughout Tanzania (TNRF, 2008), Loliondo is the only locale that has actually rejected a formal proposal for establishment of a WMA on village lands.

National policy context: Tourism growth, pastoralism contraction

The past decade has witnessed the continuing growth of the economic importance of wildlife tourism in the Serengeti ecosytem, with revenues generated by SNP increasing from about US$6 million in 2000/01 to over US$20 million by 2006/07 (TANAPA, 2007; Honey, 2008). Since 2006, a number of new tourism developments have been authorized and constructed in the park, as the government has sought to increase the tourist capacity and revenue generation from the Serengeti. For example, the government has publicized plans to increase the number of hotel and lodge bed-nights in SNP from the current 950 to about 4,500 by 2012 (Ihucha, 2009).

At the same time, the national policy context for local pastoralists has ranged from ambivalent to expropriative (Matee and Shem, 2006). New reforms in livestock policy and legislation have tended to promote restrictions on the mobility of pastoralists and more individualized or 'modern' ranching models, while land policy and implementation measures continue to prioritize making lands available for private investment and securing individual title so that land can be used as collateral (Ibid.). Collective tenure over communal properties such as pasto-ralist rangelands has remained insecure and subject to threats of alienation, despite Tanzania's relatively enabling legal framework for communal land tenure. As Tanzania has pursued a set of development policies designed to increase commercial investments in high-potential areas such as the Serengeti ecosystem, and the lines between private investment and public institutions become increasingly blurred (see Nelson and Blomley, this volume), villages in Loliondo face a continued and often multiplying set of state and non-state claims to local resources.

This then provides some of the historical context for continuing local struggles over land rights and wildlife management in Loliondo. The next section reviews a more recent series of conflicts and debates wherein we examine the strategic responses of local communities, working with a range of allies and facilitators, to address the continuing land tenure conflicts that seem to break out over Loliondo with the regularity, and often the intensity, of the April rains.

Contesting local land and resource rights: Recent cases from Loliondo

Wildlife legislative debates

The wildlife of the Serengeti ecosystem is the resource that attracts most outside investors, and thus government authorities' interest, into the Loliondo area. This interest is a result of Loliondo's attractiveness for tourism and recreational hunting, and its strategic importance for conserving the Serengeti's migratory wildlife outside the national park boundaries. During the 1990s, Tanzania adopted reforms to its wildlife and tourism policies that called for increasing local benefits from wildlife through community-based tourism and devolved user rights over wildlife on village lands (Nelson et al, 2007). Starting in 1999, though, the institutional environment began to change in unanticipated ways towards reconsolidating central control over wildlife and tourism (Nelson and Blomley, this volume).

The Ministry of Natural Resources and Tourism made regulatory changes, starting in 2000, that formally limited the rights of villages situated in designated hunting concessions, such as exist in Loliondo and most of wildlife-rich northern Tanzania, to enter into contracts with tourism operators (Ibid.). The regulatory measures released in 2000 effectively stated that such tourism activities were prohibited inside any centrally-designated hunting concessions, including those on village lands, without the express permission of the Ministerial Wildlife Division (Masara, 2000). This posed a direct and unambiguous challenge to existing village rights to determine land access and land rights, legally establishing the precedence of central bureaucratic and national interests in hunting concessions over locally negotiated arrangements.

These regulatory changes signalled a somewhat informal shift in national policy in relation to local access to benefits from tourism and wildlife, and precipitated a great deal of concern among local communities and their civil society allies, partic-ularly with regard to future revenue flows, which by 2001 had become substan-tial in some villages. Legal opinions were sought by several interested local and international NGOs to clarify the legality of the regulations in question, given the apparent conflict of jurisdictional authority between village rights to manage land under the land legislation, and ministerial authority over wildlife as administered through trophy hunting concessions (Masara, 2000; Nshala, 2002). The local response was to wait and see if the regulations would be implemented, and despite several confrontations in the field between local government officials and tourism companies, they generally were not, at least in the Loliondo area.[3] Implementation would have provoked a direct confrontation between villagers' economic interests and central authorities, which at this time the latter appeared to prefer to avoid. In subsequent years the number of village-tourism agreements in Loliondo actually increased considerably, despite the nominal illegality of all these enterprises. This increased local stakes in controlling wildlife, tourism and land use in Loliondo.

It was not until 2007 that this issue resurfaced in formal policy debates, with the release of a new set of ministerial regulations ('The Non-consumptive Tourism Regulations'). These regulations effectively reconfirmed ministerial authority to regulate tourism activities on private village lands, but rather than simply proscribing tourism activities in hunting concessions, the 2007 regulations took a different approach. These regulations established a formal schedule of payments that tourism companies operating in these areas are required to pay for different activities such as walking, camping and establishing lodges. These payments effectively replace existing fees paid by operators directly to villages, who are instead to be granted a proportion of the revenues paid to the Wildlife Division. Payments for access to village lands by tourism operators would thus be centralized and prices and/or fees made uniform across the different village areas, which vary in their attractiveness for tourism. The central government defended these changes as being necessary to prevent tourism investors from taking advantage of villagers who had limited ability to negotiate commercial contracts. For villagers such as those in Loliondo, whose rapidly increasing tourism revenue flows during the preceeding decade seemed to indicate a reasonable competence in contract negotiation, the regulations came across as a sweeping disempowerment and loss of control over revenue generated by local lands and resources.

By the time ministerial authorities released the 2007 regulations, having spent years drafting these regulations and with a clearer focus on increasing government revenues from tourism outside protected areas, government was much more committed to enforcement. Tourism company payments were expected to begin immediately and largely cease being made directly to villages. For the villages, a strategy of passive resistance was not possible since it was the tourism companies that were being pressured to comply. For those companies, many of which were high-end foreign-owned businesses, they had few options to resist such regulatory directives if they wished to continue operating. If villages wished to defend their claims they would be forced to take a more pro-active approach.

Several strategies were pursued by villagers in Loliondo and elsewhere in northern Tanzania, where most affected communities were situated given the importance of tourism in the region. In terms of formal policy engagement, a process of debate and discussion was initiated between the communities and private tourism operators on the one hand, and the government on the other, with facilitation provided by the Tanzania Natural Resource Forum and the African Wildlife Foundation.[4]

At the local level in Loliondo, the villages initiated a process of counter-negotiation. If the Ministry would claim the right to charge fees on tourism companies on village lands, the villages would re-focus attention on revenue flows from the holder of the tourism hunting concession situated on the village lands, Ortello Business Corporation (OBC). Villages and OBC began a contentious process of negotiating contracts acknowledging OBC's rights and responsibilities in hunting on village lands, which had resurfaced as an issue for negotiation largely because of the pressure the government had applied to the villages through the claims on tourism income. The negotiation process was complicated and ridden with conflict, with district government officials intervening to try to control the content of the contracts in a way favourable to OBC, for example by negotiating with Village Chairmen at district headquarters instead of publicly at the village level. The results were equally complex; two villages refused to agree to contracts, deeming the drafts presented unacceptable, while four villages signed contracts, although in some cases these were not approved by Village Assemblies but only signed by Village Chairmen. In Arash village, the village government negotiated effectively until OBC agreed to sign a contract that recognized the villages' rights to carry on land use activities as locally planned and desired in the 'hunting concession'. This contract was notable in that it provided formal contractual acknowledgement by OBC that the village was entitled to carry out tourism activities in its village lands without external interference.

An even more important legislative process that the villagers in Loliondo have been forced to address recently has been new national wildlife legislation, the Wildlife Conservation Act, which was published in the government gazette in mid-2008, prior to its first reading in Parliament, and eventually passed by Parliament in early 2009. This Act consolidates and extends centralized control over wildlife, and lands used by wildlife. Several new provisions in the draft bill, at its first tabling in Parliament, provided for major extensions of ministerial authority over land uses on community lands, particularly in pastoralist areas of northern Tanzania. One measure would have made illegal any livestock grazing in Game Controlled Areas, which overlap with village lands throughout northern Tanzania (e.g. all of Loliondo Division is within Loliondo Game Controlled Area), without authorization of the Wildlife Division. This would have effectively made all pastoralism in northern Tanzania illegal or at least dependent on the discretionary authority of wildlife officials. Other provisions provided for new protected land use categories such as wildlife 'corridors' and 'dispersal areas' which were to be created outside core state protected areas. Ultimately the proposed legislation posed a major challenge to livelihood security and land tenure rights of pastoralist villagers.

The stark nature of the Bill's provisions prompted widespread village-level mobilization and engagement with the legislative process, in a way that is rarely seen in Tanzania. With ministerial officials having produced the Bill with little public participation, at least at the village level, the entry-point for villagers was the Parliamentary Environment Committee, which had scheduled a public hearing on the bill in Dar es Salaam. In order to assure that local concerns were heard by parliamentary representatives, villagers from Loliondo and other locales in northern Tanzania, working with civil society coalitions such as the Pastoralist

Indigenous NGO's Forum (PINGOS), mobilized to attend and organize formal critiques of the Bill and recommendations for changes. Money to pay for advocacy activities including the costs of travel and accommodation to Dar es Salaam from northern Tanzania was raised locally, with some villages in Loliondo raising in excess of US$10,000 through individual villager contributions provided by cattle sales.

As a result, the public consultation on the Bill was dominated by concerns from communities in northern Tanzania, with support from various NGOs, and an additional public consultation was agreed to be held in Arusha. This meeting provided even more intense discussion of the Bill, with community representatives stating publicly that passage of such measures would result in loss of votes for both the ruling party as a whole and individual Members of Parliament more specifically (Ihucha, 2008a).

When the Bill arrived in Parliament for its second reading and presumptive passage in early 2009, the debate over the Bill's provisions was intense, with some MPs arguing that it provided greater protection for wildlife than the country's citizens and demanding a range of changes be made prior to passage (Kiishweko, 2009). NGOs and community leaders continued to pressure northern Tanzanian MPs to introduce various amendments which addressed key concerns. In the end, the bill was passed, as is virtually inevitable given the dominance of Tanzania's Parliament by the ruling CCM party, but one key amendment was made that safeguarded village land rights in Game Controlled Areas (URT, 2009). A combination of local collective action and civil society-led policy engagement helped spur a vibrant public debate over the Bill and led to at least one important change aimed at supporting local livelihood interests and limiting the proposed expansion of centralized authority.

Tourism investors and villagers' land access

The legacy of the land claims and allocations of the 1980s continues to haunt the communities in Loliondo in the form of a number of ongoing disputes over certain properties. In recent years, the most problematic dispute has come to involve the Sukenya Farm.

The Sukenya Farm is a roughly 12,000-acre property located in Soit Sambu village in northwestern Loliondo, in the sub-village location of Sukenya. The property was originally acquired, in circumstances which are still disputed, by the parastatal Tanzania Breweries Ltd (TBL), in 1984 at the height of the regional scramble for land in Loliondo. In 2006 TBL, which had never made use of most of the property for barley production as ostensibly had been the original intention, sold the lease on the property to one of Tanzania's leading tourism operators, Thomson Safaris, at a reported cost of US$1.2 million (Juma et al, 2008). Thomson purchased the property with the intention of developing a 'private nature reserve' and a tourism tented camp or lodge (O'Kasick, n.d.).

The acquisition of the property precipitated a land use conflict with the local community. Despite the property's acquisition by TBL, the fact that TBL had never used most of the land (TBL was financially insolvent in the 1980s and was later acquired by South African Breweries when the government divested many parastatals) meant that the community continued to use the property in accordance with customary range management practices for livestock grazing. The area holds several permanent sources of water and provides grazing to Soit Sambu villagers and also residents of Engusero Sambu village to the east, and is also used for moving livestock between these two communities and various livestock markets. Thus when Thomson took over the property and attempted to begin development of a nature reserve which, in its operational vision, meant excluding use by livestock, a conflict was created. Since 2006 the conflict has intensified, with Thomson working with the district officials and police to prevent entry of livestock onto the property. This has led to numerous imprisonments of Soit Sambu village residents, and in one case a shooting where a herder was shot through the jaw and subsequently hospitalized for three months, although both Thomson property guards and the police deny responsibility for the shooting (Nkwame, 2008).

Central to this conflict is not only divergent interests in how land uses are determined, but also a legal conflict over rights over the property. As Ihucha (2008b) reports, the 'tourist firm claims that the land was legally ceded to them by former owner, Tanzania Breweries Ltd, while the villagers on the other hand maintain that even TBL itself had acquired the farm in controversial circumstances.' Specifically, the villagers claim that 'the farm was leased to TBL by a group of people who pretended to be leaders of Soitsambu village, but in actual fact these people have never been in such a position' (Ibid.) The precise circumstances that surrounded the allocation of the disputed Sukenya Farm in the 1980s may never be definitively known, but it is well documented that during this period fraudulent land allocations were widespread throughout northern Tanzania and in Loliondo in particular (Shivji, 1998; Ojalammi, 2006).

During the past three years the residents of Soit Sambu have confronted their most serious land use and land tenure conflict since the 1980s, given the size of the disputed property in question and its strategic importance for local livestock producers. The situation may have considerable long-term negative implications for local livelihoods in terms of access to resources used by livestock through seasonal rotational grazing patterns. The community has effectively mobilized to address this challenge, but this mobilization has taken time and required focused local efforts.

Initially many community members recognized the nature of the problem, and were angered by loss of access to the property. However, two obstacles to collective action limited the community's ability to develop an effective response. The first was the presence of internal divisions within the community that were effectively exploited by Thomson and their allies in local government. Soit Sambu village, like the Loliondo area in general, is largely inhabited by the *Purko* section (or 'clan') of the Maasai, which is also the predominant section across the adjacent Kenyan border. However, a small minority section within the area, the *Laitayok*, is also present, as is the *Loita* section.[5]

In Soit Sambu, the community in general and village government organs in particular are numerically dominated by *Purko* Maasai, with *Laitayok* a distinct minority within the community. In the year or so immediately after Thomson's acquisition of Sukenya Farm, various *Purko* members of the community's dominant grouping began to organize opposition to the company's plans and presence, in light of the growing list of local grievances. Some *Laitayok* residents, however, saw an opportunity to improve their position by supporting the company. Thomson allied itself with these *Laitayok*, hiring community members from this section as employees on the farm, for example as security guards paid to keep other village residents from grazing livestock on the property. The situation thus evolved into one where the community was internally divided and unable to collectively organize to challenge Thomson's claim.

The second problem undermining local action was the community's own elected village government, particularly the Soit Sambu Village Chairman who had become unresponsive to the broader community's interests and grievances. Because of the Chairman's power over the convening and agenda-setting of the village government, this impeded village residents' ability to use the Village Council and Village Assembly meetings as a forum for organizing strategies to legally or politically challenge Thomson's claim to the disputed property.

Both of these challenges were addressed through formal local political and electoral processes, backed up with extensive informal negotiation within the community. The result was the resolution of internal conflicts and a new-found level of local unity and accountability in Soit Sambu. The division between the *Purko* and *Laitayok* village members was addressed by ameliorating the prevailing *Laitayok* sense of marginalization by electing three *Laitayok* residents to the Soitsambu Ward CCM (ruling party) Committee, which as the local ruling party organ is a key political representative body. This unprecedented level of *Laitayok* representation in the local party committee (the committee was now evenly split between *Purko* and *Laitayok* members) was the result of a focused campaign led by a Soit Sambu village resident with a history of activism, both within the village and working with local NGOs, to convince fellow *Purko* villagers that the community needed unity to address its external threats, which in turn required reaching out and empowering the *Laitayok* minority within the village in some tangible way. The result of this move was profound, with many *Laitayok* soon joining the *Purko* residents in a more unified opposition to Thomson's management of Sukenya. Symbolically, a number of *Laitayok* employed on the farm soon left their employment at the community's insistence, including Thomson's local community liaison officer.

Once the inter-sectional division was improved, the problem of the Village Chairman was easily negotiated by the unified Village Assembly. The village informally, through local social sanctions, excluded the Chairman from the village government meetings; when meetings were called the villagers simply elected an acting chair for each meeting. Faced with widespread and constant social sanction and criticism, the Chairman effectively abdicated his role as head of the village government and did not stand for re-election at the next Village Council elections which were held in August 2009.

By overcoming the internal divisions that undermined collective action at the local level, the village has been able to deploy a wide range of advocacy strategies in its efforts to regain rights over Sukenya Farm. Working with some local and regional NGOs, community leaders have held press conferences to present their perspectives on the dispute (Ihucha, 2008b). A delegation of villagers met with the Prime Minister to discuss the problem in mid-2008, which resulted in the formation of a formal government enquiry into the status of the farm and the nature of the conflict with the villagers (Ibid.). The villagers have also used local governance organs to press their case. In March 2009, the Ngorongoro District Council approved a formal motion suggesting 'that Thomson Safaris Ltd [...] be left with only a few acres for their use in the area' with the rest of the farm's acreage returned to the villagers (Juma, 2009). This motion was further ratified by the regional administration, with the community's case at the regional level pursued by the Ngorongoro constituency Member of Parliament. While the case remains subject to ongoing local and national deliberations, the community has developed a unified position and been able to use a range of local and national governance organs, including elected representatives at village, district and parliamentary levels, to advance their claims.

Protected area boundaries and expansion

A final recent case involving contested resource claims in Loliondo and adjacent areas involves local attempts to defend their lands from enclosure by state protected areas. As noted above, the community has been historically affected by the establishment of SNP and the relatively rigid boundary this imposes with respect to livestock movements and access to pasture and water. This boundary is also the subject of long-running conflict and negotiation between the SNP management authority and the Loliondo villages.

Periodically there have been efforts to effect a boundary extension, in either legal or practical terms. In the 1980s SNP, as with some other national parks, began to try to impose a 10km-wide 'buffer zone', partly to prevent the encroachment of agriculture and livestock grazing up against the park's actual boundary. More recently the park has undertaken at various points to re-demarcate its boundary, often in ways that are not congruent with local understanding of the officially recognized boundary between park land and village land. In 2008 the SNP formally undertook a new boundary demarcation exercise which involved surveying the border and placing boundary beacons on the land. Villagers in Loliondo considered some of these beacons to be within their village lands, and claimed that the new boundary did not conform with the official gazetted boundary of SNP. In response, villagers physically removed and destroyed the beacons. This led to SNP staff, through their local Klein's Gate ranger post, arresting several villagers for destroying park property in the form of the beacons. This precipitated a physical confrontation between residents of Ololosokwan village and the park ranger post, with several hundred villagers armed with spears demanding the release of the arrested village members. Confronted with a choice to back down or escalate the situation into a likely physical clash, and given that the beacons had been placed on village land without a strong legal basis for doing so, the park staff chose the former option. A direct physical confrontation, organized quickly and decisively and backed up by a clear potential for violence based on villagers' determination to secure their lands and resources, was able to prevent the extension of state lands onto community lands in this instance.

Local negotiations over resource rights in Loliondo

The core theme in the contemporary history of natural resource governance, conservation and development in Loliondo is one of progressively intensifying competition between different actors for the area's resources. This competition is driven by the increasing value of the area in relation to the growth of the tourism industry in Tanzania during the past 20 years. The fact that Serengeti National Park and Ngorongoro Conservation Area are, along with Mount Kilimanjaro, two of the three most valuable tourism sites in the country and generate hundreds of millions of dollars in economic activity and investment, accounts for the intensity of interest in Loliondo and the scale of the challenges facing village-level claims on land and resources. The link between tourism investment and wildlife conservation continues to drive the steady expansion of state protected areas in Tanzania, in a country where 30 per cent of the land is already set aside as exclusive national parks, game reserves and forest reserves (Nelson et al, 2007). It is important to highlight that in Loliondo, in contrast to global and national discourse on the widespread adoption of decentralization, the policy and management trend is overwhelmingly one of expanding state and external private control over land and natural resources, and contracting local resource rights.

Diverse actors and shifting alliances

The actors attracted to Loliondo's natural assets are diverse and form an ever-shifting mosaic of competing and compatible interests, which result in equally fluid alliances amongst different groups. Although today there is a clear and relatively polarized conflict between central governmental authorities and villagers with respect to land and wildlife use, the reality is far more complex than this state–local tension. In the 1980s and much of the 1990s, local communities, their elected leaders and state conservation agencies were common allies. The main threat to both local land use and central conservation interests was the threat of agricultural encroachment into Loliondo by external farming interests, as exemplified by the TBL acquisition of Sukenya Farm and many similar land claims or requests made during the mid-1980s. A donor-funded government conservation programme, the Serengeti Regional Conservation Strategy, even assisted the villages to obtain title deeds in the early 1990s to demarcate and secure their lands (Ojalammi, 2006). The Serengeti National Park authorities, through their outreach efforts initiated in the late 1980s, helped Ololosokwan village establish a campsite for tourists so that the community could share in the ecosystem's tourism revenues as an incentive to conserve wildlife outside park boundaries.

It was only from 2000 onwards that the Ministry of Natural Resources and Tourism asserted jurisdiction over tourism activities on village lands and declared tourism carried out without official sanction to be illegal. The reason for this shift was the increase in competition for access to valuable wildlife areas such as Loliondo. By the end of the 1990s, the volume of tourism was rapidly increasing throughout northern Tanzania. Holders of centrally-allocated hunting concessions faced increasing incursions into 'their' areas from non-consumptive tourism companies allied to villages through contractual access agreements. Companies such as OBC in Loliondo began to demand that ministerial authorities prevent this competition for access and use of these areas. This iterative negotiation between ministerial authorities and local communities, and hunting operators and tourism companies, continues to this day and has framed wildlife governance issues and conflicts in northern Tanzania for the past decade (Nelson et al, 2007).

Villages have been allied with their business partners, the tourism companies, but only because those companies depend on the villages for access to communities' lands. In instances where tourism operations do not respect local land rights and attempt to control lands through externally-rooted claims, most notably in the case of the ongoing controversy surrounding Sukenya Farm, the conflicts between tourism investors and local villages can be as intense and polarized as any others.

NGOs also exhibit diverse allegiances and interests, both supporting and inhibiting local interests and agency. The early debate over WMA implementation saw the villages resisting pressure from the Frankfurt Zoological Society, which has a long history of supporting state protected areas in the Serengeti and Ngorongoro ecosystems, to accede to the government proposal (Nelson and Ole Makko, 2005). More recently, community efforts to project their voice into national policy debates that impact their resource management practices have been supported by Tanzanian and international NGOs with both natural resource conservation and human rights orientations.

Framing legitimacy through 'community-based conservation'

Despite the widely divergent interests evident in Loliondo in relation to land use, wildlife governance and the flow of resource benefits, and the protracted conflicts between many parties for access and control of these, it is highly notable that virtually all parties justify their actions with reference to practising 'community-based conservation'. Villagers and their local allies contend that traditional rangeland management practices embody a form of indigenous 'community-based conservation'. Tourism companies involved in village-level contracts originally developed those local agreements as a financial incentive for villages to maintain integrated livestock and wildlife land uses and exclude agriculture, and thus defend their arrangements as models of 'community-based conservation'. Thomson Safaris, while apparently engaged in a very different type of tourism venture that is not based on supporting extant pastoralist land use practices, nevertheless portrays the Sukenya Farm as 'a community-based conservation area' which 'aims to implement programs for habitat restoration, wildlife preservation, and community empowerment' (O'Kasick, n.d.). That the company can describe its activities as 'community-based conservation' even while its main interaction with surrounding communities is characterized by rigorous law enforcement efforts leading to the violent imprisonment of many community members, is indicative of both the power and malleability of the set of ideas and imagery that comprise the contemporary 'community-based conservation' narrative.

Similarly, international NGOs and government wildlife authorities describe WMAs as a framework for 'community-based conservation' even when the communities themselves reject such a framework due to perceived incompatibility with existing local resource governance systems. Ultimately each actor in Loliondo seeks legitimacy for pursuing their own interests within the increasingly wide ambit of 'community-based conservation', a concept which consequently has become as starkly contested as the lands and resources themselves.

Local agency and collective action

The degree to which natural resource governance in Loliondo reflects local interests and values is largely a function of local agency in shaping both the physical landscape and the discursive battle of ideas, and in resisting the impositions of external interests. Such agency is in turn a function of the capacity for local collective action, meaning the ability of local groups to organize to influence resource governance decisions made at different scales. As the various episodes recounted here show, local collective action is enhanced and constrained by a range of factors in Loliondo. Within communities, various forms of ethnic, gender or class division can present barriers to collective action, but these may also be overcome through focused efforts to strengthen local unity as the recent case of Soit Sambu village in the Sukenya Farm conflict demonstrates.

The accountability of elected leaders in representing constituents' interests is a critical factor in enabling local collective action in pursuit of shared interests, and is often highlighted as a key factor in the sustainability of decentralized natural resource governance arrangements (e.g. Roe et al, 2009). Recent experiences in Loliondo demonstrate the fluid and evolving nature of accountability in local governance processes. In different villages the performance of elected governance bodies waxes and wanes during different periods. For example, Soit Sambu village has used the Sukenya Farm crisis as a rallying point to demand better performance and representation from the Village Council and its Chairman. In neighbouring Ololosokwan, by contrast, the past five years have witnessed a marked decline in village government transparency and accountability in managing tourism revenues, from what was previously a model example of accountable local decision-making (cf. Nelson, 2004). As a result, during the 2009 village government elections the Ololosokwan villagers forced the previous Village Chairman, who had voluntarily retired from service after his last term ended in 2004, back into action as the Village Chairman during the current period of heightened conflict over village lands and resources, in order to 'rescue' the community's leadership from the troubles of the past five years.

While local factors shape communities' ability to organize and pursue shared interests in important ways, the broader national and increasingly globalized political and economic context also shapes local agency in both enabling and disabling ways. The single most important political-economic trend influencing resource governance patterns in Loliondo is the rapidly increasing commercial demand and value attached to the Serengeti ecosystem in relation to the global tourism market. In the 1990s the rise of community-based tourism ventures empowered local communities by providing them with new forms of collective and individual income through locally-controlled ventures, and achieved this without displacing the communities' established seasonal livestock grazing practices. This income could be translated into political capital, for example by using revenue to take legal action in defence of land claims. During the past decade, however, the growing value of Loliondo as a tourism destination, combined with its existing value as a tourist hunting concession, has transformed economic opportunity into the growing threat of land and resource alienation. To draw on a point made in much broader global and African contexts by Ribot (2004) and Alden Wily (2008), respectively, Loliondo's lands are gradually becoming 'too valuable to allow communities to own', at least within the context of the current manifestation of the Tanzanian state and its formal and informal development policies and political-economic configurations. Tanzanian pastoralist communities today are thus politically marginalized as a result of their own resource endowments.

At the same time, the increasingly globalized flow of information presents new opportunities for local advocacy efforts. National and international media and NGOs play an increasingly visible and effective role supporting local campaigns and amplifying community-level voices. For example, international NGOs and networks have played an instrumental role in enabling the Sukenya Farm dispute to be presented before the United Nations Committee on the Elimination of Racial Discrimination, which in turn has requested formal responses and actions on the part of the Tanzanian government.[6] The ability of communities to engage with government policy-making processes has been substantially enhanced by the increasing sophistication of Tanzanian NGOs, stronger NGO coalitions and better links between NGOs and media bodies.

One final concluding point bears emphasizing. The strategies used by rural communities in contesting resource tenure conflicts in northern Tanzania today are diverse and range from informal forms of passive resistance, or as Scott (1985) famously termed them, 'weapons of the weak', as well as sophisticated political advocacy, lobbying, electoral campaigning, and legal challenges. Indeed, at times it seems there is relatively little difference in form between the strategies employed in such a remote rural locale in northern Tanzania, and those deployed in many activist efforts in western developed nations. Perhaps a greater difference lies in the democratic context such advocacy efforts take place within, although even this is changing albeit in non-linear and unpredictable ways. One apparent change that has occurred in Tanzania lies in the importance attached to formal electoral processes. In the mid-1990s Pietilä et al (2002) could say of Loliondo that 'the elections themselves did not have much importance' to community members' lives and livelihoods. This is clearly not the case today, at least with respect to village, ward, district and parliamentary representatives. Elections are a focus of local politics, campaigns and collective engagement, with the potential to create meaningful change in the performance of elected officials and thus of local collective action in relation to contested lands and resources. These elected representatives are judged by their constituency in large part based on how well they represent villagers' land and resource claims and help prevent higher-level appropriations from taking place. Struggles over natural resource governance lie at the centre of democratic contests and these local democratic institutions and processes are increasingly relevant and influential avenues as local communities organize to pursue and defend their interests.

Notes

1   Unlike the other protected areas in the ecosystem, the NCA is a multiple-use area allowing human residence.
2   www.ccafrica.com/destinations/tanzania/kleins/.
3   There was only one locale where the regulations were implemented, in the West Kilimanjaro area, with the result being charges were brought against a tourism company engaged in a contract with Sinya village. Eventually this operator was forced out of the area, resulting in a loss of nearly $40,000 in annual income to Sinya village from tourism access payments (Honey, 2008).
4   The former is a national coalition of over 2,000 member organizations and individuals which works to improve accountability in natural resource governance and enhance local benefits and participation, while the latter is an international conservation NGO which has invested heavily in promoting community–private wildlife-based tourism ventures in Tanzania and elsewhere in East Africa.
5   In the past, these sections have been the basis for wars fought between different Maasai groups, as in the famous *Iloikop* wars of the mid-19th century when the *Ilkisongo* section became dominant throughout north-central Tanzania and pushed other Maa-speaking peoples to the fringes of the Maasai Steppe. While contemporary violence between Maasai sections in northern Tanzania is rare, there are some disputes over land and resource access between the different sections in Loliondo.
6   Letter sent 13 March 2009 from Fatimata-Binta Victoire Dah, Chairperson of the UN Committee on Elimination of Racial Discrimination, to His Excellency Mr Marten Lumbanga, Permanent Representative for Tanzania at the United Nations Office at Geneva. Available at: www2.ohchr.org/english/bodies/cerd/docs/early_warning/Tanzania130309.pdf (Accessed 26 August 2009).

References

Alden Wily, L. (2008) 'Custom and commonage in Africa rethinking the orthodoxies', *Land Use Policy*, vol 25, pp43–52

Alexander, C. (1993) 'The Brigadier's shooting party', *The New York Times*, 13 November 1993, www.nytimes.com/1993/11/13/opinion/the-brigadier-s-shooting-party.html Accessed 24 August 2009

Brockington, D. (2002) *Fortress Conservation: The Preservation of the Mkomazi Game Reserve*, James Currey, Oxford

Campbell, H. and Stein, H. (1991) *The IMF and Tanzania*, SAPES Trust, Harare, Zimbabwe

Dorobo Tours and Safaris and Oliver's Camp Ltd (1996) 'Potential models for community-based conservation among pastoral communities adjacent to protected areas in northern Tanzania', in N. Leader-Williams, J. Kayera, and G. Overton (eds) *Community-based Conservation in Tanzania*, Occasional Paper of the IUCN Species Survival Commission No. 15, IUCN, Gland and Cambridge, Switzerland and UK

Dowie, M. (2009) *Conservation Refugees: The Hundred-Year Conflict between Global Conservation and Native Peoples*, MIT Press, Cambridge, MA

Goldman, M. (2003) 'Partitioned nature, privileged knowledge: Community-based conservation in Tanzania', *Development and Change*, vol 34, no 5, pp833–862

Grzimek, B. and Grzimek, M. (1960) *Serengeti Shall Not Die*, E.P. Dutton, New York

Homewood, K.M. and Rodgers, W.A. (1991) *Maasailand Ecology: Pastoralist Development and Wildlife Conservation in Ngorongoro, Tanzania*, Cambridge University Press, Cambridge

Homewood, K., Kristjanson, P. and Trench, P.C. (2009) *Staying Maasai? Livelihoods, Conservation, and Development in East African Rangelands*, Springer, New York

Honey, M. (2008) *Ecotourism and Sustainable Development: Who Owns Paradise?* 2nd Edition, Island Press, Washington, DC

Igoe, J. (2004) *Conservation and Globalization: A Study of National Parks and Indigenous Communities from East Africa to South Dakota*, Wadsworth/Thomson Learning, Belmont, CA

Igoe, J. (2003) 'Scaling up civil society: Donor money, NGOs and the pastoralist land rights movement in Tanzania', *Development and Change*, vol 34, no 5, pp863–885

Igoe, J. and Brockington, D. (1999) *Pastoral Land Tenure and Community Conservation: A Case Study from North-east Tanzania*, Pastoral Land Tenure Series, International Institute for Environment and Development, London

Igoe, J. and Croucher, B. (2007) 'Conservation, commerce, and communities: The story of community-based wildlife management in Tanzania's northern tourist circuit', *Conservation and Society*, vol 5, no 4, pp534–561

Ihucha, A. (2009) 'Dar faces 62pc hotel shortage', *IPP Media.com*, 17 May 2009, www.ippmedia.com/frontend//index.php?l=2216 Accessed 20 July 2009

Ihucha, A. (2008a) 'Wildebeests will vote for you in 2010', *IPP Media*.com, 22 October 2008, www.ippmedia.com/ipp/guardian/2008/10/22/124905.html Accessed 30 October 2008

Ihucha, A. (2008b) 'Arusha villagers awaiting PM's land probe findings', *The Guardian*, 20 December 2008, p3

Juma, M. (2009) 'Council wants President to trim down Thomson's area,' *The Arusha Times*, 4–10 July 2009, pp1–2

Juma, M., Nkwame, V.M. and Ndaskoi, N. (2008) 'Tanzania: Former TBL farm brews new crisis', *The Arusha Times*, 9 August 2008, http://allafrica.com/stories/200808110013.html Accessed 27 August 2009

Kiishweko, O. (2009) 'Wildlife bill back to drawing table', *The Citizen*, 4 February 2009, p2

Lane, C. (1996) *Pastures Lost: Barabaig Economy, Resource Tenure, and the Alienation of their Land in Tanzania*, Initiatives Publishers, Nairobi, Kenya

Masara, Y.B. (2000) 'The Conflict of Legislations and Collision of Jurisdictions: An impediment to the realization of community based conservation in Tanzania?', Unpublished consultancy prepared for the African Wildlife Foundation, Arusha, Tanzania

Mattee, A.Z. and Shem, M. (2006) *Ambivalence and Contradiction: A review of the policy environment in Tanzania in relation to pastoralism*, Drylands Issue Paper No. 140, International Institute for Environment and Development, London

Mitchell, J., Keane, J. and Laidlaw, J. (2008) *Making success work for the poor: Package tourism in northern Tanzania*, Overseas Development Institute and SNV, London

Nelson, F. (2004) *The Evolution and Impacts of Community-based Ecotourism in Northern Tanzania*, Drylands Issue Paper No. 131, International Institute for Environment and Development, London

Nelson, F. and Ole Makko, S. (2005) 'Communities, conservation, and conflict in the Tanzanian Serengeti', in B. Child and M.W. Lyman (eds) *Natural Resources as Community Assets: Lessons from Two Continents*, Sand County Foundation and The Aspen Institute, Madison, WI, and Washington, DC

Nelson, F., Nshala, R. and Rodgers, W.A. (2007) 'The evolution and reform of Tanzanian wildlife management', *Conservation and Society*, vol 5, no 2, pp232–261

Neumann, R.P. (1998) *Imposing Wilderness: Struggles over Livelihood and Nature Preservation in Africa*, University of California Press, Berkeley, CA

Neumann R.P. (1997) 'Primitive ideas: Protected area buffer zones and the politics of land in Africa', *Development and Change*, vol 28, no 3, pp559–582

Neumann, R.P. (1995) 'Local challenges to global agendas: Conservation, economic liberalization and the pastoralists' rights movement in Tanzania', *Antipode*, vol 27, no 4, pp363–382

Nkwame, V.M. (2008) 'LHRC files case in Loliondo killings', *The Arusha Times*, 7–13 June 2008, www.arushatimes.co.tz/2008/22/courts_and_crime.htm Accessed 28 June 2009

Norton-Griffiths, M. (1995) 'Economic incentives to develop the rangelands of the Serengeti: Implications for wildlife conservation', in A.R.E. Sinclair and P. Arcese (eds) *Serengeti II: Dynamics, Management, and Conservation of an Ecosystem*, University of Chicago Press, Chicago, IL

Ojalammi, S. (2006) 'Contested lands: Land disputes in semi-arid parts of northern Tanzania', PhD Thesis, University of Helsinki, Finland

O'Kasick, J. (n.d.) 'Tales of the wily, wild dog of Tanzania', www.thomsonsafaris.com/newsletter_signup.shtml Accessed 27 August 2009

Pietilä, T., Ojalammi-Wama, S. and Laakso, L. (2002) 'Elections at the borderland: Voter opinion in Arusha and Kilimanjaro Tanzania', in M. Cowen and L. Laakso (eds) *Multiparty Elections in Africa*, James Currey, Oxford

Ribot, J.C. (2004) *Waiting for Democracy: The Politics of Choice in Natural Resource Decentralization*, World Resources Institute, Washington, DC

Roe, D., Nelson, F. and Sandbrook, C. (2009) *Community Management of Natural Resources in Africa: Impacts, Experiences and Future Directions*, IIED Natural Resource Issues No 18, International Institute for Environment and Development, London

Sachedina, H. (2008) 'Wildlife is our oil: Conservation, livelihoods and NGOs in the Tarangire Ecosystem, Tanzania', PhD thesis, University of Oxford

Scott, J.C. (1985) *Weapons of the Weak: Everyday Forms of Peasant Resistance*, Yale University Press, New Haven, CT

Shivji, I.G. (1998) *Not Yet Democracy: Reforming Land Tenure in Tanzania*, IIED/HAKIARDHI/ Faculty of Law, University of Dar es Salaam, Dar es Salaam and London, Tanzania and UK

Shivji, I.G. and Kapinga, W.B. (1998) *Maasai Rights in Ngorongoro, Tanzania*. IIED/HAKIARDHI, London

Sinclair, A.R.E. and Arcese, P. (1995) *Serengeti II: Dynamics, Management, and Conservation of an Ecosystem*, University of Chicago Press, Chicago, IL

TANAPA (Tanzania National Parks) (2007) *Annual Report and Financial Statements 2006/07*, TANAPA, Arusha, Tanzania

TNRF (Tanzania Natural Resource Forum) (2008) *Wildlife for all Tanzanians: Stopping the Loss, Nurturing the Resource and Widening the Benefits. An Information Pack and Policy Recommendations*, TNRF, Arusha, Tanzania

URT (United Republic of Tanzania) (2009) *The Wildlife Conservation Act*, Government Printer, Dar es Salaam

Western, D. (1989) 'Conservation without parks: Wildlife in the rural landscape', in D. Western and M. Pearl (eds) *Conservation for the Twenty-first Century*, Oxford University Press, Oxford

Part 4

Looking Forward

13

A Changing Climate for Community Resource Governance: Threats and Opportunities from Climate Change and the Emerging Carbon Market

Maxwell Gomera, Liz Rihoy and Fred Nelson

Introduction

Climate change is the defining environmental issue of the present era, both a product and embodiment of the increasing interconnectivity of global economic, technological and ecological processes falling under the rubric of 'globalization'. As a physical process, changes in the global climate present a wide and complex range of ecological, social and economic implications. Climate change, along with other different yet linked forms of ecosystem shifts such as deforestation, has contributed to the growing integration of thinking about the environment and the global economy. With climate change assuming the central position in the global environmental discourse, transnational efforts to mitigate the impacts of greenhouse gas (GHG) emissions are poised to reshape institutional arrangements for natural resource governance at local, national and global scales. How this reshaping takes place is, however, very much uncertain and contingent on ongoing negotiations, changing narratives and discourses, and the ability of different groups of people, and groups of nations, to influence efforts to regulate the global climate 'commons'. What is clear, however, is that there are both major risks and opportunities for local resource governance regimes in places such as sub-Saharan Africa, and that the imperative to address global climate change is shifting the institutional scale of environmental management to the transnational level, away from local and even national concerns and controls.

In this chapter we highlight some of the ways in which global responses to climate change provide potential opportunities and impetus for transforming African agrarian economies, including local rural economies that have hitherto remained marginalized from regional and global market-places. We note, however, that efforts to address climate change, particularly those that relate to land use issues such as forest management, also have the potential to undermine community rights and access to resources. Particularly important in the context of rural Africa is the effort to incorporate global financing for forest conservation in developing countries into a post-Kyoto protocol under the United Nations Framework Convention on Climate Change (UNFCCC). This integration of climate change concerns with the problem of deforestation, through measures targeting so-called Reduced Emissions from Deforestation and Forest Degradation (REDD), has the potential to radically affect the distribution of costs and benefits in relation to forest management in places such as sub-Saharan Africa. REDD aims to create new markets for forest-based land uses by channelling resources to developing nations experiencing high levels of deforestation, and, potentially, local forest-dependent communities living amidst or along those frontiers of deforestation. However, without clarity on land and natural resource rights and tenure, there is a real and increasingly recognized danger that these policy and governance responses to climate change will contribute to an emerging new 'scramble for Africa' driven by the growing commercial value of rural landscapes for REDD as well as the conversion of land for growing crops, to supply an expanding bio-fuels markets, commercial agricultural investments and other natural resource uses.

The situation is further compounded by the characterization of the climate itself as a 'global commons' with as yet unclear institutional structures to regulate access, responsibilities and benefit streams related to it. Such threats are not unique to Africa. Reports from the Amazon indicate that bio-fuel production, as one strategy being advanced as a means to both secure energy supplies and reduce GHG emissions, is threatening livelihoods of small farmers through displacement for plantations and pollution of local water resources (Christian Aid, 2009). Bio-fuel production has also emerged as a major concern in Africa in the context of weak and contested local land rights and the growing commercial value of rural lands (Cotula et al, 2008). Despite these growing threats, achieving stabilization of GHG emissions and supporting the social and economic development of communities in Africa is not a zero-sum game. Securing local rights to ecological infrastructure and optimizing new production systems arising from climate change concerns – such as new energy economies and technologies and 'carbon farming' – makes good economic and developmental sense in many African settings (Stiglitz, 2006).

Much of the global debate on climate change focuses on the political negotiations between developed and developing nations over the new climate governance regime. However, beyond this arena of international negotiation is the reality that any new climate-related policy and regulatory measures will be fundamentally shaped, in their implementation and outcomes, by the institutional and political-economic context of different national and local settings. Such local contexts will shape the outcomes of developments such as transnational REDD payments or bio-fuels investments, in relation to both the local winners and losers as well as the ultimate impact such initiatives have in relation to their global environmental goals.

With reference to the highly contested arena of rural land tenure and resource rights as documented by the cases presented in this volume, we highlight some of the likely impacts of emerging climate governance regimes, as well as the impacts of climate change itself in a biophysical sense. While many scientists and activists are calling attention to the necessity of ensuring that the principal beneficiaries of REDD are local communities who inhabit rural African landscapes, there is a greater need to anticipate the institutional struggles that will inevitably emerge as a result of the growth of the global carbon market and new ways of assigning economic value to lands and land uses. There is a basic need for greater political understanding of these dynamics if REDD and similar strategies are to avoid a further marginalization of Africa's rural poor. Drawing on the experiences of community-based natural resource management (CBNRM), which in southern Africa go back over three decades, is essential to designing and implementing climate governance institutions that are able to achieve their aims.

Climate change in Africa: Implications and adaptation

A fundamental reality in the 21st century is that the environment has assumed an immense transformative influence over global economies. Climate change and ecosystem degradation increasingly occupy public and scientific discourse. Previous assumptions regarding the independence of economic growth and development from ecosystem services are increasingly untenable. In 2007, the Intergovernmental Panel on Climate Change (IPCC) concluded that the relationship between global warming and human (economic) activity is 'unequivocal' (IPCC, 2007, p30). The IPCC also estimated that climate change mitigation will cost the global economy about 0.1–0.2 per cent of gross world product (Ibid.). Stern (2006) concludes, from an economic perspective, that climate change is the greatest market failure the world has ever seen and the cost of mitigation today would be around 1 per cent of gross world product.

The IPCC also predicts that climate change will result in discriminate effects – with poor countries suffering the most. Africa, the continent that has contributed the least to greenhouse gas emissions, is the most vulnerable but least prepared for the challenges that climate change will bring. Food and water security, shelter and livelihoods, environmental management and biodiversity conservation, the spread of diseases and population migrations will all be adversely affected by climate change (IPCC, 2007). Conversely Africa, the continent that is best positioned to take advantage of renewable energy opportunities, is the one that to date has recorded the least investment. In 2008, 20 per cent of global investments in energy were in the renewable energy sector, but less than 5 per cent of the renewable energy investments were in Africa (UNEP, 2008; Worldwatch Institute, 2009).

It is the poor who are the most vulnerable with the least ability to adapt. Climate change is expected to compound the many development challenges already confronting African people (Boko et al, 2007; see Box 13.1) and will constrain Africa's ability to achieve the poverty reduction and sustainable development targets set out in the Millennium Development Goals. Many parts of Africa already experience highly variable rainfall and other climatic extremes and, although African communities have developed coping strategies to deal with this variability, these are likely to fall short of what is required to deal with the impacts of climate change. Climate change will likely increase conflicts over resources such as water,

---

Box 13.1 Key predicted climate change impacts in Africa

- 75–250 million people will experience greater water stress by 2020
- Rain-fed agricultural yields could be reduced by up to 50% by 2020 in some countries
- 10–30% reduction in average river run-off and water availability by mid-century
- Drought affected areas will increase in extent
- Increased risk of extreme weather events leading to natural disasters such as floods
- Changes in ecosystem structure and loss of biodiversity
- Human health deteriorates as vector-borne diseases spread.

Source: Boko et al, 2007

---

rangelands and forests, and will place new stresses on the local and national institutions that mediate those conflicts.

The ability of African institutions (especially local institutions) and people to adapt to climate change impacts is limited by widespread poverty, fragile ecosystems, weak rights and attitudinal and knowledge barriers within and between government agencies, political representatives and local communities. Persistent centralized control over land and resource tenure in particular acts as a major constraint to local efforts to craft adaptive resource governance regimes that can enhance resilience in the face of changing environmental conditions. Despite the serious implications, there is relatively little emphasis on climate security coming from African governments and civil society.

Correcting global environmental market failures

As noted by the Stern (2006) review, climate change fundamentally represents a failure of global economic markets to account for the externalities of industrial production, and is part of a broader set of interrelated environmental market failures. For example, the Millennium Ecosystem Assessment comprehensively documents the extent of global ecosystem degradation and associated environmental and socio-economic losses (MEA, 2005). It concludes that human activity has changed the world's ecosystems, for the worse, more rapidly and extensively in the last 50 years than at any other time in recorded history (Ibid., p1). The report measures the effect of such losses on national economies – concluding that 39 countries have experienced a decline of 5 per cent or more in net wealth once unsustainable forest harvesting, depletion of non-renewable mineral and energy resources and damage from carbon emissions are taken into account, and 10 countries recorded a decline of up to 60 per cent (see also Worldwatch Institute, 2008). The MEA thus highlights how the supply of ecosystem services, in all their constituents – material sufficiency, health, good social relations, security and freedom of choice and action – is now a key driver of economies and the degradation of ecosystems represents a barrier to achieving developmental goals.

This emerging reality about our ecosystems demonstrates that conservation is essential for sustaining economic success, particularly in the context of Africa's agrarian and resource-dependent communities and national economies (see Nelson, this volume, Chapter 1). The climate change issue is thus not only about negotiating an unfolding environmental crisis, but encompasses an economic, developmental and policy agenda informed by science that requires restructuring global markets to take account of and internalize GHG emissions and other environmental impacts. The ultimate imperative of climate change interventions is to fundamentally reform global markets and engender new forms of economic interaction and accounting for growth and wealth. Central to this process are new markets and market concepts which are emerging as older conventions are being transformed. Payments for ecosystem services (PES), based on the conditional remuneration for ecological assets, goods and services, has emerged as a way to create viable market signals for the production of economically valuable ecosystem services (Engel et al, 2008). PES initiatives have assumed centre stage as a potentially critical opportunity for developed countries to pay substantial volumes of money to developing countries for maintenance of ecological services and assets valued at the global scale.

PES concepts and frameworks are central to efforts to develop global markets in carbon that assign a cost to carbon emissions and a value to emission reductions, and mechanisms for exchange between buyers and sellers of those reductions. Only a decade ago the carbon market did not exist, but recent years have witnessed a growth in its value from US$11 billion in 2005, US$30 billion in 2006 to US$64 billion in 2007 (Capoor and Ambrosi, 2008), providing a dramatic example of how new environmental markets and PES arrangements can be created. In comparison, net Overseas Development Aid (ODA) to Africa in 2007 amounted to only US$38.7 billion (African Economic Outlook, 2009).

Carbon markets exist because of regulatory requirements under the Kyoto Protocol or the voluntary desire of individuals, companies or governments to reduce their carbon emissions. Carbon markets involve three major market segments:

1   the compliance market, which includes the Clean Development Mechanism (CDM) of the Kyoto Protocol;
2   other compliance or pre-compliance markets such as emissions trading platforms created by national-level legislation;
3   the voluntary carbon market which mainly trades in emissions reductions that cannot be traded in the compliance markets.

Notably, the latter includes many emission reductions generated by forestry or land use activities since REDD was not allowed under the CDM.

Even more novel market concepts and production systems have emerged largely in response to climate stress. For example, 'carbon farming' – the notion that farmers can be paid for storing increased amounts of carbon by maintaining agricultural practices and certain plant species which sequester carbon on their farms – is gaining momentum. Carbon farming can also potentially have high levels of co-benefits such as improved organic content in the soil and improved agricultural productivity.

Climate change and the globalization of governance

Climate change is part of a broader discussion about global economic governance that includes trade rules, security interests and international financial regulation. Just as growing patterns of transnational commerce and financial flows create both threats and opportunities for African economies, given their place in the global economic 'order' (Ferguson, 2006), a key question for climate change is how global and national responses can contribute to the economic options of developing countries. Tensions between protecting local or national interests and being a 'good' global citizen also abound, as fundamental debates between countries such as India and China on the one hand, and western countries on the other, suggest. Such tensions can play out in ways that challenge democratic and local rights. Within the context of climate change discussions in today's globalized world, democratic societies are often portrayed as a democratic 'society of organizations' rather than of individuals, with politics more than ever a struggle for power over organized political and social agents.

Climate change discussions are also attracting a new range of global stakeholders and interest groups to environmental management issues, some seeking to imagine new patterns of social and political organization under conditions of global interconnectedness, and others with interests and goals that conflict with those of local peoples. The urgency associated with climate change results in discussions taking place and decisions being made in fora where the interests of rural communities tend to go unrepresented; and at speeds and with commitments that do not reflect local realities. This dynamic is introducing potential threats, from what are noble intentions, to poor people's livelihoods.

In 2008, the global economy fell into three crises often characterized as the most significant since the Great Depression of the 1930s. These comprise a *financial* crisis, fermented in the American sub-prime mortgage securities market; a *fuel* crisis, reflected in the large fluctuations of the price for crude oil; and a *food* crisis, reflected in the increase in the prices of grains in many parts of the world. These crises have underscored the extent to which the global economy has underinvested in assets that bring value to society at large and especially how vulnerable poor countries and communities are to sudden shocks occurring at global scales and over which most people have little or no influence.

Meanwhile, underinvestment in shared assets fundamental to society – a stable climate, biodiversity, productive soil, cleaner air and water, renewable energy sources, waste management capacity, among others – threatens poor countries and constituent local communities. Estimates suggest that investments on the order of US$1 trillion can stop greenhouse gas emissions from rising to dangerous levels, while at the time of writing global fiscal stimulus packages totalling around US$3 trillion had been proposed or implemented to stimulate the economy and restore jobs (Jowit and Wintour, 2008). The decisions over such future economic regimes and regulatory mechanisms do not seem to be explicitly taking account of poor people's needs and run the risk of creating in developing countries economic systems that consume capital, create unacceptable climate threats, perpetuate extreme poverty and which are inherently unstable.

The end of the Cold War in the early 1990s ushered in nearly two decades of economic globalization. The climate and ecosystems crisis and the recent global financial crisis create growing demands to address governance challenges whose origins and solutions lie beyond the boundaries of the nation state. Political institutions at local and national scales are gradually becoming less relevant, and this trend seems set to continue well into the future.

Local tenure and global commons: Community resource rights and climate change

As the cases in this volume detail, the contested status of communally held lands and resources is central to many existing social and political conflicts in African countries (Alden Wily, 2008). For the past century or more, most land has been managed as state property (public land), as a result of the historic appropriation of rights over land by colonial governments, and the general retention of centralized land ownership by independent African governments (see Murombedzi, this volume). The result is that the ecological assets and infrastructure that support rural communities' livelihoods are often legally and practically contested, subject to competing claims pursued in settings where the rule of law often does not serve to peacefully mediate such conflicts. This situation favours groups able to rapidly mobilize resources, and effectively facilitates the continued alienation of resources to non-local actors with access to power and money. In this context, insecure and contested land and resource tenure in African countries prevents local groups from capitalizing on natural resource wealth to develop their economies and also undermines incentives for conservation at the local level (USAID, 2004). This problem is not confined to Africa; globally, up to 2 billion people depend on customarily managed lands but lack recognized rights to these areas, and at least two-thirds of all the current conflicts throughout the world are driven in part by contested claims to land (Alden Wily, 2008; see Nelson, this volume, Chapter 1).

Development and conservation problems linked to insecure resource tenure and property rights are also central to the likely impacts of efforts to mitigate the impacts of climate change in African counties (Cotula and Mayers, 2009). It is through increased exploitation of local communities' institutional weaknesses and marginal tenurial position that global responses to climate change may pose a significant threat to the livelihoods of rural Africans. Many of the policy responses being developed to address climate change will give significant new economic value to land and natural resources, particularly forests. Such values will be further enhanced by increasing global demand for food, fibre and bio-energy. As the case studies in this volume demonstrate, governments and private companies already have multiple incentives to take advantage of insecure local resource rights and weak frameworks for enforcement in rural areas to lay claim to lands and resources on which the poor depend for their livelihoods. These incentives will almost certainly significantly grow over the next several decades. The outcome may be that rural communities will lose access to their main capital asset – land – pushing millions of people further into poverty and conflict.

CBNRM and the centrality of local resource tenure

Over the last 30 years, community-based natural resource management (CBNRM) initiatives in southern Africa have effectively demonstrated that sustainable utilization of natural resources based on local management and governance regimes can be the most economically, socially and environmentally sustainable form of land use in arid and semi-arid lands (Roe et al, 2009). CBNRM is an approach to conservation and development that recognizes the rights of local people to manage and benefit from their natural resources. Valuable lessons have been learned relating to the sustainable governance of the natural resource base in a wide range of biophysical and socio-economic settings. Foremost amongst these lessons is that sustainable natural resource management depends on appropriate forms of devolution or decentralization of control over natural resources to local users (Murphree, 1993; Roe et al, 2009). This requires local governance institutions that are representative of and accountable to a local constituency but which also have vertical and horizontal linkages to institutions at higher scales (Murphree, 2000). Equally important is that legally recognized ownership rights be vested with those locally representative institutions to ensure appropriate incentives are in place for sustainable use.

The experiences of CBNRM in southern Africa also reflect broader findings about collective resource governance regimes and sustainable use of natural resources throughout the world. For example, research carried out over the past 20 years increasingly documents the importance of local rights to make and enforce rules governing use in relation to sustaining forest cover and productivity (Ostrom and Nagendra, 2006). This emerging body of knowledge has led to issues surrounding local rights and tenure coming to play a central role in global forest conservation efforts, and by extension initiatives to reverse deforestation as a component of global carbon emission reductions (Agrawal et al, 2008; Sunderlin et al, 2008; Cotula and Mayers, 2009).

CBNRM is fundamentally premised on the assumption that the ability of local groups of people to manage resources sustainably is linked to institutional arrangements that confer rights over resources to these groups. But, as is highlighted over and over again throughout this volume, such rights over land and natural resources are subject to contests and trade-offs between the various interest groups which struggle to gain control of these resources. The result of these contestations, both globally and particularly within African countries, has often been the failure by communities to secure legally recognized rights (see also Ribot, 2004; Roe et al, 2009). For example, Sunderlin et al (2008) found that despite a continued transition towards recognizing local forest land access and ownership, only a few of the 30 most forested countries in the tropics (mostly in Latin America) have made significant changes in community forest tenure since an earlier 2002 study (cf. White and Martin, 2002). The chapters in this book highlight how multifaceted political and commercial interests, in the context of broader global political-economic and institutional factors, limit the ability of rural communities across the region to secure rights over resources. As noted in the previous section, the vested interests of these state and non-state actors are poised to grow in their scale and influence as greater economic values and a host of new competing interests are introduced as a result of global responses to climate change.

The natural resource and development problems facing southern African countries in the 1980s and early 1990s, and which gave rise to local formulations of CBNRM, were generally amenable to localized solutions. Indeed, many innovative southern African experiments with devolved natural resource governance arose within a context of relative regional and international isolation for countries such as South Africa, Zimbabwe (then Southern Rhodesia) and Namibia (then South West Africa) (see Suich et al, 2008). Within this context, environmental governance tended to focus on 'cleaning up' localized problems, developing and commercializing wild resources as complementary sources of income to agriculture. In the 1990s, with increasing value of wildlife enterprises such as sport hunting, 'farming' of wild species, photographic safaris and community-based tourism, wildlife emerged as a major source of transnational commerce. The apparent success of CBNRM experiments in Zimbabwe and other CBNRM programmes in southern Africa made wild species more valuable to communities as well as at the national scale. It was at that point that environmental governance began to attract interests broader than local communities and national agencies. International instruments such as the Convention on International Trade in Endangered Species (CITES) became major concerns to regional wildlife enterprises and communities, as global interests in how wildlife was used in other countries emerged to challenge national programmes and their constituent local resource management regimes (Hutton and Dickson, 2000).

Today, global processes such as climate change are transforming what it means to be a 'local community' in today's increasingly complex world and expanding the suite of global claimants on local resources. On the one hand, this increasing globalization of environmental conservation would seem to be pulling the locus of resource governance away from the type of localized regimes that southern African CBNRM models have worked to promote. At the same time, though, it is increasingly clear that local incentives, rights and responsibilities are fundamental to sustainable natural resource governance and thus to the effectiveness of any new global regimes designed to maintain resources such as forests (RRI, 2008). We now explore this somewhat paradoxical interaction between global environmental governance aims and local management regimes in relation to efforts to design a framework for REDD.

REDD regimes: Threat or opportunity?

Forest conservation, and particularly issues surrounding tropical deforestation, has returned to centre stage globally because of the link between forests and climate change. Forests are relevant to both mitigation and adaptation dimensions of the climate issue, but are assuming increasing importance as a component of emission reduction efforts because of the reality that GHG emissions from land use changes (mainly deforestation) account for approximately 17 per cent of the total global emissions, second only to the energy supply sector whose total proportion is 25.9 per cent (IPCC, 2007). Therefore maintaining and protecting forests and using wood from sustainably harvested forests is an important way of reducing one of the main anthropogenic emissions of carbon to the atmosphere.

Forestry is recognized along with other human-induced land use change activities in the Kyoto Protocol, and the CDM provides for developed nations to buy emission reduction credits from developing nations from afforestation or reforestation projects. Avoided deforestation was however not included in the Kyoto Protocol; nor is REDD allowed under existing national and/or regional mechanisms such as the European Union Emission Trading Scheme. The exclusion of avoided deforestation from the Kyoto regime served to exclude one of the major sources of global carbon emissions, and at the 13th UNFCCC Conference of Parties held in December 2007, in Bali, Indonesia, a general agreement was reached to include REDD activities in the post-Kyoto UNFCCC protocol (Angelsen, 2008).

Despite this general consensus, debate continues to revolve around REDD including a wide range of general and specific issues. Divergent opinions include those arguing that REDD would be difficult to monitor or operationalize in a way that creates viable permanent reductions in carbon emissions without creating perverse incentives amongst countries that have historically low levels of deforestation, to those who believe that avoiding dangerous levels of climate change would be virtually impossible without an efficient mechanism to contain and reduce forest emissions. For the former group REDD is difficult to consider in international and national instruments due to issues such as the permanence of forest-based reductions, leakage of emissions from one site to another site, and governance challenges. Proponents of REDD agree that these issues pose difficulty and need creative solutions but are not in themselves sufficient for excluding REDD in a post-Kyoto climate agreement (see Angelsen, 2008).

Local communities and REDD

Under a post-Kyoto REDD regime, it is anticipated that developing nations will be paid for the opportunity costs of protecting forests and ecological restoration of natural forests in order to store more carbon and reduce net carbon emissions. Much of the discourse surrounding REDD focuses on technical design issues such as monitoring and verification of changes in forest cover, establishing baseline rates of deforestation and the scope and structure of payments (Angelsen, 2008). Forest governance issues are also increasingly recognized as critical to any operational effectiveness of REDD, with Bond et al (2009, p20) noting that:

> *The successful implementation of an international REDD scheme depends upon the will and ability of states to govern their forests effectively. There is a well-established consensus that failures of governance are underlying causes of deforestation and degradation...*

As such, ongoing negotiations over REDD design include many critical elements relating to broader local rights, tenure and governance similar to those that CBNRM initiatives in southern Africa have faced over the last several decades. For example, the poor reputation of forest-related projects under the CDM has been linked to the issue of the uncertainty over longevity of forests. Unlike other forms of climate change mitigation, carbon stored in forests is non-permanent in that sooner or later, the sequestered carbon will be released into the atmosphere.

In the case of forests this could be because of weak governance structures and accompanying risks of changes in carbon stocks (Engel and Palmer, 2008; UNEP, 2008).

In addition to broader recognition of the need for effective forest governance institutions, some observers highlight the key role that local forest governance regimes must play in order for a global REDD regime to succeed. For example, Robledo et al (2009) conclude that 'forest (and carbon) tenure and user rights need to be in favour of local stakeholders if forest resources are to be used for addressing climate change.' The recognition that local forest governance regimes must provide part of the foundation for effective REDD in developing countries stems from two basic realities. First, an increasing area of forest, particularly in tropical developing nations, is falling under local jurisdictions (Agrawal et al, 2008). Estimates suggest that 420 million hectares of forests around the world are now locally owned and managed – nearly as much as the amount of forest enclosed within state-protected areas – and that based on current trends about half of all forests in developing countries will be managed by communities within the next decade (White and Martin, 2002; Molnar et al, 2004; see also Sunderlin et al, 2008). Local communities are thus now increasingly in charge of the forest estate that could form a significant proportion of a REDD regime.

A second critical factor in relation to linkages between global REDD objectives and local forest tenure is the reality that local groups' increasing share of the world's forests is partly a function of communities' ability to manage forests more sustainably than public state agencies. State forestry departments often perform poorly in terms of sustaining notionally protected forests as a result of weak incentives and capacity, particularly in African countries. Such governance problems, where resource rights are domiciled with organizations that have little to do with day-to-day management of forests, compound REDD design challenges involving leakage, monitoring and risks of over-harvesting. Local ability to set and enforce rules governing forest use is a key factor determining changes in forest condition in a range of circumstances (Hayes, 2006; Chhatre and Agrawal, 2008). In places as diverse as Mexico, Nepal and Tanzania, enabling local communities to secure rights over forest use and exploitation has been the key to forest recoveries and more sustainable institutional arrangements (Ostrom and Nagendra, 2006; Sunderlin et al, 2008). This growing body of findings suggests that without situating issues of tenure and forest rights at the centre of the emerging REDD regime, the objectives of REDD payments in relation to forests and climate change will not be attainable (Bond et al, 2009; Cotula and Mayers, 2009).

Carbon claims: The potential for growth and conflicts under REDD

REDD provides a major opportunity to link global financial flows and environmental priorities with rural African landholders in a virtually unprecedented manner. Carbon markets are potentially a frontier opportunity that will enable local communities to participate more in the regional and global economies. REDD provides an opportunity for the North to pay 'proper money' to the South to maintain forests and for rural African communities to obtain economic benefits from the ecosystem services that they are best situated to produce. The financial potential of these ecosystem products is staggering. Eliasch (2008, p213) suggests that 'if deforestation is to be halved by 2020, additional public/private finance of US$11–19 billion a year may be required.'

The Norwegian government recently made available US$2.5 billion for capacity-building for 'REDD readiness', including approximately US$100 million for Tanzania over the next five years. The World Bank has also set aside a US$300 million Forest Carbon Partnership Facility to catalyse the REDD market, while the African Development Bank has set up a Congo Basin Forest Fund to support REDD-related initiatives in the Congo Basin. The United Nations recently set up a REDD programme to support REDD initiatives. These are just the beginning of such initiatives.

REDD therefore represents an opportunity to introduce payments for global ecosystem services on a massive scale. But the crucial question underlying the sustainability, impact and effectiveness of REDD revenues is: who will be the beneficiaries of such payments (Robledo et al, 2009)? There is widespread concern, particularly amongst local activists and indigenous groups, that REDD might benefit those engaged in logging activities and exclude forest communities (e.g. Rai, 2009).

As described in the previous section, it is increasingly clear that forest governance in general, and local property rights and resource tenure in particular, are essential for a workable REDD framework that links global, national and local interests and actions. This creates a potentially important paradox for REDD, one which is eminently familiar to CBNRM practitioners in southern Africa (e.g. Murphree, 2000; see also Nelson and Agrawal, 2008).

Operationalizing REDD requires clarifying and in some instances securing rights over land, forests, and carbon production, so that rewards (payments) for producing forests and carbon can be effectively channelled to producers. For local producers to obtain financial rewards that translate into incentives for conserving forests, they need to be able to capture benefit flows as well as to control the forests themselves. As Bond et al (2009, p21) note, 'without clear land and carbon rights the local co-benefits that could help ensure the permanence of forest emission reductions are unlikely to be realised.'

However, by introducing new forms of financial benefits and economic values which may be derived from the control of forests, and the carbon those forests store, revenues generated under REDD stand to generate claims over forests that will compete with the claims of local communities. As many CBNRM experiences in Africa have demonstrated (Roe et al, 2009), as natural resources become more commercially valuable they may attract a wider set of competing actors with incentives to 'capture' those resources. The chapters in this volume amply demonstrate that natural resource governance outcomes are subject to political competition and linked to the relative powers of different groups or individuals to impose their preferences on others. Local communities in African polities are often constrained by a range of structural political, organizational, and informational factors in their ability to secure rights over such contested resources.

Even in countries that have reformed natural resource tenure, the granting of local rights has not guaranteed effective local control. As Rihoy and Maguranyanga (this volume) illustrate, in Botswana the government has backtracked on guaranteeing access rights to local communities by recentralizing control over natural resources, in this case wildlife. Whilst in Zimbabwe, the government is failing to prevent illegal incursions into communal areas. What is clear is that even where the government may be willing to recognize community rights, political imperatives and the interests of the economic élite, as well as technical constraints, hinder progress.

Ultimately whilst REDD aims to link carbon emission reductions, forest conservation and poverty reduction, it is poised to increase competition over control of Africa's forests and landscapes in a context where local communities' claims are often easily marginalized. REDD may thus contribute to turning low-value real estate of the rural poor into the high-value property of the rich. While global environmental interests are premised on the ability of REDD revenues to translate into reductions in local and regional deforestation, political élites in neo-patrimonial governance systems will likely attempt to capture these revenue flows and use them to pursue private political and economic interests. It is these private political interests, as well as bureaucratic interests in using REDD funds to expand authority and resources, that will drive the claims of non-local parties on REDD funds and the forests that they are linked to.

Recognizing and securing rights to land and other natural resources, strengthening civil rights and strengthening democratic governance systems will be critical to ensuring that this scenario does not unfold and that REDD can be effectively linked to incentives for conserving forests at multiple scales of society (Bond et al, 2009). This will need to involve mechanisms to ensure that space is created to enable the voices and perspectives of local people to be addressed. The provision of stronger tenurial rights will be foremost amongst mechanisms to achieve this, but as noted above, will be largely incompatible with the interests of many government decision-makers. REDD will thus create incentives in the political realm which may work to undermine its operational objectives and principles.

This paradox is deeply reminiscent of African experiences with CBNRM, which as amply demonstrated throughout this volume, has struggled with similar political-economic dynamics. CBNRM initiatives have struggled with these issues – access and rights, governance, equity, market access and securing involvement of smallholders in policy negotiations – for some 30 years. And whilst it would not be true to claim that solutions have been found, there is now a wealth of invaluable implementation experience that it is imperative is fed into and used to inform global and national processes. The governance challenges facing REDD are thus largely 'new wine in an old bottle'. Enthusiasm for REDD and PES approaches more broadly should perhaps be tempered with the knowledge that prior international interventions to support forest conservation have had limited impacts in reducing forest loss and degradation (RRI, 2008). This has mainly been due to ineffective or insufficient efforts to strengthen human rights, clarify resource rights and encourage the transparency and accountability necessary for equitable markets and governance arrangements to develop. Pervasive poverty, corruption and social tension not only have generated violent conflict and a concentration of forest wealth, but also create a situation where new, additional investments risk catalysing new discord and conflict unless they are carefully and equitably targeted.

States as brokers of local rights

Eliasch (2008) highlights the strong role that national governments should and can play in brokering equitable and effective regimes for REDD. There are three basic roles played by African states in REDD negotiations and implementation. The first one is in the international negotiations for REDD, and ensuring that the agreement for a post-Kyoto climate protocol reflects citizens' interests. Second is the extent to which the state can act as a broker between interests at national level, including creating strong incentives for local participation and accountability. The final role relates to the ability of the state to attract appropriate international financing.

In all three areas, many African states are in a profoundly weak position. The examples provided in this volume of natural resource governance dynamics in eastern and southern African countries all clearly indicate that despite rhetoric to the contrary, none of these countries, with the possible notable exception of Namibia, are expanding the space for citizen participation in natural resource management, and nor do these states have the means to inform and facilitate such a process. As Pocock (1992) remarked, 'equality is something of which only a few are capable', and certainly equal participation has remained an idealistic notion in most of post-colonial southern Africa rather than an operational democratic principle. Neither is there evidence that the countries in the region are playing an active role in international policy debates, with the exception of South Africa. As a result, the state in southern Africa is likely to be a net consumer of global policy prescriptions. The end result will be that the state, and by extension, its citizens and local communities, will once again lose out.

Second, most states in southern Africa are unlikely to be able to broker equitable outcomes. Again, there is ample evidence provided in the preceding chapters that in many states, such as Zambia, Zimbabwe, Kenya and Tanzania, it is in the instrumental interests of centralized policy-makers to retain authority over natural resources and limit decentralization. In others countries, such as Mozambique and Botswana, it is in the economic interests of the political élite to ensure the contraction of space for communities to extend rights over resources. But in many cases, even if states' interests and incentives were different, they do not have the capacity to prepare themselves for entry into schemes such as REDD without substantial and strategic forms of external support.

Finally, the capacity of countries in southern Africa to mobilize appropriate financial resources and ensure that those resources are responding to actual local needs is limited. Transnational forces are increasingly challenging the traditional concepts of the state and the rights and duties of citizens within a country (Ferguson, 2006). National borders are increasingly irrelevant to today's crises and emergent forms of global political organization. Technological changes such as high-speed internet which increasingly includes various communications media (e.g. audio and video calls and conferencing) render state boundaries, and the political controls that underpin them, increasingly obsolete. The growing importance of transnational capital flows suggests an emerging shift in power from elected governments to private shareholders. Governments now control a progressively lesser proportion of ODA funds than private and market-based mechanisms such as the CDM.

Conclusion

Climate change, in its biophysical, social, economic and institutional dimensions is poised to exert an immense transformative influence on African societies. For local communities in rural African landscapes, they will be impacted in manifold ways and will be forced to adapt to climatic changes according to the financial, human and natural resources at their disposal. Adaptation clearly depends largely on local responses in concert with national and global actors and forms of support, and in many respects the adaptation agenda for rural people is almost indistinguishable from southern African regional CBNRM approaches of the 1980s and 1990s, although adaptation demands a more holistic approach than the often sectorally parochial CBNRM programmes (Murombedzi, 2008).

Mitigation efforts also have a strong link to local resource governance regimes, primarily through the emerging mechanism of REDD payments designed to stem deforestation. REDD is unlikely to succeed unless there is a renewed commitment to securing the rights of local communities to lands and forests, and conservation strategies that fail to recognize the importance of local interests in forests undermine the types of long-term local incentives that resource stewardship depends on. At the same time, REDD will enhance the commercial and financial value of forests in rural Africa, and is likely to attract a wide range of new public and private claimants. This trend is already emergent across much of Africa as a result of interest in securing land for bio-fuels (Cotula et al, 2008), and carbon markets are likely to further catalyse this contemporary 'scramble for Africa'. This presents a paradox for REDD: effectively combating the impacts of climate change requires strengthening of local resource rights so that communities can capture benefits from those resources, but the greater those benefits become the more contested those resource rights are likely to become.

Ultimately climate change, even while shifting the locus of debate and governance to the global scale, is re-emphasizing the centrality of local resource rights and tenure. Just when community-based resource governance regimes seemed destined for obsolescence in the age of globalization, local institutions have become essential to piecing together, from the ground up, effective conservation measures that can help sustain the climate 'commons'. As such, the climate change adaptation and mitigation agenda presents a new opportunity for making greater progress in terms of decentralizing local rights over resources.

References

African Economic Outlook (2009) 'Growth of aid to Africa', www.africaneconomicoutlook.org/en/outlook/growth-of-aid-to-africa/ Accessed 30 September 2009

Agrawal, A., Chhatre, A. and Hardin, R. (2008) 'Changing governance of the world's forests', *Science*, vol 320, pp1460–1462

Alden Wily, L. (2008) *Whose Land is it? Commons and Conflict States, Why the Ownership of the Commons Matters in Making and Keeping Peace*, Rights and Resources Initiative, Washington, DC

Angelsen, A. (2008) *Moving Ahead with REDD: Issues, Options and Implications*, Centre for International Forestry Research, Bogor, Indonesia

Boko, M., Niang, I., Nyong, A., Vogel, C., Githeko, A., Medany, M., Osman-Elasha, B., Tabo, R. and Yanda, P. (2007) *Africa. Climate Change 2007: Impacts, Adaptation and Vulnerability*, Contribution of Working Group II to the Fourth Assessment Report of the Intergovernmental Panel on Climate Change, M.L. Parry, O.F. Canziani, J.P. Palutikof, P.J. van der Linden and C.E. Hanson (eds), Cambridge University Press, Cambridge

Bond, I., Grieg-Gran, M., Wertz-Kanounnikoff, S., Hazlewood, P., Wunder, S. and Angelsen, A. (2009) *Incentives to Sustain Forest Ecosystem Services: A Review and Lessons for REDD*, Natural Resources Issues No. 16, International Institute for Environment and Development, London with CIFOR, Bogor, Indonesia and World Resources Institute, Washington, DC

Capoor, K. and Ambrosi, P. (2008) *State and Trends of the Carbon Market 2008*, The World Bank, Washington, DC

Chhatre, A. and Agrawal, A. (2008) 'Forest commons and local enforcement', *Proceedings of the National Academy of Sciences of the United States of America*, vol 105, no 36, pp13286–13291

Christian Aid (2009) *Growing Pains: The Possibilities and Problems of Biofuels*, Christian Aid, UK www.christianaid.org.uk/images/biofuels-report-09.pdf Accessed 15 September 2009

Cotula, L. and Mayers, J. (2009) *Tenure in REDD: Start-point or Afterthought?* Natural Resource Issues No. 15, International Institute for Environment and Development, London

Cotula, L., Dyer, N. and Vermeulen, S. (2008) *Fueling Exclusion? The Biofuels Boom and Poor People's Access to Land*, FAO/IIED, Rome and London

Eliasch, J. (2008) *The Eliasch Review – Climate Change: Financing Global Forests*, UK Office of Climate Change, London

Engel, S. and Palmer, C. (2008) *'Painting the Forest REDD?' Prospects for Mitigating Climate Change through Reducing Emissions from Degradation and Deforestation*, Institute for Environmental Decisions, Zurich, Switzerland

Engel, S., Pagiola, S. and Wunder, S. (2008) 'Designing payments for environmental services in theory and practice: An overview of the issues,' *Ecological Economics*, vol 65, no 4, pp663–674

Ferguson, J. (2006) *Global Shadows: Africa in the Neoliberal World Order*, Duke University Press, Durham, NC

Hayes, T.M. (2006) 'Parks, people, and forest protection: An institutional assessment of the effectiveness of protected areas', *World Development*, vol 34, no 12, pp2064–2075

Hutton, J. and Dickson, B. (2000) *Endangered Species, Threatened Convention: The Past, Present and Future of CITES*, Earthscan, London

IPCC (Intergovernmental Panel on Climate Change) (2007) *Climate Change 2007: Synthesis Report*, Contribution of Working Groups I, II, and III to the Fourth Assessment Report of the Intergovernmental Panel on Climate Change, IPCC, Geneva, Switzerland

Jowit, J. and Wintour, P. (2008) 'Cost of tackling global climate change has doubled, warns Stern', *The Guardian*, 26 June 2008, www.guardian.co.uk/environment/2008/jun/26/climatechange.scienceofclimatechange Accessed 30 September 2009

MEA (Millennium Ecosystem Assessment) (2005) *Ecosystems and Human Well-being: Synthesis*, Island Press, Washington, DC

Molnar, A., Scherr, S.J. and Khare, A. (2004) *Who Conserves the World's Forests? A New Assessment of Conservation and Investment Trends*, Forest Trends and Ecoagriculture Partners, Washington, DC

Murombedzi, J. (2008) *Climate Change, Natural Resources and Adaptation in Southern Africa*, ResourceAfrica/FFI Report, ResourceAfrica, Johannesburg, South Africa

Murphree, M.W. (2000) *Boundaries and borders; the question of scale in the theory and practice of common property management*, Paper presented at the Eighth Biennial Conference of the International Association of Common Property (IASCP), Bloomington, IN

Murphree, M. W. (1993) *Communities as Resource Management Institutions*, Gatekeeper Series No. 36, International Institute for Environment and Development, London

Nelson, F. and Agrawal, A. (2008) 'Patronage or participation? Community-based natural resource management reform in sub-Saharan Africa', *Development and Change*, vol 39, no 4, pp557–585

Ostrom, E. and Nagendra, H. (2006) 'Insights on linking forests, trees, and people from the air, on the ground, and in the laboratory', *Proceedings of the National Academy of Sciences of the United States of America*, vol 103, pp19224–19231

Pocock, J.G.A. (1992) *The Ideal of Citizenship since Classical Times: in Queens Quarterly*, vol 99, no 1, pp35–55, reprinted in and quoted from R. Beiner (ed) (1995) *Theorizing Citizenship*, Albany, State University of NY Press, pp25–52

Rai, M. (2009) 'REDD and the rights of Indigenous Peoples: Ensuring equity and participation in World Bank funds,' The Brettonwoods Project, www.brettonwoodsproject.org/art-564322 Accessed 15 September 2009

Ribot, J.C. (2004) *Waiting for Democracy: The Politics of Choice in Natural Resource Decentralization*, World Resources Institute, Washington, DC

RRI (Rights and Resources Initiative) (2008) *Seeing People Through the Trees: Scaling Up Efforts to Advance Rights and Address Poverty, Conflict and Climate Change*, Rights and Resources Initiative, Washington, DC

Robledo, C., Blaser, J. and Byrne, S. (2009) 'Climate change: What are its implications for forest governance', in L. German, A. Karsenty and A.M. Tiani (eds) *Governing Africa's Forests in a Globalized World*, Earthscan, London

Roe, D., Nelson, F. and Sandbrook, C. (2009) *Community-Based Natural Resource Management in Africa: a Pan-African Review of Impacts and Experience*, IIED Natural Resource Issues No. 18, International Institute for Environment and Development, London

Stern, N. (2006) *Stern Review: The Economics of Climate Change*, Her Majesty's Treasury, London

Stiglitz, J. (2006) *Making Globalisation Work*, Penguin Books, London

Suich, H., Child, B. and Spenceley, A. (2008) *Evolution and Innovation in Wildlife Conservation: Parks and Game Ranches to Transfrontier Conservation Areas*, Earthscan, London

Sunderlin, W.D., Hatcher, J. and Liddle, M. (2008) *From Exclusion to Ownership? Challenges and Opportunities in Advancing Forest Tenure Reform*, Rights and Resources Initiative, Washington, DC

UNEP (United Nations Environment Programme) (2008) *Making Forests Competitive: Exploring Insurance Solutions for Permanence*, Concept paper by the UNEP FI Climate Change Working Group and the UNEP FI Insurance Working Group, www.unepfi.org/fileadmin/documents/Exploring_Insurance_Solutions_for_Permanence.pdf Accessed 15 September 2009

USAID (United States Agency for International Development) (2004) *Nature, Wealth, and Power: Emerging Best Practices for Revitalizing Rural Africa*, USAID, Washington, DC www.usaid.gov/our_work/agriculture/landmanagement/pubs/nature_wealth_power_fy2004.pdf Accessed 15 September 2009

White, A. and Martin, A. (2002) *Who Owns the World's Forests?*, Forest Trends, Washington, DC

Worldwatch Institute (2009) *State of the World 2009: Into a Warming World*, W.W. Norton, New York

Worldwatch Institute (2008) *State of the World 2008: Innovations for a Sustainable Economy*, W.W. Norton, New York

14

Democratizing Natural Resource Governance: Searching for Institutional Change

Fred Nelson

The aim and focus of this volume has been on examining the ways that institutional arrangements for governing natural resources have been negotiated in different African states, across various scales of both society and time. The cases highlight the political dimensions of natural resource use and governance processes and how resource management outcomes are related to political and economic interests amongst particular groups or organizations. The motivation for assembling these cases has been a practical one: to use comparisons across cases to generate an improved understanding of how and why natural resource governance reform efforts play out the way that they do, and to contribute to the development of more effective strategies for influencing institutional changes which empower local people to secure their livelihoods, lands and environmental assets. This concluding chapter attempts to synthesize the key outcomes and patterns from across the cases in order to capture key lessons and contribute towards more effective reform efforts in the future.

Several key conclusions emerge. First, although patterns of institutional change and governance reform are variable and non-linear in nature, the general trend within eastern and southern Africa is towards reconsolidating central authority over natural resources and consequently eroding or subverting existing local claims and rights. This stands in marked contrast to the prevalent narratives of decentralization and devolution that spread across the region in the 1990s, and the expectations of further democratization in relation to natural resource governance.

Second, the causes of recentralization across different countries varies, but in all cases is linked to broader macro-political and macro-economic dynamics within states and regions. In some cases commercial patterns of investment in tourism and wildlife utilization have fuelled efforts by central agencies and political élites to strengthen control over lands and wildlife use. In other countries, notably Kenya and Botswana, the interplay of particular ideological interests or policy discourses with political interests and structures has driven recentralization and the marginalization of local interests. In all cases, however, it is the continuing concentration of political authority in the executive branch of the state that effectively dominates policy processes and governance decisions. The current dynamic of recentralizing control over natural resources is thus linked to and reflective of broader political patterns in African countries. This suggests that natural resource governance trends at local and national levels may be symptomatic of a wider erosion or reversal of democratic governance in Africa at present as a result of various national, regional and global forces. The limitations of decentralization in natural resource governance reform mirror wider dynamics in relation to African governance. The chapter also briefly discusses these African governance dynamics in a broader comparative global context in relation to natural resource decentralization and institutional change in Latin America and Asia.

The chapter's final section builds on the analysis of the volume's contents to develop some strategic recommendations for facilitating more effectively efforts at natural resource governance reform in African countries. Current trends highlight the urgency of rethinking existing modes of external support, revisiting assumptions about reform processes, and priorities for further research. New strategies that build collaborative organizations and processes informed by deep and up-to-date knowledge of the formal and informal political dimensions of natural resource policy and governance are urgently needed. Reform efforts themselves should be treated as experiments in adaptive management, with impacts in relation to objectives constantly evaluated and revised in a cyclical process that generates knowledge which feeds back into collective action processes. Ultimately, developing more resilient, adaptive and decentralized natural resource governance arrangements in African countries is largely contingent on changing the evolving relationship between states and citizens in ways that promote greater accountability from central to local actors.

Decentralization or recentralization?

Earlier analyses of community-based natural resource management (CBNRM) evolutions in eastern and southern Africa highlight the non-linear and unpredictable nature of local resource governance changes, in their various social and institutional dimensions (e.g. Alden Wily and Mbaya, 2001; Hulme and Murphree, 2001; Fabricius et al, 2004a). Natural resource governance regimes are constantly being negotiated by different parties with competing or complementary interests, and as the balance of power within society shifts to favour one group or another, so too do opportunities to access, use, control and conserve resources.

These shifts and oscillations are evident from local to national levels, and occur both gradually and suddenly. Indeed, a major challenge for a number of the contributors to cases in this book has been to ensure that changes in local resource governance dynamics are adequately captured, so that the published analysis accurately reflects the evolving situation on the ground. This is particularly notable in the case of Zimbabwe, where local and national political configurations have been in a near-constant state of flux and uncertainty in recent years (Rihoy et al, this volume).

Despite recognizing that patterns of change are non-linear, many reviews of natural resource governance carried out since the early 1990s, both in Africa and globally, generally describe existing dynamics as trending towards greater local participation and empowerment in relation to tenure and decision-making. For example, Fabricius et al (2004b, p281) conclude assuredly, with specific reference to southern Africa, that 'Governments and donors have embarked on a process of devolution and democratization of natural resources from which there is no turning back'. Alden Wily (2000, p1) similarly invokes a narrative of inevitable democratization of governance configurations across the region:

> *The new millennium is witnessing evidence of a social and political watershed in Africa, and one which is marked by a potent alteration in the relations between government and people. Through one mechanism or another, ordinary citizens are beginning to play a greater part in the management of society and its resources. The change is uneven, hesitant, contentious and contradictory, but nevertheless underway in a fundamental and unstoppable fashion.*

At a global scale, Snyder (2001, p93) claimed roughly a decade ago that 'we live an age of decentralization' characterized by a 'devolution revolution'.

In marked contrast with such assumptions that initial reform efforts supportive of local rights and participation in natural resource management would be deepened and consolidated, this volume provides ample evidence of reversals of devolutionary processes. These reversals notably include wildlife governance in Botswana (Rihoy and Maguranyanga, this volume), Zambia (Lubilo and Child, this volume) and Tanzania (Nelson and Blomley, this volume). Whereas Namibia once seemed like the shape of things to come in terms of its far-reaching wildlife policy reforms (Jones, this volume), the country's communal conservancies now appear more as a conspicuously isolated case of sustained devolution in a region characterized by broadly reconsolidating centralized discretionary authority. Even in relatively successful cases, such as participatory forest management in Tanzania, the limits of top-down policy and legal reforms are apparent in the face of emergent competing, and largely informal, political-economic interests (Nelson and Blomley, this volume).

Despite the widely documented experience of power and authority over resources and benefits shifting back from local to national scale, the drivers of such changes are hardly uniform across the different countries (Table 14.1). In Tanzania, for example, recentralization of control in the wildlife sector since the late 1990s is closely tied to the neo-patrimonial character of the state's governing network of fused public and private interests, combined with the growing value of wildlife through tourism and tourist hunting within that context of public–private patronage (Nelson and Blomley, this volume). Lubilo and Child (this volume) provide a similar explanation for the recentralization of control over revenues from commercial uses of wildlife in Zambia, but also note the role played by foreign donors in changing their approach to supporting natural resource reforms in that country. Clearly, centralized interests in controlling valuable natural resources such as wildlife for private economic and patronage purposes remain a critical determinant of reform outcomes in a number of countries (see also Nelson and Agrawal, 2008).

In other countries, similar patterns of centralization or recentralization are evident but are linked more to particular policy discourses, narratives or ideologies, rather than crude instrumental interests. In Botswana, the trend since 2001 is towards recentralization of benefits from wildlife use on communal lands, but there is little evidence that private political capture of public resources is a driving factor (Rihoy and Maguranyanga, this volume). Rather, a complex set of cultural and political factors, combined with the political weakness of local communities (Madzwamuse, this volume) and the absence of a strong actor network supporting local management regimes, underlies contemporary developments in Botswana. Of particular salience is the 'diamond debate' in Botswana which has presented a fundamental challenge to those seeking to localize management of wildlife.

In Kenya, a combination of centralized political authority, chronic budgetary deficits on the part of the state wildlife authority, and strong vested interests in the national tourism industry and international animal welfare lobby work to limit space for reform and greater local rights to manage wildlife. While reformists linked to local and community interests were nearly able to achieve a major decentralization of wildlife governance in the wake of Kenya's 2002 general election, and the political reconfigurations it produced, in recent years wildlife policy reforms once again point towards expanding central regulatory authority.

The case studies in the volume that focus more on micro-level contests over resource access and tenure generally tell a similar story. In South Africa, the Madimbo corridor case suggests that national interests in wildlife tourism and expansionist transfrontier conservation areas may, at least in some settings, be prevailing over local efforts to reclaim lands lost during the apartheid era (Whande, this volume). In northern Tanzania, pastoralist communities continue to experience constant threats to local land and resource tenure and access, much of which is driven by expanding state and commercial interests in wildlife-based tourism (Ngoitiko et al, this volume). Although local people demonstrate considerable sophistication in devising and pursuing political strategies to defend their claims, the external balance of political and commercial interests that rural communities must confront is at times overwhelming.

In Zimbabwe, the macro-political changes of the past decade have had profound implications for the functioning of the CAMPFIRE programme, promoting more personalized patterns of local governance and undermining previously accountable resource governance institutions at the community level (Rihoy et al, this volume). Nevertheless, it is highly notable that despite the increasingly authoritarian political environment in Zimbabwe during the past decade, with numerous measures passed to reinforce central control over information, resources and people, direct control over wildlife in communal areas has not been legally or administratively recentralized as has happened elsewhere. This may reflect the relative strength of the various local proprietary interests in wildlife in Zimbabwe, which include district councils, local communities and traditional leaders, all of whom compete to control wildlife's value but collectively provide a powerful constituency against imposition of direct central control (Rihoy et al, this volume; Rihoy and Maguranyanga, this volume).

Table 14.1 *Key findings from select national cases regarding patterns of change and reform in natural resource governance, and the underlying drivers of those changes*

Country	Key Institutional Trends in Relation to Local Resource Rights	Drivers of Institutional Trends
Botswana	1989–2001: Initiation and expansion of national CBNRM programme, creating numerous local trusts with user rights over wildlife and substantial generation of local income from wildlife-based enterprises 2001–present: Centralization of revenues from wildlife in local areas that previously were captured by local trusts	• Substantial external donor interest and funding • Strong southern African CBNRM narrative and regional network of policy-makers and technical experts • Supportive national context e.g. high quality civil service, rapidly growing ecotourism industry, stable business environment, limited informal rent-seeking in wildlife industries • Growing influence of policy argument in favour of treating wildlife revenues as a national resource as is the case with diamonds • Allegations of widespread local mismanagement of revenues fuels argument for more paternalistic central control • Limited support among élites for common property regimes in rangelands in favour of individualized cattle production • Weak domestic constituency for CBNRM due to dominance by foreign donors and technical advisors • Weak political influence at local level, particularly amongst San/Basarwa hunter-gatherer communities who predominate in CBNRM areas
Kenya	Entrenched central control over wildlife with prohibitions on consumptive use since 1977; windows for reform widened during period following 2002 general election and loss of power by KANU ruling party, leading to parliamentary passage of new wildlife Bill which was eventually vetoed by the President	• Concentration of power in the executive branch leading to historic central control over governance decisions • Influential and well-resourced foreign animal welfare lobby committed to an ideological agenda in support of prohibiting wildlife use and maintaining strict central control over wildlife; effective political production of this 'preservationist' policy argument at key levels of government and broader society during the past 20 years • National tourism industry also generally supportive of centralist wildlife governance institutions

Country	Key Institutional Trends in Relation to Local Resource Rights	Drivers of Institutional Trends
Namibia	Sustained expansion of communal conservancies (now covering nearly 15% of the country) and increasing local wildlife revenues within a secure and devolved legal framework since mid-1990s	• Political shift from racially-based minority rule pre-1990 to majority franchise, set against a background of devolved wildlife user rights on white freehold properties since the late 1960s • Desire from local communities for equal user rights to wildlife as those enjoyed on freehold lands • Strong ideological commitment to devolved wildlife governance framework within key élite actor network of ministerial policy-makers and national NGOs as a result of earlier experiences with wildlife population recoveries on private lands and community conservation initiatives • Sustained support for conservancy development from foreign donors through effectively coordinated local/national actor network
Tanzania	Forestry sector: Major policy and legislative reforms passed 1998–2002 and steady expansion of communally managed forests to now comprise over 10% of non-reserved forest in the country; despite enclosure of these forests through secure local rights, continued exclusion of local communities from commercial timber trade Wildlife sector: Recentralization of local revenues from wildlife-based tourism and expansion of state protected areas and central regulation onto community lands; limited devolution of rights and benefits through formal community-based conservation initiatives	• Strong donor support for reform coupled with limited incentives on the part of forestry bureaucracy to expand control over low-value degraded *miombo* forests and lack of a centralized timber concession system for extracting forests' economic values from community lands • Informal political resistance, particularly at district level, to enabling communities to fully control commercial forest values through licensed timber sales from locally-controlled forests; indicates a willingness of government officials to support local enclosure of forests but not local control over commercial activities and revenues • Increasing value of tourism and tourist hunting combined with high levels of institutional corruption and rent-seeking associated with wildlife-based enterprises, and a heavily centralized tourist hunting concession allocation system

The cases do, however, also provide important contrasting cases of governance reforms continuing in ways that shift greater authority to the local level. Namibia's communal conservancies, unlike CBNRM programmes in neighbouring Botswana and Zimbabwe, have maintained the region's most devolved wildlife governance framework, with broad local user rights over wildlife including 100 per cent of revenues generated. The conservancy programme, grounded in a strong network of national NGOs, supportive government bureaucrats and foreign donors, has steadily increased the scope and volume of local benefits, both commercial and subsistence, from wildlife (Jones, this volume). It is important to highlight the importance of several unique contextual factors in terms of explaining Namibia's divergent trajectory. First, the reforms carried out in the 1990s were strongly shaped by the earlier devolution of user rights to wildlife on white freehold lands in Namibia starting in the 1960s. This provided strong empirical evidence that such devolved management policies led to wildlife recoveries as a result of local economic incentives to conserve and produce wildlife, and convinced a range of key Namibian policy-makers and conservationists that expanding such measures to communal lands would lead to both economic and environmental benefits. Majority franchise in 1990 provided the opportunity to do precisely this, and the political imperative amongst the new regime to extend the same privileges to communal lands as already existed on white-owned private lands. Foreign donor and NGO support has played an important role in facilitating the expansion of Namibian communal conservancies during the past decade, but it is important to highlight that the original crafting of the key wildlife governance reforms in Namibia was dominated and directed by domestic actors and constituencies.

In Tanzania, forestry governance reforms initiated in the 1990s and bolstered through legislative reforms in 2002 have led to a steadily expanding area of forest under local proprietary control and management. This has led to widespread ecological recoveries of degraded forests and woodlands through enhanced local stewardship and enforcement measures. However, it is increasingly clear that even a relatively enabling policy and legal framework is insufficient to facilitate local capture of the commercial value of forests, even when those forests are situated on village lands (Nelson and Blomley, this volume). The core problem in Tanzania is that despite the enabling policy and legal framework, informal processes tend to dominate forest governance at the local level. For example, informal and illegal trade in forest products is widespread and often creates disincentives for local government officials to support community forest rights and capture of rents and benefits. This is a major reason why, despite over a decade of expanding communally-managed forests, formal village-level commercial exploitation of these increasingly valuable forests remains almost totally undeveloped. Although communities in Tanzania have clear legal rights, what they lack, in the Tanzanian political context, is sufficient forms of power and leverage to enforce and capitalize upon those rights.

In summary, the cases highlight the limitations of the natural resource governance reform processes that have been carried out across the region. Most community-based reform initiatives have not had the intended impacts in terms of shifting rights and authority over natural resources, with a number of initially successful cases of devolved benefits or tenure being recentralized by national legislative or administrative measures. The most recent case study material suggests that, on balance, trends towards recentralization of control over valuable resources such as wildlife, and land that those resources are found on, are becoming more distinct across east and southern Africa at present. The next sections further discuss some of the factors that account for those trends.

Recentralization, markets and bureaucratic imperatives

Central governments and state agencies continue to play the pivotal role in natural resource governance dynamics across the region, with more authority, as well as direct physical control over landscapes, accruing to these actors. This highlights two basic realities about governance processes in east and southern Africa, which are relevant not only to natural resource management but also to broader issues of democratic transformations in political authority.

Firstly, increasing commercial values of resources such as wildlife, forests, and land itself are increasing the incentives for central governments, individual élites and private investors to claim jurisdictional control over those resources. These commercial values are in turn being driven upwards by global patterns of trade, affluence and scarcity, be it demand for timber and ivory in China or for ecotourism destinations in American and European travel markets. Simply put, the economic stakes in controlling African landscapes are rapidly rising as a result of a range of global economic changes. Emerging 21st-century markets such as bio-fuels and carbon will continue to increase these stakes.

Secondly, in the context of increasing competition amongst actors for control over valuable lands and resources, local communities in rural areas are fundamentally marginalized and disempowered within the region's existing political context. This context is characterized by poverty and limited resources and infrastructure, which inhibit collective action in rural areas, and structural factors which continue to circumscribe democratic governance processes. Even while multiparty elections have become the norm across much of sub-Saharan Africa during the past two decades, the fundamental structural elements of the centralized post-colonial state have often been little altered. Patterns of natural resource governance and recentralization are simply reflective of broader limitations of democratization in Africa during this period (Bratton and van de Walle, 1997; Villalón and VonDoepp, 2005; Mbaku and Ihonvbere, 2006). The ability of local groups of citizens to demand rights and accountability remains limited by these enduring structural impediments.

Despite the power imbalances they confront, local communities across the region do display considerable capacity for effective collective action and political sophistication in confronting challenges to their rights and livelihoods. Local communities, even relatively marginalized groups such as indigenous hunter-gatherers in Botswana or pastoralists in northern Tanzania, are skilled at using both formal and informal mechanisms to advance their claims, and at working with national and global networks to gain allies and various forms of support. While communities have always practised 'adaptive management' of natural resources, it is clear that such adaptive behaviour extends to contemporary negotiations over resource governance arrangements and processes of institutional change (Rihoy et al, this volume). The problem is that despite such strategic responses, the current parameters of citizenship in African states provide limited leverage on non-local decision-makers; the post-colonial state remains relatively inured from local forms of sanction.

Thus the expanding penetration of global commerce – and in some cases, markets for products that did not exist at all a decade ago – into rural landscapes increases incentives for control over resources by government agencies, political élites and private entities, and the enduring structural power imbalances in African states limit local agency in shaping, adapting to or resisting these processes. These factors lie at the heart of the political-economic processes that underlie current patterns of recentralization, in a stark contrast to the prevalent narratives of devolution, community-based management and decentralization from a decade ago. The political-economic terrain upon which natural resource governance arrangements are negotiated has changed considerably and, in contrast to the reformative period following the end of the Cold War, is not fostering greater space for local interests.

Privatized states and ordered polities

As noted in the introductory chapter to the volume, the state in Africa has long been characterized by fused public–private relations and functions, whereby the state effectively becomes a vehicle for the pursuit of private accumulative interests by those exercising power (Bates, 1981; Ake, 1996). Such accumulative interests clearly continue to play a major role in shaping natural resource governance institutions, and processes of institutional change, in ways that alienate local groups of people from their lands and resources. As trade and investment grows, these private patterns of appropriation and accumulation may become more entrenched and effectively institutionalized. The importance of private capture of public resources in shaping resource governance decisions is an important element in a number of the cases documented in this volume.

Nevertheless, it is important to highlight some of the differences in political dynamics that exist across different states in eastern and southern Africa. It is implicit that states which are highly privatized are ones where formal institutions are less influential in a governance sense, and where corruption is widespread and the rule of law is weak. As Figure 14.1 demonstrates, the countries in eastern and southern Africa fall into two distinct groupings when various governance indicators are used to plot their respective rankings. Most countries in the region are characterized by high levels of corruption and are around the median or below on the Ibrahim Governance Index, which scores African countries based on a range of governance factors. However, Botswana, South Africa and Namibia all have relatively low levels of corruption and strong rule of law by African standards, with Botswana performing at a high level by global standards according to Transparency International's Corruption Perceptions Index.

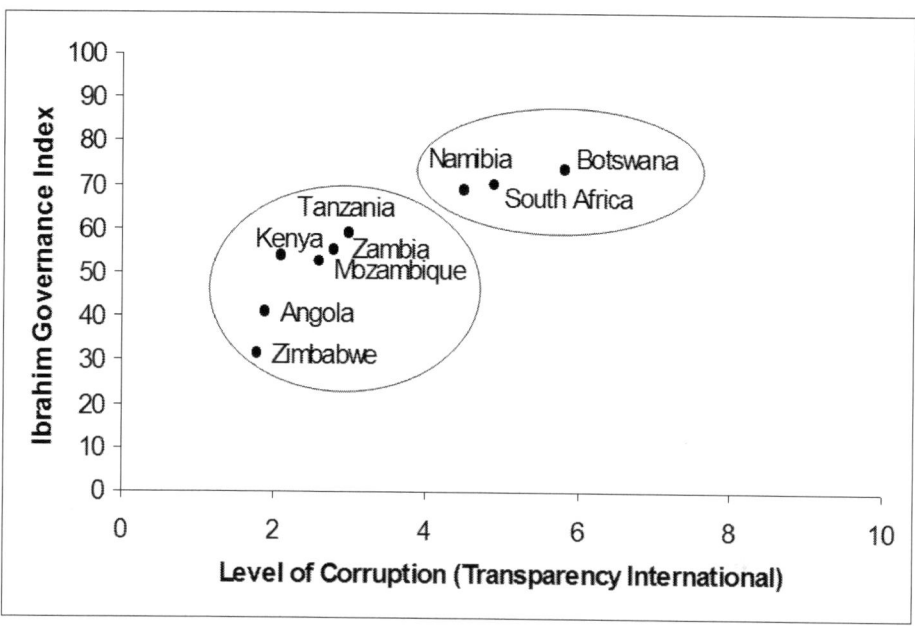

Sources: Mo Ibrahim Foundation, 2009 and Transparency International, 2008

Figure 14.1 *Differences in quality of governance across eastern and southern African nations as measured by the Ibrahim Governance Index (y-axis) and Transparency International's Corruption Perceptions Index (x-axis)*

These governance differences are important in relation to natural resource use and policy-making processes. Essentially, Botswana, South Africa and Namibia are countries where public officials cannot as easily claim or capture public resources, in contrast to the highly informal polities of most African states. This does not mean that these countries are inherently more democratic or decentralized, but it does mean that public officials are likely to make decisions based less on personalized patronage interests and more out of technocratic or public interest considerations (Nelson and Agrawal, 2008). All three countries have embarked on some of the most substantive efforts in the region to democratize land and natural resource governance, including Namibia's communal wildlife conservancies and post-apartheid South Africa's land reform process (Jones, this volume; Whande, this volume). In Namibia, wildlife governance reforms in the 1990s were led by relatively enlightened bureaucrats and their allies among regional and national NGOs and scholars. In Botswana, even through recent reforms have recentralized control over revenues from natural resources, there is little evidence that this has occurred because of private accumulative interests in the bureaucracy, but is rather a function of much broader public debates about governance and sharing of resources in the country.

Zimbabwe is a highly notable case because it has effectively shifted from being a relatively formalized and bureaucratically ordered polity in the 1980s and 1990s, to a state dominated by informal political processes where the rule of law has collapsed in violent fashion over the course of the past decade.[1] This has severely undermined the ability of many local communities to benefit from wildlife under the CAMPFIRE programme and led to a collapse of formal wildlife governance systems in many areas (Rihoy et al, this volume). Despite this, CAMPFIRE has proven institutionally resilient, with some communities responding to crises by developing new approaches to negotiating for their rights and interests (Taylor and Murphree, 2007).

Macro-political context plays a key role in shaping the incentives of different actors, particularly state actors, to pursue different policy or governance options. The evidence collected here suggests that governance reforms which decentralize authority to local actors are more likely to occur in a macro-political environment characterized by stronger formal institutions, the rule of law and lower levels of private appropriation of public resources.[2] One implication of this is that efforts to transfer positive outcomes linked to institutional reforms which have occurred in certain places to other countries with very different governance environments are unlikely to succeed. Thus while Namibia's communal conservancies may inspire advocates of CBNRM and inform project design, as well as empirically informing broader debates about wildlife management and conservation outcomes, efforts to encourage other countries in the region to adopt the Namibian model have not worked and are unlikely to work. This is particularly the case where policy-makers have strong disincentives to devolve rights and benefits to the local level, as is the case in Zambia and Tanzania, for example. Namibia's relatively technocratic approach to devolving rights over wildlife to the local level, which arose out of its unique history and political context in the early 1990s, will not produce the same results in those very different contexts, as over 20 years of community-based wildlife management reform efforts in Zambia and Tanzania amply demonstrate.

The paradox of the market: Globalization and local rights

Natural resource governance reform efforts seeking to promote CBNRM have operated throughout eastern and southern Africa on two basic parallel tracks. Firstly, to increase local economic benefits from natural resources, and secondly, to strengthen local rights to govern how resources are used. As Murombedzi (this volume) notes, in much of southern Africa the focus has been on generating commercial benefits from resources such as wildlife, although this varies across the region, with for example community-based forest management efforts in Tanzania initially emphasizing tenure reform over benefit flows (Alden Wily and Mbaya, 2001). A core assumption underlying CBNRM has been that increasing benefit flows and strengthening local property rights are synergistic; as benefits increase, this increases the incentives for local investments in resource management (Bond, 2001), while stronger tenure enables communities to control economic activities and markets based on natural resources. Indeed, this basic model of linking rights and benefits informs not only CBNRM but wider emerging models of Payments for Ecosystem Services (PES), which include efforts to establish markets for biodiversity, water, and forest carbon. Thus a defining characteristic of modern conservation and development thinking is that the growth of markets, and the penetration of capital into rural areas in Africa and other parts of the world, is central to both environmental and poverty reduction challenges (Brockington et al, 2008).

The problem with this 'neo-liberal' narrative on the role of markets in supporting local economic and environmental interests lies in the politically contested nature of markets themselves. The neo-liberal discourse assumes that property rights are either secured, or can be made so through technocratic reform processes that see secure local rights and resource tenure as an objective. The narrative generally does not take into account the way that institutions, such as property rights, which play a key role in shaping participation in the market-place,[3] are constantly being negotiated and renegotiated in the African governance context. It also often does not explicitly recognize that rising economic resource values increase the incentives for claims on those resources through renegotiation of institutional arrangements governing ownership, access and use. In other words, the more valuable resources become, the greater the incentives for external powerful claimants to alter property rights arrangements. As incentives rise for local communities to participate in markets for certain resources through growing resource values, so do the incentives for external actors to appropriate local rights to those same resources. Africa's heavily centralized governing institutions enable property rights to be restructured in this way relatively easily. Thus because of this political economy of natural resource governance in African countries, the more valuable a resource is the greater the likelihood that local resource users will be dispossessed. Thus the growth of markets can act to undermine local property rights, even as the growth of markets is understood to depend on securing those same property rights.

This is a fundamental paradox for nearly all market-based development and conservation approaches, but it is particularly pronounced in the case of communally-held and -managed natural resources. Those resources tend to be subject to much less secure local property rights than individually-owned resources such as, say, agricultural land (Alden Wily, 2008). Nevertheless, it appears that the threat of wholesale dispossession of rural agricultural and pastoral communities in sub-Saharan Africa is currently on the rise from external investments ranging from bio-fuels and agriculture to mining and tourism. The trends discussed here in relation to natural resource governance, particularly wildlife, may simply be a harbinger of emergent trends in the broader arena of land tenure in rural Africa.

African resource governance in comparative perspective

If global patterns of market penetration and commerce are serving in Africa to weaken local resource tenure and drive the recentralization of natural resource governance arrangements, it is important to note that this does not appear to be the case, at least to the same degree, in all other regions of the world. Indeed, RRI (2009, p7) notes in a review of trends in expanding local forest tenure, referring to this shift towards local control over forests as a global 'forest tenure transition', that 'In comparison to other regions of the world, Africa has made very little progress in the forest tenure transition.' While many countries in Asia and Latin America have progressively secured growing areas of forests with local and indigenous communities, in Africa governments still claim ownership over 98 per cent of all forests (RRI, 2009; see also Sunderlin et al, 2008).

These resource governance disparities highlight social and political differences between much of Africa and other developing regions such as Asia and Latin America, and the implications these differences have on natural resource management outcomes and institutional arrangements. In much of Asia and Latin America, there has been a marked expansion in recent years in recognition of local communities' territorial rights over lands and forests (White and Martin, 2002; Agrawal et al, 2008). Conservationists increasingly recognize the major contributions made by local communities in places such as India to biodiversity conservation through local management practices or 'community conserved areas' (Kothari, 2006). Across different regions, local communal management regimes are contributing to a rethinking of the advantages and disadvantages of state protected areas in relation to more decentralized institutional arrangements (Ostrom and Nagendra, 2006).

Some community-based regimes in Latin America and Asia are rooted in long-standing historical forces and have a strong social underpinning as a result. One of the most prominent examples is community-based forestry in Mexico, which has its roots in the Mexican revolution of the early 20th century and has evolved based on agrarian peasant movements and demands, particularly since the 1970s (Bray et al, 2005). In India, some local forest management regimes are rooted in historical resistance to British colonial policies (Agrawal, 2005), but more recent events also demonstrate the continued potency of rural resource-based constituencies.

India's 2006 Forest Rights Act provides, for the first time, broad recognition of the customary rights of forest-dependent communities and represents a major reformist achievement by advocates of local collective rights to natural resources. The Act came about following earlier attempts to resolve the status of communities living in protected areas through nationwide evictions following a decision by the country's Supreme Court. This prompted a broad popular backlash, as the land and resource rights of millions of people were imperilled, and catalysed the formation of a popular movement geared towards formal recognition of those local rights. Springate-Baginski et al (2008, p12) highlight the importance of collective action by rural communities, including links to armed rural resistance movements, in influencing the adoption of the 2006 Act by the state:

> *After the attempted evictions in 2002 the ensuing uproar radicalised and mobilised popular movements and a new common cause was recognised between forest dependent groups across the country...Ameliorating civil unrest in tribal areas also definitely seems to have been a consideration in enacting the law, as a lack of recognition of forest rights is a major cause for the extensive Maoist movements across India's forested tribal regions.*

The popular roots of community-based resource management reforms in parts of Asia and Latin America, both in the past and present, provide a useful comparative reference point for studies of African resource governance, mainly because such popular rural influences are so starkly absent from much of Africa. Indeed, the cases in this volume generally describe policy and legislative processes dominated by government bureaucrats and foreign donors, and in some cases a few urban NGOs. While local communities show considerable ability to influence outcomes at the local level, there appears to be limited national-level engagement or influence by resource-dependent communities, and in some cases (e.g. Botswana) this is specifically identified as a major weakness of CBNRM initiatives (Rihoy and Maguranyanga, this volume).

Two factors in particular bear highlighting in relation to the African context and its apparent divergence from the politics of natural resource governance in other developing regions. First, sub-Saharan Africa is now distinctly less democratic overall than Latin America and Asia. As Figure 14.2 illustrates, levels of accountability and citizens' voice in sub-Saharan Africa are considerably below those of regions such as East Asia and Latin America.[4] Second, the influence of external interests in Africa, particularly foreign aid agencies and transnational NGOs, is generally greater.[5] African governments are the most dependent on foreign aid of any developing region, and the financial resources that both public (governmental) and private (NGO) forms of aid are able to mobilize can translate into significant influence in certain contexts. One impact of this aid dependence can be the 'crowding out' of domestic political constituencies as governments are more functionally accountable to external donors than their own citizens, and the domination of policy-making processes by the central state and foreigners (e.g. Gould and Ojanen, 2003). The recent history of wildlife governance reform in Kenya is an instructive case of external private NGO influence (Kabiri, this volume). Experiences with forestry and wildlife reform in Tanzania, and CBNRM in Zambia, all highlight significant influence by foreign donors, although this influence is shaped in turn by its interaction with recipient governments' own political imperatives.

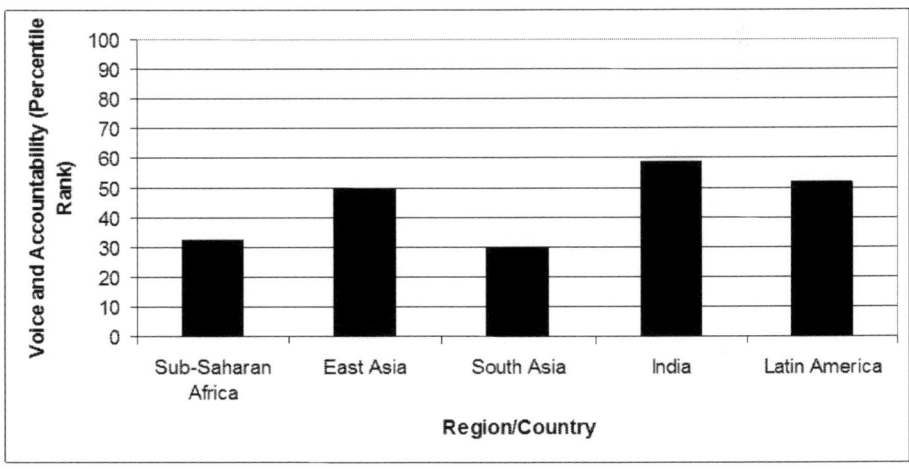

Source: Kaufman et al, 2009

Figure 14.2 *Levels of 'voice and accountability' across different developing areas, as ranked by the World Bank's Governance Indicators database*

Democratization, 'good' governance, and models of change

Recent trends in natural resource governance in Africa reflect challenges relating to democratization and governance reform in the wider social arena. Anstey and Rihoy (2009) note that existing contests over natural resources, and the limitations of CBNRM across the region, reflect broader struggles over local governance and efforts to build more meaningful democratic processes beyond periodic public participation in national elections as a manifestation of democracy.

As scholars such as Shivji (1998) and Boone (2007) point out, the nature of land and resource tenure has major implications for democratic relations and meanings of citizenship in African countries. Natural resource decentralization and related reforms such as CBNRM were, at the global scale, part and parcel of the spread of democratic governance during the 1990s (Alden Wily, 2000). In Africa, this period of democratization was particularly dramatic, not only due to the spread of multiparty elections but also to the end of racially-based minority rule in South Africa in 1994. The end of apartheid not only liberated South Africa but also contributed to wider peace and democratic reform in the region through the independence of Namibia in 1990 and the end of Mozambique's long civil war in 1992.

This period of rapid democratic change created major opportunities for reconfiguring institutional power and authority, including many of the natural resource reforms described in this volume. CBNRM initiatives fed off and contributed to broader social and political reforms across the region. This contributed to the general perception that such natural resource reforms were part of a long-term process of democratization (e.g. Alden Wily, 2000). At the same time, scholars and development agencies developed a deeper understanding of the links between governance institutions and economic development (e.g. North, 1990). This work, combined with the evident failure of development efforts in sub-Saharan Africa in the 1970s and 1980s, highlighted the need to transform governance dynamics in Africa through a range of reforms promoting multiparty elections, strengthened rule of law, property rights, reduced bureaucracy and curtailed corruption (World Bank, 1989).

Kelsall (2008) points out that the 'good governance' agenda, generally emphasizing technocratic reforms aiming to strengthen formal governance measures as embodied by the rule of law, has made limited progress since the 1990s across many African countries. The transformative agendas of CBNRM and natural resource decentralization, more narrowly, and 'good governance', more broadly, thus both emerged in the context of democratic movements during the 1990s but both appear to be losing traction. This suggests that efforts to democratize natural resource governance, and governance more broadly, are meeting with common constraints, and that the processes of recentralization of resource governance documented in this volume may be indicative of broader political shifts in African societies.

Towards more effective conceptual and practical models for reform

Developing more effective approaches to promoting natural resource decentralization, as well as democratization more broadly, requires confronting and negotiating existing structural barriers to change. This volume has described the political dimensions, and their roots in historical and social forces, of a range of ongoing institutional processes and reform efforts.

Two key points, with reference to both natural resource reforms and broader debates over governance in Africa, bear emphasizing. Firstly, natural resource reform efforts are fundamentally about changing the relationship between the state and its citizens (cf. Shivji, 1998). This means that initiatives such as CBNRM, where they involve reconfiguring rights over natural resources, are inherently linked to and influence broader questions of democracy and citizenship (Anstey and Rihoy, 2009). Secondly, what is notable about natural resource reform efforts in many African countries is the extent to which they have *not* been transformative in their orientation and in their impacts (cf. Murombedzi, this volume). Thus a core challenge facing a wide range of activists, conservationists, development agencies and local communities going forward is how to develop more transformative and impactful models for supporting institutional change and structural reforms.

Models for reform

During the past 20 years, the great majority of natural resource reform efforts occurring across the region have been designed, initiated and directed by central government agencies, often with high levels of foreign donor and external NGO support. The basic model for many of these initiatives, in a highly simplified form, is illustrated in Figure 14.3a. The salient feature of this operational reform model is that the key actors are central government, which is responsible for transferring rights and authority over resources to local communities, and the external agent (i.e. donor agencies), which provides resources to government to design and implement reforms. Clearly, where political circumstances favour such reforms, this model is viable, as generally was the case in Namibia in the early 1990s with respect to wildlife sector reform, or in Zimbabwe during the initial formulation and roll-out of CAMPFIRE. However, where political interests at the centre do not favour democratic or devolutionary reforms, this model is not viable.

Anstey and Rihoy (2009, p46) highlight the problematic assumptions inherent in this model and in relation to much of the discourse surrounding decentralization and devolution, which they claim

> ...act to privilege the centre as a starting point and create a 'mental model' around which central power and authority are the negotiating start and control the direction and speed of the process. In privileging the centre they reinforce a bureaucratic view of the state and a subject rather than citizen approach to democracy.

The point here is that the state often cannot be the starting point for democratic reforms that involve shifting power relations from the centre to the periphery. Furthermore, it follows that in struggles over resource rights between local communities and national élites or state agencies, providing resources to those centralized actors, as is the case with most donor programmes, is likely to impede rather than catalyse devolutionary institutional changes.

Figure 14.3b provides a simplified alternative framework for external support to natural resource reforms that empower local communities, by simply shifting the locus of support from those who are more likely to resist reform (central actors) to those who are decentralization's explicit constituency (local communities).[6] Several other basic differences between Figure 14.3a and Figure 14.3b are important. First, Figure 14.3a suggests that the process of institutional change is a relatively linear one, whereby rights are transferred from the centre to the local level in a fairly orderly and technocratic fashion. Figure 14.3b, by contrast, depicts the interaction between central and local actors as one of non-linear give and take, as struggles over resource rights occur over time and change according to various factors. This model is fundamentally non-linear, does not assume that the centre is inclined towards empowering the periphery, and also fundamentally has no end-point but recognizes that institutional changes of a decentralist or centralist nature may occur at any time based on the changing balance of power and changing incentives amongst groups.

Secondly, Figure 14.3b does not assume that external support is necessarily financial. Shifting external support from central to local actors does not presume routing large amounts of money to local actors who may not be in a position to receive such financial aid. Rather, it highlights that the role of external actors needs to focus more on building local capacity through training, knowledge, organizational support and networking in ways that increase local political capital and thus local ability to demand accountability (these forms of support may be routed through intermediary organizations – i.e. NGOs – provided the political-economic interests of those intermediaries are sufficiently aligned with and accountable to local communities' interests). Figure 14.3b is thus a simplified conceptual and operational model for placing local communities at the centre of governance reform and gearing external support towards supporting local interests and capacity.

A final point bears highlighting in terms of the way external support is organized between these two models. This is that the organizational norms of many external donors, and particularly multilateral and bilateral government development aid agencies, strongly favour the centralized (Figure 14.3a) over the decentralized (Figure 14.3b) model. There are a range of reasons for this, including continued use of linear planning frameworks and project models (Wallace et al, 2007), the association of large-scale expenditures with prestige and promotion within many aid agencies, and the resultant 'pipeline effect' that encourages development agencies to keep funding flowing as planned or budgeted (Jansen, 2009). These organizational norms exert a profound influence on the behavioural choices and policies of development aid agencies (Gibson et al, 2005). To the degree that these agencies are unable to adapt their organizational preferences and investment patterns to support more decentralized models of locally-driven reform, there may be a need to de-emphasize the potential for governmental donor agencies to effectively support natural resource governance reforms.[7]

(a)

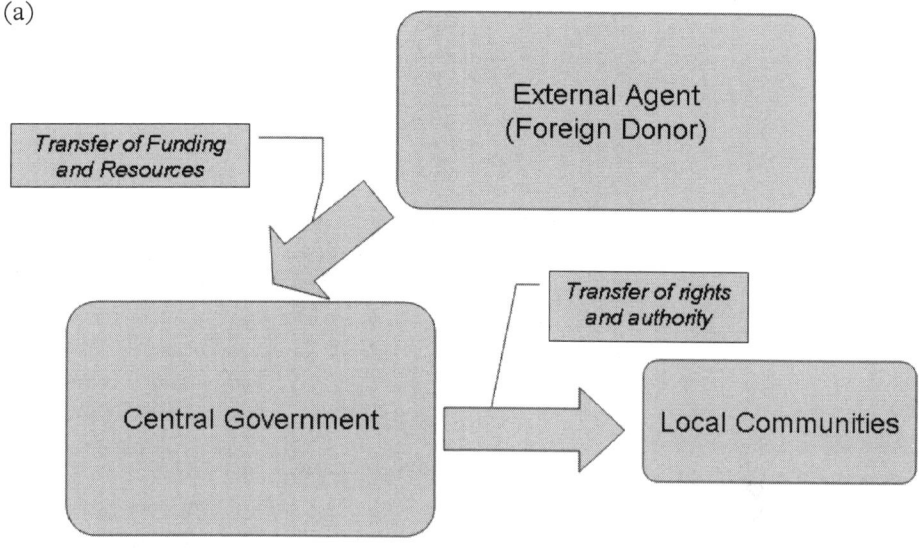

(b)

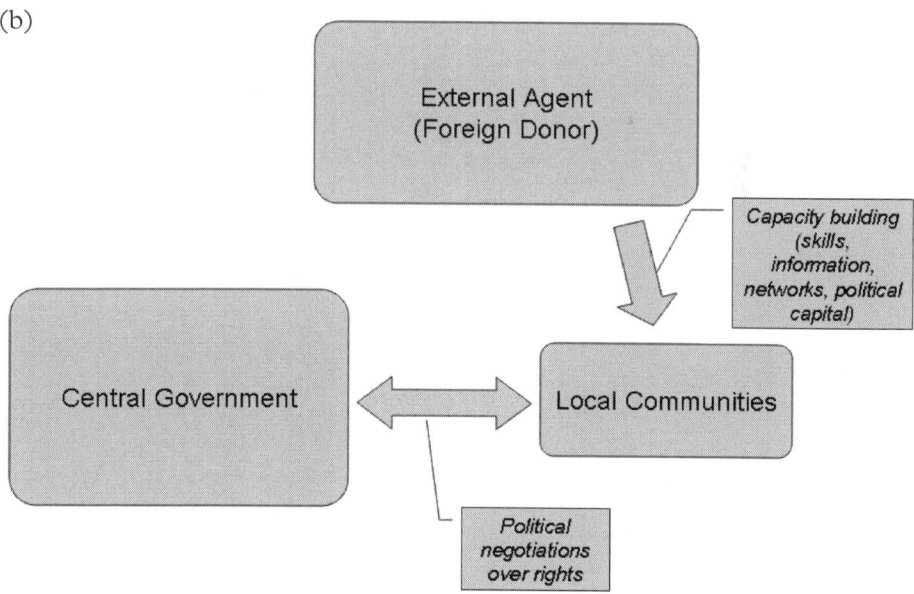

Figure 14.3 *Simplified alternative models for providing external support for natural resource decentralization reforms*

Ultimately it is essential that natural resource governance reform efforts place greater emphasis on providing direct support to local communities, and their allies within civil society, in building their voice and leverage to demand accountability and to advocate for their rights and interests. Conceptually, the emphasis needs to be on building political capital at different scales that can work to negotiate for institutional changes.

Reform and crisis

Natural resource reform processes are generally non-linear, with local and national opportunities for change opening and closing according to broader political trends and developments. Most of the major reforms that have occurred in eastern and southern Africa in relation to natural resource governance institutions have emerged during periods of macro-political crisis or reconfiguration. Post-apartheid land reform in South Africa, community wildlife initiatives in Namibia and Zimbabwe, and land, wildlife and forestry reforms in Mozambique all occurred immediately following the end of long-term liberation movements or civil wars, in periods characterized by radically new national political orders. In Tanzania and Zambia, periods of economic crisis in the 1980s and shifts to political pluralism in the 1990s had a significant influence on natural resource reforms and opportunities for change agents at local and national levels to promote experimental new institutional arrangements. In Kenya, the nearest the country has come to overhauling its maladaptive wildlife governance institutions occurred in the period immediately following the 2002 electoral transition, which saw the defeat of the monopoly on executive authority held by the Kenya African National Union party since independence in 1963.

Such periods of major transition and reconfiguration break up existing networks of patron–client relations and political interest groups to create opportunities for change which may not otherwise emerge. Essentially, reformists are faced with the task of building political capital (knowledge, networks, coalitions) which can then be deployed at these strategic moments. It should be emphasized that it is periods of crisis, which may be political or economic or both, which are key to creating opportunities for institutional change. By contrast, periods of relative stability are less enabling of institutional reconfiguration. The present period of recentralization across eastern and southern Africa may reflect the relative political stability and economic improvements that have characterized most of the region, with the notable exception of Zimbabwe, for the past ten years or so. Such stability and growth reinforces the position of those in power and discourages reforms that redistribute power and authority. However, the present period of stability and growth may give way to future crises due to, for example, rising inequality, political marginalization of certain groups, or environmental impacts from unsustainable resource use or climate change. Current patterns of recentralization are unlikely to be sustained indefinitely, but as ever it is difficult to predict future patterns of crisis and change.

Emerging issues and a research agenda for change

The experiences documented and analysed in this volume, as with any cross-section of local and national experiences, may be indicative of broader political-economic trends in sub-Saharan Africa, and perhaps elsewhere in the world, but also may reflect particular features of eastern and southern Africa. The cases generally focus on landscapes and wildlife populations valued for tourism, including tourist hunting, which are particularly a feature of eastern and southern Africa's savannahs. As described in this chapter, it is the combination of increasing commercial economic values and global capital flows, combined with the region's structural political characteristics, which appears to be driving recentralization of control over those lands and resources across much of the region, thereby undermining local efforts to secure rights, tenure and access to benefits. This political economy of resource governance varies, though, within the region, particularly between relatively patrimonial, informal states such as Tanzania, Zambia and Mozambique; and the more ordered bureaucratic states of South Africa, Botswana and Namibia. Wildlife-based tourism may be a key factor in encouraging expanding central control over lands and resources across both groups of countries, but the political dynamics have important differences.

A range of questions emerge from these national and regional trends and dynamics, which have been explored in this volume, in this chapter and in the national and local case studies, but which would greatly benefit from further research. First, it is unclear from existing studies to what degree to which the trends identified here are occurring in other regions of sub-Saharan Africa. Although useful analyses of natural resource decentralization in central Africa exist (e.g. Oyono, 2004), it is unclear if existing trends point towards recentralization, or if the local rights of access to and control over forests are so limited that such recentralization is unnecessary to maintain and expand central extractive interests. Given the high economic value of the region's forests, and the likelihood for that value to increase under operational rules for Reducing Emissions from Deforestation and Forest Degradation (REDD), coupled with the weakness of democratic institutions in the Congo Basin states, reforms favouring decentralization seem highly unlikely.

In west Africa, decentralization to district and sub-district level appears to be proceeding in some areas, such as Niger (Mohamadou, 2009). However, in much of the Sahel there are few valuable natural resources – with the exception of underground minerals – which create incentives for direct central control over large areas. In Senegal, though, Ribot (2008, p*iv*) describes how incentives to control the charcoal trade continue to circumscribe local rights over woodlands, leading him to call forestry governance in Senegal 'a last frontier of decolonization'.[8]

Inevitably there are many similarities and differences between different regions, and comparative studies between eastern, western, southern and central Africa are generally of great use, particularly between French- and English-speaking nations (e.g. Roe et al, 2009; Torquebiau and Taylor, 2009). Within countries, greater attention needs to be paid to connecting natural resource governance outcomes and local political ecology analyses to broader political-economic factors and trends. Are trends in natural resource governance in African countries indicative of broader advances and retreats in local and national democratic governance, or are valuable natural resources particularly resistant to reform?

As global markets for African resources such as wildlife (tourism), bio-fuels and agricultural land, and forests (timber and carbon) spread and grow, changing economic incentives and market relations will continue to influence political contests over rights and tenure. How these changes play out in different local and national contexts will continue to be a priority for research, and for linking that research to ongoing efforts by social movements, local communities, activists and civil society organizations to influence institutional change.

Conclusion

Today, at the end of the first decade of the 21st century, the emerging reality is that natural resource governance regimes grounded in local interests, incentives, indigenous knowledge and adaptive governance capacity are needed more than ever in order to address global processes of ecosystem degradation operating at wide and interconnected scales. Climate change is emblematic of this challenge. While the impacts of climate change are global in nature, and difficult to predict in their precise timing and spatial extent, adaptation and mitigation will both depend heavily on local actions. It is therefore a major challenge for all actors, from local to national to global scales, to strengthen local resource governance regimes. At present, the existing configuration of political-economic incentives across much of eastern and southern Africa is leading to recentralization of rights and authority in ways that are unlikely to support resilient and adaptive resource governance systems. The core challenge is to transform existing institutional incentives from a scenario in which increasing resource values and patterns of trade create greater incentives for further central control and capture of resource rents, to one where such values can reinforce local rights, voice and collective action. This transformative challenge is political in nature and stands as a priority bridging development, conservation and democratic interests and constituencies.

Notes

1   This is evident in Zimbabwe's decade-long freefall in nearly all governance indices, to its present ranking as one of the most corrupt and badly governed countries in the world. Although the changes in Zimbabwe should not be understated, its current ranking probably owes more to the nature of the changes that have occurred in the past nine years, than to the quality of governance in Zimbabwe as such.

2   This echoes Ruitenbeek and Cartier's (2001, p23) suggestion that devolution is 'an emergent property of a democratising society'. See also Oyono (2004, p108), who comments in reference to forestry reforms in Cameroon that, 'there is no chance for democratic decentralisation when representatives of the central administration live off corruption'.

3   By 'participation in the market-place' I simply mean the right and ability to sell a given good or service, such as those related to the use of lands or natural resources. The rights governing resource use, access and tenure, are fundamental determinants of this participation.

4   South Asia, which includes, among other countries, Pakistan, Afghanistan and Bangladesh, is the only region which scores lower than sub-Saharan Africa for this governance indicator; although India, the largest country in South Asia, scores above the global median value and well above sub-Saharan Africa.

5   It should be noted that these two issues are not necessarily unrelated, with an increasing number of scholars and activists arguing that the high proportion of government

budgets comprising of foreign aid is an important limitation of greater citizen account-ability in Africa. See Mwenda, 2006 for a particularly lucid presentation of this argu-ment, and Bräutigam and Knack (2004) for a more analytical treatment.

6   This simplified model effectively adapts the operational reality of most decentraliza-tion reform initiatives, which route resources through state bureaucracies, to Chhatre's (2008, p12) critical observation that 'decentralisation is about community agency'.

7   Donor agencies differ and, while nearly all recognize the importance of building the capacity of non-state actors to demand accountable forms of governance, the effective-ness of pursuing such aims varies. The World Bank, which directly supports only client governments, has few means at its disposal for supporting demand-driven reforms. Britain's Department for International Development, by contrast, is among the bilateral European donors that have developed a range of mechanisms for supporting civil society and for investing in both learning and action in the realm of governance reform.

8   This suggests that broader democratic processes are advancing in Senegal, and that the forestry sector is an institutional outlier. In Tanzania, by contrast, it is unclear if expanding central control of wildlife is an anachronistic outlier or rather embodies the broader erosion of the limited democratic reforms enacted during the 1990s, which may well be the case. See for example Mmuya, 1998; Lissu, 2000; Cooksey, 2003.

References

Agrawal, A. (2005) *Environmentality: Technologies and the Making of Governmental Subjects*, Duke University Press, Durham, NC

Agrawal, A., Chhatre, A. and Hardin, R. (2008) 'Changing governance of the world's forests', *Science*, vol 320, pp1460–1462

Ake, C. (1996) *Development and Democracy in Africa*, Brookings Institute, Washington, DC

Alden Wily, L. (2008) 'Custom and commonage in Africa rethinking the orthodoxies', *Land Use Policy*, vol 25, pp43–52

Alden Wily, L. (2000) *Making Woodland Management more Democratic: Cases from Eastern and Southern Africa*, International Institute for Environment and Development, London

Alden Wily, L. and Mbaya, S. (2001) *Land People and Forests in Eastern and Southern Africa at the Beginning of the 21st Century: The Impact of Land Relations on the Role of Communities in Forest Future*, IUCN-Eastern African Regional Office, Nairobi, Kenya

Anstey, S. and Rihoy, L. (2009) 'Beacon and barometer: CBNRM and evolutions in local democracy in southern Africa', in B.B. Mukamuri, J.M. Manjengwa and S. Anstey (eds) *Beyond Proprietorship: Murphree's Laws on Community-Based Natural Resource Management in Southern Africa*, Weaver Press, Harare, Zimbabwe

Bates, R.H. (1981) *Markets and States in Tropical Africa*, University of California Press, Berkeley and Los Angeles, CA

Bond, I. (2001) '"CAMPFIRE" and the incentives for institutional change', in D. Hulme and M.W. Murphree (eds) *African Wildlife and Livelihoods: The Promise and Performance of Community Conservation*, James Currey, Oxford

Boone, C. (2007) 'Property and constitutional order: Land tenure reform and the future of the African state', *African Affairs*, vol 106, pp557–586

Bratton, M. and van de Walle, N. (1997) *Democratic Experiments in Africa: Regime Transitions in Comparative Perspective*, Cambridge University Press, Cambridge

Bräutigam, D.A. and Knack, S. (2004) 'Foreign aid, institutions, and governance in sub-Saharan Africa', *Economic Development and Cultural Change*, vol 52, pp255–285

Bray, D.B., Merino-Pérez, L. and Barry, D. (2005) *The Community Forests of Mexico: Managing for Sustainable Landscapes*, University of Texas Press, Austin, TX

Brockington, D., Duffy, R. and Igoe, J. (2008) *Nature Unbound: Conservation, Capitalism and the Future of Protected Areas*, Earthscan, London

Cooksey, B. (2003) 'Marketing reform? The rise and fall of agricultural liberalisation in Tanzania', *Development Policy Review*, vol 21, no 1, pp67–91

Cotula, L., Vermeulen, S., Leonard, R. and Keeley, J. (2009) *Land Grab or Development Opportunity? Agricultural Investment and International Land Deals in Africa*, FAO/IIED/IFAD, Rome and London

Fabricius, C., Koch, E., Magome, H. and Turner, S. (2004a) *Rights, Resources, and Rural Development: Community-based Natural Resource Management in Southern Africa*, Earthscan, London

Fabricius, C., Koch, E., Turner, S., Magome, H. and Sisitka, L. (2004b) 'Conclusions and recommendations: What we have learned from a decade of experimentation', in C. Fabricius, E. Koch, H. Magome, and S. Turner (eds) *Rights, Resources, and Rural Development: Community-based Natural Resource Management in Southern Africa*, Earthscan, London

Gibson, C.C., Andersson, K., Ostrom, E. and Shivakumar, S. (2005) *The Samaritan's Dilemma: The Political Economy of Development Aid*, Oxford University Press, Oxford

Gould, J. and Ojanen, J. (2003) *'Merging in the Circle': The Politics of Tanzania's Poverty Reduction Strategy*, Institute of Development Studies, University of Helsinki, Finland

Hulme, D. and Murphree, M.W. (2001) *African Wildlife and Livelihoods: The Promise and Performance of Community Conservation*, James Currey, Oxford

Jansen, E. (2009) *Does Aid Work? Reflections on a Natural Resources Programme in Tanzania*, U4 Anti-Corruption Resource Centre, Chr. Michelsen Institute, Bergen, Norway

Kaufmann, D., Kraay, A. and Mastruzzi, M. (2009) 'Governance matters VIII: Aggregate and individual governance indicators, 1996–2008', http://info.worldbank.org/governance/wgi/mc_chart.asp Accessed 28 September 2009

Kelsall, T. (2008) 'Going with the grain in African development?', *Development Policy Review*, vol 26, no 6, pp627–655

Kothari, A. (2006) 'Community conserved areas: Towards ecological and livelihood security', *Parks*, vol 16, pp3–13

Lissu, T.A. (2000) *Repackaging Authoritarianism: Freedom of Association and Expression and the Right to Organize Under the Proposed NGO Policy for Tanzania*, Lawyers' Environmental Action Team, Dar es Salaam, Tanzania

Mbaku, J.M. and Ihonvbere, J.O. (2006) *Multiparty Democracy and Political Change: Constraints to Democratization in Africa*, Africa World Press, Trenton, NJ, and Asmara, Eritrea

Mmuya, M. (1998) *Tanzania: Political Reform in Eclipse*, Friedrich Ebert Stiftung, Dar es Salaam, Tanzania

Mo Ibrahim Foundation (2009) 'Ibrahim index of African governance 2008', www.moibrahimfoundation.org/en/section/the-ibrahim-index/scores-and-ranking   Accessed 6 October 2009

Mohamadou, A. (2009) *Decentralisation and Local Power in Niger*, IIED Issue Paper No. 150, International Institute for Environment and Development, London

Mwenda, A. (2006) *Foreign Aid and the Weakening of Democratic Accountability in Uganda*, Foreign Policy Briefing No. 88, Cato Institute, Washington, DC

Nelson, F. and Agrawal, A. (2008) 'Patronage or participation? Community-based natural resource management reform in sub-Saharan Africa', *Development and Change*, vol 39, no 4, pp557–585

North, D.C. (1990) *Institutions, Institutional Change and Economic Performance*, Cambridge University Press, Cambridge

Ostrom, E. and Nagendra, H. (2006) 'Insights on linking forests, trees, and people from the air, on the ground, and in the laboratory', *Proceedings of the National Academy of Sciences of the United States of America*, vol 103, pp19224–19231

Oyono, P.R. (2004) 'One step forward, two steps back? Paradoxes of natural resource decentralization in Cameroon', *Journal of Modern African Studies*, vol 42, no 1, pp91–111

Ribot, J.C. (2008) *Authority over Forests: Negotiating Democratic Decentralization in Senegal*, Working Paper 36, Representation, Equity, and Environment Working Paper Series, World Resources Institute, Washington, DC

Roe, D., Nelson, F. and Sandbrook, C. (2009) *Community Management of Natural Resources in Africa: Impacts, Experiences and Future Directions*, IIED Natural Resource Issues No. 18, International Institute for Environment and Development, London

RRI (Rights and Resources Initiative) (2009) *Who Owns the Forests of Africa? An introduction to the forest tenure transition in Africa, 2002–2008*, RRI, Washington, DC

Ruitenbeek, J. and Cartier, C. (2001) *The Invisible Wand: Adaptive Co-management as an Emergent Strategy in Complex Bio-economic Systems*, Occasional Paper No. 34, Centre for International Forestry Research, Bogor, Indonesia

Shivji, I.G. (1998) *Not Yet Democracy: Reforming Land Tenure in Tanzania*, IIED/ HAKIARDHI/ Faculty of Law, University of Dar es Salaam, Dar es Salaam and London, Tanzania and UK

Snyder, R. (2001) 'Scaling down: The subnational comparative method', *Studies in International Comparative Development*, vol 36, no 1, pp93–110

Springate-Baginski, O., Sarin, M., Ghosh, S., Dasgupta, P., Bose, I., Banerjee, A., Sarap, K., Misra, P., Behera, S., Reddy, M.G. and Rao, P.T. (2008) *The Indian Forest Rights Act 2006: Commoning enclosures?* Paper presented to the 12th Biennial Global Conference of the International Association for the Study of the Commons (IASC), held in Cheltenham, UK, 14–18 July 2008 Available at: http://iasc2008.glos.ac.uk/conference%20papers/ papers/S/Springate-Baginski_233001.pdf Accessed 2 September 2009

Sunderlin, W.D., Hatcher, J. and Liddle, M. (2008) *From Exclusion to Ownership? Challenges and Opportunities in Advancing Forest Tenure Reform*, Rights and Resources Initiative, Washington, DC

Taylor, R.D. and Murphree, M.W. (2007) *Case Studies on Successful Southern African NRM Initiatives and their Impacts on Poverty and Governance. Zimbabwe: Masoka and Gairezi*, International Resources Group, Washington, DC

Torquebiau, E. and Taylor, R.D. (2009) 'Natural resource management by rural citizens in developing countries: Innovation still required', *Biodiversity and Conservation*, vol 18, no 10, pp2537–2550

Transparency International (2008) 'Corruption perceptions index 2008', www.transparency.org/policy_research/surveys_indices/cpi/2008 Accessed 1 October 2009

Villalón, L.A. and VonDoepp, P. (2005) *The Fate of Africa's Democratic Experiments: Elites and Institutions*, Indiana University Press, Bloomington, IN

Wallace, T., Bornstein, L. and Chapman, J. (2007) *The Aid Chain: Coercion and Commitment in Development NGOs*, Practical Action Publishing, Warwickshire, UK

White, A. and Martin, A. (2002) *Who Owns the World's Forests?*, Forest Trends, Washington, DC

World Bank (1989) *Sub-Saharan Africa: From Crisis to Sustainable Growth*, The World Bank, Washington, DC

Index